D0899083

GENES, WOMEN, EQUALITY

Genes, Women, Equality

Mary Briody Mahowald

New York Oxford
OXFORD UNIVERSITY PRESS
2000

Oxford University Press

Oxford New York
Athens Auckland Bangkok Bogotá Buenos Aires Calcutta
Cape Town Chennai Dar es Salaam Delhi Florence Hong Kong Istanbul
Karachi Kuala Lumpur Madrid Melbourne Mexico City Mumbai
Nairobi Paris São Paulo Singapore Taipei Tokyo Toronto Warsaw

and associated companies in
Berlin Ibadan

Published by Oxford University Press, Inc.,
198 Madison Avenue, New York, New York, 10016
http://www.oup-usa.org

Library of Congress Cataloging-in-Publication Data
Mahowald, Mary Briody.
Genes, women, equality / Mary Briody Mahowald.
p. cm. Includes bibliographical references and index.
ISBN 0-19-512110-4
1. Medical genetics—Moral and ethical aspects. 2. Medical
genetics—Social aspects. 3. Women—Health and hygiene—
Sociological aspects. 4. Women—Diseases—Genetic aspects.
I. Title.
RB155.M3135 2000
616'.042'082—dc21 99-14296

2 4 6 8 9 7 5 3 1

Printed in the United States of America
on acid-free paper

To my favorite geneticist

PREFACE

Genes, Women, Equality—these are the central topics of this book in order of their generality. To some extent, this title also indicates, in reverse order, the importance that I impute to the three topics. Equality is the main ethical concept that concerns me; women form the societal group that I am particularly concerned about with regard to applications of that concept; and genes, or genetics, is the sphere of application that has most concerned me in my recent work. The conjunction of these concerns describes the position or standpoint from which I view the issues discussed. Although that standpoint is both feminist and egalitarian, it is also, quite inevitably, the standpoint of a particular person whose account is influenced, for better or worse, by her particular experience. Accordingly, to enable the reader to recognize some of the strengths and weaknesses of my standpoint, I will explain it more fully.

A philosopher by profession, I worked in a regular philosophy department for 13 years before moving to a medical school–hospital complex in 1982. In both academic settings, my teaching, research, and writing have focused on concepts and issues relevant to women. Theoretical considerations of these topics have been informed and facilitated by my involvement in cases that raise ethical dilemmas for women and the clinicians who treat them. My research focus on genetics has been reinforced by having a geneticist as my life partner.

I am a U.S. citizen by birth, married, with three grown children, white, heterosexual, currently able, and moderately affluent. Except for my sex, all of these characteristics represent advantages that may obscure for me the standpoints of those less advantaged. Conscious of that limitation, I have attempted to improve my vision by learning from those whose standpoints are different from mine, particularly from those whose standpoints tend to be ignored. I hope my nearsightedness has thereby been reduced; I realize that it has not been eliminated.

My desire to articulate and assess the impact on women of advances in genetics was precipitated in part by the observation that concerns about discriminatory applications concentrated almost exclusively on specific ethnic and socioeconomic groups. Only rarely have women been identified as possible targets of discrimination in genetics; instead, a gender-neutral rhetoric prevails in the analysis of specific issues. If men and women were equally affected by genetics and genetic technologies, the gender-neutral rhetoric would be appropriate. In fact, however, this is not the case.

Given limited funding for research and inadequate coverage of basic health care for millions of citizens, I question whether the decision by the U.S. Congress to allot $3 billion to the Human Genome Project was a wise or just distribution of resources. Nonetheless, when I learned that 3%–5% of the allotment would be devoted to examination of the ethical, legal, and social issues associated with the project, I decided to see if I could obtain a very small piece of that very large pie to support the area of research that I had identified as virtually unaddressed. To that end, in 1990 I prepared and sent to the National Institutes of Health (NIH) a research proposal focusing explicitly on the implications of the Human Genome Project for women. The panel that approved the proposal may have been convinced by my rationale (elaborated further in Chapter 1) or they may have considered the topic politically correct and useful; perhaps both considerations conspired in my behalf.

The first phase of the project involved the development of an exhaustive bibliography and organization of the information available through those sources on gender differences in genetic research and its applications.[1] The second phase addressed the normative question raised by the gender differences that had been identified: Are the burdens that the Human Genome Project involves or is likely to involve for women ethically justified? Consideration of this question required analysis of what is meant by justice in relation to differences, particularly gender justice in relation to genetic differences. The analysis proceeded from both theoretical and practical perspectives, basing the former on traditional principles of bioethics and different conceptions of justice and the latter on case studies of cystic fibrosis, sickle cell anemia, and breast cancer. With all three diseases, genetic aspects, clinical manifestations, and modes of treatment were examined, as were the psychosocial implications of the diseases for those affected and their caregivers. Participation by women who either had the disease or were caregivers of those who had the disease contributed greatly to these discussions.

Theoretically, analysis of whether the burdens of genetics for women are justified requires consideration of ethically relevant features and their interrelationships. These features include the preferences of individual women, the expected benefits to others, and the expected benefits to society as a whole. All these features may be viewed as falling within the purview of four major principles: respect for autonomy, beneficence, nonmaleficence, and justice. Although these principles have been extensively elaborated in the literature of bioethics and articulated in institutional policies regarding medical research and treatment, just what they mean and whether they are adequate or appropriate have rarely been scrutinized in the context of a commitment to gender justice, an essential subset of justice.

A case-based analysis illustrates the casuistic approach that many bioethicists have favored in recent years. It also reflects the emphasis on context that feminism and pragmatism entail. Of the three conditions studied, sickle cell disease is most informative and provocative with regard to ethical and social issues because the history of sickle cell testing in the United States reveals discriminatory practices to be avoided with regard to current and future genetic information. The more recent history of cystic fibrosis screening provides an example of the uncertainty that remains even when new tests are available and of the difficulty of respecting the autonomy of parents, prospective parents, and their children.

Genetic testing for breast cancer is associated with even more uncertainty, no matter what the test result. Unlike cystic fibrosis and sickle cell anemia, breast cancer affects mainly women and may be cured through early detection. Genetic testing for this disease illustrates issues that apply to other forms of cancer and other multifactorial late onset disorders that affect individuals of both sexes. While breast cancer affects women in all ethnic and socioeconomic groups, cystic fibrosis and sickle cell disease prevalently affect specific ethnic and racial groups. Adequate consideration of the impact of advances in genetics on women necessarily includes consideration of differences that do not exclusively affect them but affect many women in those different groups.

The third phase of the project focused on policy issues, especially those related to access to genetic services, abortion, gene therapy, and insurance and employment. These have specific implications for women, as do issues that have surfaced more recently, such as preimplantation genetic diagnosis and the possibility of human cloning. For a limited number of women, preimplantation diagnosis may present definitive genetic information and a means of avoiding prenatal diagnosis and termination of pregnancy; even for them, however, it is costly, invasive, and often fails to produce a newborn because of the low success rate of in vitro fertilization. Human cloning, if it is developed on the model that has already produced nonhuman clones, will require women to provide the eggs and the uterine environment that are necessary to produce a cloned human, whether male or female.

The content of this book draws heavily on material gleaned from the different phases of my NIH-supported project. In writing it, however, I have felt more free than I did in the course of that project to develop the standpoint that I bring to issues here discussed more fully. My standpoint has not only been influenced by my colleagues and participants in the NIH project but also by colleagues, friends, and students with whom I have interacted for many years. My family have of course been influential as well, in ways that extend much further than the genes we share. Nonetheless, my standpoint is one for which I am finally responsible because neither genes nor environment, nor both together, determined it for me. Rather, I have chosen an understanding of feminism and equality that I consider morally and logically perferable to the alternatives, and I have applied that understanding to the issues addressed. While I realize that the views that emerge from this standpoint are fallible and limited, I believe that its key component, a commitment to gender justice, is shared by most of my potential readers.

Chicago, Ill. M. B. M.
January 1999

Note

1. The gender differences identified in our research are explained and documented in Mary B. Mahowald, Dana Levinson, Christine Cassel, Amy Lemke, Carole Ober, James Bowman, Michelle LeBeau, Amy Ravin, and Melissa Times, "The New Genetics and Women," *Milbank Quarterly* 74, 2 (1996): 239–83. This article includes an extensive bibliography on the topic.

ACKNOWLEDGMENTS

With gratitude, I acknowledge support from a number of institutions in preparing various drafts of this book: the National Institutes of Health (NIH), the American Council of Learned Societies (ACLS), Creighton University Center for Health Policy and Ethics, the Rockefeller Foundation, and of course, my own university. NIH funded the initial research through a grant from the Ethical, Legal, and Social Issues Program of the National Institute for Human Genome Research. The ACLS and Creighton University supported me during a leave from the University of Chicago to write the bulk of the book. By offering me a month-long residency at the Bellagio Study Center, the Rockefeller Foundation provided me an opportunity to revise the manuscript in an unforgettably supportive and intellectually stimulating environment. The University of Chicago, through the Department of Obstetrics and Gynecology, made it possible for me to complete the work by agreeing to my leave from regular duties in the department and in the MacLean Center for Clinical Medical Ethics.

I also acknowledge, with thanks, permission from the publishers to print the cartoon that appears at the end of the Introduction, and the tables in Chapter 7. The cartoon first appeared in *Science,* Vol. 248 (4958), May 20, 1990, p. 1023; *Science* is published by the American Association for the Advancement of Science. The tables appeared in the *Journal of Women's Health,* Vol. 6, 1997, pp. 639–47; this journal is published by Mary Ann Liebert, Inc., Publishers.

Beyond institutions, I am indebted to all of the people who helped bring the book to fruition. While I here name many of them, I probably, regretfully, miss some to whom I am nonetheless grateful. Among the many I will name are secretaries who sequentially assisted by faithfully fulfilling diverse and sometimes tedious tasks: Joan Hives, Sandee Butler, and Tim Jacobs, all at the University of Chicago. In addition, Joan Hives contributed her expertise and indispensable assistance in compiling the indices. At Oxford University Press, Edith Barry and Laurel Edmundson guided the manuscript through its early stages, Nancy Wolitzer expedited the production process, and Carole Schwager did a fine job of copy editing the completed manuscript. Gail Isenberg at the Greenhill Library in my department, and Christa Modshiedler, ably assisted by Rebecca Woolbert, generously tracked down answers to many of my odd queries at the Crerar Library of the University of Chicago. Lisa Jewell, also at the Greenhill Library, drew on her considerable computer skills to provide the book with its attractive cover. Sincere thanks to all of them.

Co-investigators who came from different disciplines to collaborate in my NIH project contributed greatly to my understanding of the topics addressed. These include James Bowman, Christine Cassel, Michelle LeBeau, Amy Lemke, and Carole Ober. A longstanding colleague and friend, Dr. Bowman was helpful not only in connection with my chapter on sickle cell disease, but also in my discussions of eugenics, cultural differences, and the impact of poverty on issues raised by advances in genetics. Although Funmi Olopade was not formally a co-investigator, she actually did the work of one by organizing our efforts to understand the impact of breast cancer on women. Dr. Olopade also took time to review and make suggestions on Chapter 11. Dana Levinson, coordinator for the last few years of the project, could not have done a better job of organizing and enabling the project, and co-authoring an important article related to it. Without her and research assistance from Karen Vergoth as well as Melissa Times, I would hardly have been able to develop an adequate account of the empirical impact of the Human Genome Project on women. Neither would I have obtained the data tabulated in Chapter 7 without Amy Ravin and Carol Stocking. I am grateful to them not only for permission to use these tables but also for their constructive input in early stages of our NIH project. I am also grateful to Helen Bequaert Holmes for inviting me to a conference on genetics and women, at which I not only learned a great deal of pertinent information but was inspired by the commitment of others to feminist analysis of issues in genetics.

Other individuals graciously read and provided me with feedback on specific chapters. June Peters did this for Chapters 3 and 11, Shelly Cummings for Chapter 11, Ed Cooke for Chapter 14, and Anthony Mahowald for Chapter 16. Gail Geller and Bridgit Bell provided useful comments on several chapters. Lucy Lester was an indispensable resource for Chapter 9, as well as for our consideration of cystic fibrosis in the NIH project. Through his expertise in computer graphics, Michael Mahowald generated the pedigrees used in Chapters 9, 10, and 11. Marion Verp, Jaideep Singh, Peter Angelos, and Terri Knutel were all quick to respond when I needed reliable answers to questions related to their different areas of expertise. Eric Meslin, while at the Ethical, Legal, and Social Issues Program of the National Institute for Human Genome Research, and Eric Juengst, who had preceded him in that post, facilitated my efforts to document the numbers of women involved in research genetics and the number of studies that focus on women. By inviting my involvement in projects related to women with disabilities, Kristi Kirschner and Anita Silvers facilitated my work on Chapter 8.

Ruth Purtilo, director of the Center of Health Policy and Ethics at Creighton, deserves special thanks for inviting me to Omaha, where I met and conferred with some wonderful colleagues at the center (Judith Kissell, Winifred Pinch, Amy Haddad, Jos Welie) and in the Philosophy Department (Jeanne Schuler, Kevin Graham, Patrick Murray, Gene Selk). Thanks too to Tim Moore, who helped me with my computer and with library searches there, to the administrative staff at the center (Rita Nutti, JoAnn Maynard, Melanie Wood), who supported my efforts through their warmth and efficiency, and to the staff at Media Services (Joyce Sheehan, Alice Smith, Steve Garcia), who were warm and welcoming as well.

Two fellows in the MacLean Center for Clinical Medical Ethics, Katie Watson and Angela Scheuerle, took the time to read the entire book and give me the benefit of their comments. As a pediatric geneticist, Dr. Scheuerle has also been a wonderfully available and reliable resource with whom to check on clinical examples and descriptions of genetic conditions. Constructive suggestions to improve the style as well as content of the book came from Jeffrey House, along with two anonymous reviewers at Oxford University Press. Laura Purdy, another reviewer, was generous, critical, and insightful in her comments and suggestions on each of my many chapters. I took all of these reviews with me when I traveled to Bellagio to revise the text. I do believe the book was improved by this effort, but of course my reviewers should not be blamed for the flaws that remain. While apologizing for these, I believe they count as further evidence of the need for implementing standpoint theory, discussed in Chapter 1 and subsequently, to reduce the myopia that afflicts us all.

CONTENTS

GENES, WOMEN, EQUALITY

The human genome belongs to the entire human race.

George F. Cahill, 1989

I realized recently that I suffer from a genetic condition. Although I have not actually had my genome screened, all the anatomical signs of Double-X Syndrome are there. And while I could probably handle the myriad physiological disorders associated with my condition—bouts of pain and bleeding coming and going for decades, hair growth patterns that obviously differ from "normal" people's—the social downsides associated with it are troubling.

Ever since the passage of the Americans with Disabilities Act, people with Double-X remain more likely than others to live below the poverty line, more likely to be sexually assaulted, and are legally prohibited from marrying people with the same condition. Some potential parents have even screened fetuses and aborted those with Double-X in an effort to avert the tragic life the syndrome brings. Perhaps you know Double-X by its more common name: womanhood.

Alice Dreger, "When Medicine Goes Too Far in the Pursuit of Normality," *New York Times,* July 28, 1998

Whether this new genetic knowledge is an advantage or a cross depends . . . upon where one is located in the social order.

Troy Duster, 1990

What the science of genetics has historically done is to frame the questions themselves in the language of the dominant culture, and the questions themselves . . . carry the power to define personhood, or rather, successful personhood.

Laurie Zoloth-Dorfman, 1989

Introduction

"GENETICS IS NOT GENDER NEUTRAL"

ALTHOUGH different species share many of their genes, each species has a unique genetic makeup in comparison with other species. In every species, however, there are genetic differences based on sex and unique genetic combinations in members of the same sex. In humans, further differences are associated with gender as a socially induced set of behaviors and attitudes.[1] Many differences are also associated with disproportionate risks, burdens, and benefits for men and women. The disproportionate differences make it clear that genetics, to the extent that it is associated with inherited conditions, is not gender neutral in its impact.

The Background

Strictly speaking, genetics as an academic discipline or area of research is as gender neutral as any area of scientific research.[2] Popularly, however, the term is often equated with heredity, that is, the transmission of characteristics from parents to offspring, which is not gender neutral. As the "science of heredity," genetics is by no means a new area of study. Even in ancient times, there was widespread awareness of inherited differences. Taboos against marriage between first-degree relatives apparently originated from an understanding of genetic flaws induced by inbreeding. In Plato's time, infanticide was practiced as a means of eliminating genetically undesirable offspring. Just as longstanding is the desire to promote inherited differences that confer social advantages.[3] In the nineteenth century, Francis Galton coined the term "eugenics" to describe these practices. Attempts to increase the number of socially desirable individuals in the world are called positive eugenics; attempts to reduce the number of those considered socially undesirable are called negative eugenics.[4] Although both types of practice are morally problematic, positive eugenics is generally viewed more negatively. In either case, however, those who hold dominant positions in society determine the criteria of social desirability.

Charles Darwin is well known for his concept of the survival of the fittest; Gregor Mendel is equally well known for his contributions to the development of genetics as a science. Although Mendel himself did not intend it, his research suggested a means by which survival of the fittest may be promoted in humans. Through simple but careful experiments in his monastery garden, Mendel showed how certain characteristics (now called phenotypes), such as flower color and plant height, could be predicted and determined. He also observed that some characteristics were expressed even when bred with a different variety of plant, and others were expressed only if bred with a plant of the same type.[5] In language used by later geneticists, Mendel thus demonstrated the distinction between dominant and recessive traits.

Early in the twentieth century, scientists identified chromosomes within the nuclei of cells as the bearers of inherited traits and diseases. Wilhelm Johannsen called these inherited factors "genes."[6] John Haldane, Julian Huxley, Lancelot Hogben, and Herbert Jennings all attempted to calculate the physical and behavioral traits of individuals and populations in accordance with the mathematical models developed by Mendel. Applying their findings to humans, some scientists explicitly supported positive eugenics. Consistent with Galton's definition of eugenics as "the science of improvement of the human race germ plasm through better breeding," they proposed that women be artificially inseminated with the sperm of "particularly estimable men" so as to improve the quality of their progeny.[7]

The Holocaust, along with more recent genocidal atrocities, offers tragic proof that eugenics did not die with the Greeks or with Galton and his colleagues. No rational, moral person countenances such practices. Nonetheless, positive eugenics seems to be encouraged through institutions such as Robert Graham's Repository for Germinal Choice in Escondido, California. Potential parents come to the repository to obtain the sperm of Nobel laureates, through which they hope to maximize their chance of having exceptionally bright offspring.[8] Whether their expectations are fulfilled depends crucially on factors over which the repository has no control: the genetic and gestational contribution of women and the impact of other environmental factors on the offspring's expression of a genetic endowment. Even for a cloned organism, different gestational and environmental factors may lead to unexpected phenotypic expressions of the genome.

In 1953 James Watson and Francis Crick published their famous description of the molecular structure of the genetic material as a double helix.[9] Their account of how four nucleotides, commonly referred to as A, C, T, and G (formed from different bases: adenine, cytosine, thymine, and guanine), are paired within our strands of deoxyribonucleic acid (DNA) made it possible to examine the mechanism of genetic coding in humans without requiring breeding experiments. Gradually, human genetics developed into a specialty of its own, with successes such as identification of an extra twenty-first chromosome in persons with Down syndrome, discovery of sex determinants in the nuclei of cells, and recognition of the relationship between sickle cell trait and protection against malaria. By the 1960s, Victor McKusick published the first edition of *Mendelian Inheritance in Man,* which listed 1487 inherited characteristics, or "mendelizing phenotypes." The current edition of McKusick's book lists more than 6678 phenotypes, associated with various modes of inheritance.[10] The phenotypes associated with specific conditions vary considerably in kind, severity, and onset of their expression. Normal human variation is also influenced by inheritance. However, the majority of human diseases, including various forms of cancer and heart disease, as well as behavioral traits and traits of appearance, are influenced by multiple genetic and environmental factors. In other words, genes alone do not determine a person's health, ability, or personality. In Table I–1, I delineate different modes of inheritance and manifestations of heredity, providing examples that represent its broad range of impact, both positive and negative, on people's lives. To readers who lack a background in the principles of inheritance, this is intended to facilitate understanding of material treated in subsequent chapters.

In 1985 molecular geneticists meeting in California proposed that the entire human genome should be not only mapped but sequenced. The mapping task involves the location of all human genes on human chromosomes; the sequencing task involves determination of the different arrangements of nucleotides that define each gene. By 1990 the U.S. Congress had launched the Human Genome Project (HGP), appropriating funds for the research to two federal agencies, the Department of Energy and the National Institutes of Health. Three billion dollars was designated for a 15 year program to map and sequence all of the 50,000 to 100,000 genes that occur on the 23 pairs of human chromosomes.[11] Watson, Nobel laureate and first director of the National Center for Human Genome Research (now called the National Human Genome Research Institute), buttressed his argument for federal support of the project by proposing that a small fraction of the funding be set aside to address the social implications of the project. This suggestion, unique in the history of sci-

TABLE I–1. Modes of Inheritance and Their Manifestations

Modes of Mendelian Inheritance

1. Autosomal dominant Autosomes are chromosomes that do not determine sex. An autosomal dominant condition is one that may be transmitted to offspring from either affected parent; this means that each child has a 50% chance of being affected. Brown eyes is an autosomal dominant trait; Huntington disease is an autosomal dominant disease.

2. Autosomal recessive An autosomal recessive condition is one that requires both parents to be carriers. Although they themselves are not affected, each of their children has a 25% chance of being affected, a 50% chance of being an unaffected carrier, and a 25% chance of being neither a carrier nor affected. Blue eyes, cystic fibrosis, and sickle cell disease are autosomal recessive conditions.

3. Sex-linked Sex-linked conditions are determined by the sex chromosomes. Hemophilia, for example, is a recessive condition in females but dominant in males. Each daughter of a woman who is a carrier for hemophilia has a 100% chance of not being affected and a 50% chance of being a carrier also; each son has a 50% chance of having the condition.

4. Chromosomal Chromosomes are structures within the cell nucleus that contain genes. Normal human beings have 46 chromosomes, half of which come from their mothers, the other half from their fathers. Twenty-two of these pairs are autosomes; the other pair are sex chromosomes. A normal female has two X chromosomes; a normal male has an X and a Y chromosome. Chromosomal abnormalities occur randomly when a chromosome is missing (monosomy, which usually leads to spontaneous abortion) and when there are extra chromosomes, as in trisomy 21 (Down syndrome). Down syndrome and other chromosomal abnormalities may also occur in a predictable pattern when either parent has the usual amount of genetic material but it is rearranged.

5. Mitochondrial Mitochondria are cytoplasmic structures containing genetic material. Women transmit mitochondrial DNA to all of their children, but men do not. The mitochondrial DNA accounts for < 1% of the human genome. Mitochondrial mutations, while rare, are associated with muscle disorders such as Leber optic neuropathy and myoclonic epilepsy.

(continued)

ence and research funding, undoubtedly strengthened the chance of approval not only in the halls of Congress but also in the minds of the public. The Ethical, Legal, and Social Issues (ELSI) Program of the National Human Genome Research Institute constitutes the implementation of Watson's proposal.

Areas identified for study by ELSI investigators include the privacy and confidentiality of genetic information, protection from discrimination based on genetics, and the safe introduction of genetic tests into mainstream medical practice.[12] Many of the funded proposals have been empirical studies of psychosocial aspects of the HGP, for example, through questionnaires or interviews asking patients or practitioners about their attitudes and practices involv-

TABLE I–1. *(continued)*

Modes of Non-Mendelian Inheritance

1. Polygenic Determined by more than one gene, e.g., skin pigment.

2. Multifactorial Determined by one or more gene plus environmental factors, e.g., fingerprints and complex diseases such as cancer and diabetes.

3. Codominant Phenotypes produced by both maternal and paternal genes, e.g., blood types.

4. Spontaneous mutations Genetic changes that occur randomly, triggered by environmental factors or by errors in DNA replication.

Manifestations of Heredity[a]

1. Somatic function or impairment, e.g., low cholesterol level, sicklelike cell structures.
2. Mobility or impairment of mobility, e.g., dexterity, lack of muscle control
3. Cognitive and creative ability or impairment, e.g., artistic talent, intelligence, mental retardation
4. Sensory ability or impairment, e.g., visual acuity, color blindness
5. Reproductive ability or impairment, e.g., tendency to twinning, infertility
6. Body structure and appearance, e.g., tallness, achondroplasia, eye and hair color
7. Susceptibility to disease, e.g., tendencies to Alzheimer disease and alcoholism.

[a]Manifestations of heredity may be major or minor in their impact; may be beneficial, neutral, or deleterious for individuals; and are often influenced by nongenetic factors.

ing genetic diagnosis, or about circumstances in which genetic tests are most likely to be offered or desired. Projects assessing knowledge of genetics and aimed at developing education in genetics for the public and for practitioners have been strongly encouraged, and some projects aim at development of tools for education and counseling.

Few ELSI projects have focused on ethical issues through a philosophical methodology, that is, through careful development and analysis of arguments for different positions.[13] Possibly this is due to the desire to avoid association with controversial positions. A book entitled *Assessing Genetic Risks,* written by a committee of the Institute of Medicine and funded in part by the ELSI program, apparently attempted to provide a critical ethical account.[14] Despite the prestige that the highly respected Institute of Medicine lends to it, this book is disappointing, at least to those who hoped for a clear, coherent, and well-developed approach to the important ethical and social issues generated by the HGP. Its deficiencies may have been unavoidable because of its many authors from different disciplines. Multiple, overlapping principles, representing different levels of generality, are delineated, with little or no argument in support of the principles or positions recommended. Ironically, one recommendation of the authors would fund criticism of their own work: "The committee endorses the concept that the ELSI program support 'meta-analyses' of what has been learned in the key areas of its program investment."[15]

In light of the longstanding neglect of women in medical research, it is not surprising that ELSI projects dealing explicitly with the impact of the HGP on women have been extremely few in number. This is particularly troublesome because of the different, and often more burdensome, impact of genetic progress on women. In this book, I attempt to reduce this overall neglect. My descriptive goal is to delineate specific implications for women of advances in genetics; my prescriptive goal is to examine the extent to which these implications are consistent with the principle of justice in general and gender justice in particular.

The Book

I begin by elaborating the meaning of "standpoint theory," which underlies my approach to various issues treated in the book. This theory involves epistemological and ethical rationales for inputing a "privileged" status to the view of nondominant groups or individuals. Although standpoint theory is supportable by traditional theories of justice, proponents of those theories often neglect nondominant standpoints such as those of women.[16] The term "feminist" is frequently associated with nontraditional theoretical approaches; yet different versions of feminism espouse different theoretical approaches, some of which are quite traditional. In light of its focus on women and gender justice, the term "feminist" identifies the standpoint from which this book is written. I believe, however, that any adequate account of justice, as inclusive of gender justice, is feminist in content even if the term is not employed.

The focus on women calls for specification of the empirical impact of advances in genetics on women. I have provided this illustratively but not exhaustively by describing the impact on women of specific genetic conditions. The goal thus pursued is to identify gender-specific differences that might be overlooked or underestimated if a gender-neutral stance were maintained. The focus on gender justice calls for consideration of inequities that arise from gender differences. To that end, specific issues in which the impact is, or is likely to be, more burdensome to women than to men are considered. Such cases, I argue, offer prima facie grounds for granting privileged status to the input of women in the development of policies regarding genetics. Because women are a nondominant group, feminist standpoint theory imputes that status to them.

The version of feminism that underlies my standpoint is an egalitarian version: it assumes a conception of equality that is applicable to everyone regardless of gender, race, class, ability, or sexual orientation. While gender equality is its central focus, an egalitarian feminist standpoint necessarily views racial equality, class equality, and other forms of equality as demanded by the same principle of justice that requires gender justice. However, an egalitarian feminist standpoint allows for the possibility that in some cases, others-than-women may be nondominant or may be more burdened; in such cases, women's interests may be subordinated to those of others. In other words, an egalitarian feminist standpoint does not maintain that women's interests always trump those of others.

While explicating the meaning of an egalitarian feminist standpoint, I do not purport to provide a methodology that dictates specific answers to questions involving public policy and ethical decision making. Rather, I believe that that standpoint provides privileged and essential input into such policy development and decision making. As will be evident in the chapters that follow, in some cases this standpoint yields fairly clear guidance; in others, it does not provide definitive guidance because the moral parameters of the situation are dependent on more variables than those described. In all instances, however, a focus on women and on gender justice reduces the gap found in much of the literature on ethical issues in genetics.

Two broad topics are explored before targeting specific issues: research and its clinical applications. With regard to research, I identify gender differences associated with specific conditions and consider whether women "do" science differently with regard to these or other issues. I also discuss reasons for the exclusion of women from research protocols and efforts to increase their participation. With regard to clinical applications, I delineate gender differences in the medical and psychosocial impact of specific conditions on those affected, on nonsymptomatic carriers, on those at risk of being affected, on caregivers, and on social attitudes and practices. Gender differences in genetic counseling as well as the feasibility and desirability of nondirective counseling are also explored.

On a more theoretical level, I discuss alternative meanings of justice and the relationship between differences and equality in a just society. Using mathematical and algebraic equations as analogues, I propose that different chromosomal arrangements suggest a way of understanding gender justice in genetics. While relating different versions of feminism to different conceptions of justice, I argue for versions of both that are conducive to gender justice in genetics. Employing that model, I address the problem of just allocation of genetic services. Because the majority of the poor are women and their children, justice demands efforts to overcome this limitation to their access to services that may benefit them; it also demands that poor women not be subject to technological interventions that may not benefit them.

Because decisions about genetic services are obviously influenced by cultural differences, I examine how attitudes, practices, and laws about reproductive rights and responsibilities for fetuses or children vary in different cultural settings. The ethical dilemma presented in such settings is how to respect cultural differences while addressing the possible social pressures that may compromise women's autonomy. Sex selection is treated as an example of this dilemma.

A relatively unaddressed gender difference in genetics arises from the fact that women may be related to their offspring through gestation and lactation as well as genetics, whereas men can be related to their children biologically only through their genes. I discuss implications of this gender difference for genetic counseling and for reproductive decisions by carriers of autosomal recessive disorders. I also examine the apparent tension between advocacy for those who are disabled and support for a woman's right to terminate a pregnancy because of fetal disability. The two positions are compatible, I argue, so long as the disability alone does not determine the decision.

Three diseases are discussed with regard to their specific impact on women: cystic fibrosis, sickle cell anemia, and breast cancer. For each of these I consider a case with an accompanying pedigree—a diagram, using standard symbols—of an individual's genetic relationships across and between generations. Cystic fibrosis and sickle cell anemia are found prevalently in Caucasians and African Americans, respectively, while breast cancer occurs in women of various races or ethnic groups. I discuss the generic issue of misattributed paternity in the context of a case involving cystic fibrosis, and prenatal testing of women who are carriers in the context of a case involving sickle cell disease. I argue against clinicians' disclosure of misattributed paternity to husbands (in the absence of women's consent to doing so) and in support of prenatal testing of women even if their partners cannot or will not be tested. Citing an innovative and provocative model utilized by the U.S. Department of Defense in evaluating proposals for research on breast cancer, I propose this model as a means of implementing feminist standpoint theory in policies and decisions about genetics.

Preimplantation genetic diagnosis and possibilities for altering the genome represent clinical innovations that portend advantages as well as disadvantages for women. The former is a means by which prenatal testing and termination of affected fetuses may be avoided, and the latter, if effective, may reduce burdensome symptoms for potentially affected individuals. In both cases, however, women may be pressured to undergo costly and invasive diagnosis and treatment for the sake of others. Moreover, both types of genetic technology raise issues such as the moral status of embryos and responsibilities to future generations, the answers to which tend to affect women more significantly than men.

The development of behavioral genetics has revived the old controversy of nature versus nurture. Nature may be identified with genetics; nurture with environmental influences. Neither set of factors is gender neutral, and both affect the capacity of individuals to make morally autonomous decisions. I examine alcoholism as a behavioral condition that is influenced by both genetics and environment, and I discuss the conflict this raises for treatment of pregnant women whose consumption of alcohol threatens the welfare of their potential children.

Because increased access to genetic information raises problems of discrimination in employment and health insurance, I consider the risk this raises for women in particular. While critiquing the public–private distinction on which claims of confidentiality are often based, I argue against the right of employers and health insurance companies to access genetic information concerning their employees or customers. A case involving familial risk for Huntington chorea is used to illustrate this argument. The final issue examined in the book is human cloning, which involves potentially different risks for women than for men. I argue against the genetic bias of human cloning in support of a more demanding conception of parenthood, one not necessarily based on genetic ties.

The concluding chapter recapitulates the overall argument of the book and offers suggestions for maximizing gender equality in the face of the inequitable differences that are bound to increase in the years ahead. As the accompanying cartoon illustrates, progress in genetics involves both good news and bad news

"The good news is we have the human genome. The bad news is the computer alphabetized it."

for all of us.[17] A just social order does not mean that we regard all news as if it were neutral. Neither does it mean that differences among people are to be treated in as simplistic a manner as ordering them by alphabet. Rather, a just social order requires that we distinguish between the good news and the bad news for specific groups and individuals and attempt to reduce the disparities that the news entails.

Notes

1. To the extent that nonhuman animals are social, gender differences in their behavior may be socially induced in them as well.
2. The *OED* defines genetics as "that branch of biology which is concerned with the study of natural development when not complicated by human interference" and as "the scientific study of heredity and variation." Heredity is defined as "the property of organic beings, in virtue of which offspring inherit the nature and characteristics of parents and ancestors generally." *The Oxford English Dictionary,* 2nd ed. (Oxford: Clarendon Press, 1989), vol. 6, p. 440, and vol. 7, p. 163.
3. Kurt Bayertz, *GenEthics,* trans. Sarah L. Kirkby (New York: Cambridge University Press, 1994), p. 23.
4. Daniel Kevles, "Eugenics," in Warren T. Reich, ed., *Encyclopedia of Bioethics* (New York: Simon and Schuster Macmillan, 1995), p. 765.
5. George F. Cahill, "A Brief History of the Human Genome Project," in Bernard Gert, Edward M. Berger, George F. Cahill Jr., K. Danner Clouser, Charles M. Culver, John B. Moeschler, George H. S. Singer, *Morality and the New Genetics* (Boston: Jones and Bartlett, 1996), pp. 2–3.
6. Cahill, p. 3.
7. Diane B. Paul, "Eugenic Anxieties, Social Realities, and Political Choices," in Carl F. Cranor, ed., *Are Genes Us?* (New Brunswick, NJ: Rutgers University Press, 1994), pp. 144, 146.
8. Richard A. McCormick, "Blastomere Separation," *Hastings Center Report* 24,2, (March–April 1994): 14–16.
9. Larry L. Deaven, "Mapping and Sequencing the Human Genome," in Carl F. Cranor, ed., *Are Genes Us?* (New Brunswick, NJ: Rutgers University Press, 1994), p. 13.
10. Victor A. McKusick, *Mendelian Inheritance in Man,* 11th ed., vol. 1 (Baltimore: Johns Hopkins University Press, 1994), p. xvii.
11. Deaven, p. 12. The project is now slated to be completed two years ahead of schedule. Nicholas Wade, "In Genome Race, Government Vows to Move Up Finish," *New York Times,* September 15, 1998, p. B10.
12. Francis S. Collins and David Galas, "A New Five Year Plan for the U.S. Human Genome Project," *Science* 262 (October 1, 1993): 43–46.
13. An early exception to this tendency was a project developed by Bernard Gert, a philosopher at Dartmouth University. A number of projects have examined specific concepts or incorporated philosophical ethical considerations into empirical studies, and some projects have addressed legal and policy considerations. For a list of projects funded by the ELSI program, see http://nhgri.nih.gov/About_NHGRI/Der/Elsi /grant_index_html.

14. Lori B. Andrews, Jane E. Fullarton, Neil A. Holtzman, and Arno G. Motulsky, eds., *Assessing Genetic Risks* (Washington, DC: National Academy Press, 1994).

15. Andrews et al., p. 298.

16. A utilitarian perspective, for example, supports the attribution of a privileged perspective to those most affected by particular decisions. Although classical American pragmatism is not always construed as "traditional," it clearly calls for the inclusion of nondominant perspectives to reduce the "fallibilism" of dominant perspectives. I develop this point in Chapter 1.

17. *Science* 248 (May 20, 1990): 1023.

1

A FEMINIST STANDPOINT FOR GENETICS

BOYS and girls are never genetically identical, even when they are twins. Neither are women and men affected in the same way, physiologically, psychologically, or socially, by advances in genetics. A tendency to ignore these or other differences between the sexes may be based on a laudable commitment to gender justice; it may be defended on grounds that equal treatment of men and women demands gender neutrality in policies and practices. Ironically, however, gender justice cannot be achieved or maximized by social practices that are entirely gender neutral because differences between the sexes may be associated, sometimes unavoidably, with gender inequity. Only when the differences are identified and their associated inequities removed, or at least reduced, is gender justice possible.

A focus on women while examining the implications of advances in clinical genetics is thus indispensable to gender justice.[1] In this chapter I develop the rationale for this claim by considering the notion of "standpoint theory," particularly "feminist standpoint theory." To the extent that any approach to bioethics affirms justice as a crucial consideration, it is feminist if gender justice is recognized as a subset of justice. Because feminism has many different versions, however, the term does not adequately identify the philosophical orientation I bring to the issues. My overall orientation is an egalitarian version of feminism, which necessarily calls for consideration of the standpoints of others besides women and, indeed, others besides feminists.[2] In other words, my views constitute *a* feminist standpoint, not *the* feminist standpoint. Different feminist standpoints represent different points of view located within the common locus in which all feminists stand.

In this chapter I first discuss the meaning of "standpoint" and "standpoint theory"as developed by feminist as well as nonfeminist authors. I then consider feminist standpoint theory in relation to different views of feminism and propose an extension of the theory that embodies my own egalitarian perspective. This chapter is more theoretical than the others (except for Chapter 4) because I wish thereby to explain the rationale that underlies my approach to the issues addressed in subsequent chapters. However, I illustrate my approach through discussion of a case involving a recessive genetic disorder that may disastrously affect the offspring of affected women but not those of affected men.

Standpoint and Standpoint Theory

The term "standpoint" has been used to define any perspectival view of the world.[3] "Standpoint theory" refers to the theoretical justification for utilizing particular standpoints and strategies to implement them. Classical pragmatists such as William James and Charles Sanders Peirce insisted that human knowledge is unavoidably perspectival.[4] In light of a doctrine he called "fallibilism," Peirce argued for collaborative inquiry, based on scientific method, in order to maximize our potential for understanding reality.[5] However, he did not use the term "truth" or "knowledge" to signify the result of his pragmatic, maximizing method; rather, he called the result "belief," defining this as a plan or habit of action.[6] Peirce thus distinguished between truth as the ultimate goal of inquiry and the conclusions that human beings reach in their ongoing search for knowledge. What is known and knowable through experience in this unfinished world is inevitably partial, but not relative. Although we cannot achieve omniscience, we can minimize our errors or mistakes through collaboration.

Because of the intellectual advantage that results from collaboration, Peirce considered it illogical to be antisocial in the quest for knowledge. "Logic," he wrote, "is rooted in the social principle," which requires that the interests of investigators not be limited to their interests as individuals or even to their own area of research.[7] Consistent with the pragmatic tenet that theory and practice are inseparable, he affirmed the congruence of the two in his conception of inquiry. The goal of inquiry, he wrote, is to enhance "the whole community," that is, "all races of beings with whom we can come into immediate or mediate intellectual relation."[8] Pursuit of this goal through a collaborative methodology requires a certain selflessness—a willingness to sacrifice one's own ego satisfaction to increase the total fund of human knowledge. Peirce viewed science as a kind of religion in the demands it makes of the individual: "He who would not sacrifice his own soul to save the whole world, is as it seems to me, illogical in all his inferences, collectively."[9]

While stressing the practical importance of generalizations, or "generals," as he called them, Peirce did not insist on universalizability. "Generals" are generalizations that are epistemologically necessary and indispensable to resolution of ambiguities or conflicts, but they do not demand applicability always and in all circumstances, as they would if they were universalizable. In contrast, most nonpragmatist philosophers have maintained that universalizability and impartiality are not only achievable but essential to the justification of ethical decisions. Immanuel Kant is one of the strongest exemplars of this view, but the majority of contemporary bioethicists, whether trained in philosophy or not, follow suit. For example, in all four editions of a widely cited work that has undergone substantial changes through the years, Tom Beauchamp and James Childress identify universalizability as a necessary condition of moral decision making.[10] Impartiality, as reflected in the image of justice as blind, is construed as a condition of universalizability. If and when the interests of one party are the same as those of another, weighing the interests of either as greater than those of the other compromises the impartiality and universalizability that ethical judgments demand.[11] Justice, which some consider the most important of Beauchamp and Childress's proposed principles of biomedical ethics, is thus dependent on universalizability and impartiality. As they recognize, however, justice is open to a number of conflicting interpretations.[12]

Impartiality is also interpreted as requiring that we prescind from personal considerations in moral decision making. Thomas Nagel, for example, distinguishes between a personal and impersonal standpoint, arguing that the latter is indispensable to ethics.[13] A personal standpoint inevitably involves particular relationships and a unique position in the world. Ethics and political theory, according to Nagel, begin with the ability "to think about the world in abstraction from our particular position in it."[14] Only from this "impersonal standpoint" can we recognize and pursue values that are common to all persons, whatever their relationships and position. In other words, morality requires persons to act impersonally, with deliberate disregard for whatever needs or interests may be unique to them. Yet if ethics focuses on the moral responsibility of *persons*, it seems ironic as well as illogical to insist that personal considerations be excluded from ethical judgments.[15] Moreover, personal considerations are not equivalent to individualistic considerations; the former often address the interests of others, whereas the latter address only those of the lone individual.

Other approaches to ethics and bioethics deny either the possibility or desirability of universalizability and impartiality. Narrative approaches, for example, insist on attention to the stories of individuals such as patients, to capture details and experiences that are inevitably missed in others' accounts of the same events.[16] Listening to patients' stories is of course the usual way in which clinicians learn about each patient's health status; telling stories through case histories is the usual way in which they communicate to their colleagues. There is thus important overlap between case-based learning, sometimes identified with casuistry,[17] and a narrative approach to ethics: both involve stories told by individuals in particular contexts. While either may be used in conjunction with principle-based reasoning, neither affirms an essential role for universalizability or impartiality, and both have been criticized as entailing ethical relativism.

Another approach that has been associated with ethical relativism is care-based ethics. This also focuses on the contexts in which most individuals find themselves most of the time: enmeshed in multiple relationships to which different evaluations are attached.[18] Although care, like love, is a vague concept, it may be construed as an ethical principle in its own right. Care would then be universalizable, but not impartially, because it demands attention to the particularities of unique relationships. It also demands attention to the particular standpoints of individuals and groups.

Through their insistence on attention to the particularities of cases, casuistry, narrative, and a care ethic all lend support to the emphasis on the "uniqueness" of the doctor–patient relationship, which has been defended by the medical establishment and desired by the public. Using the term "uniqueness" in this context is misleading because *the* relationship is in fact regarded as a generic one between doctors and their patients. Nonetheless, partiality is not only defensible but demanded in the clinical setting because each patient must be treated differently from every other to be treated effectively.[19] In other words, each patient and each clinician has a unique standpoint to represent in the context of their relationship.

While stressing attention to context and the uniqueness of clinician–patient relationships, none of these approaches identifies the disparity that usually occurs in that relationship as a significant consideration. Clinicians, however, generally occupy privileged positions or positions of power with regard to their patients. The nonprivileged status of patients stems from their virtual ignorance regarding diagnosis, treatment, and prognosis, as well as the more vulnerable position that actual or potential disease entails. Often, the privileged status of the professional is enhanced by race, sex, socioeconomic status, and a system whose norms and structures have been defined by those similarly situated.

In the 1980s, Nancy Hartsock developed a notion of standpoint that identifies the disparities that arise between those who occupy different positions vis-à-vis one another.[20] Applying Karl Marx's view of the relationship between the bourgeoisie and the proletariat to the relationship between men and women, Hartsock imputed the following related claims to the standpoint she proposed:

1. Material life or social position structures and limits everyone's understanding of social relations.
2. When material life is structured in fundamentally opposing ways for two different groups, the vision of each represents an inversion of the other, and in systems of domination the vision available to the rulers is inevitably partial.
3. The vision of the ruling or dominant group structures the material relations in which all parties participate.
4. Members of the nondominant or marginalized group are capable of seeing beneath the surface of the oppressive social relations they experience; this vision is facilitated by the educative impact of their struggle to change those relations.
5. The standpoint achieved by the dominated group allows them to see beyond the present, exposing to others as well as themselves the dehumanizing aspects of existing social relations; this enables them to fulfill "a historically liberatory role."[21]

The fourth and fifth of Hartsock's claims provide the rationale for seeking and utilizing marginalized standpoints to reduce the inevitable nearsightedness of those who occupy the privileged or dominant side of a relationship, which is the side that defines its terms. Hartsock would reverse the privileged status of the parties involved, granting superior status to the nondominant or dominated point of view because it constitutes a means of overcoming the inevitable limitations of the dominant view. Both groups are advantaged through the reversal of privilege: members of the dominant group are empowered to correct and expand their vision, members of the dominated group are empowered to liberate themselves. Although Hartsock's original account targeted the man–woman relationship, her later work acknowledges the need to extend this analysis to other dominant–nondominant relationships. "My focus on a simplified model of masculinist and feminist perspectives," she writes, "left out of the account other important social relations."[22] Other groups to whom a privileged status should be assigned to overcome the nearsightedness of the dominant perspective are ethnic minorities, those who are disabled or poor, people of color, gays and lesbians. Hartsock has thus amended her view to account for the plurality of dominant and nondominant standpoints that an egalitarian version of feminism needs to address.

While supporting Hartsock's rendition, Donna Haraway observes that "the standpoints of the subjugated are not 'innocent' positions." Nonetheless, she considers them "preferred positions because in principle they are least likely to allow denial of the critical and interpretive core of all knowledge."[23] This "core" derives from their widespread and diverse experience of nondominance in a culture of dominance. Nondominant standpoints are justified or, rather, demanded, on ethical as well as epistemological grounds because of the relationship between knowledge and decision making. Ethical decisions, after all, require an adequate grasp of pertinent information, which can be obtained only through the corrective lens of those who are nondominant.

Admittedly, nondominant groups and individuals are sometimes so suppressed that they are incapable of recognizing, let alone utilizing, the perspective that is available to them. Whether they are able to access the core of knowledge to which Haraway refers depends crucially on the degree in which they are intellectually and psychologically capable of comparing and contrasting their own situation with that of the dominant group. Women, for example, need to be free enough to recognize their marginalization vis-à-vis men. Increased education and consciousness-raising techniques serve the purpose of enabling women to identify their own standpoint as different from, and dominated by, the supposedly impersonal standpoint of men.

For Nagel and his ilk, an impersonal standpoint is achieved through a process of abstraction that is indispensable to moral judgment. Referring to the majority of those who embrace this view, Hartsock calls the process one of "abstract masculinity."[24] Other standpoint theorists concur in her denial that an impersonal standard is feasible or desirable. Haraway, for example, affirms the "embodied nature of all vision" against the pretense of objectivity that denies the overall situatedness of human experience.[25] The concept of an impersonal standpoint, she says, suggests the "god trick of seeing everything from nowhere."[26] To a believer, then, performers of this "god trick" act blasphemously. Moreover, their attempt to impose their vision on everyone, on grounds that judgments drawn solely from their experience are universally applicable, is ethically objectionable because it fails to respect the autonomy of those whose standpoints are different from their own.

Haraway's proposed alternative is a doctrine of "embodied objectivity" that involves "partial, locatable, critical knowledges." These "knowledges" sustain "the possibilities of webs of connections called solidarity in politics and shared conversations in epistemology."[27] Only through such partial perspectives, she claims, can we approach genuine objectivity. Haraway defends her proposal against the anticipated charge of relativism by pointing out that, like the concept of an impersonal standpoint, relativism is "a way of being nowhere while claiming to be everywhere equally."[28] Her concept of "situated knowledges" does not conform to this definition of relativism because it denies the adequacy of anyone's inevitably partial perspective. The difference between partial knowledge and relativism thus supports the epistemological validity of standpoint theory.

Critics of an impersonal standpoint include authors who are not explicitly feminist. John Ladd, for example, develops a distinction between objective and subjective points of view that is comparable to feminist accounts of dominant and nondominant standpoints. Like Haraway, Ladd equates the "God's eye point of view" of those who claim to be objective with the dominant perspective of "social engineers," who see themselves, and whose supporters describe them, as "sincere and dedicated public servants selected on the basis of their professional expertise."[29] Although their approach is inevitably speculative, the social engineers or programmers regard their perspectives as overwhelmingly superior to those of ordinary, nondominant individuals. As objectivists, they think that their own "formal organizations of expert administrators" are indispensable to achievement of their goal, a true and adequate account of "the way things are."[30] Participation by those who see the world subjectively—differently, or from nondominant perspectives—can only impede that achievement.

For Ladd, the preceding rationale ignores the fact that, typically, the individuals who formulate decisions and policies are fallible human beings like the rest of us and "frequently misinformed and stupid to boot."[31] However, the most significant flaw of this approach is that dominant individuals often "lack the kind of involvement in the outcome that is forced on the recipients of the decision," who are nondominant.[32] While the latter are fallible also, they have a personal moral stake in what is decided, which in itself constitutes a moral argument for their participation. On democratic as well as utilitarian grounds, their input should be weighed more heavily than that of those who are less affected precisely because of the differential impact.[33]

The critical question that Ladd's objectivist fails to address is "Who is to decide?" This question, he says, is even more important today than in the past because those who make decisions are further removed than ever from those to whom their decisions apply. As proof of a longstanding tendency to ignore the question, Ladd offers examples of old men who decide that young people should kill innocent people in war, rich men who decide what kind of welfare the poor should receive, and white men who decide who should police the streets in a black neighborhood.[34] All of his examples are pertinent to standpoint theory, as is one not mentioned: men in general decide what women in general may do or not do.

Aware that the "objective approach" threatens the autonomy of nondominant groups, Ladd maintains that participation in decision making is a means of reducing the alienation they experience through domination. He credits minorities, students, and workers with contributing to "disalienation" through their demands for participation in the communities to which they belong, at home, school, or their places of employment,[35] imputing to them a position of ethical as well as epistemological privilege. The same point may of course be made for women whose efforts to participate in various levels of community governance serve as an antidote to the alienation that might otherwise prevail.

In short, the epistemological reasons for subscribing to standpoint theory reflect recognition that the experiences on which knowledge is based are incomplete and partial; they also reflect the pragmatists' insistence on collaborative inquiry as a means of overcoming the limitations of individual quests for knowledge. The ethical warrant for standpoint theory derives from prima facie obligations to respect the autonomy of, and practice beneficence and nonmaleficence toward, those who are nondominant as well as those who are dominant. While acknowledging the liberatory potential of standpoint theory for dominant groups, the theory assumes that justice has priority in ethical and social decision making.

As Albert Camus observed, both oppressors and oppressed are diminished through oppression. "I rebel," he wrote, "therefore we exist."[36] Applying that remark to the practice of health care, clinicians and patients alike may be liberated by imputing privileged status to the standpoint of the nondominant group. Patients in general are nondominant vis-à-vis clinicians, but many clinicians (e.g., genetic counselors and nurses) are nondominant vis-à-vis other clinicians (e.g., physicians). Standpoint theory is thus applicable to different groups within the health care setting. As we shall see in the next section, however, justice toward all of the individuals for whom the theory is intended requires its extension beyond dominant and subjugated groups.

Feminist Standpoint Theory and Its Extension to Individuals

Women in general are a nondominant group because they are hugely underrepresented among those in positions of power in the world. Feminist standpoint theory involves the arguments cited above for imputing privileged status to women in decisions and policies that affect them along with men. However, these arguments are even more compelling when women are affected more significantly than men, as in many areas of reproduction and genetics. The ethical argument is rendered stronger still by the rejection of relativism that feminism, in all of its diverse manifestations, adds to Haraway's refutation through its affirmation of gender equality as an objective, universalizable ethical norm.[37] As Susan Sherwin puts it, even if feminists remain relativist on other moral matters, they remain "absolutist on the question of the moral wrong of oppression."[38] So long as feminism is absolutist on that matter, it is in fact incompatible with relativism.

Sara Ruddick posits the roots of a feminist standpoint in the experience and activity of mothering. She develops a concept of "maternal thinking" that is applicable to men as well as women. Maternal thinkers do "maternal work" through preservative love, nurturance, and socialization of those for whom they care.[39] This work necessarily involves resistance to the spirit and practice of militarism, which impedes the growth and development of oppressed or vulnerable people. For Ruddick, a feminist standpoint thus involves pacifism. Not all women, of course, are pacifists, and not all women are feminists. Women's standpoint differs from a feminist standpoint in that the latter entails a prescriptive element—resistance to oppression.

Acknowledging the difference between a feminist standpoint and women's standpoint, Hartsock embraces the former rather than the latter because she interprets women's experience and activity as including both negative and positive aspects. In contrast, a feminist standpoint "picks out and amplifies the liberatory possibilities" contained within women's standpoint, that is, the negative aspects that may be effectively changed into positive possibilities for women.[40] On such a reading, a feminist standpoint is narrower than women's standpoint unless the former includes the standpoint not only of women as a group but also of women as individuals who belong to other nondominant groups and, in many cases, to dominant groups as well. Thus understood, a feminist standpoint embraces the standpoint of all of those who are nondominant or marginalized, whether by gender, race, class, ability, or sexual orientation.

Hartsock admits that her delineation of a feminist standpoint assumes commonalities among women despite their differences. In general, those commonalities are associated with nondominance. However, a narrow interpretation of a feminist standpoint cannot adequately reflect all of the standpoints of individual women, who, in addition to the above, are distinguishable by size, age, politics, religion, and multiple other factors. Like men, women are unique in the compilation of standpoints that each embodies. A broad interpretation of a feminist standpoint collects all of the nondominant standpoints together and imputes to them a privileged status vis-à-vis whatever dominant standpoint prevails, regardless of whether gender or another characteristic, or set of characteristics, determines the dominance.

Hartsock's feminist standpoint applies to groups rather than to individuals. However, an extension of standpoint theory to individuals is consistent with most versions of feminism because of their common emphasis on attention to context and relationship, as well as their critique of gender roles, stereotypically conceived. It also serves as a response to a criticism of Hartsock's account that it leads to a form of essentialism, representing women from different cultures and classes as if they were fundamentally the same.[41] Hartsock defends herself against this criticism when she asserts that "a standpoint is constituted by more than oppression and cannot be reduced to identity politics as usually understood."[42] In other words, other characteristics are relevant to the standpoints of diverse oppressed groups. While this acknowledgment makes Hartsock's position more acceptable to those other groups, extending the theory to individuals constitutes, in my view, an even stronger defense.

Individual women are not adequately definable as a group or even as members of multiple groups because of the uniqueness of each one's context and relationships. An adequate feminist standpoint calls for attention to the variety of contexts and of relationships in which women find themselves. While insisting on the importance of relationships that women alone have to others (e.g., pregnancy, motherhood), a broad interpretation of feminist standpoint theory maintains a critical attitude toward relationships and roles that support the subordination of women to men, whether as individuals or as a group. Simultaneously, it maintains a critical attitude toward generalities that mask the disparate needs and advantages of individual women.

Contemporary feminist scholarship has been self-conscious about its own limitations, attempting to reduce them through careful, critical consideration of the diversity of women's experience. Among others, Maria Lugones and Elizabeth Spelman offer compelling arguments for paying attention to cultural, racial, and class differences among women.[43] But generalizations regarding cultural, racial, and class differences may ignore significant differences among women who belong to the same culture, race, and class. Lesbian women and women with disabilities, for example, are often overlooked when cultural, racial, and class differences are addressed.

Taking account of differences among women also means taking account of different versions of feminism. Alison Jaggar suggests that consideration of women's "standpoint" may provide a criterion for evaluating different feminist theories.[44] For Jaggar, the "socialist feminist concept of the standpoint of women" is crucial to such evaluation.[45] In general, I agree with this view. Among other versions of feminism, however, postmodern feminism is most strongly supportive of an extension of feminist standpoint to individuals. For postmodern feminists, the privileged standpoint of women is borrowed from Simone de Beauvoir's category of otherness, which they extol rather than reject.[46] For de Beauvoir, the category of otherness applies to women as a group; for postmodern feminists, the category applies to individuals as well. Rosemarie Tong describes the more positive interpretation of women's otherness as enabling "individual women to stand back and criticize the norms, values, and practices that the dominant culture (patriarchy) seeks to impose on everyone, including those who live on its periphery."[47] In other words, the very otherness of women, both as individuals and as a group, introduces a potential for change and difference that justifies the privileged status of their standpoints.

Through its link with deconstruction, postmodern feminism is anti-essentialist. The anti-essentialism entails a rejection not only of universal definitions, but also of traditional male-defined dichotomies between reason and emotion, beautiful and ugly, self and other, and of rigid boundaries between disciplines such as art, biology, and psychology.[48] A dichotomy between maleness and femaleness can be challenged not only on postmodernist grounds but even on biological grounds because of the different chromosomal arrangements that may characterize members of either sex.[49] Whereas categorizations may be inevitable and useful, rigid distinctions and dichotomies tend to be stereotypic and artificial, betraying the complexity of real individuals and adequate accounts of them.

Through its insistence on uncategorizable differences among individuals, postmodern feminism may be particularly supportive of nondirectiveness in genetic counseling. However, so radical a critique raises enormous epistemological and communicative problems. Some postmodernists even reject the term "feminism"; nonetheless, their views are profoundly feminist in that they propose for women the most fundamental liberation of all: "freedom from oppressive thought."[50] Individual women, after all, cannot be adequately defined by the thoughts of others, even when the others are feminists.

Taking account of differences between individuals as well as groups means proceeding on two tracks at once. On one track we pay attention to the actual standpoints of individuals; on the other, we also look for patterns of oppression or domination in different groups in order to identify and rectify systemic injustice or exploitation. Sandra Harding recognizes the tension that occurs when the standpoint of an individual is at odds with that of a group with which she is identified. She maintains, however, that this "apparent tension in feminist thought is simply one we should learn to live with."[51] On both tracks, women's experience is the starting point of the critique.

Feminist standpoint theory applies to women as a group and to women as individuals through an egalitarian perspective that takes account of all of the differences that arise in people's lives. Genetics provides multiple examples of the need to identify and evaluate these differences to limit inequities that might otherwise exist. As the following case illustrates, even when we think we have done that, our inevitable nearsightedness may cause us to miss inequitable gender differences.

A Feminist Standpoint in Genetics: The Case of Maternal PKU

Julia Smith Andre is a 27-year-old woman who, through a routine newborn test, was discovered at birth to have phenylketonuria (PKU). PKU is an inborn (genetically determined) error of metabolism which usually entails severe mental retardation unless the child's diet is restricted to ensure low serum phenylalanine levels. The required diet is exceedingly bland, consisting mainly of breads, cereals, fats, fruits, and vegetables, supplemented by a formula containing amino acids and other nutrients with no phenylalanine. If phenylalanine intake is well-controlled after the condition is identified within the first few days of life, development is normal. The dietary restrictions must continue at least until late childhood or adolescence, when they may be eliminated gradually without severe deleterious consequences. However, discontinuation of the diet has been associated with reduced achievement levels and with peripheral and central neuropathies. Consequently, current policy is to recommend ongoing dietary restriction.[52]

A significant caveat to the prevention of phenotypic expression of PKU applies only to women. Unless an affected woman, whether symptomless or not, continues her restrictive diet, or returns to it early in her pregnancy or before becoming pregnant, her fetus has a very high probability (>90%) of acquiring an even more serious disease, maternal PKU (MPKU).[53] Because phenylalanine concentrates in the fetus, the recommended diet prior to and during pregnancy is even more restrictive for women with PKU. MPKU in their children is a teratogenic rather than genetic condition. In 92%–95% of cases it involves severe mental retardation; it also carries a 73% risk of microcephaly and an increased risk of congenital heart disease and low birth weight.[54] These problems are not correctable after birth through diet.

Unfortunately, the tragic potential of what was initially thought to be a dietary cure for PKU was not recognized until decades after the newborn test was first offered and dietary restrictions recommended in response to positive results. Women who had avoided symptoms and eventually returned to a normal diet began to have children who were severely symptomatic. Today, testing for PKU is mandatorily performed within days of birth in most jurisdictions, and dietary restrictions are observed to avoid its expression in those who test positive. Through the routinization of testing and dietary control, symptoms of the disease have been virtually eliminated for those affected. But, many women who were apparently "cured" as infants or young children were never told or may have forgotten that they should return to their restrictive diet to avoid having a severely impaired child. Julia Smith Andre was one of these women. Unlike affected children, who, if "treated" soon after birth, may not miss foods they have never had, women with "treated" PKU find it difficult to return to a low-phenylalanine diet after having enjoyed a normal diet.[55] This was clearly the case for Julia.

During her first pregnancy, Julia was contacted by an organization that scanned wedding announcements in local newspapers to identify women whose medical records indicated that they had tested positive for PKU as newborns. The women were notified of the risk to children they might have if they did not return to their childhood diet. By the time Julia was contacted she was already six weeks pregnant.

Julia attempted to follow the recommended diet, but the PKU formulas nauseated her, making it difficult for her to consume enough protein to sustain a healthy pregnancy. Brain development of fetuses can be severely compromised by inadequate nutrition.[56] Charles, Julia's husband, was an unemployed chef, who detested the blandness of the diet. At 10 weeks gestation, nocturnal nasogastric infusions were begun, producing lower phenylalanine levels. Because this regimen could not be tolerated over a long period, a percutaneous feeding gastrostomy was placed at 12 weeks gestation, and this was maintained for the duration of the pregnancy.[57] At 38 weeks gestation, intrauterine growth retardation was diagnosed and a cesarean section was performed for the sake of the fetus. Although the baby was small for gestational age, there were no neonatal problems. At follow-up two years later, the child showed normal growth and development.

When her daughter was nearly three, Julia became pregnant again. This time she was aware of the recommendation to return to her PKU diet before conception, but she did not do so. Although she voluntarily reduced her phenylalinine intake when she learned she was pregnant, her level rose to a point that her clinicians thought dangerous to her fetus. Influenced by her previous experience, however, Julia refused nasogastric infusions and placement of a gastrostomy. Special phenylalanine-free protein pills were recommended as a dietary supplement; 240 pills per day were required to provide adequate protein intake. At 16 weeks gestation, it was evident that Julia was not taking all of the pills and was probably supplementing her diet with high-protein foods. Her serum phenylalanine was at a level associated with fetal microcephaly and mental retardation. When intravenous infusions of phenylalanineless supplements were recommended, Julia refused. Her caregivers questioned whether they might legally and morally coerce her to accept treatment they considered essential to avoid severe impairment of her newborn. While it is possible that her reasoning process was compromised by not adhering to the diet, she could hardly be judged incompetent on that basis.

The illegality of coercion in this case was clear enough. To some extent the case parallels other situations of "maternal–fetal conflict"[58] in which pregnant women's competent and informed refusal of treatment must be respected at least until fetal viability. The ethics of coercion to accept treatment is more problematic, depending on variables such as the degree of discomfort and duration of interventions required to minimize risk to the fetus. Clearly, the standpoint of the person most affected is crucial to this assessment. From the standpoint of an outsider to the case, the inconvenience of temporary dietary restriction may seem a small burden, and therefore easily overridable by the benefit of avoiding profound retardation in a newborn. Julia, however, is likely to weigh these factors differently on grounds of her actual experience of their impact.

Both legal and ethical rationales for giving priority to the patient's autonomy in this case are supportable by the extended version of feminist standpoint theory outlined above. Patients generally belong to a nondominant group to whom privileged status may be imputed because the recommendations that govern their care are made by the dominant group. Accordingly, to the extent that patient autonomy is given greater weight currently than in past times and in other cultures, feminist standpoint theory has been implemented. Its epistemological justification stems from the fact that patients know best what they experience with regard to their condition and its treatment or nontreatment. What clinicians know, by and large, consists of generalizations developed through the years from their studies and experiences with other patients. All of this knowledge is pertinent but not enough, which explains why physicians in training are often warned to be wary of the limitations of their learned or acquired generalizations. As experienced doctors often put it: "When in doubt, look at the patient." Feminist standpoint theory would require more: to remain in doubt until one examines and listens to the particular patient.

While patients as such generally belong to a nondominant group, they often belong to nondominant groups in other ways as well. Julia was apparently dominated in one of those ways. Caregivers did not recognize this form of domination until after she had her second daughter, who unfortunately was severely affected with MPKU. At a conference where the possibility of coercive treatment during a potential third pregnancy was discussed, a geneticist who had counseled Julia informed the group: "Julia will probably become pregnant again because her husband wants her to have a son and insists that they keep trying to have one." In light of Charles's insistence, along with his views about diet and Julia's apparent unwillingness to conform to medical recommendations, the geneticist considered it highly likely that Julia would have another affected child. Moreover, if her third child were a daughter, the geneticist thought that Julia would go on having affected daughters until she had a son, whether affected or not. Describing Julia's relationship to her husband in the context of the demands of caring for an affected child, the geneticist compared her situation to that of a battered woman.

Feminist standpoint theory would impute privileged status to Julia not only as a patient herself but as the mother of a severely compromised child and apparently as a dominated wife. Her desires about becoming pregnant, the possibility of pregnancy termination, and conformity to medical recommendations before or after pregnancy might well have altered in the months following the birth of her second child. Accordingly, her caregivers would be obliged not only to inform her as fully as possible of the risks and recommendations for reducing them, but also to ask for and listen to her views on the matter, attempting to facilitate a truly autonomous decision and to respect that decision as coming from the one most affected by it.[59] Engaging Julia's husband in the process would be appropriate as well—as a possible support to Julia in maintaining her diet and as acknowledgment of his partial responsibility for the outcome. Although dominant with regard to Julia, Charles is probably nondominant vis-à-vis her caregivers.

Granting privileged status to nondominant individuals or groups does not imply that their decisions should always prevail. Some nondominant individuals are unable to make decisions for themselves; however, their interests are morally relevant to others' decisions that affect them. Julia's older daughter, for example, was undoubtedly affected by having a sister who is severely compromised, but whether the impact of this is positive or negative depends largely on how her parents deal with the situation. The life prospects of Julia's second daughter have apparently been compromised by Julia's inadequate compliance with dietary recommendations during pregnancy, but whether that possibility would have justified coercive treatment of Julia is doubtful.

The criterion by which conflicting desires or interests should be resolved is the mediating principle of justice or equality, which in this case requires equitable distribution of burdens and benefits. Other factors being equal, then, the desires or interests of the individual or group most significantly affected should have priority over the desires and interests of others. Patients are not only nondominant but also more significantly affected than nonpatients, and mothers too tend to be nondominant and are generally more significantly affected than fathers by caregiving responsibilities for their children.

Granting privileged status to Julia Smith Andre's decision regarding diet control and medical interventions during pregnancy, and to her decisions about a future pregnancy, is supported by feminist standpoint theory. So long as the impact of her decision does not disproportionately burden others, an egalitarian version of feminism further supports her decisions. In subsequent chapters I extend this egalitarian feminist analysis to a variety of issues in genetics.

Notes

1. To the extent that differences in genetics are associated with inequities toward men, they need to be identified and addressed as well, but that is not the focus of this book.

2. I have elaborated this perspective more extensively in Chapter 1 of *Women and Children in Health Care: An Unequal Majority* (New York: Oxford University Press, 1993), pp. 3–19.

3. Some of the material developed here is drawn from my article "On Treatment of Myopia: Feminist Standpoint Theory and Bioethics," in Susan W. Wolf, ed., *Feminism and Bioethics* (New York: Oxford University Press, 1996), pp. 95–111.

4. John J. McDermott, ed., *The Writings of William James* (New York: Modern Library, 1968), pp. 629–45, 227–32, 136–52.

5. Justus Buchler, ed., *Philosophical Writings of Peirce* (New York: Dover Publications, 1955), pp. 4, 38, 42–59, 160, 288, 356.

6. Buchler, pp. 9–10, 28.

7. Charles Hartshorne and Paul Weis, eds., *The Collected Papers of Charles Sanders Peirce,* vol. 2 (Cambridge: Belknap Press of Harvard University Press, 1960), #654.

8. Hartshorne and Weis, #654.

9. Hartshorne and Weis, #654.

10. Tom L. Beauchamp and James Childress, *The Principles of Biomedical Ethics* (New York: Oxford University Press, 1979, 1983, 1989, 1994).

11. The "if" in this statement is intended to allow for the possibility that the interests of one party are never precisely the same as those of another.

12. Beauchamp and Childress, pp. 330–40.

13. Thomas Nagel, *Equality and Partiality* (New York: Oxford University Press, 1991), pp. 10–20.

14. Nagel, p. 10.

15. Nagel could respond to this criticism by claiming that the things that matter most to individual persons matter to all of them (p. 11). My rejoinder to this response is that morality asks more, and sometimes less or other than merely dealing with what matters most to everyone.

16. Katherine Montgomery Hunter, "Narrative," in Warren Reich, ed., *The Encyclopedia of Bioethics* (New York: Macmillan, 1995).

17. Albert R. Jonsen, "Casuistry and Clinical Ethics," *Theoretical Medicine* 7 (February 1986): 65–73.

18. See Carol Gilligan, "Moral Orientation and Moral Development," in Eva Feder Kittay and Diana T. Meyer, eds., *Women and Moral Theory* (Totowa, NJ: Rowman and Littlefield, 1987), pp. 19–33.

19. Of course, patterns emerge in treatment and ethical dilemmas and in ways of addressing them effectively; these patterns are useful and necessary but inadequate to the particularities of each situation. Laura Purdy (personal communication, August 3, 1998) believes that partiality and universalizability are compatible so long as the partiality practiced is judged permissible for everyone in that situation. As suggested above, however (n. 11), no one is ever in precisely the same situation as any other.

20. Nancy C. M. Hartsock, *Money, Sex, and Power* (Boston: Northeastern University Press, 1985), and *The Feminist Standpoint Revisited and Other Essays* (Boulder, CO: Westview Press, 1998), pp. 105–32.

21. Hartsock, *The Feminist Standpoint Revisited,* p. 108.

22. Hartsock, *The Feminist Standpoint Revisited,* p. 235.

23. Donna Haraway, "Situated Knowledges: The Science Question in Feminism and the Privilege of Partial Perspective," *Feminist Studies* 14 (1988): 584.

24. Hartsock, *The Feminist Standpoint Revisited,* pp. 117–25. Hartsock draws on psychoanalytic theory in developing this critique.

25. Haraway, p. 581.

26. Haraway, p. 581.

27. Haraway, p. 584.

28. Haraway, p. 584.

29. John Ladd, "The Ethics of Participation," in J. Roland Pennock and John W. Chapman, *Participation in Politics* Nomos 16 (New York: Lieber-Atherton, 1975), p. 101. Ladd imputes this view to Kurt Baier in *The Moral Point of View* (New York: Random House, 1965), p. 107.

30. Ladd, p. 102.

31. Ladd, p. 103.

32. Ladd, p. 103.

33. The democratic justification for participation may be construed as a deontological argument, e.g., one based on the inalienable right of persons to participate in the development of social policies that affect them. Admittedly, utilitarian arguments may be invoked to curtail as well as to demand participation by nondominant groups. The utilitarian rationale for their participation gives priority to the greatest number of subjects to whom utility is to be applied; this is a democratic interpretation of utilitarianism. The

utilitarian rationale opposing their participation gives priority to the best consequences (greatest happiness), which may be achieved undemocratically by allowing the exclusion of specific groups or individuals.

34. Ladd, p. 103.

35. Ladd, p. 102.

36. Albert Camus, *The Rebel,* trans. Anthony Bower (New York: Alfred A. Knopf, 1956), p. 22.

37. Note that I have identified equality as an *ethical* rather than *psychological* or *empirical* norm. Paradoxically, equality deserves to be supported, and is in fact supported, as an ethical norm by people who are *psychologically* attracted to inequality and pursue it in their empirical affairs. Most of us tend to promote the advantaged side of inequality in our own behalf.

38. Susan Sherwin, *No Longer Patient* (Philadelphia: Temple University Press, 1991), p. 75.

39. Sara Ruddick, *Maternal Thinking: Toward a Politics of Peace* (New York: Ballantine Books, 1989).

40. Hartsock, *Money, Sex and Power,* p. 232.

41. Hartsock, *The Feminist Standpoint Revisited,* p. 231.

42. Hartsock, *The Feminist Standpoint Revisited,* p. 238.

43. Maria C. Lugones and Elizabeth V. Spelman, "Have We Got a Theory for You! Feminist Theory, Cultural Imperialism, and the Demand for 'The Woman's Voice,'" *Women's Studies International Forum* 6 (1983): 573–81, and Elizabeth V. Spelman, *Inessential Woman: Problems of Exclusion in Feminist Thought* (Boston: Beacon Press, 1988).

44. Alison Jaggar, *Feminist Politics and Human Nature* (Totowa, NJ: Rowman and Allanheld, 1983), p. 371.

45. Jaggar, p. 377.

46. Simone de Beauvoir, "The Second Sex," in Mary Briody Mahowald, ed., *Philosophy of Woman* (Indianapolis: Hackett, 1992), p. 82.

47. Rosemarie Tong, *Feminist Thought* (Boulder, CO: Westview Press, 1998), p. 7.

48. Linda J. Nicholson, ed., *Feminism/Postmodernism* (New York: Routledge, 1990), is an excellent collection of articles on postmodern feminism.

49. For example, while most women and men are chromosomally defined as XX and XY, respectively, some are XO, XXX, XXY, or XYY. Moreover, gender identity and sex identity (as defined by chromosomes) may be different in the same individual.

50. Tong, p. 223.

51. Sandra Harding, *The Science Question in Feminism* (Ithaca, NY: Cornell University Press, 1986), p. 195.

52. W. B. Hanley, R. Koch, H. L. Levy, R. Matalon, B. Rouse, C. Azen, and F. de la Cruz, "The North American Maternal Phenylketonuria Collaborative Study, Developmental Assessment of the Offspring: Preliminary Report," *European Journal of Pediatrics* 155, Suppl. 1 (July 1996): S169–72; R. Koch, C. Azen, E. G. Friedman, K. Fishler, C. Baumann-Frischling, and T. Lin, *European Journal of Pediatrics* 155, Suppl. 1 (July 1996): S90–92; and R. Koch, H. Levy, W. Hanley, R. Matalong, B. Rouse, F. Trefz, and F. de la Cruz, "Outcome Implications of the International Maternal Phenylketonuria Collaborative Study (MPKUCS)," *European Journal of Pediatrics* 155, Suppl. 1 (July 1996): S162–64.

53. W. B. Hanley, J. T. R. Clarke, and W. Schoonheyt, "Maternal Phenylketonuria (PKU)—A Review," *Clinical Biochemistry* 20 (June 1987): 149–56.

54. E. Waisbren, B. D. Hamilton, P. J. St. James, S. Shiloh, and H. L. Levy, "Psychosocial Factors in Maternal Phenylketonuria: Women's Adherence to Medical Recommendations," *American Journal of Public Health* 85, 12 (1995): 1636.

55. "Treatment" of PKU means dietary restriction that avoids the onset or exacerbation of symptoms.

56. J. Dobbing, "Maternal Nutrition in Pregnancy and Later Achievement of Offspring," *Early Human Development* 12 (1985): 1–8; W. B. Hanley, L. Linsao, W. Davidson, and C. A. F. Moes, "Maturation with Early Treatment of Phenylketonuria," *Pediatric Research* 4 (1970): 318–27.

57. Prolonged use of a nasograstric tube for feeding involves risks of dislodgement and aspiration into the esophagus.

58. Some authors have questioned the term "maternal–fetal conflict" on grounds that the disagreements to which the term refers generally occur between clinicians and pregnant women. Typically, both want what is best for the fetus but they have different views on how to pursue that goal. Ellen J. Stein, "Maternal–Fetal Conflict: Reformulating the Equation," in Andrew Grubb, ed., *Challenges in Medical Care* (Chichester: John Wiley and Sons, 1992), pp. 91–92.

59. It may of course be argued that the fetus or potential child is more drastically affected by Julia's decision than she is. Among those who are autonomous, however, Julia is clearly the one most affected. Whether the impact on the fetus is morally compelling depends on the moral status attributed to it, an issue that appears irresolvable by philosophical or public consensus.

2

WOMEN IN GENETICS RESEARCH

STEREOTYPICALLY, a scientist is a white male. Like other stereotypes, this one includes both valid and distortive elements. Most scientists are in fact white and male, but many are neither. The medical research pursued by these mainly white male scientists has prevalently focused on men's health rather than women's, and some studies have erroneously assumed that their results are applicable to women even when men alone are studied.[1] This is not surprising because people are naturally inclined to define others' interests as coincident with their own.[2] The prevalence of white male researchers and reviewers is thus likely to influence decisions about what research is done and what research is funded. Broader participation of minorities and women as investigators and reviewers is a means of reducing the nearsightedness associated with these decisions.

Men are also more likely than women to be enrolled in research studies. Because women are reported to be more inclined toward affiliative and altruistic behavior than men, this difference is somewhat surprising.[3] This chapter explores reasons for such discrepancies. I begin with an empirical account of the extent to which women are involved as researchers in biology and genetics. Having documented the limited number of women who are researchers, I delineate five areas in which issues particularly or exclusively applicable to women need to be targeted by researchers. More provocatively and speculatively, I then consider whether the style, content, and methods of science tend to be different for women than for men, and possible implications of such differences for advances in genetics. With regard to participation of women as research subjects, I assess reasons for their exclusion, and discuss efforts to extend their participation.

Women in Human Genome Research

A question sometimes asked in connection with human genome research is "Whose genome is to be mapped and sequenced?"[4] The answer to this question suggests that the research itself is gender neutral: the genome targeted is a generic composite, developed mainly from existing cell lines of healthy individuals of both sexes from different races and ethnic groups. The DNA regions that are of particular interest to researchers involve diseases that are symptomatic, either exclusively or predominantly, in either sex, such as X-linked diseases in men and breast cancer in women. On a trivial level, it may be argued that the genome to be mapped and sequenced is male because the Y chromosome, which women lack, is included in the generic genome.[5] But this argument is defeated by the claim that adequate understanding of the human genome requires studies of all of the different chromosomes present in human beings. It is further defeated by efforts to clone the mitochondrial genome, which is inherited exclusively from females.

In the United States, federal funding for genomic research is obtained through grants and contracts from the Department of Energy and the National Institutes of Health (NIH). At the NIH, in which the National Human Genome Research Institute (NHGRI) is located, the number of women who apply for grants is considerably less than the number of men who apply. This may be a matter of gender inequity in its own right, but it is not one over which NIH has control. Despite the gender imbalance of applicants, the percentage of grants awarded to men and women is not substantially different. In fiscal year 1997, for example, 5500 applications were submitted to NIH by women, and 28.7% of them were successful. During the same period, 16,849 proposals were submitted by men, and 30.6% were successful.[6] The Ethical, Legal, and Social Issues (ELSI) Program, a small part of the NHGRI at NIH, has an excellent track record for grants to women. In 114 successful grants from 1990 to 1998, the principal investigators of 58 were women.[7] Topically, grants that address predisposition testing for breast cancer or Alzheimer disease, prenatal testing, and carrier testing for hemophilia or cystic fibrosis implicitly focus on women because women comprise the majority of study participants. Projects that target nurses or master's-prepared genetic counseling focus implicitly on women for the same reason. As of this writing, however, only two grants have acknowledged and addressed the differential impact of genetics on women in other areas of genetics by identifying women as their explicit focus.[8]

Although the research involved in mapping and sequencing the human genome appears to be gender neutral, differential impact undeniably occurs with regard to specific genetic conditions. The sex differences that are observable across the spectrum of genetic diseases are categorizable in five ways: (1) conditions that primarily or exclusively affect one sex only, (2) conditions affecting the sexes in unequal ratios, (3) conditions determined by the sex or some other characteristic of the transmitting parent, (4) conditions affecting fertility differently in men and women, and (5) conditions in which pregnancy poses particular risks to affected women. Table 2–1 elaborates these differences in more detail.

All of these sex differences are relevant morally as well as clinically because they are often associated with discrepant impact. Because they are determined by biology, the differences themselves are virtually unchangeable. Nonetheless, the inequity or disadvantages for women with which some differences are associated may be ameliorated even if not eliminated through social measures that reduce the inequity of their impact. If justice is an important social goal or ethical imperative, society in general is morally obliged to look for ways of reducing inequities or disadvantages associated with differences in whomever they occur.

In general, Table 2–1 shows that the conditions in which men and women are differently affected may entail inequitable impact for either sex. For many phenotypes, the sex ratio is abnormal even though the causative gene is autosomal because the milieu in which the gene is expressed is conditioned in part by sexual constitution. However, different prenatal and postnatal survival data may skew the observed sex ratio for specific genetic conditions; that more males are born but proportionately more females survive may be due to factors other than genetics.[9]

Because X-linked diseases are symptomatic only or mainly in males, men are directly affected by more genetic diseases than women. From an egalitarian perspective, the psychological onus that mothers experience by being "responsible" for transmitting X-linked diseases to their children—as fathers are not—seems less onerous than the burden of the disease experienced by their sons (and some of their daughters). Women are also "responsible," as men are not, for transmitting mitochondrial disorders to their offspring. To the extent that some men are more disadvantaged than women by specific genetic conditions, gender justice calls for efforts to reduce the inequity associated with these conditions. From an egalitarian feminist standpoint, their standpoint deserves the privileged status of any nondominant group.

In a number of ways, however, women tend to be more disadvantaged than men by genetic diseases; to the extent that this is so, they too deserve privi-

TABLE 2–1. Types and Examples of Sex Differences in Clinical Manifestations of Genetic Disease

1. *Conditions affecting one sex only or primarily*
   a. Most X-linked diseases (affected male, unaffected female carrier)
      Examples: Duchenne muscular dystrophy, Hunter syndrome, hemophilia A
   b. Sex-limited diseases (due to the nature of the disease)
      Examples: Breast cancer (mainly women), ovarian cancer (only women)
      Prostate cancer, hypospadias (only men)
2. *Conditions affecting the sexes in unequal ratios*
   a. Male> female
      Example: Posterior urethal valves
   b. Female> male
      Example: Anencephaly
3. Conditions determined by the sex or other characteristic of the transmitting parent
   a. Triplet repeat expansion diseases
      Examples: Fragile X, myotonic dystrophy (maternal inheritance increases severity)
      Huntington disease (paternal inheritance increases severity)
   b. Imprinting diseases
      Examples: Angelman syndrome (deficiency of maternal contribution)
      Prader-Willi syndrome (deficiency of paternal contribution)
   c. Parental age effect
      Examples: Down syndrome (older mothers)
      Achondroplastic dwarfism, Marfan syndrome (older fathers)
   d. Mitochondrial inheritance (always transmitted by mothers)
      Examples: Myoclonic epilepsy, ragged red muscle fiber disease
4. *Conditions affecting fertility in males and females*
   a. Infertility in males
      Example: Cystic fibrosis
   b. Infertility in females
      Example: Congenital adrenal hyperplasia
5. *Conditions in which pregnancy exacerbates risks for affected women*
   Examples: Cystic fibrosis, sickle cell anemia, Marfan syndrome, neurofibromatosis

Sources: Mary B. Mahowald, Dana Levinson, Christine Cassel, Amy Lemke, Carole Ober, James Bowman, Michelle Le Bean, Amy Ravin, and Melissa Times, "The New Genetics and Women," *Millbank Quarterly* 74, 2 (1996): 244–46, Mary Buyse, ed., *Birth Defects Encyclopedia* (Cambridge, MA: Blackwell Scientific Publishers, 1990), and Victor A. McKusick, *Online Mendelian Inheritance in Man,* http://www3.ncbi.nlm.nih.gov:80/0mim/.

leged status based on their nondominance. Two types of disadvantage for women are associated with their role in reproduction. As illustrated by the last type of difference in Table 2–1, pregnancy exacerbates the symptoms, occasionally to a life-threatening degree, of some genetic diseases. Ironically, the success of medical technology in extending the life span of affected persons has been accompanied by this increased risk for women only. Another biology-based disadvantage for women is that fetal tests and interventions for any of the diseases mentioned can be conducted through their bodies only; men never experience the risks and discomforts of these procedures, even though they may be genetically "responsible" for the condition being identified or treated.

Beyond sex-based differences in clinical manifestations of genetic conditions is the possibility of gender-based differences in how research in general and genetics research in particular is conducted. Because the experience of women is inevitably different in some respects from the experience of men, it seems reasonable to think that their different experiences are reflected in the topics they choose to study and in the ways in which they pursue their studies. But do women in fact pursue science differently than men? Although the next section supports an affirmative answer to the question, a negative answer is defensible as well. Moreover, even if there were utterly compelling evidence of generalizable differences in the research practice of men and women, this would not imply that either type of difference is conducive to better research. Nor would it imply that all women or all men "do" science or choose their research questions in correspondence with the differences attributed to their gender. From a feminist standpoint, the argument for inclusion of women in developing and pursuing a research agenda has a remedial intent: it is necessary to reduce the unfortunate but inevitable myopia of the dominant group.

Do Women Conduct Research in Genetics Differently from Men?

According to Evelyn Fox Keller, this question is difficult to answer because it is impossible to separate women and men from the different cultural contexts in which their lives are imbedded.[10] Possibly the dearth of women who pursue careers in science is influenced by those features of its practice that exemplify the characteristics attributed mainly to men. Although Keller is credited with the claim that women and men approach science differently, she considers this a "mistranslation" of her view. Rather, she wants to improve the quality of science by articulating the deficiencies of a stereotypical male model of the scientist as detached and unfeeling.[11] She cites Nobel laureate Barbara McClintock as an example of a scientist whose methodology combined elements of both masculine and feminine approaches. McClintock, according to Keller, seemed to develop a relationship with the corn she studied, "listening" to what it had to tell her even when she "heard" things that contradicted prevailing dogma. By joining her intuitive strengths to the rationalist model of science, McClintock succeeded beyond those who employed only the latter approach. Men as well as women, Keller says, are fully capable of and do in fact employ both approaches to science. The approaches combined are more likely to be successful than either alone. Because of the pervasive association of science with masculine stereotypes, however, the combined model is less likely to be followed by men.

The question of gender differences in the conduct of science is not unrelated to the question of whether men and women think differently in moral matters. On this question, the literature of moral psychology, bioethics, and feminism has been burgeoning in recent years.[12] Women in general are described as more attentive to particular relationships and responsibilities borne of those relationships; men are more likely to affirm individual rights and abstract, universal principles. The former has been dubbed a care ethic; the latter a justice ethic.[13] If women exemplify a care ethic in science, they are more likely to be collaborative than competitive in their research.[14] Women may thus be more inclined to share data with colleagues and to practice the altruistic commitment to knowledge that Charles Sanders Peirce declared essential to scientific progress.[15] Although many women do not conform to this characterization, those who do may be more likely, through greater attention to context and relationships, to pick projects that are wholistic and complex rather than atomistic and simple. This tendency, in whomever it occurs, has its drawbacks as well as advantages because no one individual can see the whole picture with all of its complexity. The collaborative strategy that classical pragmatism and feminist standpoint theory both support is a practical means of reducing that limitation.

As we saw in Chapter 1, a feminist standpoint also involves critique of the concepts of objectivity and rationality, which are seen as integral to science. "Objectivity" refers to the status of the knowledge gained through scientific method as well as to the method itself. With regard to both, it means that reason and facts alone determine the conclusions reached. "Rationality" refers to the means by which facts are related, organized, and interpreted, through logical analysis moving inexorably from its premises to its conclusions. Of course, the truth of a conclusion depends on that of the premises, and, to the extent that scientific reasoning is inductive rather than deductive, its conclusions are inevitably provisional. Rationality and objectivity are nonetheless tied to science and to each other. They are also tied to the assumption that subjective biases and emotional factors are eliminable in the practice of science.

Despite the prevalence of "faith" in objectivity and rationality, most scientists are likely to agree with Ruth Bleier's observation that there is "hardly a significant area of science however remote from gender or race or other social issues, that does not engender wildly differing opinions, intense passions, irrational responses, and personal antagonisms." Further, according to Bleier, "Most scientists would not be happy in their work nor would science have accomplished so much as it has in understanding natural phenomena and applying the knowledge to social uses were these passions and drives absent from the laboratory."[16] Scientists, in other words, are not Platonic minds or Cartesian thinking machines. Rather, they are mind–body composites in whom reason and passion commingle—fortunately.

Related to the alleged "emotionlessness" or objectivity of science is the notion of value neutrality in the pursuit and attainment of knowledge. Some scientists see this feature as a significant distinction between their discipline and ethics. At least in its prescriptive form, ethics affirms and argues for specific moral positions, principles, or values. While knowledge is a value, it is not necessarily a moral value. Unless virtue is knowledge, as Plato maintained,[17] it is not what we know but what we do (or don't do) with what we know that counts as moral right or wrong, good or bad. Hence, in the name of scientific neutrality, some scientists divorce themselves from consideration of the moral questions raised by their advances, leaving the analysis of those implications to others.[18] In doing so, they fail to acknowledge or demonstrate their own status as moral agents.

Further reinforcement of a separation between ethics and science comes from the very different kinds of analysis that each undertakes. Scientists are comfortable working with empirical data, experimental design, and technical equipment; humanist/philosopher types are comfortable working with concepts, distinctions, books, and arguments. Understandably but regrettably, one group often underrates or distrusts the expertise and importance of the other. Scientists sometimes avoid listening to nonscientists, and vice versa. For example, I once asked a sociologist who was planning a workshop on social aspects of genomic research how he would ensure that participants had sufficient understanding of its basic genetics to address its implications. To my dismay, he replied: "We don't need to know about the science to discuss policy issues."

Similarly dismaying is Arthur Kornberg's defense of the reluctance of fellow scientists to communicate with the public. The typical scientist, he said, is "immobilized only when he steps into the social and political arena." Attributing this reluctance to the demands of science itself, Kornberg added: "The biochemist who deals with molecules cannot afford any time away from them."[19] The demands of science may well be too great to allow some of its practitioners to have a life beyond the laboratory. Because of their discrepant roles in reproduction and child rearing, such demands are likely to discourage more women than men from pursuing careers in science. To the extent that women are more context-oriented than men, they are also less likely to overlook the moral and social implications of their research.

Some well-known and respected scientists rebut Kornberg's view through their success both in and out of the laboratory.[20] In fact, success in one realm may facilitate success in the other. Either physical or psychological "time away" from one's own discipline or specialization is required to broaden one's standpoint and overcome the limitations of a single perspective. In clinical practice as well as research, however, generalists are seldom as highly esteemed as specialists, and women comprise a proportionately greater number of generalists in practice.[21]

Even if knowledge is morally neutral, choices regarding topics pursued and methods for pursuing them may not escape the influence of gender stereotypes. For example, many biologists have studied fertilization by concentrating on the activity of sperm while neglecting the active role of the egg; to some scholars this suggests stereotypical thinking about female passivity.[22] Nor are the choices themselves always morally neutral. While the quantitative nature of genetics lends itself to pretensions of neutrality, objectivity, and rationality, reproductive genetics inevitably raises morally controversial and emotionally charged issues such as abortion and "surrogacy."

Admittedly, the mathematical model of genetic predictability is purely rational; genetic counseling endorses a moral neutrality that supports this model. Genetic reductionism, by which human beings are defined solely on the basis of their genetic composition, provides a way of ignoring the complexity and unpredictability of life and the moral quandaries that life entails for most individuals. Conclusions reached through a reductionist methodology are supposedly uninfluenced by the perspectives or experiences of those who reach them. Because of the clarity that reductionism affords, many are tempted to accept its erroneous conclusions, thinking they thus understand a whole when at best they have grasped but a part of a part.

In the early days of genetics, the reductionist thesis was buttressed by the fact that most of the conditions identified by genetic researchers were single gene disorders.[23] Once it was learned that a disorder was homozygous or heterozygous, its predictability (e.g., one in two or one in four) was mathematically determinable. Of course, as Ruth Hubbard has explained, we still do not know just when and how a particular disease will be expressed.[24] Sickle cell disease and cystic fibrosis, for example, affect some individuals much more severely than others who have the same genetic mutation.[25] Indeed, through recent advances in genetics, we have discovered individuals who are symptomless despite mutations identical with those found in affected individuals.[26] Even predictable traits may be expressed in various forms (e.g., different hues of blue eyes in the same family). Nowadays we know that most genetic conditions, whether diseases or normal variations, are polygenic, multifactorial, or inherited in complicated, non-Mendelian patterns. Still, comparatively little is known about how genetic and environmental factors affect each other. The reductionist model that has been attributed both to genetics and to a masculine model of reasoning is therefore not only inadequate but misleading.[27] Only a broader sense of context and of the limits of mathematical prediction can reduce the ignorance that remains through application of that single perspective.

To the extent that women are more context-oriented and relationship-oriented than men, they are less likely than men to accept a reductionist model of genetics and more likely to pursue their research collaboratively rather than individualistically. To the extent that women tend to value emotion more highly than men, they are more likely to reject a purely rational, objective, or emotionless model of science. Because of unique aspects of their experience as women, women are also more likely to identify areas of research that are relevant to them but not relevant or less relevant to men. As Alison Wylie observes, men are often unaware, or if they are aware, little interested in the circumstances that put women at a disadvantage vis-à-vis themselves.[28]

That said, the avoidance of stereotypic interpretations of gender differences is morally and epistemologically as necessary to research as it is to other areas of life. Whether or not gender-defined differences are present in real individuals of either sex, the goals of research are facilitated through critique of longstanding assumptions and methods derived from a model of rationality and objectivity that forecloses new ways of thinking about and practicing science. From their different standpoints, nondominant scientists can envision these new ways and implement them more effectively, thus enabling science to stretch beyond the limits defined solely from the standpoint of those who are dominant.

Increasing the number of women who do research in genetics may lead to more research on issues relevant to women. However, such research demands greater participation of women as research subjects. As we will see in the next section, this raises questions of gender justice based not only on past practices of underinclusion but on the potential for overinclusion of women in research protocols.

Women as Research Subjects in Genetics

Women have prevalently been excluded from human subjects research for good, bad, inadequate, and fallacious reasons.[29] Good reasons include those based on pejorative risk-to-benefit ratios, lack of consent, and irrelevance of the research to women. Bad, inadequate, or fallacious reasons include fears of liability, biases favoring men, avoidance of complexity, paternalism, and the presumption that data applicable to men are applicable to women. Not only pregnant and potentially pregnant women have been excluded from research; those who are definitively infertile such as postmenopausal women and very young girls have been excluded because of age or incompetence to consent. Regardless of the reasons for exclusion, the overall result is that many women are treated unscientifically, that is, through means that have not been proved effective or safe for them. Had a feminist standpoint been introduced into review processes for research excluding women, it is doubtful that their virtual disenfranchisement from participation would have occurred.

Concern about even a slim possibility of pregnancy, and distrust of women who have indicated that they have no intention of becoming pregnant, is widespread among reviewers of research protocols. According to guidelines of the Federal Drug Administration (FDA), the exclusion of any woman "of childbearing potential" applies to all women capable of becoming pregnant, whether married or single, regardless of whether they are on "oral, injectable, or mechanical contraception, " even if their "husbands [*sic*] have been vasectomized or . . . have received or are utilizing mechanical contraceptive devices."[30] At times, the apparent anxiety about this issue is totally unsupported by the facts. Consider, for example, the following remark by a member of an Institutional Review Board (IRB), during discussion of the board's policy regarding inclusion of potentially pregnant women in drug studies: "The worst thing that could happen is that someone enrolled in a study would get pregnant and not have an abortion."[31] Because this attitude may be fairly prevalent but rarely articulated, it deserves further analysis.

First, the remark seems to ignore the high probability in a given case that the embryo or fetus would not be deleteriously affected by the pregnant woman taking the drug under study. While some drugs are toxic to some fetuses, depending on the type of drug, dosage, means of ingestion, and stage of gestation, most are not. Second, the remark suggests that a woman *should* have an abortion if she becomes pregnant during a drug study. Obviously, this view would not be legally enforceable, but the moral support it entails for abortion is surely questionable in its own right. Many people, including pregnant women, would disagree that terminating a pregnancy because of the possibility of fetal anomaly is morally *worse* than continuing the pregnancy; some would even see continuation as morally demanded.[32] Moreover, institutional endorsement of the sentiment expressed by the IRB member could lead to pressure on pregnant women in such circumstances, compromising the autonomy of their decisions. Finally, the remark implicitly negates the right to life and value of life of those who are disabled: it suggests, in fact, that it would be better for them not to be born. Chapter 8 examines this apparent implication more fully.

Facilitated by human genome research, genetic testing unrelated to reproduction has increased in recent years, and this is likely to continue as tests for late onset and multifactorial disorders proliferate. Even so, the fact that genetic testing unrelated to reproduction can and does occur does not eliminate the possibility of prenatal testing for the same disorders that can be postnatally detected and possibly prevented or treated before birth. Prenatal tests for Huntington chorea, for example, have been available and utilized for several years, and prenatal tests for susceptibility to adult cancers are also available. Although there are important differences between Huntington disease and adult cancers, in both cases those affected experience normally healthy childhoods. Nonetheless, a pregnant woman whose fetus tests positive for a late onset disorder has the legal option of termination, an option that is foreclosed to her once an affected child is born.

Genetic tests for different diseases raise different kinds of issues, in part because the knowledge obtained through testing often involves ignorance about its implications, regardless of whether the results are positive or negative. Once the specificity and sensitivity of each new test is determined, the recurrent questions raised are whether it should be offered, and if so, to whom and under what conditions.[33] Because of their central role in reproduction, women are more significantly affected than men by the answers to these questions. In contrast to their underrepresentation in other areas of medical research, women are thus the principal subjects of research in genetics, particularly reproductive genetics. The fact that more women than men are needed for this research (because of their distinctive reproductive roles) does not necessarily lead to women's being overrepresented. Women are overrepresented in genetics research if their involvement exceeds this necessity or if the potential for men to participate is ignored or neglected. Susan Rosser suggests that an overrepresentation of women in reproductive research stems from "men's interest in controlling production of children."[34] Research in genetics may provide another means of assuming such control.

From a feminist perspective, the commonality between underrepresentation of women in nonreproductive research and overrepresentation of women in reproductive research is that the interests of the dominant group prevail in both cases. Whether advertently or not, the interest that has prevailed in nonreproductive research is the promotion of men's health, while the interest that has prevailed in reproductive research is the promotion of the health of their offspring. In neither situation is the promotion of women's health an essential goal. Moreover, pursuit of the prevailing interests of men and their potential children may at times conflict with women's interests. For the interests of men to be promoted through reproductive research, the direct involvement of women is indispensable, whereas their own involvement is typically minimal or unnecessary. Reproductive genetic tests are but one means of involvement; prenatal interventions for the sake of the fetus are another.

One of the factors considered in determining whether a particular test should be offered to women (prenatally or postnatally), to men, or to children is the possibility of prevention or therapy. For the majority of genetic diseases, effective therapy is unavailable and prevention is impossible or dubious. In the case of children, the Institute of Medicine (IOM) and the American Academy of Pediatrics have explicitly recommended that testing not be offered unless effective therapy is available.[35] However, there are some conditions of fetuses that can be treated in utero and some conditions for which gene therapy may be effective only if it is administered prenatally. This means that women are treated for the sake of their fetuses or potential children, while men undergo no comparable risk or pain for the fetuses or potential children to whom they are genetically related. As we will see in the next chapter, most of the currently available means of fetal therapy or surgery, as well as gene therapy, are experimental; through the Human Genome Project and increasing availability of genetic tests, more experimental protocols for treatment of fetuses are likely to surface. In each case, women will be asked or expected to participate as research subjects.

In general, then, women may be discriminated against through either exclusion or inclusion in medical research. Although exclusion has been the pattern of the recent past, gender discrimination in the new genetics is more likely to occur through overinclusion. Because women play an irreplaceable role in that research—one that men are unable to play even if that is their desire—women may be pressured to participate in the development of genetic diagnostics and treatment that are not in their interests.

Admittedly, there are benefits to those who participate in research protocols. For example, research subjects tend to get better care and attention than nonparticipants, even with respect to areas that are not essential to study goals.[36] Study subjects may not be required to pay for the care associated with their participation and may even be compensated for their participation. Knowledge obtained through their participation may thus increase the options and may benefit some women and their potential children, as well as women and their children who benefit by that knowledge in the future. None of these benefits, however, is certain. Moreover, the fact that access to good health care on the part of poor people may require their participation in studies suggests that their consent to participation is not entirely free. From an egalitarian standpoint, access to good health care should not depend on participation in research.

Recent efforts to ensure the inclusion of women in research studies have helped to reduce the gap in medical knowledge relevant to women. As we will see in the next section, however, these efforts do not entirely solve the problems raised by past and ongoing discriminatory practices in research with human subjects.

Efforts to Include Women in Research

In the nineteenth century, medical researchers in the United States commonly used African-American women as their unanesthetized subjects.[37] Following the Civil War, prisoners became their principal subjects for experimentation. Gradually, public perceptions of research as a threat rather than aid to human health led to a policy of protectionism for vulnerable populations. The Nuremberg code of 1949 articulated widespread abhorrence of Nazi experimentation and desire to avoid any repetition of those atrocities. "Voluntary consent of the human subject" was held "absolutely essential" to medical research.[38]

Initially, pregnant women were not identified as a vulnerable population. However, the tragic consequences of lack of surveillance in drug development became evident through use of two new drugs for pregnant women, thalidomide in Great Britain and diethylstilbestrol (DES) in the United States. By 1973, the abuse of subjects who participated in the Tuskegee Syphilis Study had become public knowledge, and the *Roe v. Wade* decision of the U.S. Supreme Court stirred fears of widespread research with human fetuses. These events contributed to a policy of virtual exclusion of pregnant women from research protocols.

According to Karen Rothenberg, recent policies about inclusion of women in research illustrate two types of movement: a policy of encouragement became one of requirement at the NIH, and a policy of exclusion became one of encouragement at the U.S. Food and Drug Administration (FDA).[39] NIH now specifically requires grant applicants to include women and minorities in clinical studies unless they provide a "clear rationale" or "compelling justification" for their exclusion. Compelling justification is defined as "strong scientific or practical reasons," which may include an "unacceptable risk for women of childbearing age."[40] Cost is designated an unacceptable reason for exclusion. Although the policy states that women of childbearing potential should not be routinely excluded from participation in clinical research, it nonetheless permits their exclusion on grounds of exposure of the fetus to "undue risks."[41] So the inclusion *requirement* of the current NIH policy applies to women in general but not to potentially pregnant women; for the latter, inclusion is still a matter of *encouragement.*

The latest FDA guidelines also call for inclusion of women in studies, specifically recognizing that women of childbearing potential are competent to give informed consent to participation in research trials. The guidelines affirm that "informed consent provides the necessary insulation to protect researcher and manufacturer from suit by mother or possible child for all but negligent enrollment practices."[42] Unfortunately, because the FDA guidelines do not have the force of law, drug companies and IRBs may still exclude potentially pregnant women from studies on whatever grounds they consider appropriate. According to those guidelines, the IRB member mentioned earlier could prevail to ensure that no study of potentially pregnant women take place at her institution.

In 1992, the IOM established a committee to examine ethical and legal policies about participation of women, including pregnant women, in clinical research. Foremost among the recommendations that resulted from the committee's deliberations was the following:

> Even when evidence concerning risks is unknown or ambiguous, the decision about acceptability of risk to the pregnancy or to offspring should be made by the woman as part of the informed consent process.[43]

Despite this clear message, existing regulations from the Department of Health and Human Services (DHHS), under which the NIH operates, still follow a presumption of exclusion of pregnant women. The regulations classify pregnant women paternalistically as a "vulnerable population" deserving of special protection against coercion or undue influence.[44] But pregnancy in most circumstances is not a disease that makes women vulnerable to coercion; on the contrary, it is a health-affirming experience for most women, who are as capable as men of resisting "undue influence." However, an important caveat to a policy of presumed inclusion of anyone in research protocols is the requirement of informed consent, which means that the potential subject should be as free to decline as to agree to participate, without jeopardizing her or his ongoing care.[45] From the standpoint of the physician/researcher, who holds a dominant place vis-à-vis the patient/potential subject, the latter should be afforded a privileged position to compensate, at least in part, for the power discrepancy between the two. Subtle pressures, whether they arise from clinicians or others, need to be identified and eliminated to the extent that this is possible.

The current DHHS regulations allow a paternal veto to the pregnant woman's participation in clinical research. From an egalitarian feminist standpoint, this is unacceptable because of the discrepancy between paternal and maternal contributions to reproduction. Paternal involvement in such decisions is appropriate because it acknowledges the potential father's shared responsibility for the pregnancy. In light of that responsibility, women themselves should seek involvement of their partners in such decisions. But involvement is not equivalent to veto. In light of their disproportionate risks and the probability that women will be the main caregivers of their children, veto power regarding their participation in research should belong to pregnant women, not their partners.

As research in genetics increases, studies involving pregnant women are necessary to ensure safety and efficacy of new tests, interventions, and therapies for the women themselves as well as their potential children. To that end, a presumption of inclusion rather than exclusion of women, whether pregnant or not, in research protocols is justified so long as their participation is in fact based on their informed choice. Where such choice is lacking, participation is (unjustifiably) overinclusive. The contrast between the IOM committee's recommendations and currently applicable DHHS regulations shows the need for change. According to Rothenberg, the committee's recommendations are still being integrated into NIH policies.[46]

An egalitarian feminist standpoint supports neither overinclusion nor underinclusion of women in research protocols. While not ideal, the newer policies at NIH and FDA are more in keeping with this standpoint than the policies that preceded them. As with development of amniocentesis and chorionic villus sampling, the changes may well have been motivated, in part at least, by the input of nondominant individuals or groups. At the FDA, for example, AIDS activists first brought to public attention the potential benefits of participation in clinical trials. At the NIH, the first woman to assume the role of director, Bernadine Healy, enthusiastically supported the development of the new guidelines, citing examples from her experience as a cardiologist to document the need for gender-inclusive research. "Being different from men," she wrote, "meant being second-class and less than equal for most of recorded time and throughout most of the world."[47] Apparently, Healy considered women's inclusion a remedial step toward gender equality. It is clear, however, that many more steps are needed. Consider, for example, the fact that women are significantly more likely to die after heart bypass surgery than men even if the men are just as old and sick as women who undergo the procedure. Although gender alone is a risk of heart surgery for women, the reasons for their greater risk have yet to be identified.[48]

Differences between men and women, whether in genetics or in any other field, do not necessarily mean that either sex is or should be treated as "second-class." In fact, gender differences in the clinical practice of genetics are entirely compatible with the egalitarian feminist perspective developed in this book. Rather than ignore them, we need to identify them and evaluate their impact. The next chapter is devoted to that task.

Notes

1. According to the Council on Ethical and Judicial Affairs of the American Medical Association, "medical treatments for women are based on a male model, regardless of the fact that women may react differently to treatments than men or that some diseases manifest themselves differently in women than in men. The results of medical research on men are generalized to women without sufficient evidence of applicability to women." See "Gender Disparities in Clinical Decision Making," *Journal of the American Medical Association* 266 (1991): 559. Cf. Institute of Medicine Committee on the Ethical and Legal Issues Relating to the Inclusion of Women in Clinical Studies, *Women and Health Research,* vol. 1 (Washington, DC: National Academy Press, 1994), pp. 36–70.

2. As a physician at the National Institutes of Health observed, "You want doctors to study what they're interested in, so you have male doctors in their fifties studying other male doctors in their fifties for heart attacks." See Leslie Laurence and Beth Weinhouse, *Outrageous Practices: The Alarming Truth about How Medicine Mistreats Women* (New York: Fawcett Columbine, 1994), p. 5, n. 10.

3. Jeanne Humphrey Block characterizes the affiliative tendency in women as "communal," distinguishing it from the "agentic" tendency of men. Carol Gilligan's studies show that women are more likely than men to base decisions on a sense of responsibility to others rather than self-interest. Block, "Conceptions of Sex Role: Some Cross-Cultural and Longitudinal Perspectives," *American Psychologist* 28 (1973): 64–78; and Carol Gilligan, *In a Different Voice* (Cambridge: Harvard University Press, 1982). Illustrating the altruistic tendency of women in health care is the fact that they comprise the majority of organ donors. Peter Ubel and Mary B. Mahowald, "Ethical and Legal Issues

Regarding Living Donors," in Warren T. Reich, ed., *Encyclopedia of Bioethics* (New York: Simon and Schuster Macmillan, 1995), pp. 1865–71.

4. Larry L. Deaven, "Mapping and Sequencing the Human Genome," in Carl F. Cantor, ed., *Are Genes Us?* (New Brunswick, NJ: Rutgers University Press, 1994), p. 28.

5. Complete mapping but not sequencing of the eukaryotic portion of the Y chromosome has already been achieved, facilitated by the fact that this chromosome is so small. S. Foote, D. Vollrath, A. Hilton, and D. C. Page, "The Human Y Chromosome: Overlapping DNA Clones Spanning the Euchromatic Region," *Science* 258 (October 2, 1992): 60–66.

6. An even larger percentage of successful applicants (34.4% of 1871) were not identifiable by gender. E-mail from Robert F. Moore, Grants Information, National Institutes of Health (*GrantsInfo@Od.NIH.GOV*), December 10, 1998.

7. These numbers are my estimate of the sex ratio of principal investigators of grants and contracts awarded by NIH to ELSI proposals, based on the names of the investigators as published in the NIH website at http://www.nhgri.gov/About_NHGRI/Der/Elsi/grant_index.html (October 15, 1998).

8. Helen Bequaert Holmes was the principal investigator of ELSI grant R13 HG-00793-01A2, entitled "Impact of the HGI on Society: A Women's Studies Approach"; I was principal investigator of ELSI grant 1RO1 HG-00641, entitled "The Human Genome Project and Women."

9. *Pediatrics* 87 (1991): 554–59 and *Critical Care Medicine* 21 (1993): 7–17.

10. Marcia Barinaga, "Feminists Find Gender Everywhere in Science," *Science 260* (April 16, 1993): 392.

11. Barinaga, p. 392.

12. E.g., Gilligan; Nel Noddings, *Caring: A Feminine Approach to Ethics and Moral Education* (Berkeley: University of California Press, 1984); Sara Ruddick, *Maternal Thinking* (New York: Ballantine Books, 1989); Eva Feder Kittay and Diana T. Meyers, eds. *Women and Moral Theory* (Totowa, NJ: Rowman and Littlefield, 1987); Susan Sherwin, *No Longer Patient* (Philadelphia: Temple University Press, 1992).

13. See Kittay and Meyers, especially Carol Gilligan, "Moral Orientation and Moral Development," pp. 19–33.

14. To the extent that Barbara McClintock pursued her research with little support from colleagues, she represents a divergence from the collaborative model. However, like many women and at least some men, she probably desired a more collaborative atmosphere than the predominant competitive model allowed. Evelyn Fox Keller, *A Feeling for the Organism: The Life and Work of Barbara McClintock* (New York: W. H. Freeman and Company, 1983).

15. Paul Weis and Charles Hartshorne, eds., *Collected Papers of Charles Sanders Peirce* (Cambridge: Belknap Press of Harvard University, 1960), vol. 2, #654.

16. Ruth Bleier, ed., *Feminist Approaches to Sciences* (Elmsford, NY: Pergamon Press, 1988), p. 4.

17. E.g., *Protagoras* 359a–361c and *Meno* 87b–89d.

18. There are of course exceptions to this tendency. In fact, some scientists and clinicians not only contribute to societal dialogue on the morality of advances in scientific research, but develop well-argued positions on specific issues.

19. Senate Committee on Government Operations, *Hearings before the Subcommittee on Government Operations on S. J. Res. 145,* 90th Cong. 2nd sess., 1968, p. 5.

20. Carl Sagan and Lewis Thomas, for example, have been widely regarded not only for their research but also for their ability to communicate scientific knowledge to non-

scientists. Nonetheless, the commitment to science of those who communicate effectively to nonscientists is sometimes questioned by their colleagues.

21. Carole J. Bland, Linda N. Meurer, and George Maldonado, "Determinants of Primary Care Specialty Choice: A Non-statistical Meta-analysis of the Literature," *Academic Medicine* 70, 7 (1995): 630.

22. Bonnie B. Spanier, *Im/partial Science: Gender Ideology in Molecular Biology* (Bloomington: Indiana University Press, 1995), p. 24.

23. Identification of single gene disorders was facilitated by their ease of detection as compared with polygenic or multifactorial disorders. A large proportion of X-linked and autosomal dominant conditions have been identified simply by tracking their occurrence in families.

24. Ruth Hubbard, *Profitable Promises* (Monroe, ME: Common Courage Press, 1995), p. 18.

25. E.g., although the average life span of individuals with sickle cell disease is shorter than that of those who are not affected by this disease, some affected individuals have been know to live beyond the normal life span.

26. E.g., it is now known that some males who are infertile but have no other symptom of cystic fibrosis have the same mutation as others who are more severely affected.

27. Admittedly, the reductionist model is also applicable to polygenic and multifactorial accounts of human behavior.

28. In fact, Wylie puts the point more pejoratively: "the beneficiaries of this disadvantage frequently deny or fail to acknowledge that any such constraints exist." Alison Wylie, "The Philosophy of Ambivalence," in Marsha Hanen and Kai Nielsen, eds., *Science, Morality, and Feminist Theory* (Calgary, Canada: University of Calgary Press, 1987), p. 64.

29. Excellent elaborations of these reasons may be found in Vanessa Merton, "Ethical Obstacles to the Participation of Women in Biomedical Research," in Susan Wolf, ed., *Feminism and Bioethics* (New York: Oxford University Press, 1996), pp. 216–51, and in Karen Rothenberg, "Gender Matters: Implications for Clinical Research and Women's Health Care," *Houston Law Review* 32, 5 (1996): 1201–72.

30. Federal Drug Administration, U.S. Department of Health, Education, and Welfare, *General Considerations for the Clinical Evaluation of Drugs,* vol. 5 (Rockville, MD: Government Printing Office, 1977), p. 15; cited by Rothenberg at p. 1237, note 243. Note that the specification of "husbands" ignores unmarried male partners even though the guideline applies to single as well as married women.

31. This statement was made at an Institutional Review Board meeting I attended at the University of Chicago in 1994. Possibly the person who made the remark felt that she would be partly responsible for a "bad outcome" of a research protocol that she had voted to approve. Of course, she would be just as responsible for a good outcome, which was in fact more likely. If her concern led to their exclusion from research, pregnant women would thereby be deprived of its fruits in their own behalf and of their prima facie right to make their own judgments regarding risk-taking.

32. Laura Purdy, "Genetic Diseases: Can Having Children Be Immoral?" In John J. Buckley Jr., ed., *Genetics Now: Ethical Issues in Genetic Research* (Washington, DC: University Press of America, 1987).

33. Specificity refers to "the proportion of people who are truly free of a specific disease and are so identified by the test"; sensitivity refers to "the proportion of people who truly have a specific disease and are so identified by the test." Clayton L. Thomas, ed., *Taber's Cyclopedic Medical Dictionary,* 16th ed. (Philadelphia: F. A. Davis, 1989), pp. 1659, 1712.

34. Susan V. Rosser, "Re-visioning Clinical Research: Gender and the Ethics of Experimental Design," *Hypatia* 4 (Summer 1989): 128.

35. Institute of Medicine, *Assessing Genetic Risks: Implications for Health and Social Policy* (Washington, DC: National Academy Press, 1994), p. 276, and American Academy of Pediatrics, "Consent for Medical Services for Children and Adolescents," *Pediatrics* 92, 2 (1993): 290–91.

36. Merton, p. 219.

37. Ruth B. Merkatz and Suzanne W. Junod, "Historical Background of Changes in FDA Policy on the Study and Evaluation of Drugs in Women," *Academic Medicine* (1994): 703, 705.

38. Cited by Rothenberg, p. 1220, n. 128.

39. Rothenberg, pp. 1229–41.

40. National Institutes of Health, Instruction and Information Memorandum OER 90-5: NIH Guidance on the Inclusion of Minorities and Women in Clinical Research Study Populations (1990), p. 30.

41. Cited by Rothenberg, p. 1231.

42. R. Alta Charo, "Protecting Us to Death: Women, Pregnancy, and Clinical Research Trials," *St. Louis University Law Journal* 38 (1993): 135, 158.

43. Committee on the Ethical and Legal Issues, Institute of Medicine, *Women and Health Research,* vol. 1 (Washington, DC: National Academy Press, 1994), p. 17.

44. *Women and Health Research,* p. 16.

45. The term "informed choice" strikes me as a better term than "informed consent" to convey this meaning. "Choice" implies a decision on the part of the one who chooses; "consent" suggests agreement to someone else's (the researcher's) choice.

46. Rothenberg, p. 1266.

47. Bernadine Healy, "The Yentl Syndrome," *New England Journal of Medicine* 325 (1991): 274.

48. "Women Found to Face More Bypass Risks," *Chicago Tribune,* July 30, 1998, sect. 1, p. 6.

3

WOMEN IN CLINICAL GENETICS

THE previous chapter identified the impact of gender differences on specific genetic conditions such as those associated with infertility in males but not in females; those that occur only in males, although only females transmit them to their sons; those that occur more prevalently in males or females; and those whose symptoms differ depending on which parent transmits the condition. This chapter considers gender differences in the clinical applications of advances in genetics.[1] The major gender differences stem from women's role in reproduction and caregiving. Additional gender differences arise in the context of genetic counseling.

Reproduction and caregiving are related but separable roles. The two are considered separately not only to demonstrate their conceptual separability but also to suggest their practical separability as a means of promoting gender justice. The reproductive role of women is not interchangeable with that of men; the caregiving role can and should be shared equally by the two sexes. As described in the next chapter, "equal shares" does not mean "same shares"; rather, it means that the shares have the same value. Before elaborating further on that concept, however, the implications for women of progress in clinical genetics need to be considered in more detail.

Gender Differences in Reproductive Genetics

The most obvious difference between men and women regarding reproduction is that women get pregnant, gestate, and give birth, whereas men do not. As a result, women alone experience the risk, discomfort, and cost of prenatal genetic tests offered to couples, and women alone experience interventions in pregnancy in response to test results. Advances in genetic diagnostics and fetal therapies have already expanded the means by which, and circumstances in which, women may undergo prenatal tests and interventions. These are bound to increase in the wake of the Human Genome Project. Even prior to pregnancy, women may be subjected to tests and interventions for which their male partners undergo no comparable risk or discomfort—through ovulation stimulation and egg retrieval for genetic diagnosis of in vitro embryos.

Many genetic tests are noninvasive or relatively noninvasive—for example, buccal smears and blood or hair follicle samples for a variety of conditions. Some tests are performed on tissue already retrieved or removed for other purposes (e.g., samples obtained for blood typing). With regard to fetuses, however, testing is complicated by the fact that access can be gained only through women's bodies. Unlike early embryos that can exist in vitro, fetuses cannot exist apart from women.[2] Once expelled from the uterus, the developing organism is no longer a fetus but an abortus, a stillborn, or a newborn.

The procedures currently available for testing fetuses for specific genetic conditions vary considerably with regard to when during gestation they may be performed, the specificity and sensitivity of test results, the invasiveness and discomfort of the procedure, its cost, and the maternal and fetal risks associated with the procedure.[3] For example, ultrasound (US) may be performed from early in gestation (five weeks) onward with virtually no risks for either the pregnant woman or her fetus.[4] Because of its low sensitivity, however, US is mainly used for screening purposes and to facilitate invasive procedures such as chorionic villus sampling (CVS) and amniocentesis.

Amniocentesis was introduced in the 1950s as a means of identifying the sex of the fetus in women who were carriers for X-linked conditions. After Down syndrome was traced to chromosome 21, amniocentesis was used more prevalently to detect this condition.[5] The procedure involves insertion of a needle into the uterus, removal of a small amount of the amniotic fluid surrounding the fetus, and examination of fetal cells contained within the fluid.[6] Because this cannot be performed effectively until about 14 weeks gestation, abortions after positive findings are more complicated (medically and emotionally) and expensive than they would be if the procedure were done earlier.

The development of CVS was motivated in part by the desire to provide reliable fetal diagnosis earlier in gestation than amniocentesis is done. This procedure is usually performed between 9 and 13 weeks gestation through analysis of tissue obtained by insertion of a catheter or needle into the pregnant woman's placenta. Although the diagnostic accuracy of CVS is high, a greater than normal incidence of fetal limb defects has been reported when the procedure is performed prior to 9.5 weeks gestation.[7] Clinicians and researchers have challenged the evidence and conclusions of these reports, apparently precipitating a waning of interest in CVS in some clinics.[8] Nonetheless, both amniocentesis and CVS are routinely offered to pregnant women over 35 years of age and to other women known to be at risk for genetic conditions (e.g., because of family history, ethnic background, or known carrier status). When a woman reaches 35, the risk of Down syndrome in pregnancy is considered high enough to warrant the risk of fetal damage or loss through the procedure.[9] Both amniocentesis and CVS entail small risks of fetal loss and maternal complications such as vaginal bleeding and infection.[10]

A feminist standpoint was apparently utilized through the participation of women in the development of CVS and amniocentesis. Historian Ruth Cowan observes that when amniocentesis first became available, some women eagerly sought the procedure from medical geneticists, becoming voluntary subjects in experimental trials intended to document its safety and efficacy. If their results were positive, some women then "sought eugenic therapeutic abortions when there was hardly any hope of finding one."[11] The input of these women, and of others who sued physicians for not offering the procedure, spurred the development of amniocentesis. Another factor that encouraged its use was the liberalization of abortion law, which was accelerated by the activism of women who supported the right to terminate pregnancies in which fetal anomalies had been detected.

Cowan describes the women who stimulated the development of CVS as different from those who stimulated the development of amniocentesis. The latter were mainly white, middle-class women whose principal reproductive risk factor was maternal age. The former often belonged to cultural or religious groups for whom second trimester abortions were particularly problematic. They desired earlier diagnosis for genetic conditions such as thalassemia, for which their ethnic background placed them at risk. Many of these women, according to Cowan, "were neither white nor middle class."[12] They included Pakistani women living in London; African women, many of them Muslims, living, in France; and Chinese, Russian, and Hungarian women. In the United States, however, by the time CVS became widely available, social pressures against development of fetal diagnostic procedures had risen in reaction to liberalization of abortion law. As a result, enthusiasm for CVS has not been as great as that which was generated for amniocentesis.

While controversy surrounding the abortion issue has by no means ended, other prenatal tests have been introduced. One of these, called a "triple screen," involves the sampling of blood from the pregnant woman for three different tests.[13] Performed routinely at approximately the same period of gestation as amniocentesis, it is less invasive but produces less definitive results.[14] Another test, used from 18 weeks gestation to term, involves aspiration of fetal blood from the umbilical cord; this is called percutaneous umbilical blood sampling (PUBS) or cordocentesis.[15] The definitiveness of results and invasiveness of PUBS is about the same as for amniocentesis, but its fetal loss rate and associated maternal complications are slightly higher (1%–2%). Because most of the conditions for which it may be performed are increasingly identifiable through less invasive and risky DNA testing, its usefulness and desirability may gradually decline. Recently, however, the use of PUBS in late gestation and for nongenetic indications seems to have escalated.[16]

Procedures used much less often than the preceding include biopsies of cells from the liver or skin of the fetus; these have approximately the same maternal and fetal complication rate as PUBS but a higher fetal loss rate (5%–7%) for fetal skin biopsy.[17] Another rarely but increasingly used technique is preimplantation genetic diagnosis. This has the advantage of being performed so early and in such circumstances that the woman is not directly affected by the procedure itself; disadvantages include the cost and invasiveness of the procedures associated with it and the risk of embryo loss after transfer.[18] This procedure is examined more fully in Chapter 12.

In addition to prenatal genetic tests, women may be subjected to fetal therapies prompted by prenatal diagnosis.[19] The available therapies include fetal blood transfusion because of Rh immunization, fetal surgery for treatment of conditions such as diaphragmatic hernia and urethral obstruction, fetal cell transplants because of conditions such as beta thalassemia major and combined immunodeficiency, and steroid treatment for congenital adrenal hyperplasia.[20] As with prenatal tests, these treatments involve a range of invasiveness and risk to the woman and her fetus, and some, such as fetal surgery, remain highly experimental. Surgical interventions on behalf of the fetus obviously entail surgery for the woman as well. Severe dietary restrictions, such as those discussed in Chapter 1 for women with phenylketonuria, and milder restrictions such as avoidance of smoking and alcohol also impose demands on women that their male counterparts do not face.[21] Advances in gene therapy will undoubtedly expand the options for treatment of fetuses in utero, comcomitantly expanding possible pressures on women to undergo them.

Ideally, prenatal testing and diagnosis should be offered after the woman or the couple has undergone genetic counseling in which the primary goal is to help individuals and couples achieve their personally defined wishes.[22] However, the very offer of prenatal diagnosis by an obstetrician may be interpreted as a recommendation to accept testing, making it difficult for women to reject these medically sanctioned technologies.[23] Such pressures may be exerted in a climate where concerns about "fetal rights" and "prenatal abuse" are viewed as overriding the right of pregnant women to autonomous decisions about their life style and medical treatment. Nonetheless, the fact that some women have refused prenatal diagnosis on moral grounds, even when tests are offered without charge through national or state health care systems, suggests that some women do exercise their autonomy in this context. Women who have allegedly been "deprived of choice" have sued physicians on the grounds of "wrongful birth," stating that physicians failed to inform them of the availability of genetic testing and of their risks of giving birth to children with genetic anomalies.[24]

The availability of prenatal genetic testing has increased third-party involvement in individual women's reproductive decision making by family members, physicians, insurance agencies, and society.[25] This again raises concerns about possible constraints on women's autonomy. Research on agreement between men and women about the purposes of genetic services demonstrates that a substantial number of them come to genetic counseling and testing for different reasons and with different reproductive agendas. Disagreement between partners has not been diminished by genetic counseling.[26] In light of the more significant burden of the decision on women, however, many laws or policies affirm women's autonomy as paramount in situations of unresolvable conflict.[27]

Admittedly, prenatal diagnostic procedures and therapies offer benefits to many women and couples and, to the extent that women have greater control over these measures, can be more advantageous to women than to men. Prenatal diagnosis provides important information to those who wish to avoid the birth of an offspring with a specific genetic condition. Even if women lack the means by which to act on that information, or if they choose to continue affected pregnancies, foreknowledge for the purpose of psychological, medical, and financial preparation may be desirable. However, despite the value of such information and the possibility that options may thereby be increased, biological differences associated with genetic testing and therapies inevitably entail greater physiological risks and burdens for women than for men.

Psychosocial Implications of Genetic Testing for Women

Biology does not define the destiny of women, yet it clearly exerts great impact on our lives. Beyond the biologically discrepant impact, the biological differences between men and women may trigger different psychosocial impact on them. Moreover, a variety of factors not contingent on biology affect women and men differently.[28] These include gender-based structures in the provision of genetic services, along with societal, cultural, and economic forces that limit or encourage women's participation in those services. An egalitarian feminist standpoint requires analysis of all of these differences.

Some social factors that impact women more significantly than men are inseparable from their biological differences. One of these is the requirement of waiting periods before genetic services may be obtained, a practice that may be motivated by the limited availability of health care personnel or by political concerns arising from the apparent connection between abortion and prenatal genetic tests. Because of this requirement, some pregnant women do not obtain relevant information in time to act on it.[29] If prenatal diagnosis is performed so late that the results are not available until the fetus is already viable or possibly viable, an abortion may not be legally or practically accessible. Access is also limited by the inability to pay for services; this is discussed further in Chapter 5.

Some women, citing moral or religious opposition to abortion, do not pursue genetic tests, or decline them when offered.[30] They usually correctly assume that genetic diseases are incurable and that, therefore, the only effective means by which the birth of a child with a genetic anomaly can be avoided is through termination of an affected pregnancy.[31] When tests are done, women's perceptions of their risk of carrying an anomalous fetus sometimes exceed the actual risk, and their apprehensiveness does not diminish through counseling and education.[32] Even if test results are normal, as happens in most cases, the psychological burden of undergoing prenatal tests may be significant.[33] While her partner may share the psychological burden, neither legally nor physically can he make the troubling decisions the woman alone must make regarding tests and interventions undertaken through her body.[34] The anxiety she experiences may be exacerbated by the fact that genetic diagnoses are typically made during the second trimester or later, when termination is both physically and psychologically more hazardous to women than first trimester terminations.

Women who terminate affected pregnancies after prenatal diagnosis tend to experience psychological sequelae similar to those of patients who suffer second-trimester miscarriages.[35] Both experiences usually involve loss of a pregnancy that was wanted and closely monitored, sometimes after having had the experience of seeing the fetus through ultrasound, feeling fetal movement, and gaining information about fetal sex.[36] The process of prenatal diagnosis thus presents the fetus as a real and separate entity, in most cases strengthening the emotional tie between the woman and her fetus.[37] Obviously, this makes the experience of termination more difficult than it would otherwise be.

With greater availability of genetic tests for a constantly increasing number of conditions, women may be pressured to undergo testing for genetic abnormalities or to abort their fetuses if such abnormalities are identified. Although their decisions and their reasons for their decisions may be justifiable, women who make them may be subjected to morally objectionable pressures. Such pressures are likely to arise from several sources: the researchers interested in the information that genetic testing generates, clinicians or institutions whose income is based on procedures performed, technology companies that stand to profit through the provision of genetic analyses, and from a social milieu that has not entirely lost its eugenic propensities. Women's social milieu includes husbands, partners, or family members who may wish not only to obtain information about potential offspring but also to ensure that decisions made on that basis are productive of the offspring they desire. That pregnant women are more likely to be influenced by these pressures than others is suggested by the fact that they have responded more positively than others to offers of new genetic tests.[38] Moreover, while eugenic practices have occurred throughout history, even in our own day, in a country where basic human rights are described as "inalienable," there have been efforts to dissuade or prevent women who suffer from anomalies such as mental retardation or epilepsy from having children. Recall, for example, Justice Oliver Wendell Holmes's infamous statement in *Buck v. Bell,* supporting compulsory sterilization of the retarded on grounds that "three generations of imbeciles are enough."[39] More recently, Laura Purdy has argued for the obligation of persons who are carriers for serious genetic disorders such as Huntington chorea not to have children.[40]

Through the influence of gender socialization, women are expected to be the main caregivers of children, whether healthy or ill. Whether expected or not, however, they do most of the caregiving of those who are genetically disabled, both formally as professionals and informally, as family members, friends, or relatives.[41] Men, on the other hand, are expected to leave these burdens to their partners; the main burden of men, stereotypically defined and culturally supported, is to earn the income necessary to pay for that care. While there is little solid documentation that care for a genetically disabled child increases the likelihood of divorce or family breakdown, this is commonly thought to be the case.[42] Women are more likely to compromise their professional ambitions and to leave jobs outside the home to care for affected children.[43] Undoubtedly, parenting responsibilities for children with severe genetic anomalies involve extra tensions for families and couples.

Social factors influence not only women's experience of prenatal testing, but also their experience of particular diseases for which genetic susceptibility tests are now available. Breast cancer, for example, is a disease whose impact is exacerbated by social factors. Beyond its high incidence in women, the extant treatment modalities of mastectomy and chemotherapy are generally disfiguring in ways that men treated similarly do not find as burdensome because society is less likely to attach importance to them for men.[44] Hair loss, even though temporary, is particularly embarrassing and sometimes humiliating for women because they are not expected to be bald; and breast removal, whether prophylactic or therapeutic, is particularly distressing because it entails the permanent loss of their womanly appearance.[45]

Treatment of gynecologic cancers for which susceptibility tests are or will eventually be available may result in loss of the ability to conceive or bear a child. Men of course may be rendered sterile through cancer treatment as well, but means of remedying this are usually less drastic, less costly, and more effective than they are for women. Moreover, the treatment of male sterility is often through women's bodies.[46] The fact that women can lose both their gestational and their genetic capability of having children doubles their potential losses with regard to reproduction. As we will see in Chapter 7, to many women, gestation is the more significant loss.

Examples of gender differences in the impact of genetic services on clients or potential clients could be multiplied beyond those mentioned here. However, lest we think that gender neutrality prevails on the other side of the relationship, I want also to consider the possibility of gender differences on the part of clinicians who provide genetic services.

Genetic Counseling and Women

In the 1980s, Dorothy Wertz and her colleagues conducted a survey of doctoral level (MD or PhD) medical geneticists in 19 countries, asking them to choose among multiple options what they would do in each of 14 clinical scenarios.[47] The respondents were also asked to give reasons for their choices. As is true of other surveys asking individuals what they would do if faced with particular situations, discrepancies between their answers and their actual behavior are probable. Nonetheless, the answers are informative regarding attitudes about specific issues. According to Wertz,

> Gender was the single most important determinant of ethical decision making and ethical reasoning, over and above all other personal and professional variables, including nationality, age, number of years in genetics, type of degree, specialty, religion, religiosity, political inclination, marital status, number of children, and number of genetics patients seen per week.[48]

The impact of gender, both their own and that of their potential clients, was evident in responses to the scenarios involving misattributed paternity, disclosure of which parent is responsible for transmission of a genetic abnormality, directive or nondirective counseling, prenatal diagnosis for maternal anxiety, and "surrogacy" as a means of avoiding transmission of a dominant condition.[49]

Medical geneticists of both sexes opposed disclosure of nonpaternity to the woman's partner, but women were significantly more likely than men (75% vs. 57%) to mention marital conflict as the reason for their position. Further, 63% of the women but only 46% of the men would identify which parent carried a translocation for Down syndrome; the main reason for disclosure cited by the women was the relevance of this information to relatives who might also carry the translocation. Both sexes strongly favored nondirective counseling, but fewer women than men (5% vs. 13%) would perform prenatal diagnosis solely to alleviate a woman's anxiety, and more men than women (22% vs. 11%) cited justice as the moral principle underlying their position. While men were more likely than women (35% vs. 52%) to present the option of "surrogate" motherhood, women were more likely to describe its negative consequences to clients (34% vs. 20%).[50]

In comparison with other medical specialties, a greater proportion of medical geneticists are women, and a greater number of these women occupy positions of leadership in medical genetics.[51] Their greater representation reflects their interest in the field and may well have been facilitated by the increase of women entering medicine in the 1970s, when medical genetics was being developed as a new specialty. In contrast to their numbers within medicine, however, women comprise a large majority (93%) of master's-level genetic counselors in the United States and Canada; comparable master's training programs do not exist in other countries.[52] It might be expected, therefore, that a survey of genetic counselors would show the impact of gender more significantly than the data obtained by Wertz and her colleagues in their 1980s survey of medical geneticists. But data comparing genetic counselors and medical geneticists from the United States show concordance as well as discordance between the two groups on many issues. For example, Deborah Pencarinha and her colleagues found 23% of master's-level genetic counselors more likely than medical geneticists to perform prenatal diagnosis or to offer a referral for sex selection, and 20% less likely to reveal a diagnosis of Huntington disease to relatives of a patient found to be at risk for the condition.[53]

In a more recent survey of nearly 3000 geneticists in 37 nations, Wertz found that cultural and class differences played a more significant part than gender in the ethical views of genetics professionals. Only 13% of women physicians differed with their male counterparts, whereas 60% of the genetic counselors differed from MDs of both sexes.[54] The physicians were more likely than the genetic counselors to be directive, less likely to preserve confidentiality, and personally more likely to abort an anomalous fetus.[55] The counselors also tended to hold more positive views than the physicians about life with a disability. Privacy and confidentiality were less important to medical geneticists around the world than to those in the United States, but within the United States, privacy and confidentiality were more important to the genetics professionals than to their clients.[56] Sex selection was more widely supported by women than by men, and women outside of the United States were more likely than men to practice directive counseling.

In general, women outside the United States (MDs and PhDs rather than master's-prepared) took a dimmer view of disability than any other group. According to Wertz, these women considered it "unfair to the child, to siblings, and to society to have a child with a disability if the birth could have been prevented."[57] The dimmer view of disabilities on the part of physicians of both sexes may be influenced by greater awareness of the long-term impact of disabilities on families and recognition that, in many countries, social supports for persons with disabilities are extremely limited. In general, MD geneticists, many of whom are pediatricians, are well acquainted with the natural history of specific genetic conditions. Their ongoing contact with families may provide them with a broader understanding of its impact than genetic counselors obtain through briefer contact.[58]

Wertz and her colleagues contrasted gender differences in genetics professionals with those identified in their clients.[59] Two findings are particularly significant: (*1*) clients, most of whom are women, tend to follow an ethic of relationships rather than a principle-based ethics; and (*2*) genetics professionals give greater priority than their clients to respect for autonomy, privacy, and confidentiality. Wertz suggested that the differences between genetic counselors and MD geneticists may be attributed to the newness of genetic counseling as a profession and to its subordinate place in the hierarchy of health care professions. The differences may also be attributable to different perceptions of the physician–patient relationship and of the counselor–client relationship.

The first finding assumes a dichotomy between relationship-based and principle-based thinking that some feminists and philosophers would dispute. The care-based ethic of Carol Gilligan, Nel Noddings, and Sara Ruddick, for example, may be viewed as proposing care as another principle to be substituted for, or added to, the four principles that Tom Beauchamp and James Childress propose.[60] Or it may be argued that relationships based on affective, autonomous, or familial ties dictate a priority to be observed in applying the principles of beneficence, nonmaleficence, justice, and respect for autonomy.

The second finding suggests a means by which the genetic counselors attempt to reduce the gap between themselves and their clients.[61] Nonetheless, the counselors' emphasis on client autonomy represents a contrast between them and medical professionals whose ethic is paternalistic. The counselors' emphasis on client autonomy may also be a mechanism for dealing with the medical hierarchy from their own nondominant position within it. As Wertz puts it, "By being nondirective, counselors can avoid conflict with physicians who may hold different opinions. Counselors cannot be faulted by physicians for presenting information and letting clients make their own decisions."[62]

Clearly, class-based, gender-based, and culture-based differences overlap in clinical genetics. All three factors (and others) contribute to the differing standpoints of women and men involved in genetics, whether they be policymakers, genetics professionals, or clients. In the United States, master's-prepared genetic counselors, most of whom are women, represent a nondominant perspective within a health care system in which doctors, including medical geneticists of both sexes, are dominant.[63] A class-based difference between the two groups arises from their different income levels, which are influenced by the greater liability, responsibility, and educational requirements of medical geneticists. Regardless of their sex, however, most genetic counselors are white and middle class, which means that they represent dominant perspectives vis-à-vis those who are nonwhite or poor—that is, many of their clients.

An egalitarian feminist standpoint requires medical geneticists to recognize their dominance and pay attention to the nondominant input of master's-level genetic counselors, many of whom have more experience of, and education relevant to, counseling than their doctoral counterparts.[64] But it also requires that master's-prepared genetic counselors of either sex recognize important differences between their standpoint and that of many of their clients. In general, their clients occupy a privileged perspective of nondominance in the counseling situation. The practice of nondirectiveness is a means of promoting that recognition.

Nondirectiveness versus Directiveness

But is nondirectiveness possible? And even if it is, is it always morally defensible? The practice of nondirectiveness, which has been central to genetic counseling since its inception, has increasingly been challenged in recent years. Ironically, it is associated with value neutrality or objectivity, which denies the inevitability and the epistemological and moral validity of a standpoint on the part of the counselor. In fact, nondirectiveness shows a value priority on the part of the counselor: respect for the client's autonomy. While insisting on the importance of nondirectiveness in the counseling process, genetic counselors themselves maintain that their relationship to clients is value-laden rather than value-free.[65] Use of the term "client" rather than "patient" in the Code of Ethics of the National Society of Genetic Counselors suggests the dominance of this value for the entire profession. Clients are thus perceived as active, patients as passive. The contrast between this value and the traditional directive emphasis of medicine recapitulates the autonomy–paternalism debate that has dominated bioethics for decades.

The situations in which nondirectiveness is most appropriate are those involving reproductive decisions and other decisions unrelated to the health of those affected. In situations where an individual's behavior is likely to influence the health outcome, genetic counselors are clearly and deliberately directive. For example, they explicitly encourage pregnant women to take folic acid to reduce the risk of neural tube defect, and they warn women against smoking and alcohol consumption which may lead to prematurity or fetal alcohol syndrome.

A genetic counselor who counsels a woman or couple whose infant tests positive for phenylketonuria or galactosemia would surely be directive about the need to restrict the child's diet to prevent the onset of symptoms. Such directiveness is neither more nor less paternalistic than comparable advice from a physician. Whether counseling is provided by physicians or genetic counselors, it is not paternalistic even if directive so long as it does not constitute imposition on the client's capacity to make her own decision.[66]

Like other health caregivers, genetic counselors are sometimes asked what they would do if they found themselves in the same situation as their clients. Implicit in the question is "Golden Rule" thinking, the rationale that we ought to act toward others as we would like them to act toward us.[67] Many refuse to answer on grounds that this would violate the imperative of nondirectiveness. A direct answer to the question might well be directive, and it might be paternalistic rather than respectful of the client's autonomy. But it may also be argued that a refusal to answer is paternalistic and disrespectful of the client's autonomy. In fact, the likelihood of paternalism in such a refusal on the part of a master's-prepared genetic counselor is probably less than the likelihood of paternalism in such a refusal on the part of a physician—because the power discrepancy in the latter case is greater than in the former. Gender stereotypes may also be influential here because the majority of clients as well as master's-prepared genetic counselors are women, whereas the majority of physicians and medical geneticists are still men.[68]

A refusal to answer the question of what the clinician would do if he or she faced the same situation is paternalistic if the answer would not sway the client unduly but would simply add to the store of information that facilitates a maximally informed and autonomous decision. Undoubtedly, numerous variables determine whether that is the case. A particular client, for example, may already be well-informed and mistrustful of the clinician's advice; another may be ill-informed and overly trustful. For the former, the refusal reduces the amount of information that the client wishes to consider; for the latter, the refusal may reduce the impediments to the client's autonomy.

In situations where clients are not autonomous (e.g., where they are profoundly retarded), paternalism is impossible because it necessarily entails the overriding of, or intention to override, someone's autonomy. Instead, the clinician's obligations of beneficence and nonmaleficence take precedence. Nondirectiveness, at least to the extent that it entails respect for autonomy, is impossible when a client is not autonomous. One of the essential features of autonomy is competence, but this is in itself a complex concept.[69] In general, competence can be assessed only in the context of that for which one may or may not be competent. As the following case illustrates, competence is not always determinable, and other factors are often morally relevant to the practice of genetic counseling.

Joan Taylor was 22, and had been married to Ed for two years. They both worked in a factory that hired people who were cognitively disabled. Joan's parents had requested and obtained a tubal ligation for her when she was 16 years old. Joan's mild retardation had no known genetic etiology; neither did Ed's. Joan visited the obstetrics clinic to ask that her sterilization be reversed so that she and Ed could have a baby. The obstetrician referred her to the genetics clinic for a recommendation on whether the reversal should be attempted.

A year later, the medical geneticist involved in this case presented it for review by a group of bioethicists. Their discussion centered around the question of whether Joan was competent to be a mother. Whether this was the crucial question in the case is a question in its own right. From an egalitarian feminist standpoint, the issues raised by the case might have been more appropriately articulated in terms of whether Joan was competent to make a reproductive decision, whether Ed was competent for this as well, and whether those involved in counseling were able to overcome the nearsightedness of their own dominant perspective in providing their advice.

With regard to the question they did address, the group agreed that some cognitively normal or superior individuals were not competent mothers. They were unable, however, to define what constituted "competent mothering." Ed's competence as a father was not discussed, nor was the relevance of that factor to the welfare of the potential child. Ignored also was the fact that Joan and Ed had lived independently as a couple (probably with some help from family members) for the previous two years; this surely suggested they had basic skills of daily living. Although the possibility that a newborn would be retarded was mentioned, this was not considered morally compelling.

Personnel at the genetics clinic were apparently uncertain that the couple were capable of raising a child, but they did not believe that the referring obstetrician was obliged to attempt the reversal of Joan's sterilization. Because the procedure was elective, refusal to perform it could be justified on other grounds, such as its low success rate or, possibly, the couple's inability to pay for the attempt. However, the obstetrician's refusal was based on the recommendation that the genetics clinic provided: that the reversal not be attempted on grounds that "Joan could not be a competent mother, whatever that means."

Obviously, this recommendation was directive. In essence, Joan was told that she should not have a child. It was paternalistic to the extent that it overrode the autonomy of the client for her own sake, and it was utilitarian to the extent that it purported to do so for the sake of a greater good. Neither of these rationales figured necessarily in the decision. From an egalitarian feminist standpoint, however, if directiveness were appropriate in this case, it is appropriate for cognitively normal people also. If competence for parenthood is a morally relevant criterion in decisions about reversal of sterilization, it should be applied as well to nonretarded potential parents who request the procedure. In this case, the wrongness of the refusal is exacerbated by the fact that its grounds are acknowledged to be unclear ("whatever that means"). Further, an egalitarian feminist standpoint would have insisted on considering the relevant role of Ed and other family members in providing adequate parenting for a newborn. Ignoring Ed entirely in assessing the adequacy of parenting may be viewed as another illustration of gender injustice.

Apparently, the medical geneticist who brought this case to the bioethics group for discussion had been troubled by his own decision. To his credit, he was willing to listen to arguments for a different conclusion, and these might influence his future practice. The referring obstetrician might have benefited by the discussion as well. The very fact that the genetics clinic had accepted the referral was problematic because Joan's retardation had already been determined not to be genetic in origin. But neither clinical group was particularly qualified to answer the question that was considered ethically salient: What makes a woman competent to be a mother? Nor did either group acknowledge that in the absence of that qualification, they lacked grounds for denying the procedure.[70] An option not considered was referral to someone whom society has judged qualified to determine qualifications for parenting, such as adoption experts.[71] From an egalitarian feminist standpoint, this would have been appropriate.

Although there are cases in which the dominance of a directive approach should prevail, this surely is not one of them. Practitioners are appropriately directive with regard to medical advice because that is their area of expertise. Note, however, that directiveness is not equivalent to coercion because patients are morally and legally free to refuse to follow medical recommendations. Genetic counselors are appropriately nondirective when the impact of clients' decisions is related to personal values other than health. Except where a decision may unduly burden others, the further removed it is from the medical domain, the stronger the case for counseling nondirectively.

Notes

1. Some of the material presented in this chapter is drawn from two previously published articles: Mary B. Mahowald, Dana Levinson, Christine Cassel, Amy Lemke, Carole Ober, James Bowman, Michelle LeBeau, Amy Ravin, and Melissa Times, "The New Genetics and Women," *Milbank Quarterly, 74,* 2 (1996): 239–83, and Mary B. Mahowald, "Genetic Technologies and Their Implications for Women," *University of Chicago Law School Roundtable* 3, 2 (1996): 439–63.

2. Mary B. Mahowald, "As If There Were Fetuses without Women: A Remedial Essay," in Joan C. Callahan, ed., *Reproduction, Ethics, and the Law* (Bloomington: Indiana University Press, 1995), pp. 199–218.

3. A table relating these variables to different prenatal procedures is provided in Mahowald, Levinson, Cassel, et al., pp. 252–55.

4. M. F. Docker, "Ultrasound Imaging Techniques," in David J. H. Brock, Charles H. Rodeck, and Malcom A. Ferguson-Smith, eds., *Prenatal Diagnosis and Screening* (New York: Churchill-Livingston, 1992), pp. 69, 79.

5. Ruth Schwartz Cowan, "Women's Roles in the History of Testing," in Karen H. Rothenberg and Elizabeth J. Thomson, eds., *Women and Prenatal Testing: Facing the Challenges of Genetic Technology* (Columbus: Ohio State University Press, 1994), p. 38.

6. Marion S. Verp, "Prenatal Diagnosis of Genetic Disorders," in Norbert Gleicher, ed., *Principles and Practice of Medical Therapy in Pregnancy* (Stamford, CT: Appleton and Lange, 1992), pp. 159–61.

7. Glenn Schemmer and Anthony Johnson, "Genetic Amniocentesis and Chorionic Villus Sampling," *Obstetrics and Gynecology Clinics of North America* 20 (1993): 497, 515–16.

8. Another possible influence on reduction of interest in CVS is the availability of early amniocentesis. Although CVS is available still earlier (by several weeks), some women prefer amniocentesis because it provides a means of detecting neural tube defects as well as genetic abnormalities.

9. The risk that a 35-year-old woman will have a fetus with Down syndrome is 1 in 385; the risk of her having a fetus with other abnormalities is 1 in 434, making the total risk of chromosomal abnormality 1 in 204. As maternal age advances this risk increases, but risk of the procedure itself remains the same (see n. 10). Procedural risks are probably lower in centers where the staff is highly trained and experienced with amniocentesis, in which case it may be offered at an earlier maternal age.

10. The fetal loss rate for midtrimester amniocentesis is 1%; the fetal loss rate for transcervical CVS is 0.5%--1% over the general population risk. Schemmer and Johnson, pp. 502–4, and Verp, p. 159.

11. Cowan, p. 39.

12. Cowan, p. 43.

13. The maternal blood is tested for alpha fetoprotein, estriol, and human chorionic gonadotropin. Judith V. Hibbard and Marion S. Verp, "Maternal Serum Screening for Detection of Fetal Abnormalities and Pregnancy Complications," in C. C. Lin, M. S. Verp, and R. F. Sabbagha, eds., *The High-Risk Fetus: Pathophysiology, Diagnosis, and Management* (New York: Springer-Verlag, 1993), p. 210.

14. Amniocentesis has a false positive rate of 0.5% and CVS has a 99.6% diagnostic success rate. These figures compare favorably but not overwhelmingly with the triple marker screen, which yields 90% and 6% sensitivity and false positive rates, respectively. E. Y. Cheng, D. A. Luthy, A. M. Zebelman, M. A. Williams, R. E. Lieppman, and D. E. Hickok, "A Prospective Evaluation of a Second-Trimester Screening Test for Fetal Down Syndrome Using Maternal Serum Alpha-Fetoprotein, HCG, and Unconjugated Estriol," *Obstetrics and Gynecology* 81 (1993): 72–77; Canadian Collaborative CVS-Amniocentesis Clinical Trial Group, "Multicentre Randomised Clinical Trial of Chorion Villus Sampling and Amniocentesis," *Lancet* 1 (1989): 1–7; David H. Ledbetter, A. O. Martin, Yuri Verlinsky, et al., "Cytogenetic Results of Chorionic Villus Sampling: High Success Rate and Diagnostic Accuracy in the United States Collaborative Study," *American Journal of Obstetrics and Gynecology* 162 (1990): 495–501.

15. Peter G. Pryde, A. Drugan, M. P. Johnson, N. B. Isada, and M. I. Evans, "Prenatal Diagnosis: Choices Women Make about Pursuing Testing and Acting on Abnormal Results," *Clinical Obstetrics and Gynecology* 36 (1993): 496, 500, and Jessica G. Davis,

"Reproductive Technologies for Prenatal Diagnosis" *Fetal Diagnosis and Therapy* 8, supp. 1 (1993): 28, 34.

16. Carl P. Weiner, "Percutaneous Umbilical Sampling" in Lin, Verp, and Sabbagha, pp. 352–61.

17. Umberto Nicoloni and Charles H. Rodeck, "Fetal Blood and Tissue Sampling," in Brock, Rodeck, and Ferguson-Smith, pp. 46–49, and Weiner, p. 354.

18. Sandra A. Carson and John E. Buster, "Biopsy of Gametes and Preimplantation Embryos in Genetic Diagnosis," *Seminars in Reproductive Endocrinology* 12 (1994): 184.

19. These are explained in more detail with regard to risks, benefits, when and for what conditions they may be performed in the table provided in Mahowald, Levinson, Cassel, et al., pp. 256–58.

20. Nicolini and Rodeck, pp. 46–49, and Michael R. Harrison, N. S. Adzick, A. W. Flake, R. W. Jennings, J. M. Estes, T. E. MacGillivray, J. T. Chueh, J. D. Goldberg, R. A. Filly, R. B. Goldstein et al., "Correction of Congenital Diaphragmatic Hernia in Utero: VI. Hard Earned Lessons," *Journal of Pediatric Surgery* 28 (1993): 1411.

21. However, because of increased recognition of the teratogenic potential of secondhand smoke and of chemicals to which they are exposed in the workplace, men may also be expected to avoid certain behaviors.

22. Dorothy C. Wertz and John C. Fletcher, "Attitudes of Genetic Counselors: A Multinational Survey," *American Journal of Human Genetics* 42 (1988): 592–600.

23. Angus Clarke, "Is Non-Directive Genetic Counseling Possible?" *Lancet* 338 (1991): 998–1001; Mary S. Henifin, Ruth Hubbard, and Judy Norsigian, "Position Paper: Prenatal Screening," in S. Cohen and N. Taub, eds., *Reproductive Laws for the 1990s* (Clifton, NJ: Humana Press, 1989); Dorothy C. Wertz and John C. Fletcher, "A Critique of Some Feminist Challenges to Prenatal Diagnosis," *Journal of Women's Health* 2, 2 (1993): 173–83.

24. Lori B. Andrews, "Torts and the Double Helix: Malpractice Liability for Failure to Warn of Genetic Risks," *Houston Law Review* 291 (Spring 1992): 149–84.

25. Elena A. Gates, "Does Testing Benefit Women?" in Rothenberg and Thomson, pp. 183–200.

26. James R. Sorenson and Dorothy C. Wertz, "Couple Agreement before and after Genetic Counseling," *American Journal of Medical Genetics* 25 (1986): 549–55.

27. E.g., *Roe v. Wade,* 410 U.S. 113 (1973).

28. A list of nonmedical factors that particularly affect women in the clinical practice of genetics is presented on p. 249 of Mahowald, Levinson, Cassel, et al. While not exhaustive, this list covers more factors than are mentioned here.

29. Laurie Nsiah-Jefferson and Elaine J. Hall, "Reproductive Technology: Perspectives and Implications for Low-Income Women and Women of Color," in Kathryn Strother Ratcliff, Myra Marx Ferree, Gail Mellow, Barbara Wright, Glenda Price, Kim Yanoshik, and Margie Freston, *Healing Technology: Feminist Perspectives,* 4th ed. (Ann Arbor: University of Michigan Press, 1992), pp. 93, 100.

30. Rita Beck Black, "A 1 and 6 Month Follow-Up of Prenatal Diagnosis Patients Who Lost Pregnancies," *Prenatal Diagnosis* 9 (1989): 795–804, and Rayna Rapp, "Women's Responses to Prenatal Diagnosis: A Sociocultural Perspective on Diversity," in Rothenberg and Thomson, pp. 219, 222.

31. Admittedly, termination of pregnancy is not necessarily equivalent to abortion, either morally or clinically. I address different concepts of abortion and their implications in Chapter 12.

32. Pryde et al.: 48.

33. Barbara Katz Rothman, *The Tentative Pregnancy: How Amniocentesis Changes the Experience of Motherhood* (New York: Norton, 1993).

34. While this statement is always true with regard to the physical burden that women undergo in prenatal tests and interventions, it is not universally true with regard to their legal right to make these decisions.

35. Rita Beck Black, "Reproductive Genetic Testing and Pregnancy Loss: The Experience of Women," in Rothenberg and Thomson, pp. 271–94; S. H. Elders and K. M. Laurence, "The Impact of Supportive Intervention after Second Trimester Termination of Pregnancy for Fetal Abnormality," *Prenatal Diagnosis* 11, 1 (1991): 47–54.

36. John C. Fletcher and Mark Evans, "Maternal Bonding in Early Fetal Ultrasound Examination," *New England Journal of Medicine* 308 (1983): 392–93; Barbara Katz Rothman, "The Tentative Pregnancy: Then and Now," in Rothenberg and Thomson, pp. 260–70; N. Caccia, J. M. Johnson, G. E. Robinson, and T. Barna, "Impact of Prenatal Testing on Maternal–Fetal Bonding: Chorionic Villus Sampling vs. Amniocentesis," *American Journal of Obstetrics and Gynecology* 165 (1991): 1122–25.

37. Rita Beck Black, "A 1 and 6 Month Follow-Up," Rayna Rapp, "Constructing Amniocentesis: Maternal and Medical Discourses," in F. D. Ginsburg and A. Lowenhaupt-Tsing, eds., *Uncertain Terms: Negotiating Gender in American Culture* (Boston: Beacon Press, 1990).

38. Admittedly, women are probably influenced by other considerations as well, e.g., by their own desires to have healthy children or to avoid the burden of being principal caregivers for children who are disabled.

39. *Buck v. Bell* 274 U.S. 200, 207 (1927).

40. Laura Purdy, "Genetic Diseases: Can Having Children Be Immoral?" in John J. Buckley Jr., ed., *Genetics Now: Ethical Issues in Genetic Research* (Washington, DC: University Press of America, 1987). Purdy makes a moral rather than legal argument, stopping short of a call for mandatory avoidance of having a child with a severe disorder. In this article, she bypasses the abortion issue by maintaining that the responsibility for avoidance may be fulfilled either before or after conception.

41. Mary B. Mahowald, "Reproductive Genetics and Gender Justice" in Rothenberg and Thomson, pp. 67, 69.

42. The few studies available may be flawed by poor methodology, limited use of variables, and nonstandardized measures of assessing the costs of caregiving. They nonetheless suggest an enormous economic and social burden for family caregivers, who are usually women, in caring for disabled or ill children. See P. Jacobs and S. McDermott, "Family Caregiver Costs of Chronically Ill and Handicapped Children: Method and Literature Review," *Public Health Report* 104, 2 (1989): 158–63, and M. D. Marcenko and J. C. Meyers, "Mothers of Children with Developmental Disabilities: Who Shares the Burden?" *Family Relations* 40 (1991): 186–90. One study suggests that families caring for children with cystic fibrosis may be less likely to break up. Cf. A. T. McCollum, "Cystic Fibrosis: Economic Impact upon the Family," *American Journal of Public Health* 61 (1971): 1335–41. This contrasts with earlier studies that suggest the opposite.

43. Naomi Breslau, David Salkever, and Kathleen S. Staruch, "Women's Labor Force Activity and Responsibilities for Disabled Dependents: A Study of Families with Disabled Children," *Journal of Health and Social Behavior* 23 (1982): 169, 179–80.

44. Francis S. Collins, "BRCA1: Lots of Mutations, Lots of Dilemmas," *New England Journal of Medicine* 334 (January 18, 1996): 186, citing statistics from the American Cancer Society.

45. Breast reconstruction mitigates the impact of this loss for many women, but it does not restore breast function or sensitivity.

46. Intracytoplasmic sperm injection (ICSI) is the most recent example of a technique through which male infertility is treated through women's bodies.

47. In the United States, professional certification for genetic counseling is obtained through the American Board of Genetic Counseling, which certifies master's-level counselors. PhDs and Mds are certified by the American Board of Medical Genetics.

48. Dorothy C. Wertz, "Provider Biases and Choices: The Role of Gender," *Clinical Obstetrics and Gynecology* 36, 3 (1993): 524.

49. I put the term "surrogate" in quotation marks to challenge the suggestion that a woman who gestates and gives birth is not a real mother solely because she intends to give the child to another woman or couple to raise. The rationale for this will be more fully explained in Chapter 7.

50. Wertz, p. 525. This finding is supported by the study of men's and women's views about gestational and genetic ties to offspring (see Chapter 7), and by the fact that neither tie is physiologically burdensome to men.

51. According to a report of "Resident Physicians in ACGME-Accredited and in Combined Specialty Graduate Medical Education (GME) Programs on August 1, 1997," the percentage of women in medical genetics in the United States is 48.1%, which is higher than the percentage of women in family medicine (44.9%), psychiatry (45.4%), surgery (20.5%), and internal medicine (37%). Women predominate in pediatrics (63.7%) and obstetrics/gynecology (62.6%). "Appendix II Graduate Medical Education," *Journal of the American Medical Association* 280, 9 (1998): 836–37. These numbers do not reflect the percentage of men and women who are in leadership positions. Because medical genetics is a relatively new specialty, its leaders are more likely to come from those who have been trained more recently, i.e., the group that includes more women.

52. Currently, that percentage is probably lower. In the United States, 62% of genetics professions (which includes counselors as well as doctoral-level geneticists) are women. Dorothy C. Wertz, "Is There a 'Women's Ethic' in Genetics? A 37-Nation Survey of Providers," *Journal of the American Women's Medical Association* 52, 1 (1997): 33–38.

53. Despite this use of language, master's-prepared genetic counselors do not "perform" prenatal diagnosis; rather they counsel women who may undergo diagnostic procedures through the services of a clinician trained to provide them. D. F. Pencarinha, H. K. Bell, J. G. Edwards, and R. G. Best, "Ethical Issues in Genetic Counseling: A Comparison of M. S. Counselor and Medical Geneticist Perspectives," *Journal of Genetic Counseling* 1, 1 (1992): 19–30. In the earlier survey by Wertz and her colleagues, provider gender did not figure significantly in responses to the scenario involving disclosure of Huntington disease to a patient's relatives.

54. Wertz, "Is There a 'Women's Ethic,'" p. 34. From an egalitarian feminist standpoint, an important limitation of this survey is acknowledged by Wertz herself: "Large parts of the world are missing [because] there are currently few geneticists in sub-Saharan African and many Moslem nations" (p. 34).

55. Wertz, "Is there a 'Women's Ethic,'" p. 37. From a feminist standpoint, the question about abortion should have been framed differently for men than for women, i.e., men should have been asked whether they would like their partners to undergo abortion in such situations.

56. Dorothy C. Wertz, "Society and the Not-So-New Genetics: What Are We Afraid

Of? Some Future Predictions from a Social Scientist," *Journal of Contemporary Health Law and Policy* 13 (1997): 310. According to Wertz, "In every case where individual privacy conflicted with potential welfare of the family, counselors placed the individual's rights first" ("Is There a 'Women's Ethic,'" p. 37). The contrast between this emphasis and the views of medical geneticists both in the United States and elsewhere, both male and female, suggests the confluence of gender, professional culture, and ethnic or national culture.

57. Wertz, "Is There a 'Women's Ethic,'" p. 36.

58. Relationships between genetic counselors and their clients often end with delivery or termination. Some provide posttermination counseling, but this does not embrace the issues faced by parents who care for children with disabilities.

59. Wertz, "Is There a 'Women's Ethic,'" pp. 33–38.

60. Carol Gilligan, *In a Different Voice* (Cambridge: Harvard University Press, 1982), Nel Noddings, *Caring* (Berkeley: University of California Press, 1984), Sara Ruddick, *Maternal Thinking* (New York: Ballantine Books, 1989), Tom L. Beauchamp and James F. Childress, *Principles of Biomedical Ethics,* 4th ed. (New York: Oxford University Press, 1994).

61. As with other clinician–client relationships, the gap arises from the fact that the client needs or desires something that the counselor has to give, rather than the other way around. In most cases, however, the gap is also based on the counselor's greater knowledge of genetics and her position within the health care system. The counselor's class and race are also likely to contribute to the gap.

62. Wertz, "Is There a 'Women's Ethic,'" p. 38.

63. Unlike nurses, whose position in the health care system is well established, the position of master's-prepared genetic counselors vis-à-vis health care professionals who are not physicians is relatively unclear. June Peters, a master's-prepared genetic counselor, believes that, in comparison with nursing, "where the pecking order is better defined historically, "genetic counselors" are not as subordinate as some physicians would like" (personal communication, August 10, 1998). However, some nurses provide genetic counseling, with or without board certification; their number may well increase as the need for genetic counseling in all areas of primary care becomes evident.

64. Of course, medical geneticists are better educated with regard to diagnosis, prognosis, and management of genetic diseases, and this knowledge enhances their ability to counsel clients successfully.

65. Barbara Bowles Biesecker, "Future Directions in Genetic Counseling: Practical and Ethical Considerations," *Kennedy Institute of Ethics Journal* 8, 2 (1998): 146.

66. Such imposition assumes that the client is autonomous, which is not always the case. To the extent that autonomy is compromised or absent, paternalism is impossible; it may, however, be practiced toward autonomous surrogates for the nonautonomous person (e.g., a young child or a profoundly retarded adult). In such cases, the best interests of the nonautonomous client is the appropriate ethical guide for both surrogate decision makers and clinicians.

67. Matt. 7:12.

68. I doubt, however, that a male (master's-prepared) genetic counselor is more likely than a medical geneticist of either sex to be directive toward clients. Unfortunately, there are no data to determine whether this is so because so few men have entered the profession as master's-prepared genetic counselors.

69. See Tom Beauchamp and Ruth Faden, *The History and Theory of Informed Consent* (New York: Oxford University Press, 1986), pp. 235–69.

70. There could of course be other grounds, such as inability to pay, which deserve critique in their own right.

71. Lest it be thought that this is an unrealistic option, at least one obstetrician in the United States exercises it in situations where he questions whether to provide infertility treatment to an individual. He asks individuals to provide evidence of their competence for parenting from someone who is qualified to make that assessment. See my *Women and Children in Health Care: An Unequal Majority* (New York: Oxford University Press, 1993), pp. 101–2.

4

GENDER JUSTICE IN GENETICS

THE preceding account of gender differences in research in genetics and in clinical applications of genetics was descriptive in nature, based on empirical studies of biological, psychological, and social differences between men and women. No normative critique has yet been offered regarding the impact of those differences. Accordingly, this chapter focuses on the question of whether gender differences raised by genetics *should* prevail. The answer to this question depends mainly on whether the differences are associated with inequity or injustice. If that is not the case, then, from an egalitarian standpoint, the differences not only may prevail but probably should prevail because the diversity they represent enriches the social environment in which we all participate. If gender differences are associated with inequity, however, the situation is morally problematic. Gender differences associated with inequity raise further questions regarding the possibility of changing either the differences themselves or the conditions associated with their impact.

In addressing these questions we confront the meaning of justice in general, and of gender justice in particular. Because a feminist standpoint obviously involves feminism, and feminism, in most if not all of its theoretical formulations and practical manifestations, is centrally concerned with gender justice, our analysis also scrutinizes various versions of feminism. As we shall see, these reveal different interpretations of justice, not all of which support the feminist standpoint described in Chapter 1. I will defend a conception of justice and gender justice which does support it.

Justice in General, Gender Justice in Particular

Justice is universally accepted as a basic principle of law and ethics.[1] Some regard it as superseding all other obligations, and some identify it with virtue in general or with the virtuous life.[2] Most people agree with the formal principle of justice, based on Aristotle: equals should be treated equally and unequals unequally.[3] They robustly disagree, however, with regard to the material principle of justice, which involves the meaning of equality underlying the formal principle.[4] The questions of who should be considered equal and what it means to treat them equally are widely debated by scholars. In contrast, these questions are probably not debated enough by political leaders who champion equality as a fundamental social value. Clearly, the goals articulated in the name of equality are often at odds with one another.

The term "equity," considered by Aristotle distinct from equality, is sometimes used interchangeably with justice.[5] Equity refers to a situation in which like but different individuals or groups are regarded and treated justly but differently because they are equally valued. The relationship between equity and equality is thus definable through the concept of equal value. Equity deals with different individuals who are equally valued; inequity refers to a situation in which like but different individuals or groups are regarded and treated unjustly because they are not equally valued.[6]

To clarify the relationship further, consider how equal value is expressed in arithmetical or algebraic equations such as $(2 + 3 = 5)$ and $(x = y)$. We may think of these symbol sets as applicable to the relationship between humans who are men or women: 2 people who are men and 3 people who are women equal 5 human beings, and one woman (x) equals one man (y), or, to be chromosomally correct, XX = XY. In the first equation, we do not mean that 2 men and 3 women are precisely the same as any 5 human beings, and in the second equation we do not mean that a man is the same as a woman. In other words, the equality sign does not connote identity. Equality, then, does not imply sameness, even while it signifies the same value. The same rationale is applicable to human beings with chromosomal arrangements such as XO, XYY, and XXY.[7] Each equally represents a human being, even though each is chromosomally distinctive.

Gender justice thus refers to a situation in which men and women are equal to each other because they are equally valued but not the same. Because of unchangeable biological differences, women experience burdens and risks that men do not experience in reproduction and genetics, and those burdens and risks are not equal. Both formally and informally, however, measures can be introduced to reduce the inequitable impact of their differences. So long as reasonable efforts are made in that direction, the requirements of gender justice may be met.[8] In other words, a societal obligation to reduce the disparities among groups of people who are equally valued calls for reasonable efforts to reach a state in which X = Y, or XX = XY = XO = XYY = XXY.

In *Inequality Reexamined*, Amartya Sen provides a partial explanation for debate and confusion about equality: most ethical theories concerning social arrangements are egalitarian in some respect; the differences among them arise from the variables identified as deserving equal attention or distribution.[9] For Sen, even theories commonly considered anti-egalitarian are egalitarian in terms of one focus while inegalitarian in terms of another. Citing Robert Nozick's libertarian theory as an example, he writes:

> a libertarian approach may give priority to extensive liberties to be *equally* guaranteed to each, and this demands rejecting equality—or any "patterning"—of end states (e.g., the distribution of incomes or happiness). What is taken—usually by implication—to be a more central focus rules the roost, and inequalities in the variables that are, in effect, treated as peripheral must, then, be accepted in order not to violate the right arrangement (including equality) at the more central level.[10]

Sen considers it a "category mistake" to subscribe to the prevalent notion that one cannot maximize both liberty and equality. "Liberty," he says, "is among possible *fields of application* of equality, and equality is among the possible *patterns* of distribution of liberty."[11] The field and the pattern are simultaneously supportable.

Accordingly, the correct question to pose regarding alternative theories of justice is not whether one is more egalitarian than another but what equality is endorsed by each theory, whether implicitly or explicitly, and how the theorist defends that endorsement. Sen's own answers to these questions are congenial to a feminist standpoint because they take into account not only individual liberty and equal opportunity but the *capability* of individuals and groups to achieve the goals they define for themselves. "Capability," he says, "reflects a person's ability to choose between alternative lives, and its valuation need not presuppose unanimity regarding some one specific set of objectives."[12] In other words, capability is determined from the standpoint of the individual agent or group. It involves the power to achieve advantage over others, or at least to reduce one's disadvantage vis-à-vis others, but it is not equivalent to that power. Using that concept, we may define gender equality as a situation in which gender differences result in neither gender having greater advantage over the other, despite different capability. Formulaically, this may be expressed as follows:

$$\frac{\text{Advantage of XX}}{\text{Advantage of XY}} = 1$$

When gender differences lead to one gender having advantage over the other, there is inequality, which may be expressed as

$$\frac{\text{Advantage of XX}}{\text{Advantage of XY}} \neq 1$$

Because gender differences inevitably influence the capabilities and potential advantages of men and women, gender justice requires (*1*) identification of the differences, (*2*) determination of whether they entail inequality, and (*3*) efforts to eliminate or ameliorate the inequalities that occur. All of the differences added together = 1 or as close as possible an approximation to 1. Because gender justice extends, or ought to extend, to women and men as individuals also, the same rationale and formulas apply to individuals of either sex as to each sex considered as a group.

According to Sen, capabilities of individuals and groups are influenced by factors beyond the primary goods delineated by John Rawls. For Rawls, the primary goods include self-respect, rights and liberties, powers and opportunities, income and wealth, health and vigor, intelligence and imagination.[13] Such goods identify the *means* by which individuals may pursue their own idea of the good, but they fail to address the *extent* to which individuals are free (or unfree) to employ the means. The extent of one's freedom to employ the means is influenced by biological, social, and cultural factors that must also be considered. In other words, Rawls's account is helpful in developing a better understanding of how to promote equality of opportunity for different people to achieve different objectives, but he ignores the fact that people are not equally capable of utilizing the equal opportunities that Rawls (and Rawlsians) would set before them.

Unequal capabilities arise from many different characteristics of human beings, including sex, age, and genetic endowment. As Sen puts it, these diverse characteristics "give us very divergent powers to build freedom in our lives even when we have the same bundle of primary goods."[14] To eliminate or reduce the inequalities associated with the "divergent powers" of individuals or groups requires attention to their different capabilities and their related advantages or disadvantages. An egalitarian feminist standpoint attends to these "divergences" by privileging those whose capabilities have been associated with disadvantage.

In previous chapters, we identified some of the factors that influence the capability of women to pursue their goals in the context of genetics. As already mentioned, whether such factors *should* influence women and how they should be managed by those affected or by others are moral rather than empirical considerations. Since "ought" implies "can," an affirmative answer to the question of whether sex and gender differences should prevail is supported by the fact that the differences are inevitable or unavoidable. Such is the case for most biologically induced differences but not for the socially determined ones.[15] Even for biologically determined inequalities, their unchangeability does not suffice as justification for their inequitable consequences. Often, the inequitable impact of the consequences may be mitigated by personal or social measures introduced to accomplish that objective.

Whether differences are changeable or unchangeable, then, their mere occurrence is ethically neutral. Some differences enrich the lives of interacting individuals as well as society. Some differences make society more efficient, as one individual finds a niche that others are not suited for but need. Sex complementarity is a probable example of these positive effects; so is the variety of talents that some individuals have and others can only benefit by or appreciate. When these are the kinds of differences considered, the answer to the question of whether they should prevail is surely yes. As the French might put it, *Vive la différence!*

For other differences, however, the answer to the question of whether they should prevail is clearly no. The negative response is not only descriptive but normative because it entails a judgment based on the proposition or assumption, for which I have argued elsewhere, that human beings are equally human and deserve to be valued as such.[16] As already suggested, this does not imply that human beings are equal to one another in all respects. Every individual may in fact be superior to every other in some respect, but this implies that every individual is inferior to others in some respect. To put it differently, certain characteristics of an individual may be superior or inferior to those characteristics in another. My nearsightedness, for example, is an inferior characteristic; it does not, however, make *me* inferior to someone with perfect visual acuity, nor does it make me superior to someone who is blind.

Once the evaluative language of superiority and inferiority is introduced into a discussion of human relationships, we run the risk of interpreting differences as necessarily entailing inequities or inequality among individuals or groups. Although that interpretation is fallacious, it seems to be fairly prevalent. In health care, for example, differences are often seen as divergences from "normality" that need to be corrected if possible because the individual so affected is less valued than others. It is healthy or good to be normal; abnormalities put us in an inferior position, requiring intervention to restore normality.

In genetics, mutations are abnormalities that evoke expectations of "bad outcomes." No matter that some abnormalities or mutations have neutral, or even positive implications for individuals, depending on their goals.[17] From an egalitarian feminist standpoint, a criterion for distinguishing between differences that ought to prevail and those that should not prevail is the determination of whether the differences are associated with avoidable inequalities, that is, disadvantages between groups or individuals. The disparities occur mainly if not exclusively between those who are dominant and those who are nondominant, for example, patients or clients vis-à-vis their caregivers, wheelchair users vis-à-vis those who walk.

I am not arguing here for the elimination or reduction of capabilities on the part of some in order to equalize their capabilities with those of others. Rather, I am arguing that the advantages that accrue to some because of their capabilities ought to be equally distributed, or less unequally distributed, to those who lack such advantages because of their lesser capabilities. Where equal distribution of advantages is not possible, there ought at least to be efforts to reduce the inequality. Morally, those who are advantaged through greater capabilities bear greater responsibilities toward those who are less advantaged. In other words, equitable distribution of advantages is a social ideal worth pursuing—despite its resonance with the Marxist maxim: From each according to ability, to each according to need.[18]

Some differences *entail* inequalities; others are merely *associated* with them. For example, the health risk and discomfort experienced by women who provide gametes for reproduction are measurable, whereas men experience neither risk nor discomfort; this inequality is entailed or necessitated by one's being male or female. Once children are born, however, the unequal roles prevalently occupied by mothers or fathers are merely associated with their sex.[19] For example, the time spent with children by both parents could be the same, or the ratio could be reversed. Caregiving responsibilities for the genetically disabled would be dramatically altered if this were to happen.

What type of situation *should* prevail if differences result in inequality? If gender justice is desirable, efforts should be made to reduce inequalities occasioned by differences between the sexes. Where inequitable differences are unchangeable, as in the different reproductive roles of men and women, measures can still be introduced to reduce the inequity of their consequences. It may be argued, for example, that laws granting women alone the right to terminate a pregnancy are based on the realization that women's bodies and not men's are affected by those decisions. Where inequitable differences are changeable, then such changes should be made, or at least attempted, on grounds of gender justice as a social goal. Alternatively, the advantages enjoyed by some may be balanced by those of others, so that the overall impact of changeable differences is equitable.

Consider, for example, the conditions under which women are likely to have their personal goals thwarted by the responsibility of caring for children affected by genetic conditions. These conditions are changeable because they are not dependent on biology, but they are inequitable toward women in that men are not comparably affected in most instances. This gender inequity could be reduced, even if not eliminated, through the establishment of more effective means of support for principal caregivers and by incentives directed toward men to participate more actively in their children's care. The capability of caregivers of either sex to pursue goals beyond caregiving could surely be enhanced by social measures that encourage employers to accommodate the fulfillment of caregiving roles by their employees. Even in a free enterprise system, such accommodation may be morally and legally required of those capable of exercising corporate responsibility.

In whatever economic system it occurs, inequality is not necessarily unjust. It is not unjust, for example, that older people typically have already had a wider range of experiences and a more extended life span than younger people. Nor is it unjust that some people are more talented, more intelligent, more attractive, or more athletically gifted than others. In comparing unequal distribution of such factors among individuals, H. Tristram Engelhardt Jr. suggests that such differences are due to failures of fortune rather than failures of fairness.[20] It is unfortunate, for example, that women are exposed to the risks of pregnancy while men are not, and that some people are disabled while others are fully able, but these are not unfair differences between people. Engelhardt would probably deny that it is a failure of either fortune or fairness that women are not born male. Yet such a statement would be empirically supportable on grounds that women are more likely than men to be poor and dependent on the health care system for themselves and others, and less likely than men to be well-educated or to find positions of power and prestige.

Engelhardt's distinction between what is unfortunate and what is unfair is based on the fact that some inequality occurs naturally and, apparently, inevitably. His distinction assumes that no one is responsible for such situations. In light of possibilities for prenatal testing and termination, however, it may be argued that the "unfortunateness" of some disabilities is avoidable, and that failure to avoid them is therefore unfair to those affected. It may also be argued, as in cases addressed in Chapters 1 and 14, that women who do not take steps to ensure healthy pregnancies, even if this requires risks to them or severe impositions on their autonomy, are unfair to their potential children.

Even in instances in which Engelhardt's rationale is correct—where the situation is both unfortunate and unavoidable—this alone says nothing to what is done or not done subsequently about such naturally occurring inequality. Different conceptions of justice may be introduced to justify alternative means of responding to inequality. The alternatives range from procedure-based libertarian theories such as Robert Nozick proposes,[21] through liberal or contractarian theories such as that of Rawls,[22] to socialist theories inspired by Karl

Marx.[23] Each of these involves a different view of gender justice and is thus relatable to different versions of feminism. As we will see, not all versions of feminism are compatible with the egalitarian perspective of this book.

Theories of Justice and Feminism

A libertarian theory of justice gives priority to the liberty of individuals in choosing mechanisms for the distribution of goods. The economic system thus supported is capitalistic, individualistic, and rights-centered.[24] Self-interest is the force that motivates individuals to enter freely, continue, and withdraw from socioeconomic arrangements whose rules they are bound, by virtue of their agreement, to observe. As Nozick paraphrases Marx, the libertarian criterion for decisions regarding distribution is "From each as they choose, to each as they are chosen."[25] This conception of justice is essentially procedural rather than substantive. Depending on the different capabilities of the individuals to whom procedural justice is owed, the material gaps between them are inevitably widened through the maximization of their individual liberty in a laissez-faire environment. So long as their choices are consistent with procedural fairness, Nozick's dictum involves no restriction of the content of one's choices; it apparently permits racist, sexist, and classist choices as well as choices that are morally praiseworthy.[26]

In genetics, both libertarian and liberal feminist arguments have been applied to specific issues. From a libertarian perspective such as Engelhardt's, for example, so long as women can pay for (or have their insurance cover) prenatal diagnosis and treatment, and are fully informed about the risks they freely undertake, genetic testing is ethically justified. [27] Since the emphasis is on *individual* liberty, the tendency to treat these issues in the context of couples, ignoring inevitable differences between partners, is inconsistent with a libertarian rationale. Lori Andrews apparently recognizes this when she argues that a feminist position on a woman's right to control the disposition of her own body is contradicted by feminists who oppose the rights of *individual* women to provide ova or gestation in exchange for money.[28]

Liberalism and liberal feminism are also associated with an emphasis on individual liberty. However, liberal feminism defends an equality of opportunity that reduces the inequality that is theoretically justifiable in a libertarian system. Some of the implications of the liberal feminist position are clear, but some are not. It seems clear, for example, that women and men alike have a right to basic health care and to an environment that is free of contaminants that might damage their own or their offsprings' health. It is not clear whether equality of opportunity requires access to prenatal counseling and intervention for all women. The extent to which society is obliged to pay for the health care of those who cannot pay for it themselves is a matter on which liberal feminists are likely to disagree. Some would support a minimal level of government subsidies, leaning closer to a libertarian approach; others would support a maximal level, with a wider range of egalitarian implications.

Rawls's contractarian theory is an effort to combine the liberal's emphasis on equal individual liberty with an emphasis on other egalitarian considerations. His first principle of justice incorporates the liberal's emphasis: individual liberty should be limited only to the extent that it is necessary to ensure the same liberty for others. His second principle of justice expresses the egalitarian component: social and economic inequalities should be arranged so that they benefit the least advantaged in a situation of equality of opportunity for all.[29] Susan Moller Okin endorses both principles of justice but citicizes Rawls for assuming that families are just.[30] She develops a liberal feminist account that refutes this assumption by documenting the inherently patriarchal structure of the family and the unjust impact of that structure on women.

Okin's theoretical critique extends to "false gender neutrality" in language as well as action. She insists on paying attention to gender differences that might provoke injustice, even while arguing for an ideal of a "genderless family." Unlike most philosophers, she offers concrete recommendations:

> Because children are borne by women but can (and, I contend, should) be raised by both parents equally, policies relating to pregnancy and birth should be quite distinct from those relating to parenting. Pregnancy and childbirth, to whatever varying extent they require leave from work, should be regarded as temporarily disabling conditions like any others, and employers should be mandated to provide leave for all such conditions.[31]

The same recommendations are applicable to issues that arise in genetic testing. Okin's rationale suggests that the cost of prenatal testing and interventions should be covered for women, and carrier testing for autosomal recessive conditions should be covered for both partners.

Critics of liberal feminism may focus on either its liberal component or its feminist component. The liberal component has been critiqued for its tendency to treat individuals atomistically, emphasizing rights rather than preservation of relationships, and neglecting responsibilities for others as well as oneself.[32] The feminist component has been critiqued by feminists themselves for subscribing to an essentially male model of rationality and autonomy. One of the results of this subscription, according to Alison Jaggar, is a "normative dualism" with regard to our evaluation of the relationship between mind and body.[33] In a society that generally views activities of the mind as superior to those of the body, women are likely to be less esteemed because gestation, birth, and early nurturance of children tie them more to physical than to mental activities. Jaggar also maintains that a liberal feminist emphasis on individual autonomy provides an inadequate account of moral goodness.[34] Beyond respect for others' choices, the ends we pursue as individuals and as a society ought to promote human surviving and flourishing.[35]

The normative dualism that Jaggar criticizes is apparent in attitudes and practices with regard to genetic diseases that are mainly associated with mental retardation. For example, the desire to avoid the birth of a child with Down syndrome is the most common reason for women to undergo prenatal testing.[36] Although specific physical findings and other medical problems are associated with this condition, the most persistent problem it poses is mental retardation. Jaggar's insistence that other values besides respect for autonomy should be considered in our moral judgments is also applicable to this type of situation. The primary justification for nondirective counseling, for instance, is respect for the client's autonomy. Jaggar and other socialist feminists would argue that considerations of beneficence and social justice are relevant to the counseling situation as well.[37] To the extent that life-style changes and early detection and treatment can reduce the incidence or severity of multifactorial genetic disorders, practitioners would agree on this point.

Socialist feminists are concerned not only about women's right to abortion but also about "the social pressures that may be exerted on couples, and especially on women, to terminate a pregnancy thought to be affected by a genetic disorder."[38] They would agree with Angus Clarke's concerns about the implications of prenatal diagnosis for "society as a whole, with long-term repercussions for the status of, and provision for, the mentally and physically handicapped."[39] Consideration of these repercussions through attention to differences between individuals as well as groups is crucial to the goal of social equality.

Communitarian or socialist thinkers are the principal critics of liberal and libertarian feminism.[40] The communitarians tend to emphasize familial or affective relationships, while socialists emphasize political relationships and the importance of equality as a social goal. A communitarian ideology may be reinforced by the care models of moral reasoning that Carol Gilligan and Nel Noddings have developed.[41] Although both models are based on women's experience, some feminists are critical of them because they may promote exploitation of women's natural propensity to care for others.[42] Because women are usually the primary caregivers of persons affected by genetic conditions, possibilities for exploitation are evident in that context. If caring behavior were as esteemed and rewarded as behavior based on a justice model of reasoning, exploitation would be reduced if not eliminated.[43]

Like communitarianism, socialism emphasizes the sociality of individuals while demanding a sense of community that reaches beyond separate or separable communities to embrace all of humankind.[44] Equality, construed broadly, is the goal of socialist justice. Overcoming gender inequality is thus central to the socialist feminist agenda. From that standpoint, society and individuals alike should attempt to reduce the disproportionate burden of genetics on women. Minimizing the cost and risk of procedures and interventions while maximizing access to them as well as to genetic counseling would constitute such an attempt. As I have already suggested, however, there are many ways by which gender inequity may be reduced. A socialist feminist standpoint not only identifies the gender inequities that occur in genetics but also finds ways of ameliorating or eliminating them.

Admittedly, the term "socialist" has been in disrepute for many years in many quarters. But the term itself is not a crucial label for the critique of individualism and liberalism that many feminists support. In fact, Sen's capability theory of justice, which invokes a broader and more complex notion of individual liberty than other theories assume, is compatible with the majority of feminist critiques. What is essential to feminist and Sen's critiques is that they start with a concept of human beings not as isolated individuals but as individuals whose meaning and reality are definable and sustainable only in the context of their relationships to others. Although Sen does not develop that concept in *Inequality Reconsidered*, his advocacy of an equality that embraces capability as well as opportunity assumes that individuals are related to others who may impede or facilitate the fulfillment of their goals.

A feminist standpoint may draw on any of the diverse versions of feminism because all of these involve a remedial emphasis on women. In fact, the enrichment of perspectives derived from their inclusion can only be maximized by including representatives of diverse feminisms. Women themselves are distinguishable from one another by class, race, ability, and sexual orientation, and by size, age, politics, religion, and profession. Thus, while we belong to the nondominant group by gender, some of us belong to the dominant group by race or class or other criteria. Just as women have a privileged epistemological status vis-à-vis men, the same is true for women of color vis-à-vis white women, and clients or patients vis-à-vis the professionals who treat or counsel them. Moreover, because women as individuals are not adequately definable through any collection of categorical designations, the rationale that underlies a feminist standpoint must be extended to a recognition of each woman as a unique individual. To promote gender justice for all women, individual differences as well as gender and other group-based differences must be taken into account.

Which Theory of Justice, Which Version of Feminism?

That said, not all theories of justice and not all versions of feminism are compatible with the feminist standpoint developed here. Libertarian justice and libertarian feminism are resistant to demands for equality that extend beyond individual liberty. However, just what individual liberty or autonomy means is a problem in its own right, and various authors have questioned whether the preferences expressed by dominated individuals are adaptive rather than autonomous.[45] Consistent with their understanding of autonomy, libertarians object to any governmentally prescribed redistribution of goods or genetic services intended to reduce the inequalities that arise from different genetic endowments. Nor would they condone mandatory assistance to ensure the participation of the underserved in the development of genetic policies; in fact, they would oppose such assistance as an impediment to individual liberty. Only services that are voluntarily provided and obtained would be acceptable to a libertarian, whether feminist or not. Unless and until such a voluntarist system succeeds in overcoming the inequities that undeniably arise in the practice of genetics, a truly feminist standpoint is incompatible with these libertarian positions because they fail in their support for all of the women to whom feminism as such is committed. At best, a libertarian feminism is a partial feminism because, by limiting its advocacy to procedural freedom, it advocates only for those women who are substantively free already.

Liberal theories of justice and liberal feminism are difficult to defend or refute because they are open to diverse and sometimes conflicting interpretations and emphases. To the extent that such theories approximate a libertarian point of view, they are subject to the same criticisms and limitations as above. Some liberal theories, for example, represent a feminist standpoint because they articulate a privileged perspective. Okin's corrected version of Rawls is an example of this. Still, Okin does not extend her feminist advocacy beyond women to other nondominant groups.[46] Ronald Dworkin's theory of justice, based on equitable distribution of resources rather than opportunities, is perhaps a more egalitarian rendition of liberal theory.[47] But, as Sen suggests, Dworkin follows Rawls in identifying the means to freedom while ignoring its reach or extent in the lives of individuals or groups. From a feminist standpoint, it is crucial that the capability for freely fulfilling one's goals also be addressed.

Communitarianism and communitarian feminism illustrate a vagueness that makes it difficult to assess their compatibility with a feminist standpoint. To the extent that they stress democratic representation they would certainly support *a* feminist standpoint. In fact, they would support many feminist standpoints, and antifeminist standpoints as well, so long as these are thought to emerge from a communal context or contribute to communal interests. But the interests of an antifeminist community and a feminist community are obviously in conflict, and the former is clearly opposed to gender justice or equality. Paradoxically, support for communities with opposing goals could promote their mutual destruction. Moreover, individuals themselves generally belong to multiple communities simultaneously, and the priorities or emphases of these different communities are sometimes, quite inevitably and sometimes deliberately, at odds. Consider, for example, the geneticist who simultaneously belongs to a research community, whose priority is to obtain scientific knowledge, and to a clinical community, whose priority is the health of patients who are also research subjects.[48] Where these priorities conflict, one community's interests may justifiably be subordinated to those of another. Feminists themselves belong to different communities in addition to their communities of feminists. Communitarianism merely stipulates that communal interests take priority over individual interests; it offers no guidance for determining which community's interests have priority over another's.[49]

Socialism and socialist feminism require a sense of community and of equality that is broader than any of the preceding theories of justice or feminism. Moreover, socialism is necessarily feminist in that it is essentially committed to equality for all women. The principal difference between socialist and other theories is their different interpretations of the ideal of equality. Nonsocialist theories tend to limit the scope of that ideal. In contrast, socialist theory embraces all of the differences that occur within and among human beings: race, class, gender, ability, sexuality, and the like. Marx recognized and took account of the fact that these differences overlap in individuals as well as groups. As Sen observes, he went beyond class analysis, insisting that equality demands a balancing of the different needs and abilities of individuals. For example, when Marx criticized the German Workers' Party for not distinguishing between equality in rewards for work and equality in satisfaction of needs, he specifically acknowledged diversities within the working class. Different needs, for Sen and for Marx, lead to inequality if they are not differently met. The different needs define different capabilities for converting primary goods and resources into "freedom to do, to be, and to live the way one would like."[50] Contradicting a widespread but false interpretation of Marx, not only group differences but individual differences are relevant to a socialist egalitarian agenda.

To conclude, then, of the theories of justice and feminism here discussed, libertarian, liberal, and socialist, the first is inconsistent with and the last is consistent with a feminist standpoint that applies to all women. Liberal feminism may or may not be consistent with that standpoint. As we will see in the next chapter, class differences present a particularly significant set of needs, for women as well as others, in clinical and societal applications of genetics. A socialist account of justice and of feminism requires careful and critical attention to those needs and to the abilities of others to respond to them. My approach to the issues addressed in subsequent chapters is guided by that account. To avoid inaccurate and pejorative interpretations of "socialist," however, I have described this approach as an egalitarian feminist standpoint.

Notes

1. "Universally" is seldom an accurate descriptive; in this case, however, I use it quite deliberately. As we will see in what follows, the meanings attached to the principle vary considerably.

2. Justice may be construed as superseding other virtues because it represents a social or political, rather than individual, virtue. Aristotle's subordination of ethics to politics, or individual goods to the common good, supports this interpretation. *Nichomachean Ethics* I, 2 and *Politics* I, 1. Regarding the tendency to equate justice with the virtuous life, see *Nichomachean Ethics* V, 1: "The best man is not he who exercises his virtue towards himself but he who exercises it towards another. . . . Justice in this sense, then, is not part of virtue but virtue entire," *The Basic Works of Aristotle,* ed. Richard McKeon, trans. W. D. Ross (New York: Random House, 1941), p. 1004. Many passages of the Bible seem to identify the two as well; see Genesis 6:9, where Noah is described as "a just man and perfect in his generations," who "walked with God." Also, Isiah 26:7: "The way of the just is uprightness and holiness" and Romans 7:12: "The law is holy, and the commandment holy, just, and good."

3. See generally Aristotle's *Nichomachean Ethics* V, 3–5. Many authors cite this principle before delineating various material principles or arguing for their own.

4. E.g., Tom L. Beauchamp and James F. Childress list six principles, each designating a different criterion for distribution to individuals: equal shares, need, effort, contribution, merit, and free-market exchange. *Principles of Biomedical Ethics* (New York: Oxford University Press, 1994), p. 330.

5. Aristotle's *Nichomachean Ethics* V, 10. Equity is defined there as "a correction of the law where it is defective owning to its universality" (Ross, p. 1020). The term "fairness" is also used interchangeably with justice, a usage supported by John Rawls's well-known article "Justice as Fairness," in *The Philosophical Review* 57 (1958). Because the terms "equality," "fairness," "equity," and "justice" are used interchangeably in common parlance, I have not distinguished among them in other writings. E.g., Mary Briody Mahowald, *Women and Children in Health Care: An Unequal Majority* (New York: Oxford University Press, 1993).

6. By using the term "individuals" rather than "persons" or "human beings," I am open to the inclusion of nonpersons and nonhumans in considerations of equality.

7. XO refers to Turner's syndrome, XYY to a chromosomal anomaly associated with mental illness and aggression, and XXY refers to Klinefelter's syndrome.

8. Admittedly, the criteria for determining "reasonable efforts" are problematic, as problematic as criteria for determining the "reasonable person" (or reasonable man) standard in law and bioethics.

9. Amartya Sen, *Inequality Reexamined* (Cambridge: Harvard University Press, 1995), p. 3.

10. Sen, p. 3.

11. Sen, pp. 22–23.

12. Sen, p. 83, deleting parentheticals.

13. John Rawls, *A Theory of Justice* (Cambridge: Harvard University Press, 1971), p. 62.

14. Sen, pp. 85–86.

15. Moreover, biological and psychological as well as social differences often influence each other. For example, the onset of menarche is influenced by whether girls engage in sports. The lesser body fat of those who are athletically active leads to later

menses, extending the girls' growth period so that they tend to be taller than their more sedentary counterparts. The interaction between nature (genetics) and nurture (environment) is discussed further in Chapter 14.

16. *Women and Children in Health Care,* Chapter 1.

17. For example, unusual tallness in a basketball player or shortness in a jockey. While the goals an individual chooses are probably determined in part by her or his ability to achieve them, once the goals are set, certain "abnormalities" may be advantages.

18. Robert C. Tucker, ed., *The Marx–Engels Reader* (New York: Norton, 1972), p. 388.

19. An exception to this point is the woman's capacity for lactation. While others, including fathers, are also able to feed infants, only women can nurse them.

20. H. Tristram Engelhardt Jr., *Foundations of Bioethics,* (New York: Oxford University Press, 1996), p. 381.

21. Robert Nozick, *Anarchy, State, and Utopia* (New York: Basic Books, 1974). Nozick also dubs his view an entitlement theory (p. 153). As such, it involves acquisition and transfer of holdings as well as rectification of violations of the rules regarding acquisition and transfer.

22. *A Theory of Justice.* The more recent rendition of his theory is more weighted in the direction of the liberty principle than the equality principle. John Rawls, *Political Liberalism* (New York: Columbia University Press, 1996).

23. Tucker, especially the early writings. I would count Michael Walzer among those inspired by Marx. See his *Spheres of Justice: A Defense of Pluralism and Equality* (New York: Basic Books, 1983).

24. Clearly, not all rights-centered views are libertarian. A notable example in this regard is Alan Gewirth, who develops a broadly and demandingly equalitarian theory in *The Community of Rights* (Chicago: University of Chicago Press, 1996).

25. Nozick, p. 160.

26. Nozick might well disagree with this interpretation, possibly citing philanthropy or voluntary giving as a just and effective means of reducing racism, sexism, and classim (pp. 262–68).

27. The libertarianism that Engelhardt develops in *The Foundations of Bioethics* (both editions) is rooted in a secular morality that he considers content-less because of "the irremedial plurality of postmodernity" (New York: Oxford University Press, 1996), p. 9. He identifies "moral communities" such as those formed by religious traditions as essential to a content-based morality.

28. Lori Andrews, "Feminism Revisited: Fallacies and Policies in the Surrogacy Debate," *Logos* 9 (1988): 81–96.

29. Rawls, *A Theory of Justice,* pp. 60–61.

30. Susan Moller Okin, *Justice, Gender and the Family* (New York: Basic Books, 1989), pp. 93–109.

31. Okin, p. 176. Despite her use of the term "genderless," I don't believe Okin is arguing for the irrevelence of gender differences after children are born. Rather, she seems to be pointing out that parenting responsibilities are interchangeable as well as sharable by men and women.

32. Jean Bethke Elshtain, "Feminism, Family, and Community," *Dissent* 29 (1982): 442, 445.

33. Alison M. Jaggar, *Feminist Politics and Human Nature* (Totawa, NJ: Rowman and Allanheld, 1983), pp. 46–47.

34. Jaggar, p. 48.

35. Elshtain, p. 442.

36. Although the reason for recommending prenatal diagnosis is usually listed as advanced maternal age (AMA), the principal anomaly with which AMA is associated is trisomy 21, or Down syndrome. As indicated in the previous chapter, the risk of any chromosomal anomaly in the fetus of a woman who is 35 years of age is about 1 in 204.

37. Jaggar's socialist feminism is well developed in *Feminist Politics and Human Nature.* See also Rosemarie Tong, *Feminist Thought: A More Comprehensive Introduction* (Boulder, CO: Westview Press, 1998), pp. 94–129.

38. Angus Clarke, "Is Non-Directive Genetic Counselling Possible?" *Lancet* 338 (1991): 998–1000.

39. Clarke, p. 998.

40. In addition, as Tong observes, communitarians critique Marxist feminism and socialist feminists critique Marxist feminism (pp. 114–18). Communitarians themselves are diverse in the views they espouse, some tilting more toward a socialist conception of equality and feminism than others.

41. Carol Gilligan, *In a Different Voice: Psychological Theory and Women's Development* (Cambridge: Harvard University Press, 1993), and Nel Noddings, *Caring: A Feminine Approach to Ethics and Moral Education* (Berkeley: University of California Press, 1984), pp. 43, 79–81. Sara Ruddick also proposes a care-related model of "maternal thinking," but this is more congenial to feminism because it necessarily involves a commitment to social justice through its advocacy of peace throughout the world. *Maternal Thinking* (New York: Ballantine Books, 1989).

42. E.g., Susan Sherwin, *No Longer Patient: Feminist Ethics and Health Care* (Philadelphia: Temple University Press, 1992), pp. 49–50, and Mary B. Mahowald, "Pitfalls of an Ethic of Care," in Amy Marie Haddad and Robert A. Buerki, eds., *Ethical Dimensions of Pharmaceutical Care* (New York: Haworth Press, 1996), pp. 85–102.

43. Joan C. Tronto develops the case for this convincingly and clearly in *Moral Boundaries: A Political Argument for an Ethic of Care* (New York: Routledge, 1993).

44. Jaggar distinguishes between socialist and Marxist feminism on grounds of the primacy attributed to women's oppression. Marxist feminists, she claims, view the oppression of women as an expression of the fundamental economic oppression that separates the bourgeoisie from the proletariat, whereas socialist feminists view women's oppression as primary (pp. 125–32). In either context, the commitment of Marx to gender justice is evident in his proposal of the man–woman relationship as a gauge by which to measure the degree of humanization that has taken place in society. Tucker, p. 69.

45. E.g., Martha C. Nussbaum, "Adaptive Preferences and Women's Options," Chapter 2 of *Women and Human Development: The Capabilities Approach* (Cambridge: Cambridge University Press, 2000), and Jon Elster, "Sour Grapes: Utilitarianism and the Genesis of Wants," in Amartya Sen and Bernard Williams, eds., *Utilitarianism and Beyond* (New York: Cambridge University Press, 1982), pp. 219–38, and Amartya Sen, "Gender and Cooperative Conflicts," in Irene Tinker, ed., *Persistent Inequalities: Women and World Development* (New York: Oxford University Press, 1990), pp. 123–49.

46. A caveat to this point is Okin's account of the overall economic disparity between men and women. To the extent that her advocacy for women extends to poor women, her liberal critique applies to class as well as gender.

47. Ronald Dworkin, "What is Equality? Parts 1 and 2," *Philosophy and Public Affairs* 10 (1981), and "What Is Equality? 3: The Place of Liberty," *Iowa Law Review* (1987): 73.

48. In university-based medical institutions, this dual community membership is common. Fortunately, the research priority is generally subordinated to the health interest of the patient.

49. If it proposed "the greater community" as a criterion for determining the priority, it would seem to be endorsing a socialist model. Approvingly, I attributed a rationale like this to Josiah Royce in Mary L. Briody, "Community in Royce: An Interpretation," *Transactions of the Charles S. Peirce Society, A Journal in American Philosophy* 4 (1969): 224–42.

50. Sen, *Inequality Reexamined,* p. 121.

5

ALLOCATION OF GENETIC SERVICES AND THE FEMINIZATION OF POVERTY

RESOURCES may be allocated unjustly through overdistribution, underdistribution, or distribution of the same resources to different parties.[1] Consistent with the notion of gender justice developed in the previous chapter, just allocation necessarily involves two components: identification of differences in burdens, benefits, and preferences of individuals and groups, and distribution of burdens, benefits, and preferences in a manner by which inequality is minimized. In this chapter, I briefly explain ways in which injustice occurs in the allocation of genetic services through overdistribution or distribution of the same benefits, burdens, and respect for preferences; however, my analysis concentrates on the underdistribution that occurs because of poverty. In all three modes of allocation, a gender difference is evident.

In the context of limited resources, the three modes of allocating resources are related; one may in fact be a cause or condition of the other. For example, given a limited number of medical school graduates, an oversupply of specialists leaves fewer graduates to practice as generalists, of whom there is an undersupply.[2] Obviously, other factors are relevant here as well; principal among these is that the income and prestige of specialists tends to be greater than the income and prestige of generalists. Even if the supply of specialists and generalists were exactly the same, however, allocating the same number from each group to fulfill the health care needs of the population would in fact constitute an overdistribution of one and an underdistribution of the other because of the greater need for generalists than specialists. An identical allocation of resources to different parties with different needs does not constitute just allocation.

Unjust Overdistribution

From the standpoint of the distributee, having too much of something is undesirable if the resource being distributed is unwanted, harmful, or provided at the cost of other resources that are desired by or more beneficial to the distributee. Harm to the distributee obviously violates the principle of nonmaleficence. Overdistribution is at odds with the principle of justice if its provision entails unequal distribution of a desired resource for oneself or others. It is morally problematic, even if it is not unjust, if and when it leads to social or psychological pressures that reduce the autonomy of the distributee.

What are the resources of genetics that may be undesirably overdistributed? The funding for research in genetics may be an unjust overdistribution of limited government resources. Clearly, the three billlion dollars that the U.S. Congress allotted to the Human Genome Project reduced the funding available for other important health-related projects and may have reduced the funds available for addressing more significant social needs. At the outset of the project, some scientists suggested an undesirable, and possibly unjust, overdistribution when they argued that such funding reduced the support available for basic science research in more important areas.[3] Because some saw the project as devoted to the development of technology rather than science, they thought it more appropriately supported by the private sector, particularly by those companies whose commercial interests would be enhanced through provision of genetic tests and services.[4]

Genetic information about individuals or families may be overdistributed by being provided to individuals or groups to whom the information is not personally relevant. It may, for example, be commercially relevant to insurance companies or employers, but, from the standpoint of those being tested, this is an undesirable and possibly unjust overdistribution. Unjust overdistribution may also occur in the context of families or relatives who are interested in, but unaffected by, genetic information. The right of individuals to confidentiality with regard to their own genetic information is not absolute because there are circumstances in which disclosure is necessary to the treatment of, or to significant decisions of, others who may be affected. However, where those factors are not present, overdistribution of genetic information is undesirable and potentially unjust.

Beyond the disclosure of information that genetic counseling entails, extensive obligatory counseling may be another form of overdistribution. For example, the counseling currently required in conjunction with testing for Huntington disease may be overdistributed if the counseling is unwanted, unhelpful, or overly costly. Some medical geneticists consider the degree of counseling required an unjustifiable imposition which is likely to impede individuals who are already sufficiently prepared both intellectually and psychologically from obtaining the information they wish to have by taking the test.[5] Overdistribution occurs for those who accept unneeded counseling in order to take the test.

Genetic tests and interventions are overdistributed if they are provided in situations where they are neither wanted nor helpful. The interests of diagnostic laboratories and researchers' interests are probably enhanced by such overdistribution, but the interests of those tested are not. Unfortunately, patients are often unaware that some tests and interventions to which they supposedly give consent are not tied to their own welfare. Some prenatal genetic tests are offered and performed so routinely that neither the clinician nor the patient is aware that this may constitute overdistribution of available resources. This is surely true of ultrasound, but it is often true of amniocentesis as well. If insurance covers the procedure, neither clinicians nor pregnant women are likely to question its usefulness so long as it is considered safe.[6] As more tests become available to men as well as nonpregnant women, these may be overdistributed too.

Routinization of genetic tests and procedures, as well as overdistribution of genetic information, contributes to a milieu in which women may feel pressured to undergo counseling, tests, and procedures that they would otherwise forgo. For example, routinization of ultrasonography and proliferation of the equipment for providing it seems to have led to an increment in the incidence of abortion of female fetuses in India and China.[7] If the main reason for ultrasonography during pregnancy is to avoid the birth of healthy female infants, this is an unjust overdistribution of the technology. Some procedures, such as chorionic villus sampling, have been disseminated widely among wealthy and educated segments of Latin American countries, despite the lack of any medical rationale for the test but simply because it is available. In the absence of data demonstrating any benefits to women or children, it is possible that affluent women are unjustly overtreated through this practice. As Victor B. Penchaszadeh puts it, they may be "victims . . . of an excessive medicalization and 'geneticization' of reproduction."[8] These practices are clearly at odds with an egalitarian feminist standpoint.

Distributing the Same to Each

Distributing literally the same resources to each individual or group is ordinarily and obviously an undesirable and undesired allocation of resources. Such distribution is undesirable because it is an inefficient use of the resources, ensuring that some will be used ineffectively or not at all. A distribution scheme based on a notion of equality as sameness is undesired in most cases because the same resources are neither needed nor desired by some of the recipients. In the context of limited resources, allocation of the same resources is superflous to some, while the needs of others are not met or only inadequately met.

As we have seen in previous chapters, men and women differ in many ways in addition to biology. Their needs for genetic services are different also. To the extent that genetic conditions are found only or primarily in women or men, only one sex needs to be tested except in the case of fetuses. Because fetuses can be tested or treated only through women, few if any would argue that the identical genetic resources provided to them should be given to men also. Even if the same genetic resources were offered and provided to everyone, the distribution scheme would be unjust because it would inevitably reduce the resources available to address other needs of individuals and groups. For example, if carrier testing were offered and provided to all comers rather than to those in specific risk groups, the resources required to do this would reduce the availability of services uniquely needed by particular groups or individuals. Unless and until we are all the same, then, this distribution scheme will be unjust. Thankfully, that boring state of affairs will never occur.

Another area in which distribution of genetic services seems to be based on a model of justice as sameness involves the use of language. As already mentioned, prenatal counselors and reproductive technologists tend to speak of their clients in gender-neutral terms, as couples. This ignores the fact that clients have a specific sex, and that their sex makes a huge difference in the impact on each of the alternatives considered. Of course, every person is genetically related to two distinct parents (unless cloned from an adult cell),[9] and equally related to both parents in that (ordinarily) the same number of chromosomes is inherited from each. As any practicing parent knows, however, the child's relation to each parent entails a great deal more than those 23 chromosomes. Moreover, while every child *may* be parented equally by both father and mother, or more by their fathers than their mothers, neither of these situations prevails in today's society. Even if children are not breast fed, most are parented more by their mothers than their fathers, and many are parented only by their mothers.[10] This last fact is one of the main reasons why underdistribution of resources, to which we turn next, is related to the feminization of poverty.

Underdistribution of Resources

Decades ago, Diana Pearce coined the term "feminization of poverty" to highlight the fact that a majority of the poor in the United States are women and their children. She calculated that "nearly two out of three of the 15 million poor persons over 16 were women" and predicted that poverty would continue to spread among women.[11] Her prediction has been fulfilled in that the phenomenon of the feminization of poverty still prevails, and shows no sign of abating. The prevalence of poverty among women arises not only from their mothering role but also from a number of other factors: the caregiving of women for parents and other relatives, the extended life span of women, and social practices and attitudes that deprive them more than men of the resources they need or desire for themselves or for those for whom they are responsible.[12] For many women, underdistribution of resources is experienced on a daily basis.

Sara McLanahan and her colleagues explicitly link the poverty of women to that of children, noting that the term "feminization of poverty" is used "to describe changes in the proportion of the poor who live in female-headed families, or changes in the proportion of the poor who are female or who live in female-headed families."[13] In fact most of those who live in female-headed households are children. Thus the feminization of poverty is accompanied by the pauperization of children. Moreover, because most women live longer than most men, pauperization extends disproportionately to elderly women as well.[14] At both ends of life's spectrum, women are reduced to poverty through living costs that escalate in the absence or loss of male support. Regardless of whether their income is supplemented by transfer payments (government benefits), the poverty persists.

Women who are single parents may be widowed, divorced, separated, or never married. Although each of these situations has different economic repercussions, all of them usually leave women and their children considerably poorer than they are in two-parent families. According to Irwin Garfinkle and Sara McLanahan, three factors contribute to the disparity: the low earning capacity of single women, the lack of child support from noncustodial fathers, and the meager benefits provided by public assistance programs.[15] The low earning capacity of women is influenced by the fact that early pregnancy is associated with fewer years of education. Substantial numbers of single working mothers find it impossible to support themselves and their children at a level above the poverty line. Health care costs are frequently beyond their reach.

Although genetic testing is covered by insurance when the cost-to-benefit ratio seems to justify it, social impediments such as those discussed in Chapter 3 often impede the utilization of genetic services. When this is not so and as more genetic tests become available, the tests are unlikely to be covered for poor women. This has already proved true with regard to cystic fibrosis and breast cancer testing.[16] While new genetic tests tend to be developed relatively quickly after the discovery of mutations for particular conditions, and the tests then become available on an elective basis to anyone who can pay for them, the poor are likely to have access to the new tests only if their participation is useful to researchers.

Despite the health care benefits available through various government programs, poverty is a factor that negatively affects the health of all poor people, regardless of age or gender. As Ruth Sidel puts it, "If you're poor, you're more likely to be sick, less likely to receive adequate medical care, and more likely to die at an early age."[17] Even if care were adequate, the likelihood of its being optimal would be slim, given that, in the large urban hospital centers to which the poor usually come for care, most of their medical care is provided by those who are least experienced, least prestigious, and least rewarded—that is, physicians in training.

If health care for the poor were universally and optimally covered, the poor would still experience a greater number of health problems than the affluent. These are often triggered by social factors such as unemployment, underemployment, poor nutrition, teenage pregnancy, and drug use. Ironically and tragically, however, the poor have the lowest use of health services in comparison with their need. Where individuals from different socioeconomic brackets have the same presenting condition, "those who are better off receive more care than poorer persons in comparable states of health."[18] Income thus influences both quantity and quality of health care.

Throughout the world, even in developed countries, women's health is threatened by their gender as well as by poverty. As Carol Bellamy, executive director of the United Nations Children's Fund (UNICEF), put it, "In today's world, to be born female is to be born high risk."[19] In her report to the United Nations, Bellamy described violence against women as the world's most pervasive form of health-related human rights abuse. The following statistics are among those cited in support of her claim: 25%–50% of all women are physically abused by their partners; 130 million women and girls suffer genital mutilation, more than 1 million children, mostly girls, are forced into prostitution every year; and more than 5000 women are killed because their in-laws consider their dowries inadequate. Regardless of their illegality, some of these practices are encouraged by specific cultures; where they are illegal, sexual offenses against women are rarely pursued with rigor. In some countries, for example, a rapist can be exonerated if his victim agrees to marry him.[20] Domestic violence, which mainly targets women, occurs in all ethnic groups and nations.

Developing as well as developed nations have an affluent elite, often concentrated in urban centers, where genetic services are increasingly available but not accessible to the majority who are poor. As the affluent utilize these services, the economic gap between them and the poor widens, and poor women shoulder a disproportionate responsibility of care for those who are disabled. At the same time, poor women are more likely to experience infertility from preventable causes such as pelvic infection due to sexually transmitted diseases, unsafe abortions, and puerperal infection.[21] Although access to contraception and abortion is often limited for cultural as well as economic reasons, infertility treatment is even less available to poor women. Infertility itself is not necessarily a harm to women, but to many, whether poor or affluent, it is a considerable source of anxiety or suffering. From a utilitarian point of view it may be argued that infertility reduces the harmful impact of limited resources on the poor; for some poor families, however, having children whose labor may contribute to their livelihood is essential to survival. From an egalitarian feminist perspective, poor women as well as wealthy women have a right to infertility treatment, but neither group has an unlimited right.

As for genetic testing, its priority for poor women is understandably low, given the significance to them of other health and social needs. This does not imply that they would not desire genetic testing if it were useful and affordable within the constraints of their environment. But, according to Penchaszadeh,

> Communities where women who become pregnant face a risk of death of 1–2% and where 10% of the children who are born will die before their first birthday may not perceive a risk of 0.5% of delivering a baby with Down syndrome as something they should be concerned about. In other words, the burdens are already so formidable that there may not be room for perceiving the additional burden of having a child with a genetic defect.[22]

Women in developing countries are more likely to have children with Down syndrome not only because of the lack of availability of genetic testing and access to abortion, but also because advanced maternal age is so prevalent. Worldwide, the incidence of births to women 35 years of age or older is 11%: 9% in developed regions, 11% in less developed regions, and 14% in the least developed countries.[23]

Poor women who wish to limit their family size or avoid pregnancy because of their risk for specific genetic diseases often lack access to the means by which pregnancy can be avoided: contraception. Religious and cultural practices impede access to contraception in some circumstances. Even when this is not the case, however, contraceptive measures or procedures are not available or not affordable for many women. In the United States, for example, birth control pills are not covered by the government or by private insurance plans, and interuterine devices are generally unavailable. The required waiting period of six weeks for women who request tubal ligation but cannot pay for it themselves sometimes results in their not having the procedure at all.

The risk of some genetic disorders can be reduced by dietary practices prior to and during pregnancy. Here again, however, the costs of those practices may inhibit their availability to poor women. A phenylanaline-restricted diet, for example, is more expensive than their normal diet for women with phenylketonuria (PKU) who wish to avoid the birth of a child with maternal PKU. Folic acid supplements can greatly reduce the incidence of neural tube defects in children, but these may be unaffordable for women whose incomes are already so limited that they cannot provide adequate nutrition for children already born.

Women's own reproductive health is impacted by overdistribution as well as underdistribution of health resources. For example, a study by Veronika Kolder and her colleagues showed that poor women in the United States are more likely than other women to be subjected to coercive treatment during pregnancy.[24] For the most part, however, poor women are less likely to obtain reproductive care and much more likely to obtain their care from physicians in training than private physicians.[25] Poor women who are infertile simply cannot pay for technologies such as in vitro fertilization and gamete donation or preimplantation genetic diagnosis, which might provide the means of avoiding the gestation of an affected fetus. Even women whose income is modest but above the poverty level are more likely to be gamete donors than affluent recipients of reproductive services that are seldom covered by insurance.[26] Although prenatal diagnosis for some genetic conditions may be covered, abortions are generally not covered, particularly during the second trimester, when most prenatal diagnoses are performed.

Poverty significantly compromises the health of children, and this tends to have much greater impact on their mothers than their fathers. To cite a few examples from the United States, asthma and bacterial meningitis are twice as common, rheumatic fever twice as common, and lead poisoning three times as common in children from low-income families than in those from higher income families.[27] Not surprisingly, the severity of these and of many genetic diseases is exacerbated in low-income groups, where women predominate as single parents. In developing countries, more than 95% of the estimated 13 million annual deaths of children younger than five years of age are mainly caused by diseases for which there are effective vaccines or relatively low-cost treatment.[28] The World Health Organization estimates 90% of infants who suffer low birth weight (< 2500 grams) were subject to inadequate maternal health and nutrition.[29] Of the infants who survive, some undoubtedly require a great deal of care.

Caring for the genetically disabled, no matter what their age, mainly falls to women, seriously compromising their economic status.[30] Not surprisingly, this is especially true for minority and low-income women. In a study of the impact of caregiving on a mother's employment, Naomi Breslau and her colleagues found that care of disabled children reduces the probability of employment and increases the domestic workload of married women in low-income and black families, but the employment probability and household activities of single mothers are not significantly affected.[31] Single mothers may depend on their own employment for family income and have little flexibility for allocating additional time to the extra needs of disabled or chronically ill children.[32] However, married women or women who can rely on the economic assistance of a partner also experience the economic and social costs of giving up paid employment.[33] Nor does the burden of caregiving end with the advancing age of children, who in previous times might have succumbed to their disease before reaching adulthood. Medicine has greatly extended the lives of people with disabilities, necessitating the long-term involvement of parents in caring for their adult children who remain affected by their disabilities.

To the extent that genetic services are viewed as elective treatment of pregnant women, other adults, or children, there is little likelihood that the poor will have access to these services. Like most forms of treatment for the infertile, their proliferation will mainly enhance the options of those who can pay for them. The limited availability of genetic services is thus more likely to increase the disparities between rich and poor. To some extent this has already occurred, as fewer poor women are able or willing to undergo prenatal diagnosis for fetal abnormalities, and fewer still are able or willing to terminate pregnancies when abnormalities are identified. Accordingly, I turn to a volatile topic that is unavoidably related to considerations of just allocation of resources in genetics.

Abortion and the Poor

A sad fact about the new genetics is that despite the proliferation of genetic tests developed after specific genes are mapped and sequenced, the time gap between tests and treatment remains immense. For the great majority of genetic conditions, no cure is available. This is true for Mendelian disorders such as cystic fibrosis and sickle cell disease, for chromosomal abnormalities such as Down syndrome, for metabolic and mitochondrial disorders such as Hunter syndrome and Leber optic neuropathy, and to a great extent for multifactorial disorders such as neural tube defects, cancer, diabetes, hypertension, and cardiac disease. While research on gene therapy is progressing, it is mainly experimental in the few instances in which it has been tried.[34] This topic will be addressed in Chapter 13.

In prenatal genetic testing, an obvious consequence of the lack of curative therapy is that once a positive fetal diagnosis is obtained, the only way to avoid having a child affected with a specific genetic condition is to terminate the fetus through abortion. Women thus face a tragic choice. Although termination procedures are sometimes described and billed as "treatment," that language is misleading unless the "disease" being treated is the woman's or couple's desire to avoid the birth of an affected child. Alternatively or additionally, when the fetus has an anomaly associated with an incurable, painful impairment, the termination may be considered fetal euthanasia. Chapter 12 considers how different definitions of abortion are operable in this context. Whether or not abortion is properly defined as treatment, however, abortion is a legal option for women in the United States at least until fetal viability, and even later if maternal health is jeopardized by continuation of the pregnancy.[35] The majority of the world's population live in countries where abortion is accepted in circumstances of contraceptive failure or an unwanted pregnancy, and 40% have access at least in theory to abortion on request.[36] For poor women in the United States, a significant obstacle to exercising the right to abortion is the Hyde amendment, which in various forms allows the states to refuse to cover abortions that are not required for maternal health.[37]

When abortion costs are not covered, many women in the United States are able to raise the money to pay for the procedure themselves, but this usually exacts a high cost for them and their families. For example, in 1993, the average cost of an outpatient abortion early in pregnancy was nearly two-thirds the average maximum AFDC (Aid to Families with Dependent Children) payment for a family of three for an entire month; this was higher than a family's maximum monthly AFDC payment in eight states.[38] Because the cost of abortion later in pregnancy, when fetal abnormalities are detectable, is considerably higher (averaging $1067 at 20 weeks gestation in 1993 in a nonhospital facility), most poor women find it impossible to cover the procedure, even with help from relatives or friends.[39] By far, the great majority of abortions are performed during the first trimester for social rather than medical reasons.[40] Second-trimester abortions are undertaken not only for fetal abnormalities and maternal health, but also in extremely difficult life situations; for example, when very young girls conceal their pregnancies and when they are victims of incest.

Even for those who find the means to pay for late abortions, access is impeded by the lack of training in abortion procedures, the limited number of physicians who perform the procedure, and the limited number of clinics offering abortions, especially in rural areas. While 98% of physicians are willing to perform abortions up to 8 weeks after the last menstrual period, only 48% are willing to perform abortions at 13 weeks, and 13% at 21 weeks.[41] Abortion services are not available to 94% of women who live in nonmetropolitan areas and 51% of those who live in urban areas.[42] These obstacles to access are often insurmountable by women who are too poor to afford the required transportation, time away from work, or child care. Access is further limited by waiting periods that may be required of all women. At times this requirement extends the duration of the pregnancy to a point where the fetus is or may be viable, and abortion is no longer legally available. In either circumstance, women then continue the pregnancy and give birth to a child who may have serious health needs that must be met and paid for by them, albeit with help from the state.[43]

Their family's poverty and society's costs are thus exacerbated by their inability to obtain an abortion.

Although there are exceptions, feminists in general support the legal right to abortion.[44] So do many men and women who do not consider themselves feminists. Support of that right, however, does not imply disregard for the moral status of the fetus; rather, it implies that in cases of conflict, the woman's interests should prevail over those of the fetus. Most feminists view an unwanted pregnancy as a tragic situation precisely because there are competing moral values at stake. Some distinguish between legality and morality, arguing for the legality not only on grounds of the woman's right to decide but also because society remains divided about the moral status of the fetus.[45] Support for this argument is compatible with the view that abortion in some instances is immoral.

Legality alone does not provide access to abortion for poor women, particularly for the more expensive procedures required during the second trimester. To the extent that an egalitarian feminist standpoint entails advocacy for all women, it opposes the denial of services that the Hyde amendment allows the states to impose on women who cannot afford to pay for the procedure. In addition, it opposes the social impediments such as language barriers and transportation requirements that impede poor women from obtaining a procedure that is available to other women. While it is already true that affluent couples tend to have smaller families than poor couples, limiting the access of the latter to abortion services exacerbates that difference and thus increases the economic disparity.

Lest it be thought that an egalitarian feminist standpoint looks at only one side of the issue, advocacy for all women is just as opposed to social impediments to poor women's continuing their pregnancies. Undoubtedly, the prospect of being unable to care adequately for a genetically disabled child because of lack of social and economic supports constitutes a pressure on some women to terminate a pregnancy they would otherwise choose to continue. Access to services necessary to continue a pregnancy and care for a disabled child, or any child, is just as demanded by an egalitarian feminist standpoint as access to abortion. Indeed, until and unless both kinds of access are procured for poor as well as affluent women, the goal of justice for all women cannot be met.

Poverty, Race, and "Passive Eugenics"

In the United States as well as in other developed countries, the tie between access to health services and poverty is hardly colorless. It is not surprising, therefore, that both kinds of access appear more limited for minority women, particularly those who are Hispanic or African American. In 1990, for example, 32% of African Americans and 36% of African-American women were living in poverty, three times the poverty rate for Caucasians (11%).[46] Forty-four percent of African-American households were headed by single female parents, whose level of poverty was greater than the entire African-American population.[47] Individually, Hispanic women have a lower average income than either Caucasian or African-American women, but even in two-parent Hispanic families, the poverty rate is 26%.[48] The impact of poverty on women's health is apparently greater in both of these minority groups than in Caucasian women. Although the average life span of African-American and Hispanic women is longer than that of their male counterparts, Caucasian women live longer than either group.

Women of color in the United States are more likely to have abortions than white women, but poor women are even more likely than other women to have abortions.[49] The coincidence between poverty and color gives credence to the notion of "passive eugenics" that James Bowman uses to characterize the inferior health care that the poor receive.[50] Given the disproportionately higher number of poor who are African American and Hispanic, his strong words are relevant to race as well as class:

> Passive eugenics is the denial of appropriate medical care for more than 37 million Americans.[51]. . . Passive eugenics is the dumping of poor patients in public hospitals by so-called not-for-profit medical centers, even though some patients will suffer irreparable harm—including death. . . .Passive eugenics is the societal hypocrisy about a health care system that is inferior to that of all major industrialized countries, even though politicians and corporate czars of our health care and insurance industries equivocate in proclaiming that our health care system is the best in the world.[52]

Bowman identifies an inevitable connection between active and passive eugenics. "A society that countenances passive eugenics," he writes, "provides fertile ground for both clandestine and overt active eugenics."[53]

Admittedly, there is an apparent contradiction between poor and minority women having only limited access to abortion and the greater proportion of abortions that are attributed to them. The contradiction is not real, however, because the number of minority women who actually undergo prenatal counseling and testing is disproportionately lower than the number of majority women who obtain these services. Exacerbating the impact of the reduced availability of services for poor women is the fact that they tend to have larger families than affluent women. The greater number of abortions attributed to poor women are early terminations, unrelated to prenatal diagnosis. Whether their terminations are early or late, however, the overall result is the passive eugenic effect that Bowman identified: fewer poor children than there would otherwise be in the general population.[54] Because poverty and color are so often intertwined, passive eugenics involves racism as well as classism. The feminization of poverty adds sexism to this mix. From an egalitarian feminist standpoint, all three "isms" are targets for criticism and change. In the following cases, however, the economic disparity between social classes appears to be the main source of unjust allocation of genetic services.

Cases Involving Allocation of Genetic Services

Case 1. A Poor Couple
Maria and Reinaldo Sanchez, 27 and 30 years old, arrived in Brooklyn, New York, from Puerto Rico, with their four school-age children. Although they knew little English, both got jobs in a restaurant, earning minimum wages. Within a month, Maria discovered she was pregnant. After a routine triple screen, she was advised to see a genetic counselor and undergo chorionic villus sampling or amniocentesis. Most of her visits to the prenatal clinic were delayed by her inability to secure appointments that did not conflict with her child care and job responsibilities, and by the unavailability of a Spanish interpreter. By the time Maria was told that her fetus had Down syndrome, she was 20 weeks pregnant. The clinic did not provide second-trimester terminations, but she was given the name of a clinic in another city where she might obtain the procedure. Maria called the clinic and was told that a second-trimester abortion would cost considerably more than her family could afford.

Case 2. An Affluent Couple
Sonya and Rob Smith, both 36 years old, had two children, ages 6 and 2. Rob was a community obstetrician with a successful practice; Sonya was a full-time homemaker. Their younger child, Alex, had problems learning to walk and appeared delayed in his speech development. At a routine visit to the pediatrician with both children, Sonya expressed her concern about Alex's slow development. The pediatrician suggested consultation with a geneticist. When Sonya called the genetics center, she was asked if she would like both children to be fully evaluated. She was also asked to have her pediatrician send complete copies of both children's medical records to the clinic. During their appointment, attended by both parents, extensive family histories were taken and physical exams performed on both children. A "routine" set of genetic tests was ordered for Alex, and the result indicated that he had fragile X syndrome. His sister was tested next and found not to be a carrier for the condition. Follow-up counseling prompted Sonya to contact various relatives to alert them to the risk of fragile X syndrome in family members. The Smiths' insurance plan covered all appointments and all of the recommended testing.

More than the cases considered separately, the difference between them illustrates allocation issues raised by the new genetics: poor women will have decreased access to the benefits of genetic information, while affluent women will have greater access. If the economic situations of the two couples had been reversed, there is little doubt but that Sonya would have had prenatal diagnosis earlier than Maria had it, and would have been able to obtain an abortion even if the diagnosis had been obtained later. Maria and Reinaldo would not have been offered a test for fragile X syndrome or carrier status in their children, even if there were a family history of the condition, unless perhaps the genetics center had a research protocol which they might be solicited to join as test subjects.

Additional details might demonstrate the gap between the cases even more. For example, the Sanchez family have no car, and the clinic to which they are referred is not accessible by public transportation. Or when Maria arrives at the clinic, the physician finds her pregnancy too advanced to perform the abortion. If Maria had been Sonya, she would probably be able to travel to another state or even another country to obtain the procedure. In the United States, abortion is legal in several states during the third trimester. With regard to the fragile X test, consider the possibility that Sonya was adopted; she therefore has no family history of the disease, and neither does Rob. If, as is improbable, they nonetheless wanted to have themselves or their children tested for the condition, they could probably find someone willing to perform the test so long as they were willing and able to pay for it. Testing for cystic fibrosis and breast cancer have been offered to low-risk populations on this basis.

The options open to Maria are obviously limited by her economic situation; the lack of language facility on the part of clinicians has probably curtailed her options as well. While the case described illustrates these constraining factors, it ignores another probable constraint: anticipation that the family's already limited resources would be severely taxed by responsibility for a child with Down syndrome.[55] Ideally, the genetic counselor would have provided a positive but realistic account of children with Down syndrome and their parents, along with information on sources of assistance. In keeping with the nondirective model, however, the counselor would also convey support for a decision to terminate the pregnancy. Unfortunately, nondirectiveness does not cancel the real constraints of the situation. Maria is not as free in making this decision as she would be if she were Sonya, or if societal supports for raising a child with Down syndrome were sufficient to neutralize the decision for her. Raising a child, whether chromosomally normal or not, is never neutral; it has its rewards as well as burdens. For Maria, however, the financial burden is accentuated by the lack of resources on which to draw and the demands of raising a child with special needs.

In contrast with Maria and Reinaldo, the advantages that Sonya and Rob enjoy because of their higher socioeconomic status are manifest: access to routine health care, easy referral to a specialist, availability of complete medical records of both children, the ability of both parents to participate in the genetics appointment, sufficient time and language facility for the specialist to do a complete investigation, insurance coverage, even for expensive testing, and the ability to contact at-risk family members so that there is benefit to the extended family. Only rarely are all or even most of these options available to poor women or couples.

From an egalitarian feminist standpoint, at least some of the factors that reduce Maria's autonomy in this situation are changeable. These should be changed so that she does not feel compelled to end her pregnancy because she and Reinaldo cannot support another child, especially one with Down syndrome. By that same standpoint, Maria should neither feel nor be compelled to continue her pregnancy, and factors that might constitute pressure in that direction are wrong as well. Most probably, the sequel to the case described would show that Maria was prevented from making either decision. Rather, the fact that she could not obtain an affordable, legal abortion would itself determine the outcome: continuation of the pregnancy and giving birth in due course to an infant with Down syndrome. The sequel to this sequel would probably show an even greater economic inequality between the Sanchez and the Smith families. In other words, whether Maria continued or terminated her pregnancy, the underdistribution of resources compromised her autonomy. Affluence, probably abetted by alliances within the medical profession, allowed the Smiths to access genetic services denied to most, thereby increasing the disparity between the "haves" and "have-nots" of the U.S. health care system.

Notes

1. This view of unjust allocation was initially developed in Mary B. Mahowald, "Gender Justice and Genetics," in Yeager Hudson and W. Creighton Peden, eds., *The Social Power of Ideas* (Lewiston, NY: Edwin Mellen Press, 1995), pp. 225–52.
2. Carole J. Bland, Linda N. Meurer, and George Maldonado, "Determinants of Primary Care Specialty Choice: A Non-statistical Meta-analysis of the Literature," *Academic Medicine* 70, 7 (1995): 620.
3. E.g., Nobel laureate David Baltimore wrote that the belief that the project would not "compete with other priorities is naive." He described the HGP as a "huge, low-priority project in biology: that would undercut funding for "very high priority science." Quoted by Daniel J. Kevles in Kevles and Leroy Hood, eds., *The Code of Codes: Scientific and Social Issues in the Human Genome Project* (Cambridge: Harvard University Press, 1992), p. 25. Because of the vast amount of "junk DNA" involved in the effort, MIT biologist Robert Weinberg criticized the HGP for seeking data that would reveal little or nothing about human disease or development. Kevles, p. 24.
4. Other scientists supported government rather than private funding because they believed that the "objectivity" of science might be compromised by researchers who were hired to promote the ends of private industry.
5. Personal communication from a well-known and well-respected U.S. medical geneticist who wishes to remain anonymous.

6. The small risk of spontaneous abortion associated with amniocentesis is seldom recognized as important enough to forgo amniocentesis for maternal age.

7. I. C. Verma and B. Singh, "Ethics and Medical Genetics in India," in Dorothy C. Wertz and John C. Fletcher, eds., *Ethics and Human Genetics: A Cross-Cultural Perspective* (New York: Springer, 1989), pp. 250–70.

8. Victor B. Penchaszadeh, "Reproductive Health and Genetic Testing in the Third World," *Clinical Obstetrics and Gynecology,* 36, 3 (1993): 492.

9. As of this writing, clones from adult humans have not been reported.

10. *Statistical Abstract of the United States* 16th ed. (Washington, DC: Government Printing Office, 1996), p. 475.

11. Diana Pearce, "The Feminization of Poverty: Women, Work and Welfare," *Urban and Social Change Review* 11 (February, 1978): 28–36.

12. American women outlive their male counterparts by about seven years, and women outlive men almost everywhere else as well. Nonetheless, there are slightly fewer women than men in the world, 98.6 women for every 100 men, for reasons that will be discussed in Chapter 6. Janice Mitchell Phillips, Mary Sexton, and Janine A. Blackman, "Demographic Overview of Women across the Lifespan," in Karen Moses Allen and Janice Mitchell Phillips, eds., *Women's Health across the Lifespan* (Philadelphia: Lippincott-Raven, 1997), p. 16, and *The World's Women 1995 Trends and Statistics* (New York: United Nations, 1995), p. 1.

13. Sara S. McLanahan, Annemette Sorensen, and Dorothy Watson, "Sex Differences in Poverty, 1950–1980," *Signs: Journal of Women in Culture and Society* 15, 11 (1989): 102.

14. Ruth Sidel, *Women and Children Last* (New York: Penguin Books, 1986), p. 158, and Stephen Post, "Women and Elderly Parents: Moral Controversy in an Aging Society," in *Hypatia* 5, 1 (1990): 84, both discuss poverty among older women.

15. Irwin Garfinkle and Sara McLanahan, *Single Mothers and Their Children* (Washington, DC: Urban Institute Press, 1986), p. 11.

16. An increasing number of clinics provide genetic testing for cystic fibrosis and breast cancer for those who can pay for the test, regardless of whether the individual has a family history of the disease. E.g., OncorMed, Inc., and Myriad Genetics, Inc., are currently marketing their testing services for breast cancer susceptibility testing. David S. Hilzenrath, "Md Firm's Gene Test to Intensify Bioethics Debate," *Washington Post,* July 25, 1996, pp. D14, D16; "BRCA1: Genetic Susceptibility for Breast and Ovarian Cancer: A Reference for Healthcare Professionals," Myriad Laboratories, Inc., January 1996.

17. Sidel, p. 36.

18. Sidel, p. 137.

19. "'To Be Born Female Is to Be Born High Risk,' UNICEF Director Reports," *Chicago Tribune,* July 23, 1997, p. 12.

20. See "'To Be Born Female.'" On the global incidence and distribution of violence toward women, see Lori L. Heise, "Gender-Based Abuse: The Global Epidemic," in Alice J. Dan, ed., *Reframing Women's Health* (London: SAGE Publications, 1994), pp. 233–50.

21. Penchaszadeh, p. 490.

22. Penchaszadeh, p. 493.

23. These data were obtained electronically through the Population Information Network (gopher://gopher.undp.org:70/00/ungophers/popin/wdtrends/agespec) of the United Nations Population Division, Department of Economic and Social Information

and Policy Analysis of the United Nations Secretariat, World Population Prospects: The 1994 Revision. Cf. Victor B. Penchaszadeh, "Implementing Genetic Services in Developing Countries," in A. M. Kuliev, K. Greendale, V. B. Penchaszadeh, and N. Paul, eds., *Provision of Genetic Services: An International Perspective* (New York: Birth Defects Foundation, 1992), pp. 17–26.

24. Veronika Kolder, Janet Gallagher, and Michael Parsons, "Court-Ordered Obstetrical Interventions," *New England Journal of Medicine* 316, 19 (1987): 1192–96.

25. This is true of poor people in general, and for all areas of health care.

26. Women who rank below the official poverty line are less likely than lower middle class women to be surrogates or egg donors. In either case, however, the women tend to be poorer than the infertile couples who pay them. See Alta Charo, "Legislative Approaches to Surrogate Motherhood," in Larry Gostin, ed., *Surrogate Motherhood* (Bloomington: Indiana University Press, 1990), p. 89.

27. Barbara Starfield, "Child Health Care and Social Factors: Poverty, Class, Race," *Bulletin of the New York Academy of Medicine,* 5, 3 (1989): 300.

28. Penchaszadeh, "Reproductive Health," pp. 490–91.

29. *Reproductive Health: A Key to a Brighter Future* (Geneva: World Health Organization, 1992).

30. For a critique of women's role as predominant caregiver of the elderly, see Post, pp. 83–89.

31. Naomi Breslau, D. Salkever, and K. Staruch, "Women's Labor Force Activity and Responsibilities for Disabled Dependents: A Study of a Family with Disabled Children," *Journal of Health and Social Behavior* 23 (1982): 169.

32. Naomi Breslau, "Care of Disabled Children and Women's Time Use," *Medical Care* 216 (1983): 620–29.

33. Dorothy C. Wertz and John C. Fletcher, "Feminist Criticism of Prenatal Diagnosis: A Response," *Clinical Obstetrics and Gynecology* 36 (1993): 541–67.

34. For an account of the first gene therapy treatment for adenosine deaminase deficiency (ADA), see LeRoy Walters and Julie Gage Palmer, *The Ethics of Gene Therapy* (New York: Oxford University Press, 1997), pp. 17–22.

35. *Roe v. Wade,* 410 U.S. 113 (1973). For the legal status of abortion in other countries, see Rebecca J. Cook, "Abortion Laws and Policies: Challenges and Opportunities," *International Journal of Gynecology and Obstetrics,* Supp. 3 (1989).

36. In many instances, "abortion on request" is not available in pregnancy.

37. *Patricia R. Harris v. Cora McRae et al.,* No. 79-1268, in "Opinions Announced June 30, 1980," *United States Law Week* 48, 50.

38. Congressional Research Service, *Medicaid Source Book: Background Data and Analysis* (A 1993 Update), January 1993, p. 174.

39. Stanley K. Henshaw, "Factors Hindering Access to Abortion Services," *Family Planning Perspectives* 27, 2 (1995): 54. Charges are much higher when the procedure is performed in a hospital, even for first-trimester terminations. Henshaw reports an average hospital charge of $1757 for a first-trimester outpatient abortion in 1991 (p. 58).

40. According to the Alan Guttmacher Institute (AGI), 91% of abortions are performed for social reasons during the first trimester. *Facts in Brief: Abortion in the U.S.* (New York: AGI, 1993).

41. Henshaw, p. 54.

42. Stanley K. Henshaw and Jennifer Van Vort, "Abortion Services in the United States, 1991 and 1992," *Family Planning Perspectives* 26 (1994): 103.

43. A 1980 study reported that 20%–25% of pregnant women who could not obtain

funding for abortions continued their pregnancies to term. J. T. Trussell, J. Menken, B. L. Lindheim, and B. Vaughan, "The Impact of Restricting Medicaid Financing for Abortion," *Family Planning Perspectives* 12, 3 (1980). Jeopardizing their own health, a small number of those who cannot obtain funding attempt illegal or self-induced abortions. A. Torres, P. Donovan, N. Dittes, and J. D. Forrest, "Public Benefits and Costs of Government Funding for Abortion," *Family Planning Perspectives* 18, 3 (1986): 111–8.

44. Feminists for Life, for example, opposes the right to abortion on grounds that it implies that women alone are responsible for raising children.

45. E.g., Alison Jaggar, "Regendering the U.S. Abortion Debate," *Journal of Social Philosophy* 28, 1 (1997): 127–40.

46. Marilyn H. Gaston and Kelly Garry, "African American and Caribbean Women," in Allen and Phillips, p. 350.

47. Gaston and Garry, p. 350.

48. Aida L. Giachello, "Latino/Hispanic Women," in Allen and Phillips, pp. 385–86.

49. S. K. Henshaw, "Research Note: Abortion Trends in 1987 and 1988—Age and Race," *Family Planning Perspectives* 24, 2 (1992), and Alan Guttmacher Institute, *Facts in Brief.*

50. James E. Bowman, "The Road to Eugenics," *University of Chicago Law School Roundtable* 3, 2 (1996): 493. The term "passive eugenics" should not be confused with positive or negative eugenics. The latter distinction is commonly used to describe intentional efforts to limit a population to people with desired traits. As used by Bowman, "passive eugenics" unintentionally results in a more limited number of people in a specific population group.

51. Currently, the figure is 43.4 million. Robert Pear, "Americans Lacking Health Insurance Put at 16 Percent," *New York Times,* September 26, 1998, citing a report of the U.S. Census Bureau.

52. Bowman, p. 493.

53. Bowman, p. 493.

54. Following Bowman's rationale, the consequences of elective terminations by minority women may also be described as "passive eugenics."

55. Additional constraining factors may include Maria's husband and her religious or cultural tradition. These factors might influence not only whether she was open to prenatal testing or abortion, but also whether physical or cognitive disability is perceived as the greater burden.

6

ETHNICITY, CULTURAL DIFFERENCES, AND SEX SELECTION

GENETICS and eugenics are linked in the context of ethnic differences. These same ethnic differences may exacerbate or reduce gender inequities that would otherwise occur in the clinical practice of genetics. For example, some ethnic groups are accepting and supportive of those with specific genetic conditions; others are not. Positive cultural attitudes and practices toward those with genetic anomalies reduce the burden not only for affected individuals of both sexes, but also for their caregivers, most of whom are women. Some ethnic groups place greater value on mental ability than on physical ability or appearance; others value one or the other more. These evaluations by others contribute significantly to the self-evaluations of affected individuals. The decisions of women considering prenatal diagnosis, and their assessment of themselves as mothers and caregivers of those affected by specific genetic conditions, are similarly affected, either affirmatively or negatively, by the values and disvalues of their ethnic group or cultural milieu. A key question thus arises for clinicians who wish to respect the autonomy of women: Are decisions that reflect the same priorities as their culture or ethnic group truly autonomous? Sex selection is one of the topics that deserves scrutiny in this regard.

In this chapter I examine the relation between ethnicity, culture, and gender and offer examples of culturally defined gender differences and challenges to genetic counseling. I then address the dilemma of respect for autonomy versus respect for cultural values, which is often relevant to decisions about genetic information. Finally, I consider sex selection as a practice that raises issues of gender justice in different cultural contexts.

Ethnicity and Culture as Related Variables

Although ethnic differences and cultural differences are not often treated as distinct, in fact they refer to two different domains, the biological and the social. Ethnic differences are based on common genetic inheritance, whereas cultural differences derive from the social practices that a particular group or community develops in response to those differences as well as other factors that arise in their experience of the world and of other communities.[1] Ethnicity and culture not only overlap but influence each other, because biology affects social practices and social practices affect biological development or expression. Ethnicity is relevant to genetics because it facilitates the predictive capacity of genetic testing. Culture is relevant to genetics because it describes the value systems in which decisions about genetic information are made and interpreted. Both ethnicity and culture affect all of us. Moreover, if we were to reach far enough back into our ancestry and history, most if not all of us would see ourselves as multiethnic and multicultural. In other words, it is doubtful that most individuals are representative solely of one ethnicity or one culture.

Race and ethnicity are more closely related than culture and ethnicity because race also involves genetic inheritance.[2] "Race" has a broader meaning than "ethnicity" when it is used to refer to the entirety of a species, as in "the human race," or to major divisions within a species.[3] In humankind, racial divisions are often identified by skin color and associated with other phenotypic characteristics as well. Thus the major races may be designated as white, brown, red, and yellow. In many instances, however, racial and ethnic designations are the same, and the prejudices associated with them are the same. In this chapter we discuss ethnic differences rather than racial differences because ethnicity is genetically more informative than race.

Factors that mingle with ethnicity in influencing culture include geographical areas, religious beliefs, socioeconomic status, spoken language, and sexual orientation.[4] The cultural expressions of these diverse influences coalesce in shared patterns of thinking and behaving. Lest it be thought that the different patterns apply to others rather than ourselves, it should be remembered that a pluralistic society such as that of the United States is a culture in its own right. It is a culture comprised of many cultures that are dominant in other geographical regions. Support for this diversity is maintained through an emphasis on tolerance, individuality, and autonomy within the dominant culture. In other words, the dominant culture in the United States is one that embraces the various modes of cultural expression that its people embody as individuals.

For many other cultures, even for some of those represented in the United States as subcultures or nondominant groups, the interests of the community supersede those of the individual. In addition to conflicts that emerge from these different emphases, some cultures have other values and practices that conflict with one another and with the larger society. Logically as well as practically, it is impossible to respect all of these cultural differences.

Beyond the different cultures defined by factors already mentioned, consider the culture of modern Western medicine, which overlaps with, or forms a subset of, the various cultures of the Western world. According to Nancy Fisher, the culture (or subculture) of Western medicine arises

> from a set of shared beliefs about the nature of reality and disease. These include a belief in science and the beneficial results of technology: a belief that the mysteries of nature are ultimately knowable; a belief that the body, like a machine, can be taken apart and "fixed" when it is not working properly. . . .As a culture, Western medicine has its own "language," standards of care, and body of knowledge.[5]

Human genetics may be seen as a subculture of Western medicine; as such, it involves its own specific language of karyotyping, DNA fingerprinting, Southern blot analysis, and the like. But human genetics goes beyond the traditional medical focus on the diagnosis and treatment of individuals to include research and information about human families.[6] Genetic counseling may be seen as yet another subculture, a subculture of human genetics whose practices are additionally influenced by the overlapping "subcultures" of race, class, and gender, which pervade most if not all of the world's cultural domains. The subculture of genetic counselors contrasts with the subculture of physicians in gender, class, and ethic. In the United States, the majority of counselors are women whose socioeconomic status is lower than that of physicians, who are mostly men. And genetic counselors place greater emphasis than physicians on client autonomy.

To the extent that these cultures and subcultures overlap and their members represent conflicting values or practices, the (sub)culture of genetic counseling confronts a huge practical challenge to the respect for cultural differences that is usually associated with the tenet of nondirectiveness. This challenge arises because of a more fundamental theoretical challenge that must also be met: the challenge of cultural relativism.

Philosophers usually view cultural relativism as antithetical to the discipline of ethics as moral philosophy. Support for, or refutation of, this view depends on how the two terms are defined.[7] If ethics involves a description of the values and practices of different cultures, and if cultural relativism simply refers to the fact that different cultures have different values and practices, then the two are not only compatible, but they may even be the same. If ethics is only descriptive, it is no longer moral philosophy; it is social science. If ethics is normative, however, it can still be moral philosophy, while compatible with cultural relativism, so long as cultural relativism involves no normative claims about its descriptive data. Cultural relativism is then limited to the domain of social science as an empirical, descriptive discipline.

If cultural relativism defines moral behavior as coincident with cultural expectations, it purports to be both normative and descriptive, displacing ethics as a separate discipline. However, it is impossible to defend a normative stance on the part of the cultural relativist without contradiction. Whatever the formulation, the cultural relativist's norm would necessarily entail the claim that any value or practice found in a particular culture is ethically justified solely on the basis of its being found there. Such a claim of universalizability is incompatible with the basic assumption of relativism, that is, a denial of universal norms.

Postulating cultural relativism as ethically normative is problematic on other grounds also. First, it apparently assumes that a single culture defines each individual's behavior; this is clearly not the case for most people and probably not for anyone. Moreover, individuals themselves diverge from cultural standards, sometimes by choice and sometimes because of other influences on their lives. Second, cultural relativism allows no critique of the culture's values or practices either from within or from without, thereby sanctioning potential atrocities, as history unfortunately attests. And third, attribution of normative status to particular practices solely on the basis of cultural expectations illustrates the naturalistic fallacy, confusing an "is" with an "ought." As G. E. Moore observed, the mere fact that something is desired does not make it desirable.[8] From a feminist standpoint as well, a normative version of cultural relativism must be rejected because justice, including gender justice, is a norm to be applied to all societies. Clearly, some cultural practices are not acceptable by that standard.

Compared with other nations, the United States provides a particularly rich range of cultural diversity. Most of these cultures embody distinctive subcultures as well. So, for example, the subculture of African Americans from the south may be quite different from that of more recent immigrants from Africa, and the subculture of Mexican Americans may be quite different from that of Puerto Ricans. Variables such as language, class, age, and duration of residence in the United States undoubtedly influence the impact of culture on individuals and groups. As we shall see, this impact is often evident in matters of gender and genetics.

Culturally-Defined Gender Differences and Challenges

Because the majority of North Americans are of European ancestry, Americans of European descent tend to emulate the values that brought them or their forebears to America. These values manifestly differ according to each of the ethnic groups that Europeans represent. Nonetheless, Spencer identifies a number of values that Europeans brought to the United States; these include productivity, initiative, individualism, and equality.[9] Whether equality should be listed is questionable if the concept is applied to race, gender, and sexual orientation. Like individuals from other cultures, European Americans often uphold a stereotypic, patriarchal version of the family structure in which women raise children and do household tasks, while men work outside the home and head the family.[10] In the European-American model, families are often small, with parents heavily invested in their children's physical and intellectual welfare. As divorce and remarriage rates escalate, blended families have been added to the traditional model. Single-parent households, usually headed by women, and families where both parents work outside the home are increasingly common.[11] Although gender inequality is reduced when both parents earn wages, women still do most of the child care and housework.

According to Spencer, European Americans tend to be acquisitive, direct, mobile, and dependent on technology.[12] Some of these traits are relevant to women's involvement with genetic services. For example, high regard for genetic technology, coupled with heavy investment in a few offspring, may provoke in women a sense of obligation to undergo prenatal genetic testing and interventions. The mobility of the culture has led to lack of availability of extended family members to assist women in caring for those who are genetically disabled. Envisioning themselves as sole caregivers may motivate women to reduce the potential burden by prenatal testing and termination of affected fetuses. From the standpoint of genetic counselors, who usually share the same cultural heritage as their European-American clients, high regard for technology and investment in healthy children makes women more amenable to their services, but the mobility of families and lack of extended genetic families complicate their efforts to obtain adequate family histories.

African Americans tend to be less enamored of technology and more distrustful of medicine than European and Asian Americans. They are also more accepting and supportive of family members with disabilities. Adoption is rare because families, defined more broadly than the nuclear model of a married couple and their children, take care of "their own." However, a lack of enthusiasm for adoption has also led to greater availability of African-American children for adoption by other ethnic groups.[13] Distrust of medical technology in the African-American community is undoubtedly triggered by the history of slavery and racist practices that continue in our day. With regard to genetics, the history of testing for sickle cell anemia is particularly notable in this regard.[14] The lack of interest in prenatal genetic testing and technology that distrust generates is abetted by a belief on the part of many African Americans that "the natural function of childbearing requires no medical intervention until the delivery stage."[15]

Extended family and informal networks are more likely to be employed as sources of medical information, and religious personnel are more likely to be consulted for advice on important life decisions. Because family roles tend to be flexible, decision making may rest with either the male or female head of household. According to Joseph Telfair and Kermit Nash, however, "maternal wisdom" is a particularly valued commodity, and individuals "coming in for genetic services may have first consulted the 'mother-adviser' on the block."[16] Elderly members of the community are held in high regard, with grandmothers often acting as decision makers about medical treatment.

While most genetic counselors are as nondominant by gender as most of their clients, they are usually dominant by class and race in comparison with their minority clients.[17] To overcome the nearsightedness of their dominance, an egalitarian standpoint suggests that white genetic counselors impute a privileged status to the views of their minority clients. The practice of nondirectiveness is a means by which that status is acknowledged, but further education is also needed if counselors and clinicians are to be receptive to what may be learned from marginalized cultures. For example, African Americans are likely to identify prolonged eye contact with staring; they prefer to look away while listening, and move closer while talking. Anticipating these types of behaviors may facilitate practitioners' listening and learning from clients. Telfair and Nash suggest that, as an antidote to fears about eugenics, counselors may point out positive aspects of genetic traits, for example, the protection from malaria that sickle cell trait confers.[18]

Latino Americans are the fastest growing minority in the United States.[19] A common denominator among Latinos from different countries is that family structures are patriarchal, with men occupying an even more dominant role than in European-American culture. Like other minority ethnic groups, Latino culture places great value on families, and the sense of family extends even beyond grandparents, aunts, uncles, and cousins to godparents who may not be genetically related to the children. According to Elena Lopez-Rangel, the participation of immediate and extended family members in decision making "emphasizes interdependence over independence, affiliation over individualism, and cooperation over confrontation."[20] She also describes a tendency to express emotions when faced with a crisis or illness. For Latinos, acting "cool" or calm in such situations is inappropriate. While eye contact with authority figures such as physicians may be a sign of disrespect, physical contacts such as handshakes are expected, and a pat on the back or clasp of arm is often appropriate.[21]

In some Latino communities, superstitions regarding the cause of disease or disability (e.g., astronomical or supernatural events) lead to distrust or disbelief in genetic etiology. Although the predominance of Catholicism among Latinos has diminished in recent years, opposition to abortion remains prevalent, and many would be offended by the mere suggestion that it be considered.[22] If abortion is not an option, prenatal diagnosis may be judged unnecessary or unhelpful. In some communities, physical disabilities are much more onerous than cognitive disabilities because physical rather than intellectual work sustains the group. For all who are born, however, female relatives are virtually their only caregivers if they are in need. If mothers die or become too ill to care, grandmothers, aunts, or sisters take over caregiving responsibilities. Men are apparently so absent from the caregiving role that, according to one study, 35% of Latino fathers of children with disabilities deny that their children actually have a disability.[23]

While traditional Chinese Americans value the family more than the individual, they share with European Americans a high regard for technology, including genetic technology. Because they also tend to impute an organic cause to any medical problem, they view medical experts and technology as their main authoritative source in addressing or avoiding these problems. In fact, their faith in medical technology is so strong that, coupled with their desire to have a few maximally healthy children, hereditary factors are often considered in selection of a spouse. According to Jack Jung, there is also a tendency to attribute familial problems to genetic origins, without considering other possible causes.[24]

High regard for authority figures makes many Chinese Americans more comfortable with a directive rather than nondirective approach to genetic counseling. The directiveness expected from clinicians has its counterpart in the directedness expected from husbands, to whom women are expected to be subservient. Women not only have high expectations for their children, but are likely to be blamed for any pregnancy outcome that is less than ideal.[25] Genetic abnormalities in particular are likely to be viewed as catastrophic, and blamed on women regardless of their origin. Beyond the moral unacceptability of this practice, it betrays a selective regard for scientific knowledge.

In traditional Chinese families, age in general deserves respect, but the greatest respect is tendered to the eldest male. Formality is expected in clinician–patient interactions, and physical contact is not accepted or appreciated. The centrality of the family in defining one's identity is illustrated by the practice of uttering or writing surnames before one's given name. Genetic counseling may be facilitated by extensive family histories, but impeded by different English transliterations of the same name (for example, "Wong" and "Huang" are different dialectical pronunciations of the same family name).[26]

Judaism illustrates the distinction between ethnicity and culture, along with the significance of that distinction for genetics.[27] It also illustrates a point relevant to the preceding discussion, that is, religion plays a central role in diverse cultures and ethnic groups. While Judaism is primarily a religion, the "Judaism" of secular Jews is ethnic and cultural without being religious; others, such as converts, may be Jewish in their religious beliefs and cultural practices without being ethnic Jews. For calculating and counseling clients about genetic risk, ethnicity is more significant than religion. For example, regardless of their level of religious observance, Ashkenazi Jews are more at risk for Tay-Sachs disease than Sephardic Jews.

Although Jewishness is matrilineally defined, men usually make decisions in traditional Jewish families and work outside the home, while women attend to children and household. For important life decisions, the advice of a rabbi is often sought and followed. In general, reproductive technologies are acceptable for infertile couples because of the strong emphasis on procreation as the natural end of marriage. If gamete donation is recommended because both parents are carriers for an autosomal recessive disorder, sperm donation may be preferable to egg donation to avoid the risk of being non-Jewish by having a non-Jewish genetic mother. If donor insemination is performed, there is no need to determine whether the donor is Jewish.[28]

Multiple forms of Judaism have their counterpart in multiple forms of other religions and cultures, raising an important challenge for clinicians who want to respect the particular values and beliefs of individual patients. As already suggested, generalizations about any particular ethnic group are informative as a caution about differences to be respected, but they are woefully inadequate and simplistic when it comes to respecting the diversities within large ethnic groups. Even if a particular group were entirely homogeneous in its values and practices, individuals within that group would diverge in their interpretations of those values, and some might have values at odds with those of the group. The challenge, then, is to determine the extent to which an individual adheres to her culture's values in a particular instance. In facing that challenge, an egalitarian feminist standpoint requires recognition of cultural pressures as well as values. Genetic counselors who wish to champion the client's autonomy must recognize that autonomous decisions do not necessarily involve conformity to one's cultural or religious heritage.

Respect for Autonomy versus Respect for Cultural Differences

Respect for autonomy is a cardinal principle of contemporary medical ethics. It is usually linked with the principles of beneficence, nonmaleficence, and justice as basic to ethical decision making in the clinical setting.[29] However, while it is generally assumed that people are or can be autonomous, just what autonomy means and whether people really are autonomous are matters of controversy. In health care, it is often assumed as well that the obligation to respect autonomy is equivalent to the obligation to obtain informed consent from patients for testing or treatment. The latter assumption seems to ignore the fact that health care decisions involve others besides patients. In the health care setting, decisions also involve health caregivers and family members and may involve patients who are not autonomous. If respect for autonomy is a moral principle, it requires respect for the autonomy of all individuals; additional principles are applicable to nonautonomous individuals.

The notion of *respect* is also subject to different interpretations. To some it simply means "paying attention to" or " taking account of." To others, respect means something more demanding, such as "giving priority to" or "acting in accordance with." The latter meaning would make respect for autonomy not only a cardinal principle but the supreme principle of bioethics. A less demanding interpretation allows that respect for autonomy is one among other principles of bioethics, all of which represent prima facie rather than supreme or absolute obligations. When respect for cultural differences is considered, the same interpretations of the term are applicable. If respect is to be tendered to both autonomy and cultural differences, however, only the less demanding interpretation is possible. If the more demanding interpretation is operable, respect for cultural differences is incompatible with respect for individual autonomy.

Although the foregoing discussion has assumed that respect for autonomy and respect for cultural differences are distinct expressions of respect, it is possible to view the two as identical. Respect for autonomy is equivalent to, or overlaps with, respect for cultural differences for individuals who autonomously conform to the value systems which their cultures embody. Unless we subscribe to cultural determinism, however, we need to confront the fact that individuals can and occasionally do freely diverge from cultural dictates or expectations. The history of the women's movement in the United States and elsewhere is replete with examples of women doing just that. Fortunately, culturally sanctioned atrocities have always been challenged by individuals who act in accordance with conscience in opposition to cultural expectations or norms.

Assuming, then, that cultural values and practices are at least occasionally in conflict with the values and practices which individuals choose for themselves, we still need to ask what it means for them to make autonomous choices. The meaning of autonomy, as already suggested, is notoriously controversial and complex.[30] Minimally, it refers to the individual's *capacity to choose,* which entails cognitive and volitional abilities that are not equally present or always present in all individuals. Maximally, autonomy also requires the *ability to implement* one's choices, which is often equated with freedom or liberty.[31] In other words, both internal and external resources are necessary to fulfill one's chosen goals.[32] To some extent, albeit paradoxically, the maximal meaning of autonomy involves dependence on those who provide or constitute such resources.

An egalitarian feminist standpoint subscribes to a prima facie rather than absolute obligation to respect autonomy, acknowledging the importance of beneficence and nonmaleficence as additional prima facie obligations. Justice is the principle that mediates conflicts that arise in applications of the other principles. With regard to gender, as also with regard to race, class, sexual orientation, and ability, justice demands more than a minimal but less than a maximal conception of autonomy. In the fulfillment of obligations arising from beneficence and nonmaleficence, justice requires a distribution scheme that respects different needs and abilities, regardless of whether the recipients are autonomous.

Limitations to autonomy arise not only from differences in cognitive and volitional ability but also from different physical, educational, and economic abilities in potential decision makers, and in the information provided to them with regard to possible choices. While supporting the principle of respect for autonomy, gender justice goes further than a minimal conception of autonomy because it requires attention to the limitations on autonomy that may be imposed on women both internally and externally.[33] The goal of gender justice is to reduce these limitations as much as possible, recognizing that discrepancies between the advantaged and the disadvantaged will remain. In most instances the gap between men and women or between other dominant and nondominant groups can be reduced only by reducing the advantages of the dominant over the nondominant. In other words, men's advantages are inevitably lessened to the extent that women's are increased. This goal involves equality of respect for autonomy[34] as well as equality in the distribution of burdens and benefits. Conflicts between or among the principles of respect for autonomy, beneficence, and nonmaleficence are thus mediated through the principle of justice.

Respect for cultural differences may be construed as respect for the autonomy of different cultures, but that construal does not settle the question of whether the autonomy of an individual can or should be respected when it is at odds with the culture's "autonomy." At that point, it may be argued that the good defined by the culture is greater than the good defined by the individual whose decision is in conflict with a particular cultural value or practice. While this argument is supportable on quantitative grounds, it is hardly defensible on moral grounds. Unless we subscribe to a crude (and cruel) form of utilitarianism, few of us would support the notion that might makes right, even if might is defined by numbers alone.[35] The view that "cultural autonomy" supersedes individual autonomy is also defensible on grounds that the stability of a group is thereby maintained. Again, however, stability is not a good in its own right. Destabilization of a culture whose values or practices are morally questionable is in fact more desirable than maintaining its stability by overriding the autonomy of dissident members.

That said, the stability of a culture whose values and practices are generally moral and supportive of the majority of its members is probably a greater good than respect for the autonomy of an individual member of that culture. An egalitarian feminist standpoint concurs that the good of the majority may at times supersede the good of the few. Moreover, where contrary indications are absent, respect for individual autonomy is more likely than not to accord with respect for the culture to which the individual belongs. In situations where it is difficult if not impossible to determine the extent to which a given individual autonomously embraces the values embodied by her culture, respect for cultural differences should ordinarily prevail. However, a significant caveat to this prevalence arises from the fact that most if not all individuals belong to several overlapping, sometimes conflicting cultures. Women themselves comprise a cultural group within and beyond the ethnic cultures to which they also belong. It follows that respect for the cultural differences that women as a group embody is part of what it means to respect their cultural differences. So, while an egalitarian feminist standpoint resists absolutizing the autonomy of individual women, it insists on the necessity of respect for the specific cultural milieu of women as women. That milieu is in fact broader than the ethnic cultures in which women find themselves, where values and practices have mainly been defined by men.

Specific cultural practices that are detrimental to women are surely questioned by most of the world's women and by many men. Consider, for example, female circumcision and suttee, the practice by which widows throw themselves on the funeral pyres of their husbands.[36] Given the pressures of socialization and fears of censure or exclusion, it is doubtful that women from cultures that encourage or demand these practices participate in them with genuine or full autonomy, even when they purport to do so. Only a very thin notion of autonomy, one which identifies it with whatever someone says or does that is not physically coerced, or with "choices" between extremely constraining options, would support the view that genital mutilation or suicide is a genuinely autonomous decision.

A different culturally sanctioned practice involving gender is particularly relevant to genetics: sex selection. This may occur either before or after fertilization. As we will see in the next section, different cultures offer very different rationales in support of this practice.

Sex Selection from an Egalitarian Feminist Standpoint

When embryos are tested for specific genetic or chromosomal anomalies, the test usually reveals the sex of the organism, regardless of whether such information is sought for medical reasons. Even when the information is not medically relevant, however, whether sex selection is sexist depends on the meaning of sexism and the rationale for the selection. Whether it is ethically justified depends also on the means by which it is undertaken. Sexism may refer to a preference for one sex, usually male, when there is no morally adequate reason for the preference. In particular cases, the preference may be morally justified if it is based on overriding moral reasons, such as avoidance of serious harm to another or others. In other cases, the preference may be based on morally neutral criteria, such as the desire to have children of both sexes. Typically, however, sexism refers to a preference for one sex that is based on morally inadequate reasons. The inadequate reasons generally involve a gender bias.

According to the *Oxford English Dictionary*, sexism is "the assumption that one sex is superior to the other and the resultant discrimination practiced against members of the supposed inferior sex, especially by men against women."[37] By this definition, sexism is wrong because it denies the essential equality between men and women. If sex selection has no impact on sex inequality, it is not sexist and it may be morally neutral; if it reduces inequality, it is morally commendable. From an egalitarian feminist standpoint, selection of males is more problematic than selection of females because it reaffirms or reinforces male dominance. But selection of females is not necessarily commendable or even morally neutral; other factors may make it morally questionable or wrong.[38]

Sexism has been supported by many if not most cultures throughout history, just as racism, classism, heterosexism, and ableism have been supported.[39] In other words, women have prevalently been viewed as inferior to men and treated as such.[40] Moreover, the cultural prevalence of sexism has coexisted in many instances with an underlying consciousness in members of both sexes that women are and should be treated as equal to men. People have thus been aware that sexism is wrong, even while practicing it.

The rationale for sex selection is not sexist, although it may be ableist, if it is based solely on medical indications, such as the 50% risk that a male fetus will have hemophilia if a pregnant woman is a carrier for the condition.[41] It is sexist if the intent is to avoid the conception or birth of a child judged inferior because of sex. For either rationale, however, the means by which sex selection is undertaken raises further moral questions and controversy, depending on whether it occurs before or after conception. Except for its association with sexism, sex selection prior to conception is relatively uncontroversial. Following conception, it may be morally objectionable or acceptable solely on grounds of one's position on abortion. Except for its tie with abortion, however, sex selection is not really a morally different issue after conception than it is before conception. Cultural opposition to abortion is compatible with cultural encouragement of preconception sex selection, and cultural permissiveness of abortion is apparently compatible with opposition to sex selection, whether prenatal or postnatal.

Lest it be thought that a preference for males is limited to developing countries, data from the United States show that 84% of couples who request sex preselection want boys.[42] A recent survey of Canadians shows a much weaker preference for sons.[43] Nonetheless, studies of sex preference for children throughout the world illustrate a stronger bias in favor of male offspring. Until recently, the various methods available, such as timing of intercourse, ovulation induction medications, and artificial insemination, were generally unsuccessful.[44] A better success rate has been reported from in vitro separation of X-bearing sperm and Y-bearing sperm by gradient techniques, but these methods have not been validated by molecular techniques or controlled clinical trials. Two new techniques have proved much more reliable: preimplantation genetic diagnosis and sperm separation by flow cytometry. The latter method is less expensive and less invasive than the former because it involves artificial insemination rather than in vitro fertilization. According to Benjamin Reubinoff and Joseph Schenker, through the increased availability of sperm separation by flow cytometry, preconception sex selection "for social purposes" is likely to be sought, offered, and utilized more widely.[45]

Subsequent to implantation, the sex of the embryo is determinable through chorionic villus sampling, amniocentesis, or ultrasound. Fetuses of the undesired sex, usually female, may then be terminated. In developing countries, the practice is often explicit, with ultrasound increasingly used for sex determination.[46] In developed nations, clients sometimes manipulate a system that is mainly opposed to prenatal testing for sex selection by requesting prenatal diagnosis for another reason, such as maternal age. When clients are informed of their test results, they are also told the sex of the fetus if they wish to know. If the fetus is not the desired sex, they then ask for termination of the pregnancy, to which they have a legal right. Because most genetic counselors oppose prenatal testing for sex selection, they tend to feel manipulated by this modus operandi. Nonetheless, the number of those who support the client's right to sex selection has apparently been increasing.[47]

Christine Overall argues that "sexual similarity" or "sexual complementarity" are morally acceptable reasons for wanting a child of a certain sex. She bases her argument on the significance of sexuality, both heterosexuality and homosexuality, to interpersonal relationships. Sexual similarity, she says, "is a likeness, an affinity, of experience and capacities—the groundedness of being with one's own kind. The notion of sexual complementarity, on the other hand, . . . is not merely a matter of dissimilarity, . . . [but also] the desire for the new, for what will change and enlarge one's own experience."[48] In arguing for the moral legitimacy of sex preselection on this basis, Overall exhibits a sensitivity to the uniqueness of human relationships with which most feminists would agree. Neither for her nor for other feminists, however, does this imply support for sex selection policies.

Although Overall generally favors involvement of men in various aspects of child care, she stops short of advocating the same degree of involvement by heterosexual partners in the sex selection of their children.[49] Through its emphasis on attention to relevant differences, an egalitarian feminism would not only stop short but would insist that one partner, the woman, has a stronger claim in this regard. Since it is the woman who carries the main burden of bringing a child into the world, and usually also the main burden of child rearing, the woman's preference regarding the sex of her offspring is more compelling (but not necessarily adequate) when compared with such a preference on the part of her male partner. This reasoning would also apply to a lesbian couple in whom one partner has a different preference regarding the sex of a future child than the other: if both women plan to share child rearing, the woman who would undergo insemination, gestation, and birth has the stronger claim regarding the sex of the child.

If the practice of sex selection led to numerical predominance of one sex over another, such a result would not necessarily be inegalitarian. It is at least possible for relationships between members of a numerical minority and majority to be fair and equal. It is also possible for a minority group to be politically stronger and to form an economic majority despite its numerical minority. So even if sex selection led to a majority of males in the population, as it has in parts of China, India, and Korea,[50] it does not necessarily follow that subjugation of women to men would thereby be supported or intensified. Nonetheless, the threat of increased sexism remains a matter of concern to those interested in promoting gender justice.

Ironically, another argument arises from the egalitarian feminist claims that women have historically been oppressed and such oppression is morally wrong. Both claims are relevant to the issue of sex determination. Consider, for example, the following rationale on the part of the potential mother, who wants what is best for her future child:

> I know that girls do not generally get a "fair shake" in society. Despite an egalitarian upbringing, a female child that I might bear is likely to have fewer advantages in life than a male child. Even with natural talents equal to a son, she probably would not reach the same income or prestige level. Marriage, parenthood, and gender stereotypes would reduce her chances of success, as they would not comparably affect a man. If I choose to have a daughter despite these drawbacks, I am choosing a future that is less than optimal for my child. Perhaps, therefore, I am morally bound to choose a son.[51]

Obviously, if every potential parent thought and acted in keeping with the preceding rationale, society would in time arrive at an overwhelming preponderance of males. Although such a situation is not necessarily sexist, it is likely to reinforce the sexism that already prevails even if the rationale for sex selection is the promotion of the future child's best interests. Accordingly, while the rationale is explicative of decisions by individual parents, it does not merit universalization or social approval.

Benefits of the availability of techniques for sex selection should be acknowledged. Among those cited are the virtual elimination of sex-linked diseases, reduced likelihood that children will be unwanted because of sex, reduction of the birthrate, and possibly a better balance of males and females in the elderly population.[52] The last result would occur because of the probability that the number of men in the general population would substantially increase. The greater longevity of women might be matched by the greater proportion of the larger population of men who survive to more advanced age.[53] Of course, achievement of this end would also mean that the ratio of men to women would be greater earlier in life. So it is only in advanced age that numerical equality might be achieved, and it is even possible then that men would predominate. The anticipated numerical predominance of men is predicated on the well-supported preference of both men and women for sons, especially as firstborns.[54]

What are the potential harms of general availability of sex selection techniques? As already suggested, these have mainly to do with the reinforcement of sex role stereotypes and sexist practices.[55] They may also intensify the burden, if the technique fails, of having or being an unwanted child. Regardless of their sex, firstborns are generally more ambitious and successful than second-born children, who are often more sociable than their older siblings. If firstborns are predominantly sons and second-born children are predominantly daughters, these differences parallel the sex role stereotypes that already exist. With fewer women in the world, Amitai Etzioni maintains that the more venal traits of men, such as their tendency to violence and criminality, would prevail.[56] Women would more prevalently be treated as objects valued for their worth to men rather than for themselves, with their freedom suppressed to increase their availability. Men who least exemplify male stereotypes might also be exploited. Alternatively but improbably, women might dominate the mostly male world as supreme sovereigns. Neither scenario is acceptable from an egalitarian feminist standpoint.

It is hardly surprising that feminists as well as nonfeminists oppose sex selection for nonmedical reasons.[57] Nonetheless, many medical geneticists and genetic counselors of both sexes support the practice. Interestingly, the rationale by which some genetic counselors support prenatal testing and termination of pregnancy for nonmedical sex selection may be considered feminist because it is based on respect for the pregnant woman's autonomy. In addition, this rationale suggests respect for the cultural attitudes and practices that may influence the request. The ethic of nondirectiveness which genetic counseling has long championed is inconsistent with opposition to sex selection for any reason, so long as the practice is uncoerced. Refusal of testing or termination for sex selection is effectively directive behavior.

A survey of 19 nations conducted by Dorothy Wertz and John Fletcher found that the majority of geneticists in India and Hungary as well as the United States would offer sex selection for nonmedical reasons.[58] In the other nations surveyed, the majority would neither perform sex selection nor refer the couple to someone who would perform it. The case that elicited these responses involved a couple with four healthy daughters and no sons, requesting prenatal testing for sex determination in the absence of medical indications for the diagnosis. The couple tell the geneticist that if the fetus is female they will abort it, and if their request is not honored "they will have an abortion rather than risk having a fifth girl."[59]

In the three countries that supported sex selection in this case, the reasons were very different. In Hungary, 60% of those surveyed would offer sex selection in order to prevent the otherwise certain abortion of a healthy fetus, which might be either male or female. In India, where 52% would offer sex selection during gestation, the principal rationale on both sides of the issue was concern about social implications of the practice. Those who opposed sex selection indicated concerns about exacerbating women's unequal position and furthering the already unbalanced sex ratio. Those who supported sex selection saw the practice as a means of population control and of reducing abuse toward women who do not bear sons and their unwanted daughters. In the United States, 62% of geneticists surveyed would offer or perform sex selection on grounds of respect for the pregnant woman's or couple's autonomy. This rationale was generally framed in terms of rights: the right to this particular medical service, the right to decide, and the right to a referral.[60]

Data from a more recent survey by Wertz and her colleagues show an interesting contrast between the views of genetics professionals on sex selection and their views on other issues.[61] Women physicians were more directive than their male counterparts on most issues. On the issue of sex selection, however, U.S. women physicians were less directive than their male counterparts, genetic counselors, and non-U.S.physicians of either sex. Despite their overall emphasis on nondirectiveness, the U.S. genetic counselors were about as likely as non-U.S. physicians to refuse prenatal diagnosis for sex selection, even though they personally disagreed with the decision.[62] Wertz suggests that cultural differences and "professional locus" influence the disparate views of these groups more than gender influences them. Economic differences probably play a part as well.[63] Although some parts of the world were not included in the survey, the 37 nations that participated represent a range of cultural differences not found among the U.S. respondents. Culture, class, and professional locus undoubtedly influence the different groups, but the interplay among the factors may be more influential still, and gender is another part of that interplay.

Philosophically, cultural support for sex selection well illustrates the problem of relativism. In arguing against sex selection for nonmedical reasons, Wertz and Fletcher suggest a middle ground between ethical absolutism and ethical relativism. While cultural diversity should generally be respected, they favor restrictions against culturally "intolerable" practices, one of which is sex selection.[64] Similarly, Susan Sherwin suggests a restricted form of relativism when she describes feminism as favoring respect for all differences except those that support gender injustice.[65] Presumably, sex selection is one of these. Neither of these views is actually supportive of relativism, however, because both entail the universal or absolute claim that sex selection for sexist reasons is never justifiable. Like it or not, then, Sherwin, Wertz, and Fletcher are not relativists but absolutists.

As with most issues, sex selection is not unalterably opposed on feminist or egalitarian grounds. Selection of either males or females is justifiable on medical grounds and morally defensible in other situations so long as the intention and the consequences of the practice are not sexist. Sexist intentions are those based on the notion that one sex is inferior to the other; sexist consequences are those that disadvantage or advantage one sex vis-à-vis the other. Regardless of whether cultural attitudes condone or encourage it, either manifestation of sexism makes sex selection morally objectionable.

Notes

1. Admittedly, the term "ethnic" may be used more broadly, as in the *OED* definition of "ethnic" as a "group of people differentiated from the rest of the community by racial origins or cultural background." *The Compact OED New Edition* (Oxford: Oxford University Press, 1991), p. 535. Whatever term is used, my main interest here is to distinguish between social and biological influences, and I therefore use the term "ethnic" in a more restrictive (biological) sense. The *OED* definition of culture excludes the biological: "the civilization, customs, and artistic achievements of a people, especially at a certain stage of its development" (p. 374).

2. Cf. another definition of "ethnic" in the *OED:* "pertaining to race, peculiar to a race or nation, also pertaining to or having common racial, cultural, or religious characteristics, especially designating a racial or other group within a larger system." (p. 535).

3. Cf. *OED,* p. 1496, where "race" is defined as a "group of persons, animals or plants connected by common descent or origin," and as "one of the great divisions of mankind having certain peculiarities in common." Note also, however, that "the term is often used imprecisely, even among anthropologists."

4. Nancy L. Fisher, *Cultural and Ethnic Diversity A Guide for Genetics Professionals* (Baltimore, MD: Johns Hopkins University Press, 1996), p. xiv.

5. Fisher, p. xv.

6. Fisher, p. xv.

7. Fisher defines cultural relativism in a more positive light than philosophers are likely to define it: "learning about another belief system, [which] includes respectful behavior and communication between groups of people—in this case, between patients and their genetics professionals" (p. xiv).

8. Moore uses the term "naturalistic fallacy" to describe this view in his criticism of John Stuart Mill. George Edward Moore, *Principia Ethica* (Cambridge, UK: Cambridge University Press, 1951), pp. 10–17, 64–80.

9. Nancy Spencer, "European Culture in North America," in Fisher, pp. 6–9.

10. Spencer, p. 4.

11. Nuclear families in which the woman is the primary breadwinner have been increasing but are hardly common.

12. Spencer, pp. 8–11.

13. Interracial adoption has been challenged on grounds that it deprives the child of his or her cultural heritage. From an egalitarian feminist standpoint, however, it is surely better for a child to be adopted by caring parents of another race than to have no parents at all.

14. The history of discrimination in testing for sickle cell disease in the United States is elaborated in Chapter 10. Whether advertently or not, African-American leaders were involved in these discriminatory practices.

15. Joseph Telfair and Kermit B. Nash, "African American Culture," in Fisher, p. 46.

16. Telfair and Nash, p. 51.

17. In a recent survey of genetic counselors, medical geneticists, and their clients by Wertz and her colleagues, 91% of the clients were women. Dorothy C. Wertz, "Society and the Not-so-New Genetics: What Are We Afraid Of? Some Future Predictions from a Social Scientist," *Journal of Contemporary Health Law and Policy* 13 (1997): 336.

18. Telfair and Nash, p. 46.

19. Elena Lopez-Rangel, "Latino Culture," in Fisher, p. 22.

20. Lopez-Rangel, p. 24. The author calls this characteristic of Latinos *"familismo."*

21. Lopez-Rangel, pp. 29, 31.

22. Lopez-Rangel, p. 30.

23. Lopez-Rangel, p. 25. A possible influence on this denial is the "macho" image of the Hispanic male, whose virility is demonstrated by his having many healthy children. Of course, this image is not influential in Hispanic culture only.

24. Jack H. Jung, "Traditional Chinese Culture," in Fisher, p. 90.

25. Jung, p. 90.

26. Jung, p. 94.

27. Mark A. Greenstein and Bruce A. Bernstein, "Jewish Culture in North America," in Fisher, p. 198: "These terms ["Jewishness" and "Jews"] can refer to an individual's cultural and religious orientations—the beliefs, attitudes and customary practices that affect daily routines and the way in which life decisions are made. In addition, the terms *Jewish* and *Jews* are used to describe an ethnic group—a people with a common biological background sharing cultural traditions. Genetic counseling assumes importance in this context." The authors further distinguish between race and ethnicity: "Genetic counselors must take care to avoid confounding the concept of Jews as an ethnic group with the inaccurate notion of Jews as a separate 'race.' The world's Jewish population is clearly composed of people of different races" (p. 199).

28. Greenstein and Bernstein, p. 211.

29. Tom L. Beauchamp and James F. Childress, *Principles of Biomedical Ethics,* 4th ed. (New York: Oxford University Press, 1994).

30. Etymologically, the term derives from the Greek *autos,* which means "self," and *nomos,* which means "rule" or "governance." According to Beauchamp and Childress, the term was first used to refer to the self-governance of the Hellenic city-states (p. 120). In the context of bioethics, however, autonomy generally means personal autonomy rather than political autonomy.

31. Beauchamp and Childress provide a societally less demanding or negative concept of liberty: "independence from controlling influences" (p. 121). Isaiah Berlin's famous distinction between "freedom to" (positive freedom) and "freedom from" (negative freedom) is consistent with their view. My egalitarian orientation finds this inadequate because it supports a system in which remediable and unjust inequalities are countenanced. See Berlin, *Four Essays on Liberty*, (New York: Oxford University Press, 1969).

32. Many years ago I distinguished between these concepts as intrinsic and extrinsic freedom. Mary B. Mahowald, "Beyond Skinner: A Chance to Be Moral," *Journal of Social Philosophy* IV (1973): 1–4.

33. Susan Sherwin has developed a notion of "relational autonomy," which involves a critique of such limitations as particularly applicable to women in the health care setting. See her "A Relational Approach to Autonomy in Health Care," in Susan Sherwin, Coordinator, The Feminist Health Care Ethics Research Network, *The Politics of Women's Health: Exploring Agency and Autonomy* (Philadelphia: Temple University Press, 1998), pp. 19–44.

34. Because people are not equally autonomous, the term "equality," as used here, refers to "respect" rather than "autonomy."

35. Although democratic government may take the form of rule by the majority, history offers some horrendous examples of corrupt decisions by the majority.

36. Literally, the term "suttee" (cf. *satti* in Hindi and *sati* in Sanskrit) refers to a "chaste and virtuous wife." Cf. *Webster's New World Dictionary,* 2nd College Edition (Springfield, MA: Merriam-Webster, 1982), p. 1435. For an excellent account of female circumcision and its relation to ethical relativism, see Loretta M. Kopelman, "Female Circumcision/Genital Mutilation and Ethical Relativism," *Second Opinion* 20, 2 (1994): 55–71. For an account that reflects the ability of some U.S. physicians to respect the standpoint of African women on the issue, see Carol R. Horowitz and J. Carey Jackson, "Female Circumcision: African Women Confront American Medicine," *Journal of General Internal Medicine,* 12 (August 1997): 491–99.

37. *The Compact OED New Edition,* p. 1727.

38. Selection of females to avoid the birth of a child affected with an X-linked disease may be viewed as commendable, but this is based on selection against the disease rather than selection of the sex. Morally questionable selection of females would occur if it were undertaken as a means of serving the interests of others, e.g., through their reproductive or domestic labor.

39. "Ableism" refers to a bias or prejudice against people with disabilities, i.e., a view that such individuals are inferior to those who are "able."

40. For documentation of philosophers from classical to contemporary times who viewed women as inferior to men, see Mary B. Mahowald, ed., *Philosophy of Woman* (Indianapolis: Hackett, 1994). With few exceptions, philosophers' concepts of woman are inconsistent with their concepts of "man" or human nature.

41. If selection of females is based on the desire to avoid suffering in an affected male, it is not sexist.

42. F. J. Beernink, W. P. Dmowski, and R. J. Ericsson, "Sex Preselection through Albumin Separation of Sperm," *Fertility and Sterility* 59 (1993): 382–86. Although one recent American study of university students shows a fall in male preference over the past 15 years, the preference for sons remains strong. The fall in preference for sons is discussed in J. B. Ullman and L. S. Fidell, "Gender Selection and Society," in J. Offerman-Zuckerburg, ed., *Gender in Transition: A New Frontier* (New York: Plenum, 1989), pp. 179–87. The strong preference for sons throughout the world is explored by

T. M. Marteau, "Sex Selection," *British Medical Journal* 306 (1993): 1704–5, G. Vines, "The Hidden Cost of Sex Selection," *New Scientist* 138 (1993): 12–13, and V. Patel, "Sex Determination and Sex-Preselection Tests in India: Modern Techniques for Femicide," *Bulletin of Concerned Asian Scholars* 21 (1989): 1–11.

43. *Proceed with Care.* Final Report of the Royal Commission on New Reproductive Technologies, vol. 2 (Ottawa: Canada Communications Group Publishing, 1993), pp. 889–90.

44. Benjamin E. Reubinoff and Joseph G. Schenker, "New Advances in Sex Preselection," *Fertility and Sterility* 66, 3 (1996), 343–48.

45. Reubinoff and Schenker, p. 348. Note that blatantly sexist reasons may be included among "social purposes." Gina Kolata, "New Method Could Help Parents Choose a Baby's Sex," *International Herald Tribune,* September 10, 1998, pp. 1, 10.

46. The use of ultrasound for sex selection occurs despite governmental efforts to restrict its use for this purpose. Bob Herbert, "China's Missing Girls," *New York Times,* October 30, 1997, p. A23. In the United States as well, ultrasound for sex selection is available to individuals whose desire for sex selection is based on cultural values. Margie Slovan, "Some Go to Great Lengths to Avoid Having a Baby Girl," *Chicago Tribune,* August 3, 1977, sect. 13, pp. 1–2.

47. Wertz, "Society and the Not-So-New Genetics," p. 315.

48. Christine Overall, *Ethics and Human Reproduction* (Boston: Allen and Unwin, 1987), p. 27. The next few pages are slightly revised from my discussion of this issue in *Women and Children in Health Care: An Unequal Majority* (New York: Oxford University Press, 1993), pp. 84–86.

49. Personal communication with the author, September 25, 1989.

50. E.g., although the birth rate for girls is higher than for boys worldwide, in Korea, there are nearly 116 boys born for every 100 girls, and in China, 118.5 boys are born for every 100 girls. Sheryl WuDunn, "Korean Women Still Feel Demands to Bear a Son," *New York Times,* January 14, 1997, p. A3. Worse still is the incidence of female infants who "disappear" from the population because, in comparison with boys, they are neglected. Herbert, p. A23.

51. Mary Anne Warren suggests more compelling circumstances than I have here portrayed—e.g., societies that are extremely oppressive to women, where inheritance or other economic rights and privileges are limited to males. Warren, *Gendercide* (Totowa, NJ: Rowman and Allanheld, 1985), p. 85.

52. Warren, pp. 160–76, and Overall, pp. 29–33.

53. Other ways of increasing the number of men in the population include more medical and social attention to the most frequent causes of death among men, e.g., homicide and stress-related work roles.

54. William D. Althus, "Birth Order and Its Sequelae," *Science* 151 (January 7, 1966): 44; and Overall, p. 29.

55. Warren, pp. 108–58, and Overall, pp. 29–33.

56. Amitai Etzioni, "Sex Control, Science and Society," *Science* 161 (September 13, 1968): 1109.

57. Michael Bayles, for example, considered all cases of sex selection for nonmedical reasons sexist. Bayles, *Reproductive Ethics* (Englewood Cliffs, NJ: Prentice Hall, 1984), pp. 34–37. Even while she approves of sex selection for sex complementarity or sex similarity, Overall opposes institutional support for sex selection for nonmedical reasons.

58. Dorothy C. Wertz and John C. Fletcher, "Prenatal Diagnosis and Sex Selection in 19 Nations," *Social Science Medicine* 37, 11 (1993): 1359–66. Moreover, according to

Wertz and Fletcher, "more geneticists would perform prenatal diagnosis for sex selection in 1994 than in 1985. . . . Nevertheless, in most nations, with the exceptions of Russia, Hungary, Israel, and Portugal, fewer respondents would accede to such requests than they would in the United States." See Wertz, "Society and the Not-So-New Genetics," p. 316.

59. Wertz and Fletcher, p. 1362.

60. Wertz and Fletcher, p. 1362.

61. Dorothy C. Wertz, "Is There a 'Women's Ethic' in Genetics? A 37-Nation Survey of Providers," *Journal of the American Medical Women's Association* 52, 1 (1997): 33–38.

62. This contrasts with the data obtained in Wertz and Fletcher's earlier study, which showed a significant difference between male and female geneticists: women were two times more likely than men to support sex selection. Wertz and Fletcher, "Prenatal Diagnosis and Sex Selection in 19 Nations."

63. According to Wertz, the average annual income of the U.S. physicians was more than $100,000, whereas the average annual income of the non-U.S. physicians and of the U.S. genetic counselors was under $50,000. See Wertz, "Is There a 'Women's Ethic' in Genetics," p. 34. Of course, income is only one indicator of economic differences between groups. Moreover, as averages, these data do not reflect the wider range of income for U.S. physicians compared with genetic counselors and non-U.S. physicians. Greater socioeconomic disparity often exists between individuals with similar cultural background, such as the Hispanic mayor of a major U.S. city as contrasted with an illegal Mexican immigrant to the United States.

64. Wertz and Fletcher, p. 1364.

65. Susan Sherwin, *No Longer Patient* (Philadelphia: Temple University Press, 1992), pp. 66–75.

7

GENETIC VERSUS GESTATIONAL TIES TO CHILDREN

DO women who desire to be mothers have as much interest in genetic ties to their children as men do? Years ago, I considered this question while attending a meeting of researchers involved in reproductive genetics. At dinner with some of these researchers, I explored the issue with the women at the table by asking them this question: If you could only be related to your child either genetically or gestationally, which would you choose?

Without hesitation, all three women said "gestation." Two had had children to whom they were related both gestationally and genetically. One had never had children, either biologically or through adoption. The fact that the question could not be meaningfully asked to the man in the group was, I felt, significant in its own right. My question assumed a desire on the part of the respondents to be parents of children to whom they would be biologically related.[1] These particular women shared that assumption, which is consistent with the fact that most people desire to be parents and most succeed in doing so. However, some men and women make a conscious and positive choice not to have children, either biologically or adoptively.

From time to time in ensuing years, I asked the same question when giving talks to infertility patients, medical students, and clinicians. The fact that the question could be answered only by women in these audiences remained significant. The responses varied considerably: many women attached greater significance to genetics; at least as many attached greater significance to gestation.

In 1993, Amy Ravin, Carol Stocking, and I developed a questionnaire by which we might document the importance women attribute to gestation or genetics. At the time, Ravin was a medical student; Stocking is a sociologist with special expertise in questionnaire studies. While we could not ask men whether they attached greater significance to gestation for themselves, we could and did ask them whether their partner's gestational tie was more or less important to them than their partner's genetic tie to their child. This chapter presents our findings and discusses the implications.[2]

Distinguishing between Genetics and Gestation

Although genetic ties to offspring are often equated with biological ties, the equation is necessarily true only for men. Women may be biologically related to their children in three distinct and separable ways: genetics, gestation, and lactation. Lactating women have served as wet nurses for other women's biological children throughout history; they also have a biological tie to the children. Only recently, however, through the development of technologies for in vitro fertilization (IVF), egg donation, and embryo transfer, have genetics and gestation been separable relationships. "Surrogacy" arrangements, while not necessarily dependent on technology, also facilitate the separability of gestation and genetics.[3]

The significance of the distinction between gestational and genetic motherhood was dramatically illustrated in the United States by the case of Johnson versus Calvert. Anna Johnson had agreed to gestate and give birth to a child who would then be raised by the genetic parents, Mark and Crispina Calvert. Prior to the birth, Johnson changed her mind and challenged the Calverts for the right to raise the child. Basing its ruling on the Uniform Parentage Act of 1975, which determines parenthood by blood typing, an appellate court in California ruled that the Calverts were the "natural, biological, and legal parents" of the child. According to the court, Johnson had no parental rights.[4]

This ruling in favor of genetics has a gender analogue in court decisions such as the Baby Richard case, discussed in Chapter 16. A court in Illinois held that the genetic tie between a man and a four-year-old child should prevail over the relationship between the child and the adoptive family who had cared for him for his entire life.[5] From an egalitarian standpoint, the child's interests in this case should have been considered, but they were not. Legally, the genetic tie bestowed a parental status on the father that years of nurturance by his adoptive family did not. Ironically, the same rationale did not apply to the child's genetic and gestational mother. Because she had irrevocably consented to his adoption, she was not legally his mother even after she married the genetic father and he obtained legal custody of the child. Except that she had also gestated the child and eventually became his primary caregiver, her situation resembled that of a sperm donor, who is genetically but not legally a father to children generated through use of his gametes.

A situation somewhat like that of the sperm donor arises in the context of postmenopausal gestation, in which the genetic mother (i.e., the egg donor) is virtually ignored, while the normally, healthfully postmenopausal woman, who is no longer able to provide oocytes, is viewed as the mother solely on grounds of her gestating and giving birth.[6] Presumably, the basis for distinguishing between postmenopausal gestational mothers and "surrogate" mothers who may also be genetically related to the children to whom they give birth is the preconception agreement between the infertile woman or couple and the "surrogate." Had the infertile woman or couple not intended to have a child, the process would not have been initiated. In the legal determination of motherhood, intentionality apparently overrides gestation, and sometimes the genetic tie as well.

The separability of genetics and gestation also provides a means by which lesbian partners can both be biologically related to a child they intend to raise. One woman may undergo ovulation stimulation and ova retrieval while the other gestates the embryo formed by in vitro fertilization of her partner's eggs through donor sperm, eventually giving birth to their offspring. Because the child would not have come to be without their mutual decision to provide both genetic and gestational requirements for development, they are parents both intentionally and biologically. The sperm donor, also biologically related to the offspring, lacks the intentional component of parenthood.

The separability of genetic and gestational ties thus reduces the dependence of women on genetics to have a biologically related offspring. For how many women, however, is that important? Surely it is not important to the majority, who are capable and desirous of both relationships. Still, substantial numbers of women and couples are infertile or carriers of specific genetic conditions, and sometimes both. For those who counsel infertile or carrier couples, the priority each individual attributes to genetics is a relevant piece of information because of the possibility of distinguishing between the two in practice. Relevant also is the fact that the anguish of infertility may be greater for women than for men because of societal stereotypes about motherhood and because infertile women experience the double loss of genetic and gestational motherhood. Despite its inconveniences and discomforts, many women find pregnancy an exciting and predominantly positive experience, one that they would not want to avoid even if they could. For some, the inability to gestate and give birth represents a greater loss than the inability to have a child whose genetic complement comprises 50% of their own genes. Infertile men only experience the loss of the genetic tie, which may be mitigated by the fact that they are less likely to identify their fulfillment as persons with having children.

The separability of gestation and genetics in women is relevant not only to cases of infertility but also to genetics, because the gametes required for fertilization come from genetically different individuals.[7] Consider, for example, a couple who are both carriers for a homozygous autosomal recessive condition such as Tay-Sachs disease, cystic fibrosis, or sickle cell anemia. Although the woman may undergo prenatal tests to determine if her fetus is affected by the disorder for which the couple are carriers, and terminate a pregnancy if her fetus tests positive for the disorder, she may avoid these procedures through gamete donation from an unaffected donor. In contrast with sperm donation, which is a comparatively simple and reportedly pleasurable experience, egg donation is possible only in conjunction with IVF and embryo transfer, and ovulation stimulation is usually required as well. Sperm donation is less expensive and generally more likely to achieve the desired result—a healthy newborn. Still, if women are not as attached to the genetic tie to their offspring as are their male partners, egg donation presents a means by which they can be biologically related to their offspring by experiencing gestation and childbirth, and their partners can be biologically related in the only way open to them, by providing sperm.

Although the following data are not derived from a large study, some results are statistically significant for those surveyed, women and men who were patients or companions of patients in an urban university clinic. Even the results that are not statistically significant, however, are important for their demonstration of the weight that many women attribute to gestational as distinct from genetic ties to offspring.

Gender Differences in Attitudes toward the Genetic Tie

Our questionnaire was formulated for both men and women of childbearing age. Beyond demographic questions, we attempted at the outset to discover the weight that the respondents attached to any biological tie to offspring by asking whether they would attempt to adopt a child if they were unable to become parents through the usual route of sexual intercourse, gestation, and birth. Those who indicated that they would prefer to seek medical assistance to have a biologically related child were then asked what type of assistance they would pursue for themselves or their partner.

One hundred eighteen surveys were distributed to persons waiting in the general adult clinics area of the University of Chicago Health Service. These clinics serve a mixed population of persons affiliated with the university and those who live in the surrounding community. One hundred six of the surveys were completed and returned. Demographic information from the 106 surveys, filled out by 52 women and 54 men, is provided in Table 7–1.

When asked to imagine that they were unable to become a parent through

TABLE 7–1. Demographic Information about Survey Respondents

PARAMETER	WOMEN (N = 52) N (%)	MEN (N = 54) N (%)
Age (years)		
< 26	19 (36.5)	17 (31.4)
26–35	13 (25.0)	24 (44.4)
>35	20 (38.4)	13 (24.0)
Marital status		
Single	27 (52.9)	32 (59.3)
Married	16 (31.4)	18 (33.3)
Separated, divorced, widowed	8 (15.6)	4 (7.5)
Yearly household income		
<$20,000	11 (21.1)	21 (38.8)
$20,000–$34,999	15 (28.8)	12 (22.2)
$35,000–$49,999	8 (15.3)	11 (20.3)
>$49,999	18 (34.6)	10 (18.5)
Race/ethnicity		
African American	19 (36.5)	10 (18.5)
European American	25 (48.0)	33 (61.1)
Other	8 (15.3)	11 (20.3)
Education		
High school, attended or graduated	4 (7.7)	6 (11.3)
Some college	17 (32.7)	7 (13.2)
College graduate	12 (23.1)	7 (13.2)
Graduate education	19 (36.5)	33 (62.3)

Reprinted from *Journal of Women's Health,* Vol. 6, No. 6, 1997, with permission from Mary Ann Liebert Inc.

the "usual route of intercourse, conception, pregnancy and childbirth," 10.4% of our respondents said they would prefer to remain childless, and an additional 22.6% said they would choose adoption and not seek medical assistance. This left 71 respondents (66.9%) who answered the questions about medical assistance in our survey. Our subsequent analysis was based on these 71 respondents, 37 women and 34 men. Table 7–2 shows responses by sex.

Among those who said they would pursue neither adoption nor medical assistance, some might not have wanted to pursue parenthood through the usual route either. Within our sample, however, we were unable to identify individuals who desired not to have children regardless of their ability to do so. Of those indicating a desire to use medical assistance, some said they would accept a more limited form of intervention than those proposed in the ensuing questions. Two women and four men refused to select any option involving gestation by another woman, artificial insemination, IVF, or gamete donation, stating that if these were the only alternatives available, they would adopt or remain childless.[8]

TABLE 7–2. Preference for Childlessness, Adoption, or Medically Assisted Reproductive Technology (MART) by Sex

RESPONSE[a]	WOMEN N (%)	MEN N (%)
Prefer to remain childless	7 (13.5)	4 (7.4)
Seek adoption	8 (15.3)	16 (29.6)
Seek medical assistance	37 (71.1)	34 (62.9)

[a] Responses to the question: If you cannot become a parent through the usual route of intercourse, conception, pregnancy and childbirth, would you prefer to remain childless, or would you pursue medical assistance or adoption to become a parent?

Reprinted from *Journal of Women's Health,* Vol. 6, No. 6, 1997, with permission from Mary Ann Liebert, Inc.

As shown in Table 7–3, when women were asked to choose between gestational and genetic relationships to their children, most (51.4%), but not a significant majority, chose gestation over genetics. When men were asked which they preferred for a female partner, a significant majority (73.5%) chose the genetic tie.

Our results indicated no statistically significant difference in preferences for

Table 7–3. Genetics or Gestation?

If you could choose one of the following, which would you choose?

Option 1. Genetics

Women: To be genetically related without carrying the pregnancy and giving birth to your child.

Men: You and your partner are genetically related to your child, but your partner does not carry the pregnancy and give birth.

Option 2. Gestation

Women: To carry the pregnancy and give birth without being genetically related to your child.

Men: You are genetically related to your child, but your partner is not. Your partner carries the pregnancy and gives birth.

RESPONSE	WOMEN ($N = 37$)	MEN ($N = 34$)
Genetics	48.6%	73.5%
Gestation	51.4%	26.5%
	$p = 0.032$	

Reprinted from *Journal of Women's Health,* Vol. 6, No. 6, 1997, with permission from Mary Ann Liebert, Inc.

genetics or gestation between those who would pursue adoption if medical help failed and those who would not ($p = 0.34$). Similarly, neither marital status ($p = 0.63$) nor having already had children ($p = 0.52$, women; $p = 0.58$, men) predicted the choice of genetics or gestation.

When presented with a scenario in which the male partner's sperm could not be used, 38.9% of the women but only 14.7% of the men chose donor insemination (DI), 47.2% of the women and 70.6% of the men chose adoption, and 13.9% of the women and 14.7% of the men chose to remain childless. This difference between the responses of men and women approaches statistical significance ($p = 0.07$).

The next several questions explicitly asked respondents to assume for the moment the same risks, costs, discomfort, and success rates for the various options. If the woman's eggs could be used but she could not carry the pregnancy, 88.6% of the women and 87.9% of the men chose IVF using the genetic material of both partners and another woman to gestate and give birth. The remaining 11.4% of women and 12.2% of men chose artificial insemination of the man's sperm into another woman, who would carry the pregnancy and give birth.

If the woman's eggs could be used and she could not carry the pregnancy but had a sister willing to do so, 54.5% of the women and 66.7% of the men chose IVF using genetic material from both partners, with the sister serving as the gestational mother. Given the same context, 36.4% of the women and 18.2% of the men chose IVF with a nonrelated gestational mother and 9.1% of the women and 15.2% of the men chose artificial insemination of the woman's sister, using the husband's sperm. As Table 7–4 shows, however, no significant differences were evident between the sexes when respondents were asked to choose any of a list of procedures for which risks and success rates, along with a rough indication of cost, were specified.

Finally, when respondents were asked to choose among IVF, DI, adoption, and childlessness and were provided with approximate costs and success rates for IVF and DI, 60.6% chose IVF, 11.3% selected DI, 23.9% opted for adoption, and 4.2% chose to remain childless. As the cost of adoption was not estimated, some respondents may have incorrectly assessed the relative costs of their options. Nearly the same percentage of respondents choosing the genetic tie and of those choosing the gestational tie selected the IVF option (62.8% vs. 61.5%). Those who selected the genetic tie in the earlier question were less likely to choose DI (4.7% vs. 23.1%) and more likely to choose adoption (27.9% vs. 11.5%) than those who selected a gestational tie initially. Responses to this question varied according to the earlier selection of a genetic or a gestational tie ($p = 0.048$), but not by income level ($p = 0.29$, women; $p = 0.26$, men). Assuming that the male partner's sperm could not be used, those who selected the gestational tie in the earlier question were more likely to choose DI (42.9% vs. 18.0%) and less likely to choose adoption (50.0% vs. 64.0%) or to re-

TABLE 7–4. Acceptability of Risks and Costs of Procedures

PROCEDURE DESCRIPTION	WILLING TO CHOOSE PROCEDURE WOMEN (%) (N = 52)	MEN (%) (N = 54)
The procedure involves a series of painful shots and a small but possibly painful surgery (women) or for your partner (men).	69.4	67.7
The procedure is very expensive and paid by insurance. It has a success rate of 15%–20% and a failure rate of 80%–85%.	62.2	68.7
The procedure is very expensive and not paid by insurance. It has a success rate of 15%–20% and a failure rate of 80%–85%.	22.2	29.0
The procedure is very expensive and not paid by insurance. It has a success rate of 85%–90%.	69.4	80.6
The procedure is very expensive and not paid by insurance. It has a success rate of 15%–20% and a failure rate of 80%–85%, involves a series of painful shots, and a small but possibly painful surgery (women) or for your partner (men).	17.1	19.4

Reprinted from *Journal of Women's Health,* Vol. 6, No. 6, 1997, with permission from Mary Ann Liebert, Inc.

main childless (7.1% vs. 18.0%) than those who selected a genetic tie initially. This difference approached statistical significance.

Our survey was designed to elicit information about how individuals rank the relative importance of different biological relationships to children they intend to rear. If confronted with an inability to have a child through the usual route of sexual intercourse, pregnancy, and childbirth, a large majority (89.6%) of our respondents said that they would pursue another means of having a child. Most (74.7%) of those seeking another means would start by looking for medical assistance, thus indicating a general preference for a biologically related child. Among those who rejected the procedures listed as options (IVF, DI), some might accept other forms of medical assistance, such as fertility drugs, artificial insemination with their partner's sperm, or surgical correction of anatomic impediments to fertility.

This study differs from other studies of reproductive decisions in a number of ways. First and most important, our subjects were not actually deciding about or undergoing medical assistance for reproduction. Infertility patients may choose between egg and sperm donation if they are heterozygous for a specific genetic disorder, but their choices are usually dictated by their specific medical need—for example, sperm donation for low sperm count or ova donation for premature ovarian failure. Second, the average age of our respondents was somewhat older than that of respondents in other studies. In most studies, the subjects are in their thirties, with men somewhat older than women.[9] Over half of the women and nearly two-thirds of the men in our study were less than 30 years old. A third difference is that about two-thirds of our respondents were single, whereas most infertility patients are married.[10] Being single and younger may make individuals less likely to be currently considering parenthood. Two limitations of our study are that it was conducted in one setting, and African-American men are somewhat overrepresented among our study subjects.

Our finding of a significant difference in how each sex regards the preference for a genetic tie to offspring contrasts with the finding of J. G. Thornton and colleagues that men and women are equally divided on the issue.[11] This difference may be related to different study populations. The Thornton study took place at a university hospital in Leeds, England, using two convenience samples as study subjects. The respondents were women who were "medical and nonmedical workers and patients from the gynecology and postnatal wards" and men who were "doctors, medical students, paramedical staff and lay people visiting patients in the same hospital."[12] Only 23 of the 50 women and 26 of the 50 men were nonmedical personnel. Our study took place at a university hospital in Chicago, where all of our respondents were patients or persons accompanying patients for clinic visits. Thus our subjects were probably less informed about medical assistance procedures than the medical personnel that Thornton and colleagues interviewed in a setting where they had not come for treatment for themselves or family members. We are unable to compare the populations with regard to marital status, income, race, or educational level because these data were not provided in the Thornton study.

Another difference between the Thornton study and ours is the language used in the key question addressed. Women in the Thornton group were asked to consider this: "If you had only one pregnancy, would you prefer to be the genetic or the birth mother?"[13] This language suggests that a woman can experience pregnancy while becoming a genetic mother without giving birth, which is impossible. The corresponding question in our study was posed as a choice between being "genetically related without carrying the pregnancy and giving birth" and "carrying the pregnancy and giving birth without being genetically related." This language takes into account the fact that pregnancy is essential but not equivalent to childbirth, while both are separable from the genetic tie. For some women, the inability to experience pregnancy may be a greater loss than their inability to give birth.

Despite the differences between these studies, both make it clear that a substantial number of men and women regard the genetic tie as more important than giving birth to one's offspring, and vice versa. Different reasons support either preference.

Why Gestation?

The fulfillment of gender roles may be compelling to both men and women. Although women are often thought to have a biologically determined desire to bear children, there is no convincing evidence of a hormonal basis for maternal feelings. Some authors claim that the desire for motherhood is culturally rather than biologically rooted.[14] Influenced by deeply ingrained societal expectations that women's special role in life involves the bearing of children, a woman may wish to be pregnant to fulfill her womanhood or to prove her femininity to herself or others. In a survey of nearly 1000 couples undergoing IVF, women placed greater emphasis on the need for gender fulfillment as a reason for infertility treatment than did the men.[15] Reinforcing this reasoning by his partner, a man might desire gestational motherhood for her because he wishes to see her fulfill her feminine role. Her pregnancy may also enhance his gender identity, affirming his manhood through this obvious manifestation of his fertility.

A woman might choose the gestational tie to realize her bodily capacity for pregnancy and childbirth. She may want to experience not only the unique physical and emotional sensations of pregnancy but also the social responses and practices that pregnancy sometimes elicits. As already suggested, pregnancy is a happy, exciting experience for many women, despite its inevitable risks, discomforts, and inconveniences. Some women describe their pregnancies as "easy," and some regard it in a positive light even when the pregnancy was unplanned or involves serious complications.[16] Other women have quite the opposite experience, and this may trigger a preference for genetics over gestation. Childbirth is hardly painless for anyone, but many women look forward to it as the necessary means through which they finally get to see and hold the child they have been nurturing for so many months.

Although the desire to be pregnant is separable from the desire to give birth, and some women might desire one but not the other, pregnancy and birth are generally inseparable. Abortion and miscarriage may of course prevent childbirth, but one cannot give birth without being pregnant. Anesthesia during delivery may deny a woman the experience but not the fact of childbirth. Moreover, both the desire to be pregnant and the desire to give birth are separable from the desire to raise a child, and the desire to be a social parent may be fulfilled by means other than medical assistance.

A preference for gestation may also be influenced by the desire to control and regulate the environment of the fetus during the formative months of pregnancy. Because the developing fetus is considerably affected by maternal health and habits during gestation, some women may opt for pregnancy to ensure sufficient vitamin intake, adequate nutrition, and the avoidance of tobacco, alcohol, or other drugs. Applying the same logic, a man may select gestation for his partner because he trusts her judgments on behalf of the fetus more than he would trust someone else to make those judgments. The desire to control the first nine months of development may thus factor into the decision to choose gestation over genetics.

Why Genetics?

Passing on one's genes is commonly seen not only as the defining characteristic of the parent–child relationship but as the means through which one's own genetic material is transmitted to posterity. Following Plato, some see genetic reproduction as an expression of the desire for immortality.[17] Men and women alike may wish to see their own characteristics incarnate in those who will live after them. This desire may extend beyond oneself to one's partner. Both partners may view their genetic tie to children as an extension of their own relationship.

Social practices suggest that men are more interested than women in maintaining a genetic link to their posterity. For example, a father may strongly desire to perpetuate his lineage and name or to maintain the family business beyond his lifetime. In the Mary Beth Whitehead case, for example, William Stern was reported to be particularly interested in having a child genetically related to himself because he was the only child of Holocaust survivors. Whitehead had contracted with Stern and his wife to be artifically inseminated with Stern's sperm so that she might become pregnant and give birth to a child that the Sterns would then raise. Obviously, the child would be genetically related to only one of her rearing parents, the father, whose surname would be hers as well.[18] The genetic link between children and their fathers is emphasized by this practice of assuming the father's surname. Even in cultures where both the mother's and father's surnames are used for offspring, the father's name is socially more significant than that of the mother, who is both genetically and gestationally related to their children.

Research on the human genome, increased availability of genetic tests, and ongoing developments in gene therapies have augmented the impact of genetics on our lives. Both men and women may prefer to pass on a known family and personal history of genetic predispositions to diseases, temperament, and behavior. In our study, several respondents' comments exhibited this rationale. Two women said that if their husbands' sperm could not be used, each would like to use her sperm of their husband's brother. Apparently, they hoped thereby to preserve as close a genetic tie as possible to their potential offspring. Two people said they would remain childless if a genetic relationship to both partners could not be achieved.

A woman might choose to maintain a genetic tie to avoid pregnancy and childbirth rather than as an actual preference for a genetic tie. Some fear the physical changes associated with pregnancy, the risk of complications, difficult labor, or the pain of childbirth. Other women may view the 40 weeks of pregnancy as a significant inconvenience, slowing them down or interfering with their ability to perform their usual activities. For some, gestation involves psychological disturbances, financial hardship, and job discrimination. Any or all of these factors may motivate a woman to choose an alternative that allows her to circumvent pregnancy and childbirth.

Regardless of his partner's preferences for genes or gestation, the only biological relationship that a man can establish with a child is the genetic tie. From a man's perspective, then, the defining relationship in starting a family is genetic. Genes (sperm) determine fatherhood. If the same reasoning were applied to women, genes (eggs) determine motherhood. A man who consciously or unconsciously examines his own potential relationship to a child and transfers that understanding to a woman's relationship to a child establishes all parental claims by genetics alone. He may thus view both parents as equal contributors to prenatal development. The gestational relationship is invisible in this analysis, having no analogue in the biological tie between father and child.

Counseling Considerations

Women who have given birth may choose the gestational tie because they appreciate the psychological and physical impact of pregnancy and childbirth. However, the reverse situation may also be true: women who have not yet experienced pregnancy and childbirth may desire fulfillment of this biological capacity. In our sample, whether or not a woman had given birth did not predict her choice of a genetic or gestational relationship to a child. Women with and without children chose genetics or gestation at approximately equal rates.

A similar pattern of reasoning may apply to men: their choice between genetics and gestation might be expected to vary according to their experience with previous children's births. Yet for them, too, having biologically related children did not predict their choices. Apparently, such simple paradigms cannot predict the preference for genes or gestation. Both women's and men's views may be influenced by whether they regard their own reproductive experiences or those of others positively or negatively.

Several respondents noted that their ability to choose a costly reproductive procedure hinged on their current financial situation. In our study, however, those with low incomes were as likely as those with high incomes to choose an expensive procedure with a low success rate in an effort to maintain genetic and gestational ties. In general, the survey respondents tended to select the technique that optimized factors other than cost, noting that if the situation ever actually arose, they might need to alter that choice because of financial constraints. In a study of 121 patients who withdrew from an IVF program in Australia, cost was the most frequently cited reason for ceasing treatment, and many of the respondents wanted to return to the program at a later date.[19] It is hardly surprising that financial concerns modify the real-life choices that people make.

The most common remark on our surveys reflected a reluctance to make decisions without the partner's input. Until these respondents had a partner or had discussed the options with their partner, they were hesitant to call their decisions final even in a survey situation. This is consistent with a survey of 147 members of a national self-help organization for couples with infertility problems, in which personal beliefs ranked first and partner's beliefs ranked second among 14 factors relevant to their choice of infertility treatment.[20]

When a partner's sperm could not be used, there was a statistically significant difference in how each sex regarded DI. This parallels a difference between the sexes in the acceptability of egg donation. In a telephone survey of 501 people, 82% of the men but only 74% of the women considered egg donation acceptable for an infertile couple.[21] In each case, fertile men and women are less accepting of gamete donation by their own sex, but infertile men have a more positive attitude toward DI than do fertile men.[22]

The varied answers of our respondents highlight the importance of counseling individuals as well as couples by attending to individual as well as gender-based differences. An exclusive focus on the genetic tie to offspring seems to support an egalitarian interpretation of parental contributions to reproduction. In fact, however, the opposite is the case. The concept of equality that underlies an egalitarian approach to counseling is not one by which individuals or groups are viewed as the same and treated in the same manner. Rather, this approach means that differences between and among individuals and groups are identified and examined to determine whether these are associated with inequality or injustice.

If parenthood is defined only by genetics, parents may indeed be considered equal contributors to the biological process, and gender-neutral language is appropriate in reproductive counseling. (Even then, the difference between how eggs and sperm are obtained constitutes a morally significant sex difference.) That approach is inadequate, however, because it ignores the other morally relevant biological relationship of gestation, which more than half of the women in our study considered more important than genetics. A genuinely egalitarian counseling approach to the different reproductive contributions of men and women demands attention to the disparities that arise because of them. In that context, gender neutrality is an obstacle to gender justice.

To return to the case of Anna Johnson versus Mark and Crispina Calvert, mentioned at the outset of this chapter, the Supreme Court of California recognized "both genetic consanguinity and giving birth as means of establishing a mother and child relationship."[23] However, the court stipulated that "when the two means do not coincide in one woman, she who intended to procreate the child—that is, she who intended to bring about the birth of a child that she intended to raise as her own—is the natural mother under California law." An egalitarian feminist standpoint supports this ruling, not only with regard to its determination of legal parenthood in this case but also in its openness to determination of parenthood on grounds of gestation.

Women who agree to gestate and give birth for another are called "surrogate mothers" whether or not they are genetically related to the child. Because our study focused on the distinction between genetic and gestational parenthood, we did not deal with those who, like Mary Beth Whitehead, are related genetically as well as gestationally to offspring.[24] What our results suggest, however, is that in either case, use of the term "surrogate" is problematic because it fails to acknowledge the significance that many women and men attach to genetic and gestational ties to offspring.

As the California court affirmed, gestation and childbirth, as well as genetics, are necessary routes to biological motherhood. Our data also affirm that many people, but particularly women, would choose gestation rather than genetics if either route but not both were open to them. In an era in which awareness of the impact of genetics has been heightened through the success of the Human Genome Project, it seems more important than ever to respect that preference, remembering that biological ties are based on more than genes.

Notes

1. Because some women and men make a conscious and positive choice not to have children, either biologically or adoptively, this assumption is not true in all cases.

2. We presented and discussed our results in Amy J. Ravin, Mary B. Mahowald, and Carol B. Stocking, "Genes or Gestation? Attitudes of Women and Men about Biologic Ties to Children," *Journal of Women's Health* 6, 6 (1997): 1–9. With permission of the publisher and other authors, much of this chapter is taken from that article.

3. The term "surrogacy" is in quotation marks to call attention to its inappropriate application to biological motherhood. A surrogate is someone who stands in place of another but is not the other. Because so-called surrogates are related to the children to whom they gave birth gestationally, and sometimes genetically as well, they are in fact

biological mothers, not stand-ins. In both instances, they fulfill the traditional definition of mother as one who gives birth.

4. *Anna J. v. Mark C,* 286 Cal. Rptr. 369 (Cal. App. 4th 1991).

5. *Otakar Kirchner v. John and Jane Doe and Baby Boy "Richard,"* No. 78101 (Supreme Court of Illinois, 1994).

6. See, for example, W. E. Schmidt, "Birth to a 59-Year-Old Generates as Ethical Controversy in Britain," *New York Times,* December 29, 1993, p. A1. Postmenopausal gestation may also be induced in women who are not normally, healthfully postmenopausal, e.g., those of normal reproductive age who have ovarian agenesis, premature ovarian failure, or have had oophorectomies for treatment of cancer. I have argued elsewhere for a moral distinction between these situations and those in which women are normally, healthfully menopausal. Mary B. Mahowald, "Medically Assisted Reproductive Technology (MART): Variables, Verities, and Rules of Thumb," *Assisted Reproduction Reviews* 6, 4 (1996): 175–80.

7. If and when human cloning from adult cells occurs, this will no longer be a requisite for fertilization. Having distinct genetic parents will nonetheless remain the norm.

8. I use the term "childless" rather than "child-free" because "childless" was used in the questionnaire. The term "child-free" would have avoided the negative connotation of "childless" with regard to the one who has "less." But "child-free" may have a negative connotation with regard to the child from whom one is "free."

9. A. M. Braverman and S. L. Corson, "Factors Related to Preferences in Gamete Donor Sources," *Fertility and Sterility* 63 (1995): 543; L. R. Schover, R. L. Collins, and S. Richards, "Psychological Aspects of Donor Insemination: Evaluation and Follow-Up of Recipient Couples," *Fertility and Sterility* 57 (1992): 583; M. J. De Zoeten, T. Tymstra, and A. T. Alberda, "The Waiting List for IVF: The Motivations and Expectations of Women Waiting for IVF Treatment," *Human Reproduction* 2 (1987): 623; K. Mao and C. Wood, "Barriers to Treatment of Infertility by In-vitro Fertilization and Embryo Transfer," *Medical Journal of Australia,* April 28, 1984, pp. 532–33.

10. J. Wright, C. Duchesne, S. Sabourin, F. Bissonette, J. Benoit, and Y. Girard, "Psychosocial Distress and Infertility: Men and Women Respond Differently," *Fertility and Sterility* 55 (1991): 100; see also n. 9.

11. J. G. Thornton, H. M. McNamara, and I. A. Mantague, "Would You Rather Be a 'Birth' or a 'Genetic' Mother? If So, How Much?" *Journal of Medical Ethics* 20 (1994): 87.

12. Thornton et al., p. 87.

13. Thornton et al., p. 87.

14. G. E. Robinson and D. E. Stewart, "Motivation for Motherhood and the Experience of Pregnancy," *Canadian Journal of Psychiatry* 34 (1989): 861; A. Lalos, L. Jacobson, O. Lalos, and B. von Schoultz, "The Wish to Have a Child," *Acta Psychiatry Scandinavia* 72 (1985): 476; B. Eck Menning, "The Emotional Needs of Infertile Couples," *Fertility and Sterility* 34 (1980): 313.

15. C. R. Newton, M. T. Hearn, A. A. Yuzpe, and M. Houle, "Motives for Parenthood and Response to Failed in Vitro Fertilization: Implications for Counseling," *Journal of Assisted Reproduction Genetics* 9 (1992): 24.

16. Personal experiences.

17. Plato, *Symposium* C208.

18. After she gave birth, Whitehead returned the money paid for her "surrogacy" and challenged the legitimacy of the contract between her and the Sterns. Eventually, a U.S. judge awarded custody to the Sterns but ruled that Whitehead had the right to visit her

daughter. Ronald Munson, "Ruling on Baby M," in *Intervention and Reflection* (Belmont, CA: Wadsworth, 1988), pp. 438–43.

19. Thornton et al., p. 87.

20. D. I. Frank, "Factors Related to Decisions about Infertility Treatment," *Journal of Obstetric and Gynecologic Neonatal Nursing* 19 (1990): 162.

21. R. Lessor, K. Reitz, J. Balmaceda, and R. Asch, "A Survey of Public Attitudes towards Oocyte Donation between Sisters," *Human Reproduction* 5 (1990): 889.

22. A. Blaser, B. Maloigne-Katz, U. Gigon, "Effect of Artificial Insemination with Donor Semen on the Psyche of the Husband," *Psychotherapy and Psychosomatics* 49 (1988): 17.

23. *Johnson v. Calvert,* 19 Cal Rptr 2d 494, Cal, 1993.

24. In re *Baby M,* No. FM-25314-86E (New Jersey Superior Court Chancery Division, 1987). See also Ethics Committee of the American Fertility Society, "Ethical Considerations of the New Reproductive Technologies," *Fertility and Sterility* 73, Supp. 2 (1990): 64S, and N. Taub, "Feminist Tensions: Concepts of Motherhood and Reproductive Choice," in V. Offerman-Zuckerbert, ed., *Gender in Transition: A New Frontier* (New York: Plenum, 1989), p. 217.

8

DISABILITIES, FEMINISM, AND CAREGIVING

FROM a feminist standpoint, the topic of disabilities raises issues with regard to those affected, those who care for them, and society in general. Although most disabilities are not genetically induced, and most abortions are not performed for genetic reasons, genetic disabilities are important to women as the principal caregivers of those affected by them and because detection of genetic disabilities (broadly defined) is the principal goal of prenatal testing. Moreover, the symptoms of some genetic conditions that are episodically disabling, such as cystic fibrosis and sickle cell anemia, are exacerbated during pregnancy.

This chapter focuses on the impact of disabilities on women in relation to feminism and caregiving. The question addressed with regard to feminism is whether advocacy for women is compatible with opposition to abortion of fetuses with disabilities. With regard to caregiving, I consider the meaning of care, the implications for women of a care-based ethic, and variables relevant to an egalitarian assessment of the caregiving role. Although most research on disabilities does not distinguish between those induced by genetics and those induced by other causes, its findings are applicable to both. What follows is also applicable to both types of disability.

Feminism and Advocacy for Those Who Are Disabled[1]

Feminists have not always recognized that advocacy for people with disabilities is logically and practically required by their commitment to women and gender justice. This is unfortunate not only because so many women are disabled and most of us who are currently able will eventually become disabled, but also because we share the same battle against stereotypes of dependence, passivity, and inferiority.[2] In general, men who are disabled are dominant vis-à-vis women who are disabled. As Adrienne Asch and Michelle Fine put it, "concerns with 'emasculation' may promote efforts directed towards those at the locus of the *masculinity-dependence* contradiction, not towards those at the redundant intersection of *femininity* and *dependence*."[3]

The major issue with which some versions of feminism seem to be at odds with advocacy for those who are disabled is prenatal testing for fetal anomalies.[4] Although some feminists object to medical technologies that usurp women's control over their bodies, many feminists embrace the technologies that provide them with a means of controlling otherwise uncontrollable aspects of their lives. Prenatal testing is one of these technologies, abortion is another, and the two are intertwined. Ordinarily, abortion is the only means through which a woman whose prenatal test is positive for a specific condition can avoid giving birth to a child with that condition. Because most results of prenatal testing are negative, some genetic counselors believe that it actually decreases the incidence of abortions. The rationale for this view is that if pregnant women could not be tested, those at risk for fetal disorders might terminate normal pregnancies to avoid the possibility of having an affected child. To some who are disabled, however, abortion after detection of fetal anomalies implies judgments that their lives are not worth living. In the words of one activist, "abortion on grounds of handicap denies us an identity as equal human beings worthy of respect, and calls into question the place in society of disabled individuals."[5]

The desire to avoid having children with disabilities is not only the objective of practitioners who recommend or perform prenatal testing but also the main motivation of women or couples who seek and undergo such testing. This is clear from the fact that the majority of referrals for prenatal testing, and the majority of prenatal tests that women actually undergo, are based on maternal age, which is associated with a heightened incidence of chromosomal abnormalities, especially Down syndrome. Although congenital anomalies, particularly cardiac and intestinal defects, occur more often in infants with Down syndrome than in other infants, the only anomaly which the syndrome always entails is mental retardation.[6] Consequently, the predominant rationale that underlies prenatal testing and termination of affected fetuses is avoidance of the birth of a child who is mentally retarded. Some women choose to continue their pregnancies after a positive diagnosis of a fetal anomaly; most do not.

Does feminist advocacy for the right to terminate pregnancy imply disregard for persons with disabilities? Related to that question are others: Does advocacy for persons with disabilities imply the right to terminate an unaffected fetus to ensure (as far as possible) the birth of an infant with a specific condition, such as achondroplasia or deafness? Does advocacy for either group imply support for the right to become pregnant or to continue a pregnancy despite inability to care for an infant without public or professional assistance? Does it also imply the right to medical assistance to become genetic parents? Answers to these questions depend on the version of feminism that is operable and on different construals of "reproductive rights." Questions involving the right to terminate a pregnancy also involve the moral status that is imputed or denied to the fetus.

Different Versions of Feminism

As discussed in Chapter 4, different versions of feminism stem from different conceptions of justice.[7] Libertarian and liberal feminists affirm that justice entails equal liberty for women and men as the primary value to be promoted. Justice mainly entails the promotion of liberty for individual women by refraining from interference with their choices. Libertarian feminism does not require social measures to reduce material inequality; in fact, it opposes such measures because they allegedly compromise the liberty of those who are materially advantaged (e.g., through graduated income tax).

A libertarian framework thus supports the right of disabled women to make choices but opposes governmental requirements of means to implement their choices. In contrast, liberal feminism *may* support such requirements and egalitarian versions of feminism *insist* on them. Whether liberal feminism supports governmental requirements that reduce the disadvantages of those who are disabled depends on its willingness to accept a concomitant reduction in the advantages enjoyed by those who are currently able, that is, the dominant group. Like liberalism in general, liberal feminism encompasses a variety of positions within a range of liberal feminist positions. For example, some liberal feminists oppose restrictions on "surrogate" motherhood while others support them.[8] Because both libertarian and egalitarian versions of feminism are clearer than liberal feminism in their implications regarding advocacy for the disabled, these illustrate the stark contrast between certain versions of feminism and their compatibility with advocacy for people with disabilities. To the extent that liberal feminism emphasizes equality, it is consistent with egalitarian feminism; to the extent that it emphasizes individual liberty, liberal feminism is consistent with libertarian feminism.

Egalitarian feminists (such as I) give priority to women's material equality with men as a condition for their individual liberty. By material equality, I mean a situation in which differences associated with inequality are eliminated, or the inequality associated with them is reduced as much as possible.[9] Because women belong to different races, classes, and sexual orientations and have different abilities and disabilities, the material equality to be promoted must take account of those differences as well. As already suggested, therefore, gender justice demands racial justice, socioeconomic justice, sexual justice, and ability justice. For egalitarian feminists, the individual liberty of some women and men may be curtailed if the expression of that liberty augments or sustains material advantages for them over others.

Advocacy for persons with disabilities, like advocacy for any other nondominant group, may mean support for their choices, their welfare, or both. In other words, such advocacy is based on the principles of respect for autonomy, beneficence, and nonmaleficence, which, from an egalitarian standpoint, should be equally applied to the currently able and all of the disabled. The goal of providing equal opportunities to both groups entails advocacy of measures that enable the disabled as much as possible. The Americans with Disabilities Act of 1990 accords with this aim, covering those with susceptibility to genetic conditions as well. To the extent that the legislation applies to both women and men, it exemplifies liberal or egalitarian feminism.

Feminists with disabilities are as likely to support a pregnant woman's right to abortion as are those who are currently able. Many, however, are particularly concerned about the societal implications of abortions based on fetal disability. In general, feminists with disabilities worry that such decisions strengthen "the widely-held belief that life with a disability is not worth living," sending "a message to children and adults with disabilities, especially people who have genetic or prenatal disabilities, that 'We do not want any more like you.'"[10] Because of the priority it imputes to individual choice, a libertarian version of feminism is more likely than other versions to tolerate this view if not endorse it; in doing so it betrays the interests of many women, including those who are currently able. Accordingly, Jenny Morris observes that "It is not in the interests of either women or disabled people to rely on liberal individualism for the furtherance of our rights."[11]

All versions of feminism involve advocacy for women, but it is unclear whether "women" include female fetuses as potential women. Since no fetus is autonomous, there can be no advocacy for fetal "choice." Accordingly, in a libertarian version of feminism, fetuses themselves are not a relevant consideration, regardless of whether they are male or female.[12] They may nonetheless be relevant to persons who are unquestionably moral agents. Although an argument may be made in support of the potential woman's choice regarding tests and interventions during her fetal development, such an argument would be highly speculative and hardly convincing. However, a liberal version of feminism might include and an egalitarian version would definitely include the welfare of the fetus as a morally relevant consideration in decisions about prenatal interventions. Further considerations that are morally relevant to such decisions are the possibility of damage to the potential child and the possibility of fetal pain. These factors are relevant to liberal and egalitarian feminists because respect for autonomy does not always trump beneficence and nonmaleficence. In other words, the right to choose is not absolute. Justice is the principle needed to determine whether respect for different choices, burdens, and benefits is equitably distributed among those affected.

Reproductive Rights and the Moral Status of the Fetus

The right to become pregnant, to continue or end a pregnancy, or to obtain medical assistance with regard to any of these goals is generally considered in the context of "reproductive rights," which most if not all feminists support.[13] Although the right to raise a child is often viewed as a reproductive right, the parenting on which newborns and children rely is both legally and morally separable from the right to reproduce. The separability derives from the fact that children, unlike embryos or fetuses, have clearly established rights based on their own interests. Moreover, the extent to which reproductive rights are supported vis-à-vis other rights or others' rights varies with different versions of feminism. A libertarian version supports a woman's right to choose among reproductive options for any reason; it would not countenance the coercion of others to assist her medically or economically in implementing her choices. In contrast, an egalitarian version would maintain that the moral exercise of reproductive rights calls for consideration of the impact of their exercise on others, including potential children. To what extent, if any, that consideration should be legally mandated is debatable even within the context of an egalitarian feminism.

Whether support for pregnant women's choices is compatible with advocacy for persons with disabilities depends also on one's view of the moral status or standing of the fetus.[14] If the fetus has no moral status in its own right or as a potential child, then regardless of whether it has disabilities, the two issues are separable, and there is neither logical nor ethical connection between advocacy for persons with disabilities and denial of support for fetuses with disabilities.[15] There may be an emotional or social link between the two, and this may have ethical implications. In general, however, if the fetus has no moral status or standing, women's decisions about pregnancy have nothing to do with their decisions about newborns with disabilities; their choices may justifiably be overridden with regard to their children, but not with regard to their fetuses. Asch and Fine support this point of view. For them, birth defines the moment at which an individual with a disability has rights and responsibilities equivalent to persons who are currently able.[16]

A contrasting view is based on the assumption that the fetus has a moral status equivalent to that of a born individual. A woman's decision to terminate a pregnancy because the fetus has a disability may then be regarded as morally equivalent to terminating a born person with a disability. Like other analogies, this one is pertinent but inadequate. Its inadequacy arises mainly from the fact that the fetus is still within the body of the woman, whereas a newborn is not. From a feminist standpoint, this difference is morally significant even when a fetus at term is developmentally more mature than a premature infant. Moreover, every fetus may be considered disabled because, at least until viability, it is totally dependent on another—the pregnant woman—to sustain its life. Whether the fetus is disabled or not, however, if its moral status is equivalent to that of a newborn, terminating it is tantamount to homicide. Support for the woman's choice is therefore incompatible with support for the disabled, including those persons with disabilities who are women. Since fetuses cannot choose, this position implies support for those who can choose over those who are unable to choose.

A number of positions about the moral status of the fetus are partial or gradualist, that is, they impute some moral status to the developing human organism. Some positions are based on the potential of the embryo or fetus for full human development; these are gradualist if they relate greater moral status to increased development. Some impute moral status to the implanted embryo but not to the zygote. Others deny that early embryos have any moral status but posit some point during gestation, such as the onset of brain activity or viability, at which moral status is fully present.[17] Whether or not any of these positions supports compatibility between the pregnant woman's right to choose and advocacy for people with disabilities depends on the weight attributed to one or the other at the point when some moral status is imputed to the fetus. If the fetus achieves full or nearly full moral status in late gestation, nonmaleficence toward it may then outweigh the autonomy of the pregnant woman. If the fetus has minimal moral standing until it is viable, respect for the woman's autonomy may trump nonmaleficence toward the fetus.

The Compatibility Question

A libertarian version of feminism emphasizes the individual pregnant woman's choice as paramount; it therefore fully supports the decisions of autonomous women, whether currently able or disabled, to initiate, terminate, or continue pregnancies for any reason. In cases involving prenatal diagnosis and termination of pregnancies because of fetal anomaly, this view is incompatible with advocacy for persons with disabilities unless (*1*) the fetus has no moral status, or (*2*) obligations that follow from its moral status are not as compelling as the woman's choice. To the extent that some women lack autonomy (e.g., because of retardation or mental illness), libertarian feminism ignores their interests if those interests are not pursued by autonomous individuals, such as family members.

An egalitarian version of feminism places greater emphasis on equality, broadly construed; it thus implies that other values besides women's autonomy are morally relevant to decisions about initiation, continuation, or termination of a pregnancy. With regard to prenatal diagnosis and termination of affected fetuses, this view is consistent with the pregnant woman's right to choose and with the rights of the disabled if the fetus has no moral status. But if the fetus has moral status or standing, egalitarian feminism can be consistent with advocacy for women's choice and for the interests of those who are disabled only if (*1*) the moral status of a fetus is deemed less compelling than the pregnant woman's autonomy, or (*2*) the decision is not based on the ability or disability of the fetus. Concerning the second factor, the decision may be based on the inability of the caregiver or of society to provide adequate care for the potential child. As already mentioned, to an egalitarian feminist, choice is not an absolute value. From an egalitarian feminist perspective, therefore, pregnant women, whether they are currently able or disabled, are morally obliged to consider the welfare of the potential child in their decisions about initiating, continuing, or terminating pregnancy. However, it does not follow that they should be legally obliged or coerced to do so.

With regard to decisions to terminate pregnancies, what I have said thus far is as applicable to fetuses without disabilities as it is to those with disabilities. The applicability to both suggests a criterion to be followed if advocacy for women's choice and advocacy for persons with genetic disabilities are to be reconciled: *the mere fact of the disability is irrelevant to the choice.* Admittedly, there are cases during and beyond gestation in which suffering, whatever its cause, may be unrelievably so overwhelming that letting the suffering individual die seems like a merciful or humane act in his or her behalf. Consider, for example, an infant with a profoundly devastating, incurable, progressive, genetic condition such as Tay-Sachs disease or Lesch-Nyhan syndrome, or someone who is dying of an incurable, painful cancer. The criterion in those cases, however, is not the disability itself but the suffering of the person with the disability. Moreover, the crucial caveat in situations of overwhelming suffering is that it be unrelievable by others. As many authors attest, much of the suffering associated with disabilities is socially induced and relievable.[18] For autonomous persons with disabilities, another crucial variable is respect for autonomy; this consideration is relevant to pregnant women but not to fetuses.

My suggested criterion for reconciling feminism with advocacy for people with disabilities is also applicable to the issue of assisted suicide, which presents another possibility for discrimination against them. One disabilities activist articulated this concern by claiming that supporters of the legalization of assisted suicide "just want to get rid of us."[19] From an egalitarian feminist standpoint, however, if assisted suicide is a legal right for those who are currently able, it should also be a right of those who are disabled. For both groups, measures must be taken to ensure that the decision is made autonomously. Circumstances that compromise autonomy, such as treatable depression, which occurs more frequently in women than in men, and social causes of disability must be adequately addressed before an individual's decision is regarded as genuinely autonomous.

An egalitarian version of feminism is more coherent in its own right and more compatible with advocacy for those who are disabled than a libertarian version. It is more coherent because individual choice is not an absolute moral right; other rights and others' rights may be more compelling. Egalitarian feminism is compatible with advocacy for the disabled because it embraces all of the disabled, including those who are not autonomous. People with disabilities, like persons who are currently able, are not always autonomous or equally autonomous any more than they are equally intelligent, talented, or attractive. The goal of an egalitarian feminism is to treat different individuals fairly in the face of these differences, both changeable and unchangeable. This returns us to the notion of gender justice as essentially tied to justice toward individuals with disabilities. An obligation to treat everyone justly assumes that no one's autonomy is absolute, whether women or men, able or disabled, young or old, whatever their class, color, ethnicity, or sexual orientation. In addition, treating everyone justly requires the persistent attempt by all reasonable means to reduce whatever disadvantages individuals or groups experience vis-à-vis one another.

Asch and Fine illustrate the compatibility between feminism and advocacy for people with genetic (or other) disabilities while identifying a concrete measure by which an egalitarian feminist standpoint may be promoted: the provision of adequate and balanced information to potential parents of children with disabilities about the experience of raising such children and their potential for satisfying and productive lives. Assessing the counseling typically provided as inadequate and biased against the birth of a disabled child, they contend that "given the proper information about how disabled children and adults live, many women might not choose to abort."[20] As already suggested, however, their support for a woman's right to terminate her pregnancy depends on a denial that fetal interests ever outweigh a pregnant woman's interests. According to Asch and Fine, "we must recognize the crucial 'line' separating the fetus—residing in the body of her mother—and the infant, viable outside the womb."[21] Once the infant is born, their position shifts drastically. While staunchly defending the right of disabled infants to be treated over the objection of their parents, they argue just as forcefully for the right of every woman to abort a disabled fetus so long as she has adequate information about its actual potential.

Unfortunately, even if pregnant women are provided with adequate information about the prospects of life with a disability, they are rarely adequately supported in the caregiving responsibilities they face if they decide to give birth to children in whom serious genetic disorders have been identified prenatally. A commitment to gender justice calls for analysis of these responsibilities from an egalitarian standpoint.

Caring for People with Disabilities

Women who provide care for those who are disabled predominate in direct care roles. These roles are generally less prestigious and less remunerated than the roles occupied by those in position of power over them, who are mainly white, heterosexual, relatively affluent, currently able men.[22] Pregnant women provide the only indispensable care for their potential children, and mothers provide most of their care afterwards. As daughters, spouses, and sisters, women also provide most of the care of kindred who are sick or disabled.[23] Here too, their care often draws little notice and is seldom remunerated.

Caregiving experiences are as diverse as the experience of different disabilities. The differences in disabilities involve the origin of the condition, the type and severity of symptoms associated with the condition, the treatability of the condition, the age of onset, and duration of symptoms. Disabilities may be cognitive, sensory, or physical, with each of these comprising a range of possibilities. Some conditions are severely impairing; others only slightly so. Some constitute disabilities mainly or only because societal arrangements have been primarily designed to accommodate those who are currently able. Although the majority of genetic diseases are incurable, their symptoms may be relievable, and possibilities for curative therapies are increasing with advances in gene therapy. Some disorders are manifest at birth or even prenatally; others strike much later in life. Early detection of multifactorial genetic disorders such as cancer can facilitate effective treatment. The experience of caregiving is influenced by each of these variables in the disability itself. Before considering some variables in the caregiving experience, however, the meaning of care and women's relation to caregiving needs to be further examined.

Although the practice of care is as old as humankind, the concept of care has rarely been articulated, let alone analyzed, by philosophers.[24] Recently, however, the terms "care" and "caring" have been explicitly discussed in the literature of moral psychology and ethics. In that context, a care-based model of moral reasoning is applicable to all interpersonal relationships, not only those that occur within the health care system or between people with disabilities and their personal attendants, but also among persons who are currently able. This model should not be confused with the meaning of care that many disabilities activists deplore because of its paternalistic connotations.[25] Care in that sense is obviously unacceptable to an egalitarian feminist.

The meaning of care elaborated by moral psychologist Carol Gilligan is based on her study of the decision making of women facing an unwanted pregnancy. Her data, as reported and interpreted in her book *In a Different Voice,* have provided a major impetus for critiquing mainstream philosophers' emphasis on justice, impartiality, and individual rights as the appropriate basis for ethical decision making.[26] Lawrence Kohlberg, Gilligan's mentor, had developed a strategy for assessing moral development that fit nicely with traditional philosophical ethics, but Gilligan found the tradition wanting.[27] It failed, she claimed, to match the reasoning of most women and some men, for whom the preservation of particular relationships figured tellingly in their decisions. Gilligan called the traditional ethic an ethic of justice, contrasting it with an ethic of care.[28] Both types of moral reasoning, she maintained, are present in most individuals, but care predominates in women and justice in men.

Nel Noddings also developed an ethic of care or caring, based on her observation of maternal behavior as exhibiting a natural or genetic drive to attend to the needs of the newborn. She proposed that "ethical care" should be based on this model.[29] Unlike Gilligan, Noddings eschewed an ethic of justice, arguing that a feminine or maternal ethic of care justifiably excluded concerns about equality because it focuses on particular others whose interests one wishes to advance. While she apparently considers her view feminist, those of us who identify feminism with advocacy for gender equality do not agree. Some feminists, however, have argued for an essential relationship between care and justice. Joan Tronto, for example, argues that justice and care are not only compatible but also essentially related.[30] For Tronto, care is in fact a way of promoting social equality. Her definition of care goes well beyond that of Noddings: *"a species activity that includes everything that we do to maintain, continue, and repair our 'world' so that we can live in it as well as possible."*[31] This definition is congenial to an egalitarian version of feminism.

The concepts that Gilligan, Noddings, and Tronto construe as care and caring are not necessarily equivalent to the activities of caregiving that occur within the health care system. Their views capture a subjective or affective element in the activity of caregiving that is sometimes lost in the motivation and experience of caregivers and those for whom they care. Loss of this element is particularly evident in the tendency to equate treatment with care.[32] Nonetheless, care and caring are surely related to caregiving, and women remain the principal caregivers within society, whether or not their caring is affective as well as effective.

It may be impossible to determine whether women's predominance in caregiving roles arises from natural or culturally induced tendencies. Indeed, the assumption that the two influences are distinctive or separable is challengeable in its own right. Barbara Hillyer, for example, has challenged the "nature–culture dichotomy" as "empirically false" and "used to confine women to the private domestic sphere in contrast to men, whose ability to 'reason' supposedly fits them for the political world."[33] It is possible, however, to identify some of the areas of impact on women's lives of assuming these roles. From a feminist standpoint, these areas need to be identified and assessed so as to reduce, as much as possible, whatever inequities are associated with them. They involve, but are not limited to, the following: the type and extent of care needed by the person who is disabled; the relationship between that person and the caregiver; the age, health, and stamina of the caregiver; societal attitudes toward caregivers; and the burdens and benefits of caregiving.

With regard to the type and extent of care, some persons with disabilities (e.g., those with profound mental retardation or advanced stages of neurological disorders) require personal assistants around the clock; others (e.g., those with moderate retardation or chronic disorders such as cystic fibrosis) require assistance on a regular but not persistent basis. Some people require caregiving only occasionally, just as those who are currently able require it. Still others do not require personal assistance at all but require social accommodations or equipment to allow them to function normally within an environment designed for those who are currently able.

Some forms of caregiving entail little more than attendance and attention to potential emergencies; others require constant scrutiny and responsiveness to someone's needs. The responsibilities of caregivers may extend to individuals in institutions, in sheltered workshops, or at home. They sometimes demand physical strength (e.g., the ability to lift an adult or a wheelchair); technical skills (e.g., the ability to use and monitor medical devices or equipment); nursing skills; or therapeutic, psychological, and educational skills. More mundanely but no less demandingly, caregiving may simply require ordinary life skills performed in another's behalf, or the maintenance of personal contact, which is indispensable to anyone's survival or flourishing.

The tasks of caregiving may be as basic, and possibly as distasteful, as cleaning someone after a bowel movement, as mundane as doing laundry or tying shoelaces, or as apparently superficial as trimming someone's nails or combing her hair. Clearly, the preparation and experience of the caregiver needed to assist in the fulfillment of tasks such as reading for the blind or signing for the deaf are quite different than they are for the caregiver who provides for more basic needs.

The relationship between caregivers and persons with disabilities may be familial, friendly, professional, or a combination of these. Sometimes a relationship may develop from one into the other, as when a family member becomes a nurse, a physical therapist becomes a friend, or a person with disabilities marries a caregiver. Relationships, however, are much more complicated than these terms express. For example, familial relationships may be genetically close but psychologically distant or even hostile; they may also be complicated by the fact that the parent-caregiver is a carrier for the condition affecting her child, or the caregiver carries a familial risk for the same disorder. Friendships between the caregiver and the person cared-for may be intense or casual, constant or sporadic, and a relationship between caregiver and cared-for that starts with friendship may become unfriendly. Professional relationships may be warm or cool, chosen or coerced, with varying degrees between each of these opposing pairs. Familial relationships are always mutual in their biological dimension; in their social dimension, however, friendship may be one-sided, and the professional–client relationship is always one-sided in that one person is in need of the services of the other, and not vice versa.[34] In other ways, some caregivers seem to need to care more than the cared-for needs care.

Family relationships are particularly complex, sometimes introducing feelings of obligation or resentment on the part of the familial caregiver. Depending on the degree and type of impairment, the person with the disability often recognizes this sentiment. In other situations, the family caregiver may relish the opportunity to show love for the other through caregiving, and the person cared-for may recognize this. Professional caregivers may also act out of a sense of obligation; this is communicated to the client when caregivers perform their duties as a job rather than a choice. Both friends and professionals may have a transient relationship to the person cared-for, while family members remain family members even if the relationship becomes distant or hostile.

Mothers who care for children with disabilities may be subjected to criticism from professional caregivers, people with disabilities, and feminists. Hillyer describes this phenomenon as one of mother blaming.[35] Apparently ignoring the responsibilities of fathers, professional caregivers are prone to blame mothers for not providing children with disabilities with an exorbitant amount of attention and care. They sometimes expect an impossible expenditure of energy, ability, and resources. In contrast, and ironically, persons with disabilities and their advocates sometimes blame mothers for being overprotective of children with disabilities, impeding their full expression of autonomy. The same mother may be the target of criticism from both sides for the same behavior.

Feminist mother blaming arises from the view that mothering in general, and mothering of those with disabilities in particular, involves perpetuation of feminine stereotypes of subservience. According to Hillyer,

> The remarkable tenacity of this idea among feminists who in other contexts know perfectly well that men and patriarchal institutions have a great deal to do with

> human options is probably a result of the fact that all of us have been daughters and only some of us mothers.[36]

Feminists as well as persons with disabilities and professional caregivers who indulge in this kind of mother blaming have apparently ignored their own myopia regarding the experience of mothers of people with disabilities.

The majority of formal and informal caregivers of disabled children are young and middle-aged women. The majority of health professionals who care for the disabled of any age are also young and middle-aged women. As persons with disabilities get older, however, their informal caregivers tend to be older as well. Because of the cost of caregiving, not only psychologically but financially, many caregivers are constantly "on call," or work the "night shift" after working outside the home each day.[37] Caring for disabled adults generally requires greater physical stamina than caring for children with those disabilities.

Next to wives, adult daughters and daughters-in-law tend to be the principal caregivers of disabled parents, as well as the principal caregivers of their children or other disabled relatives. Moreover, as medical advances have extended the life span of the disabled at all ages, the duration of their lives through which women fulfill their caregiving roles toward others escalates. One example of this multigenerational caregiving is a 65-year-old woman with major caregiving responsibility for her 85-year-old mother, her 70-year-old husband, and her adult child, all living in the same home and all disabled by different manifestations of a familial form of cancer, Li Fraumeni syndrome.

Unfortunately, societal attitudes toward the majority of caregivers, whether they work in institutional or home settings, tend to be positive in rhetoric but not in practice. Occasionally, while observing attendants of people with severe disabilities (e.g., involving ventilator dependence) in the workplace, I have been troubled by what appeared to be disrespectful treatment of the attendant, totally ignoring his or her presence, as if the assistance rendered was coming from a piece of equipment or a machine rather than a person. Admittedly but unjustifiably, people in powerful or prestigious positions in the workplace often similarly fail to acknowledge the currently able people who assist them.

The discrepancy between rhetoric and practice may be measured by the gap between the income and power of a few versus the majority. The minority of caregivers who are already in prestigious positions are physicians. Most are men, with the increasing number of female physicians concentrated at the lower levels of power.[38] Physicians work in hospitals or offices where they provide care acutely or episodically rather than constantly, and are well rewarded economically. In contrast, hospital nurses, who are still mainly women, provide continuous care by shifts, are often less respected, and are usually less remunerated.[39] Within the health care system as a whole, women predominate as caregivers at the levels of least prestige and income.[40]

As already noted, women predominate as caregivers in their homes and others' homes, and here the gap between rhetoric and practice is widest. The work that women typically do in the home is not only unremunerated but expected rather than respected; when men do similar work they are often respected because it is not expected. When a member of the household becomes disabled, the person who does the work in the home is expected to extend her responsibilities to the new required tasks. Only occasionally are the extra demands of caregiving even recognized as extra. When a caregiver leaves a job outside the home to care for a relative with a disability, she loses not only prestige and income, but the social supports of the workplace.[41] In time, the self-concepts of caregivers in such circumstances are more likely than not to be depleted by these societal attitudes and practices.

Attitudes of the disabled toward their caregivers may be positive or negative as well. While there is always a certain dependence of the cared-for on the caregiver, the caregiver may be dependent on the cared-for both emotionally and financially. In many instances, persons with disabilities are better educated and more affluent than their caregivers. Because they are as human as their caregivers, persons with disabilities are also capable of conveying a disrespect for the role of caregiver. Generational differences may exacerbate this disrespectfulness, with children expecting sacrificial care from their mothers and elderly parents expecting it from their daughters. Where parent-caregivers are carriers for the condition affecting their child, they may be resented or blamed for transmitting it.

As many mothers might say, caregiving has its rewards as well as its burdens, even if the rewards include neither income nor prestige. People who care for persons with disabilities might say the same. To extend Noddings's point that mothers have a natural or genetic drive to care for their dependent infants, it may also be true that women in general have a natural or genetic drive to care for others who are dependent, including people with disabilities.[42] And if fulfillment of that natural drive entails satisfaction for mothers, women may be more likely than men to find satisfaction in caring for those who are genetically disabled.

It may also be the case that Noddings's notion of ethical care, as distinct from natural care, is the drive that motivates women to be caregivers. Through the impact of gender socialization in which maternal nurturance is equated with self-sacrifice, women tend to internalize the notion that they *ought* to be the main caregivers of their children, the aged, the sick, and the disabled. There again, fulfillment of the ought may entail satisfaction for them, although not without cost.

Costs of caregiving include payment for therapies, medications, nursing care, hospitalizations, and medical equipment, as well as stress, chronic fatigue, and lack of time for other desirable and remunerative activities.[43] The physical and psychological toll for the primary caregiver also includes ill health, guilt, and anger.[44] Symptoms of mothers who are primary caregivers are strongly influenced by their perception of how severely disabled their child is, the actual severity of the disability, and their relationship with the child's father.[45] Not surprisingly, positive relationships may be correlated with milder symptoms, and severity of disability, whether actual or perceived, with more problematic symptoms. Women who are primary caregivers are more likely to experience depression than their male counterparts, but this is true of women in general.[46] Unfortunately, studies of the psychological impact of caregiving on those who care for people with disabilities seldom address gender differences, referring only to "parental" or "family" impact. In gathering their data, however, the researchers typically interview mothers rather than fathers.[47]

Men as well as women may of course find satisfaction in caring for their infants and caring for others, whether or not the satisfaction derives from fulfillment of a natural or ethical drive. If so, how sad that so few men, in comparison with women, fulfill those drives. Beyond the possibility that men do not naturally have as great a drive toward (unremunerated, nonprestigious) caregiving as women do, another explanation for the gender imbalance in caregiving is that the financial cost for men is likely to be greater. Their income from work outside the home is typically greater than that of their wives or their female counterparts in the workplace, and that advantage would of course be lost if they were to spend their days caring for someone at home.[48]

For professional caregivers who have no other or no better source of income, an obvious benefit of caregiving is that it provides some income, no matter how meager. To persons with disabilities, the fact that basic caregiving is not well paid is an ambivalent benefit because they would probably like to see their caregivers paid better, but they may not have the means to pay them better or the power to see that others do so. From an egalitarian feminist standpoint, the inequity that caregiving responsibility usually involves for the caregiver, whether male or female, can and should be rectified by practical changes in laws and social policies. Unfortunately, the rhetoric that often favors such rectification is seldom matched by practice.

Notes

1. This section and the section on caregiving draw considerably on my contribution to *Disabilities, Difference, Discrimination: Persepectives on Justice in Bioethics and Public Policy,* co-authored with Anita Silvers and David Wasserman (New York: Rowman and Littlefield, 1998), pp. 209–51.

2. People with disabilities in the United States number from 35 million to 43 million, depending on how disability is defined. Of these, one-third are over 65 years of age, and women comprise the bulk of that population. Joseph P. Shapiro, *No Pity* (New York: Random House, 1993), p. 6.

3. Adrienne Asch and Michelle Fine, "Introduction: Beyond Pedestals," in Michelle Fine and Adrienne Asch, eds., *Women with Disabilities* (Philadelphia: Temple University Press, 1988), p. 3.

4. In addition to Asch and Fine (n. 3 above), see, e.g., Marsha Saxton, "Disability Rights and Selective Abortion," in Rickie Solinger, ed., *Abortion Wars, a Half Century of Struggle 1950–2000* (Berkeley: University of California Press, 1998), Alison Davis, "Women and Disabilities: Abortion and Liberation," *Disability, Handicap, and Society* 2, 3 (1987), and Adrienne Asch and Gail Geller, "Feminism, Bioethics, and Genetics," in Susan Wolf, ed., *Feminism and Bioethics* (New York: Oxford University Press, 1996).

5. Davis, p. 275.

6. Down syndrome is also associated with a higher incidence of hyperthyroidism, leukemia, and risk for early onset Alzheimer disease. The health problems unrelated to mental retardation would rarely be construed as warranting abortion in fetuses thought to be mentally normal.

7. I have also developed the relation between different versions of feminism and conceptions of justice in "Gender Justice and Genetics" in Yeager Hudson and Creighton Peden, eds., *The Social Power of Ideas* (Lewiston, NY: Edwin Mellen Press, 1995), pp. 225–52.

8. E.g., Lori B. Andrews, "Feminism Revisited: Fallacies and Policies in the Surrogacy Debate," *Logos* 9 (1988): 81–96, supporting surrogate gestation, and Christine Overall, *Ethics and Reproduction: A Feminist Analysis* (Boston: Allen and Unwin, 1987), pp. 11–136, opposing surrogate gestation.

9. Amartya Sen's account of egalitarianism would not be so restrictive because it accommodates "virtually all the approaches to the ethics of social arrangements." Even "pure libertarians," for Sen, "demand equality with respect to an entire class of rights and liberties." *Inequality Reexamined* (Cambridge: Harvard University Press, 1992), p. ix.

10. Susan Wendell, *The Rejected Body: Feminist Philosophical Reflections on Disability* (New York: Routledge, 1996), pp. 153, 154.

11. Jenny Morris, *Pride against Prejudice: Transforming Attitudes to Disability* (Philadelphia: New Society Publishers, 1991), p. 81.

12. To the extent that fetuses or other nonautonomous entities are capable of suffering, some libertarians acknowledge the moral relevance of beneficence toward them. H. Tristram Engelhardt Jr., for example, maintains that "One *can* have substantial concerns with beneficence toward severely mentally retarded humans." *The Foundations of Bioethics* (New York: Oxford University Press, 1986), p. 145 (italics added); cf. p. 322, 2nd ed., 1996. Strictly speaking however, the inclusion of this principle is not demanded by a libertarian framework.

13. A possible exception to this support is a group called Feminists for Life, who argue against a woman's right to abortion on grounds that it implies that women alone are responsible for children.

14. L. W. Sumner distinguishes between moral status and moral standing, but his distinction is not helpful here. *Abortion and Moral Theory* (Princeton, NJ: Princeton University Press, 1981), p. 26.

15. The same point may be made with regard to sex selection. But the potential for discrimination based on sex is different from the potential for discrimination based on disability because the latter is also associated with greater caregiving responsibilities for women.

16. Adrienne Asch and Michelle Fine, "Shared Dreams: A Left Perspective on Disability Rights and Reproductive Rights," in Fine and Asch, pp. 297–305.

17. For example, L. W. Sumner, "A Third Way" and Baruch Brody, "Against an Absolute Right to Abortion," both in Susan Dwyer and Joel Feinberg, eds., *The Problem of Abortion,* 3rd ed. (Belmont, CA: Wadsworth, 1997), pp. 88–117.

18. For example, Wendell, pp. 35–56, and Asch and Fine, pp. 5–6. The extent to which suffering associated with disability is relievable depends as well on the nature of the disability and the variability of its impact on specific individuals. Those who are able to write about their own experience of disability probably constitute both a numerical minority and a dominant group within the community of those who are disabled.

19. This statement was made by a woman with disabilities who attended a workshop funded by the Ethical, Legal, and Social Issues Program of the National Center for Human Genome Research in Zanesville, Ohio, May 16–19, 1996. The principal investigator for the workshop on Women and Genetics in Contemporary Society (WAGICS) was Helen Bequaert Holmes.

20. Asch and Fine, p. 302. Shapiro maintains that less than 50% of women told that a fetus has a serious genetic defect choose abortion (p. 278).

21. Asch and Fine, p. 302.

22. In 1994, women comprised 19.5% of the physicians in the United States. Four-fifths, or 85.6%, were in patient care, concentrating in internal medicine, pediatrics, family practice, psychiatry, obstetrics and gynecology, and anesthesia. Lillian Randolph, Bradley Seidman, and Thomas Pasko, *Physician Characteristics and Distribution in the U.S.* (Chicago: American Medical Association, 1996), p. 44.

23. Stephen G. Post, "Women and Elderly Parents: Moral Controversy in an Aging Society," *Hypatia* 5, 1 (1990): 83–85.

24. Warren Reich has tracked the history of the concept of care in the *Encyclopedia of Bioethics* (New York: Macmillan, 1995), pp. 319–29. In doing so, however, he interpreted various other terms, such as "sympathy" and "attention" as parallel in meaning. Those who chose the other terms might disagree with this interpretation.

25. For example, Shapiro remarks that "the disability rights movement consciously steers clear of" caregiver language because it "suggests that a disabled person is a sick and passive recipient of an attendant's help" (p. 254). As a person who is currently able, Shapiro imputes this view to others.

26. Carol Gilligan, *In a Different Voice: Psychological Theory and Women's Development* (Cambridge: Harvard University Press, 1982).

27. Lawrence Kohlberg, *The Philosophy of Moral Development* (San Francisco: Harper and Row, 1981).

28. Carol Gilligan, "Moral Orientation and Moral Development," in Eva F. Kittay and Diana T. Meyers, eds., *Women and Moral Theory* (Totowa, NJ: Rowman and Littlefield, 1987), pp. 19–33.

29. Nel Noddings, *Caring: A Feminine Approach to Ethics and Moral Education* (Berkeley: University of California Press, 1984). Note that Noddings uses the word "feminine" rather than "feminist" to describe her approach.

30. Joan C. Tronto, *Moral Boundaries: A Political Argument for an Ethic of Care* (New York: Routledge, 1993).

31. Tronto, p. 103. This definition was formulated with Berenice Fisher.

32. On the distinction between the two, see Mary Briody Mahowald, *Women and Children in Health Care: An Unequal Majority* (New York: Oxford University Press, 1993), p. 268.

33. Barbara Hillyer, *Feminism and Disability* (Norman: Universtiy of Oklahoma Press, 1993), pp. 164–65.

34. A caveat to this point is that some caregivers may be financially dependent on the job of caregiving, despite its low level of remuneration.

35. Hillyer, pp. 86–107. As the mother of a daughter with multiple, severe disabilites, Hillyer apparently experienced mother-blaming herself.

36. Hillyer, p. 92.

37. For an overview of the psychological and economic costs of caregiving for the genetically disabled, see Mary B. Mahowald, Dana Levinson, Christine Cassel, Amy Lemke, Carole Ober, James Bowman, Michelle LeBeau, Amy Ravin, Melissa Times, "The New Genetics and Women," *Milbank Quarterly* 74, 2 (1996): 268–70.

38. In 1994, women represented almost one-third (32.6%) of all residents in training. Surgical residents were still predominantly male (80.3%) but pediatric residents were predominantly female (62.4%). "Appendix II-Graduate Medical Education. Table 1: Resident Physicians on Duty in ACGME-Accredited and in Combined Specialty Graduate Medical Education (GME) Programs in 1996," *Journal of the American Medical Association* 278, 9 (1997): 775–76.

39. Some experienced nurses in administrative roles have higher salaries than medical residents.

40. In the United States, women comprise only 21.5% of physicians and dentists but 86.2% of registered nurses, pharmacists, dietitians, therapists, and physician assistants. Blacks and Hispanics represent an even greater discrepancy, regardless of their sex, comprising 3.7% and 4.4% respectively of physicians and dentists. *Statistical Abstract of the United States 1995* (Washington, DC: Government Printing Office, 1995), p. 411.

41. Naomi Breslau, David Salkever, and Kathleen S. Starch, "Women's Labor Force Activity and Responsibilities for Disabled Dependents," *Journal of Health and Social Behavior* 23 (1982): 169.

42. Noddings, p. 31.

43. Christine Eiser, "Psychological Effects of Chronic Disease," *Journal of Clinical Psychology and Psychiatry* 31, 1 (1990): 85–98; Susan Hillier Parks and Marc Pilisuk, "Caregiver Burden: Gender and the Psychological Costs of Caregiving," *American Journal of Orthopsychiatry* 61 (1991): 501–9.

44. Parks and Pilisuk, pp. 501–9.

45. Eiser, pp. 85–98.

46. Eiser, pp. 85–98.

47. For example, A. Kathleen Barlew, Robert Evans, and Carlton Oler, "The Impact of a Child with Sickle Cell Disease on Family Dynamics," *Annals of the New York Academy of Sciences* 565 (1989): 162.

48. On average, women in the United States earn 71 cents for every dollar earned by men. The earning discrepancy between men and women applies to blacks, Hispanics, and whites, but it is greatest between white men and white women. Charity Anne Dorgan, ed., *Statistical Handbook of Working America* (Detroit: Gale Research, 1995), p. 567.

NOTE AND NOTATION FOR CHAPTERS 9, 10, AND 11

THE common goal of Chapters 9–11 is to identify the impact on women of specific genetic conditions: cystic fibrosis (CF), sickle cell disease (SCD), and breast cancer (BC). Whereas BC mainly affects women, CF and SCD mainly affect distinct ethnic groups of men and women. As already noted, an egalitarian feminist standpoint demands attention to actual or potential gender inequity in different ethnic groups.

In the chapters on CF and SCD, both of which are autosomal recessive disorders, I have an additional goal: to address specific gender-related issues that arise in the context of genetic testing for those conditions. The issues targeted are disclosure of misattributed paternity and carrier testing of pregnant women. In the chapter on BC, a multifactorial late-onset disorder for which susceptibility testing is available, I have different additional goals: to assess different approaches to genetic testing and to describe a mechanism for involving those affected in the development of policies about testing.

To ilustrate the issues raised by all three conditions, I describe a specific case in each of the three chapters and provide the relevant genetic pedigree for each. The notation used is illustrated in the table which follows:

Notation Used in Chapters 9–11

STATUS	MALE	FEMALE	SEX UNKNOWN
Individual	□	○	◇
Affected individual	■	●	◆
Deceased individual	⧄	⊘	◇ with slash
Carrier for specific condition	◨	◑	◇ half-filled
Pregnancy	P	P	P
Proband (counselee)	↗□	↗○	↗◇

Based on Robin L. Bennett, Kathryn A. Steinhaus, Stefanie B. Uhrich, C. K. O'Sullivan, R. G. Resta, D. Lochner-Doyle, D. S. Markel, V. Vincent, J. Hamanishi, "Recommendations for Standardized Human Pedigree Nomenclature," *American Journal of Human Genetics* 56 (1995): 745–52.

A relationship between male and female partners is indicated by a horizontal line connecting them. Children or fetuses produced through that relationship are indicated by a vertical line whose origin is the horizontal line that connects their parents. Each child of a particualr set of parents is connected to that vertical line by a horizontal line to which all of the siblings are connected. For example, three generations of unaffected parents and their children might look like this:

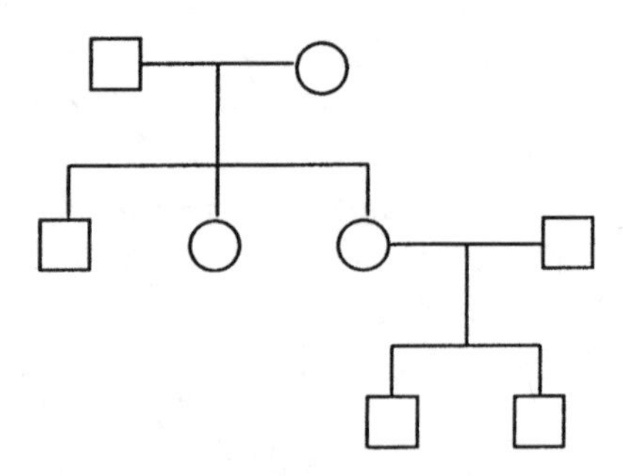

Generic Pedigree

9

CYSTIC FIBROSIS AND MISATTRIBUTED PATERNITY

CYSTIC fibrosis (CF) is the most common autosomal recessive genetic disease affecting the Caucasian population throughout the world. In the United States, its estimated incidence among Caucasians is 1 in 2500, and the incidence of carriers is about 1 in 25.[1] Although CF occurs in other ethnic groups, its estimated incidence in those groups is much less common.[2] As with any autosomal recessive disorder, a couple who are both carriers for CF face a 25% risk in each pregnancy of having a child affected with the disorder, a 50% chance of having a child who is an unaffected carrier, and a 25% chance of having a child who will neither have nor be a carrier for the disorder. Symptoms of CF include airway obstruction, chronic infections, pancreatic insufficiency, biliary tract obstruction, and infertility.[3] In 1997, the median survival age for people with CF in the United States was 32.7 years for males and 28.9 years for females.[4] The symptoms are triggered by a mutation in the gene for a chloride conductance channel, causing abnormally thick and viscid secretions in the respiratory, gastrointestinal, and reproductive tracts.[5]

CF is but one example of a single gene disorder for which one's ethnicity is a risk factor. Other genetic disorders for which this is so include Tay-Sachs disease and sickle cell disease, which mainly affect different populations and have different symptoms. While many symptoms affect men and women equally, some do not. Genetic testing for these disorders raise similar issues, including, occasionally, whether to disclose genetic information about misattributed paternity to the partners of women who are carriers for the condition. "Misattributed paternity" refers to a situation in which the man thought to be the biological father of a child is found, usually through genetic tests, not to be so. An egalitarian feminist standpoint is particularly relevant to this issue because of the gender differences associated with disclosure.

Gender Differences in the Impact of Cystic Fibrosis

Survival curves for males and females with CF seem to diverge at the onset of puberty. This suggests that the gender difference in survival is related to hormonal differences emergent at that time. However, no specific pathophysiology has been discovered in this connection, leading some to think that the poorer nutritional status of women with CF is associated with the impact of gender socialization, particularly as it affects Caucasian women. A stereotype of men as muscular may motivate them to maintain adequate body weight despite the difficulty; a stereotype of thinness as essential to feminine beauty is a disincentive in this regard.[6] In general it is difficult for patients with CF to maintain normal body weight because of their pancreatic insufficiency and malabsorption.

The major gender differences in the clinical manifestation of CF involve fertility and reproduction. Two factors have increased the significance of these differences in recent years: the longer life span of patients with CF due to advances in treatment and improved methods of assisted reproduction. Some 97%–98% of men with CF are infertile due to morphologic abnormalities in the reproductive tract, that is, congenital absence of the vas deferens.[7] Through intracytoplasmic sperm injection (ICSI) of their partners, some men with CF may have biologically related offspring, but this entails ovulation stimulation and embryo transfer in conjunction with in vitro fertilization.[8] In addition to the associated expense and low success rate, these procedures subject women to invasive treatment, risk, and pain or discomfort that their infertile partners do not undergo.

Although women with CF have anatomically normal reproductive tracts, their fertility is considerably reduced due to anovulatory cycles and secondary amenorrhea. Reduced fertility rates are also attributed to abnormally viscid cervical mucus, which impedes sperm motility. Pregnancy in women with CF occurs at less than 20% the rate of a comparable group of healthy women.[9] When women with CF do become pregnant, they face additional risks. These include the potential for respiratory failure and right heart failure brought on by the physiologic changes of pregnancy, especially in women with marginal pulmonary function. Consumption of adequate calories to maintain a healthy pregnancy is often difficult, as is chest physiotherapy late in pregnancy.[10]

Women with CF who wish to have a child face decisions not only about their own health but also about the health of their potential offspring. Fetal well being may be threatened not only by inadequate weight gain but also by the teratogenic potential of antibiotics and other medications required for women with CF.[11] Because they are obligate carriers, any child they conceive will be a carrier as well. If both partners are carriers, each pregnancy entails a 50% chance of the fetus having CF. If both partners are affected, all of their biological children will have the disease. Given the prevalence of male infertility and the reduced fertility of females, however, it is extremely unlikely that affected partners will ever have a child who is genetically related to both. For those unable to conceive and for women for whom pregnancy presents a particular risk, the usual forms of medical assistance offered to infertile couples are available: gamete donation, ICSI, and "surrogacy" with or without their own ova. Gamete donation is a means of avoiding transmission of affected or carrier status in one's offspring. "Surrogacy" is a means of avoiding the health risks of pregnancy. Adoption is another means of providing an individual or couple with a child, but that option would be considerably limited by the unwillingness of placement agencies to choose a parent whose own health is impaired and whose expected life span is shortened by her disease.

Recently, men who are infertile because of congenital bilateral absence of the vas deferens have been discovered to have a CF genotype despite having no other symptoms.[12] This finding raises questions about risks and benefits of disclosure of information to the men themselves as well as to family members for whom the information is relevant to their health or reproductive plans. Because these men are likely to have a normal life span, including them in calculations of survival increases the survival ratio of men with CF as contrasted with women with CF.

Genetic testing for CF does not definitively determine whether an individual is a carrier for the disease. More than 800 CF mutations have been identified to date, but these are not all of the possible mutations, and tests are available for only a fraction of the mutations discovered, most of which are rare.[13] Accordingly, women who wish to avoid having a child with CF cannot totally eliminate their risk even if they and their partners are not known to be carriers, and even if they obtain negative results on all available tests. Preimplantation genetic diagnosis of embryos and prenatal testing can provide relative but not absolute certainty that an embryo or fetus is affected. As the following case illustrates, however, the relative certainty of a genetic diagnosis occasionally provokes genetic counselors to suspect undisclosed paternity regarding a particular child or fetus.

A Case and a Pedigree

Marilyn and Dave Smith, both 27 years of age, visit a genetic counselor when Marilyn is 2 months pregnant with their second child. They have been referred by their obstetrician for prenatal diagnosis for cystic fibrosis (CF) because their first child, Rick, was diagnosed with CF as an infant and died at 7 years of age. If the CF mutation present in the couple is identified, the prenatal diagnosis can be made more accurately. Accordingly, tissue samples are requested from Marilyn and Dave. Marilyn is found to be heterozygous for Δ F508, the most common mutation associated with CF. Dave is not heterozygous for Δ F508, and no other CF mutation can be detected in either partner.

Genetic testing for CF can detect about 90% of the most common mutations for the disorder.[14] Although it is therefore possible that Dave contributed a nondetectable, rare mutation to Rick, there is no genetic test that could verify this, and it is much more probable that he is not Rick's biological father. If Dave is not Rick's genetic father, the risk of CF in the fetus Marilyn is currently carrying is extremely slim. To provide accurate predictive data regarding the risk of CF in this pregnancy, the genetic counselor now faces the question of whether to disclose potentially disturbing information about undisclosed or misattributed paternity to either or both partners.

The genetic counselor has diagramed the family history as in Pedigree 1. The pedigree indicates the relationship between Rick and his parents that the couple disclosed to the genetic counselor through their history and the results of their genetic tests. From a genetics standpoint, however, the pedigree is not credible because Rick could not have had CF unless Dave as well as Marilyn were carriers for the disease. Assuming that Dave is biologically related to the fetus that Marilyn is currently carrying, the diagram could be amended as in Pedigree 2 to reflect the genetic relationship that testing suggests.

Because Rick was their nephew, Dave's siblings probably consider themselves at risk of being carriers of CF also. Information regarding misattributed paternity is thus relevant to decisions they may make with regard to reproduction and genetic testing.[15] In other words, this unrequested information raises issues not only to members of the nuclear family (both social and biological) but to extended family members as well.

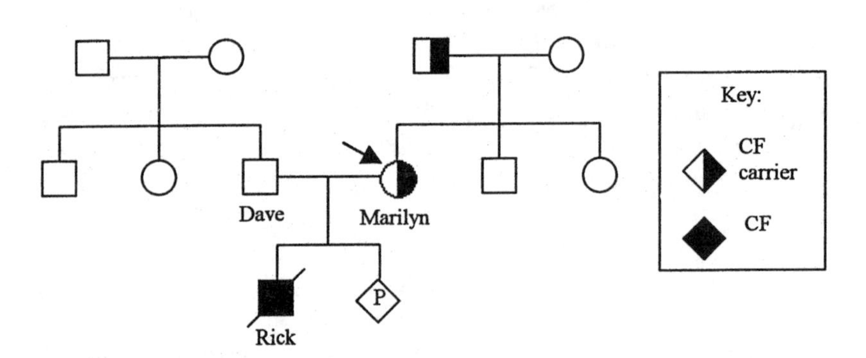

Pedigree 1

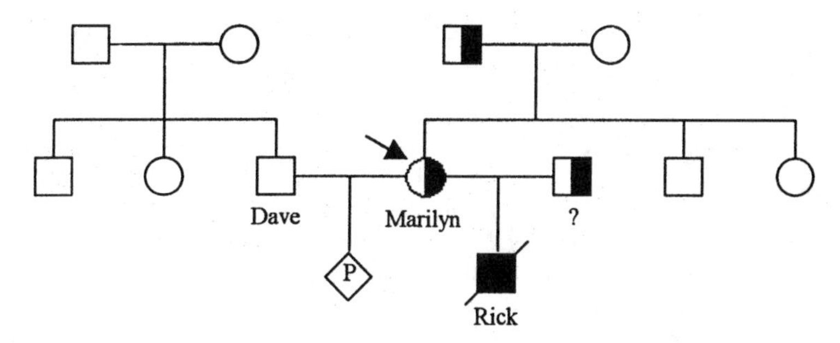

Pedigree 2

Misattributed paternity has been estimated to occur in 10%–15% of the population, but this incidence is not based on published evidence.[16] Nonetheless, parents presumed to be carriers for an autosomal recessive disorder are usually warned in advance that genetic testing may disclose unexpected information regarding paternity.[17] Either or both may then be asked whether they want to be provided with that information. Because the question itself may raise concerns on the part of either partner, asking it may likewise raise concerns for the counselor. These concerns are virtually the same as those faced by genetic counselors who have not indicated to the couple the possibility of obtaining such information. They involve confidentiality toward the woman, the man's right to know, the possibility of family disruption, and the relevance of the information to the child. From an egalitarian feminist standpoint, all of these factors are relevant to determination of whether unanticipated misattributed paternity should be revealed by health professionals to individuals who come for genetic counseling. As we will see in the next section, geneticists and genetic counselors tend to attribute different moral weight to these factors.

Attitudes of Geneticists and Genetic Counselors on Misattributed Paternity

Two sets of authors have documented the attitudes of geneticists and genetic counselors concerning misattributed paternity. In 1985–1986, Dorothy Wertz and John Fletcher surveyed medical geneticists in 19 nations, including the United States; Deborah Pencarinha, Nora Bell, Janice Edwards and Robert Best surveyed genetic counselors in the United States.[18] The medical geneticists had either PhD or MD degrees, but mostly the latter, and the majority (65%) were men. The genetic counselors had masters' degrees in genetic counseling, and the majority (93.5%) were women. The genetic counselors were presented with some of the same scenarios that the medical geneticists had considered. The scenario involving misattributed paternity was the following:

> You are evaluating a child with an autosomal recessive disorder for which carrier testing is possible and accurate. In the process of testing relatives for genetic counseling, you discover that the mother and half the siblings are carriers, whereas the husband is not. The husband believes that he is the child's biological father. Of the following options, which would you choose:
> A. Tell the couple what the lab tests reveal about the child's parentage.
> B. Tell the couple that they are *both* genetically responsible.
> C. Tell the couple that the origin of the child's disorder is not genetic.
> D. Tell the couple that you have not been able to discover which of them is genetically responsible.
> E. Tell the couple the facts about the child's parentage and try to get the name of the child's biological father so he can be told that he is a carrier.
> F. Tell the mother alone, without her husband being present.[19]

All of these options would also be available to a geneticist or genetic counselor involved in the case of Dave and Marilyn. However, there are differences between that case and the scenario presented to the geneticists and genetic counselors: one involves an ongoing pregnancy while the other does not, and testing is definitive in one situation but not the other. One case involves siblings of the affected child, the other may involve siblings of the noncarrier father. Still, the issue of disclosure to the couple or to the woman alone is raised in both instances, and the responses that Wertz and Pencarinha and their colleagues received to their queries about a hypothetical scenario would be equally applicable to the case of Dave and Marilyn.

Genetic counselors typically refer to their clients as couples or families, emphasizing client autonomy without addressing possible conflicts between family members' interests or desires. Nonetheless, an overwhelming majority of the geneticists and genetic counselors in effect affirmed women as their primary client in cases of misattributed paternity. Of the 677 respondents to the questionnaire of Wertz and her colleagues, 96% believed that protection of the mother's confidentiality overrode disclosure of misattributed paternity. Of these, 81% said they would tell the mother alone, without the husband present; 15% would effectively lie by telling the couple that they are both genetically responsible or that there is a new mutation.[20] The main reasons offered for protecting women's confidentiality were preservation of the family unit (58%) and the mother's right to decide what to do with the information (30%). Another 13% cited the woman's right to privacy as their rationale.[21] Interestingly, the women from the United States in this group of medical geneticists were 6.6 times more likely than the men to preserve the mother's confidentiality, and 2.7 times more likely than the men to mention marital conflict as a source of their concern.[22]

When the same case was presented to the genetic counselors from the United States, 98.5% of 199 respondents said they would tell the mother alone. Their reasons were the same as those of the medical geneticists: preservation of the family unit and preservation of client confidentiality.[23] A 1994–1995 survey by Wertz and Fletcher of 1084 geneticists in the United States drew similar responses: two-thirds of the geneticists indicated that they would not tell the woman's partner that he is not the biological father even if he asked for the information.[24]

These views of the geneticists and genetic counselors are supported by the Institute of Medicine (IOM) in the policy recommendation it has proposed regarding cases such as that of Dave and Marilyn. Authors of the IOM report on assessing genetic risks propose "that information on misattributed paternity be communicated to the mother, but not be volunteered to the woman's partner."[25] A practical question that arises for the genetic counselor who follows this recommendation is what to say if asked about paternity by the woman's partner. Unfortunately, the IOM does not offer guidance on this. In disclosing positive test results to the woman, however, the IOM maintains that "If misattributed paternity might alter the interpretation [of the chance of having an affected child], this should also be disclosed.[26] Acknowledging that "This extremely sensitive issue is likely to become increasingly problematic as genetic testing expands," the IOM recommends ongoing research and evaluation of policies regarding misattributed paternity.[27]

When I have presented the scenario that Wertz and her colleagues elaborated to nongeneticist audiences, I have found substantial disagreement with their view. But many are more likely to agree with the position articulated in 1983 by the President's Commission:

> Counselors would seem to have an obligation to both partners counseled. Certainly, if the man were to *ask* about the possibility of nonpaternity, it is difficult to maintain that the counselors ought to withhold the information they have unless disclosure would probably result in a serious and irreversible harm. . . . Full disclosure, combined with careful counseling that goes well beyond information-giving, would seem most likely to fulfill the principles of autonomy and beneficence.[28]

Accordingly, in the remainder of this chapter, I will elaborate arguments for different responses to the issue, assessing these from an egalitarian feminist standpoint.

Arguments For and Against Disclosure of Misattributed Paternity

Depending on who discloses what to whom, unanticipated misattributed paternity may or may not be problematic for genetics professionals. Disclosure by the professional to the woman who is her client is relatively unproblematic, as is, from the standpoint of the professional, disclosure by the woman to the man who had been assumed to be genetically related to their child or fetus. Disclosure to the man discovered through testing to be the genetic father of the child or fetus is beyond the realm of the genetics professional. For the woman-client, however, these potential disclosures may not only be difficult but may raise fears of their consequences to herself or others.

Disclosure to patients of information pertinent to their reproductive plans or health is a prima facie obligation of caregivers who have obtained such information, even when it was not requested. But prima facie obligations may at times be superseded by other prima facie obligations. Justifiable supersession may be based on a utilitarian calculation that more harm would be done through disclosure than nondisclosure or on a deontological calculation that more compelling rights would be violated if the information were disclosed to a specific individual such as the putative father or the genetic father.

The difference between the roles and moral responsibilities of the woman-client and the genetics professional is morally significant. Assuming that the woman is morally obliged to disclose misattributed paternity to her partner, it would not follow that the genetics professional incurs the same obligation in the absence of her willingness to do so. Even if the woman's partner is also a client, obligations to different clients are not necessarily equally compelling.

However, in a well reasoned article on the topic, Lainie Friedman Ross supports the President's Commission view of 1984 against the predominant view of genetic counselors, medical geneticists, and the IOM.[29] She examines the alternatives of disclosure to the woman alone, nondisclosure to either partner, and disclosure to both, finding the last the most morally defensible. While insisting that genetic counselors recognize that both partners are their clients, she adds a third client to be considered: the potential or actual child.

Ross launches her argument with a definition of genetic counseling as "the process by which individuals are informed about the risks to themselves and/or their offspring of genetic diseases and susceptibilities."[30] While this definition accurately identifies the educative role of the counselor, it fails to capture a further role, which, according to the American Society of Human Genetics, involves helping an individual or family to "choose the course of action which seems appropriate to them in view of their risk and the family goals, . . . and [to] make the best possible adjustment to the disorder in an affected family member."[31] To most genetic counselors, facilitating choice and adjustment within families is what makes them genetic counselors rather than genetic educators. Rightly or wrongly, defining counseling in the context of family goals may underlie their resistance to disclosure of misattributed paternity.

Ross is correct that this resistance is at odds with the principle of respect for client autonomy that has dominated the profession of genetic counseling since its inception. If clients are couples, it is also at odds with the American Society of Human Genetics view that genetic counselors should help all of their clients to "comprehend the medical facts, including the diagnosis, the probable course of the disorder, . . . appreciate the way heredity contributes to the disorder, and the risk of recurrence in specified relatives."[32] Respect for autonomy requires disclosure of whatever information is pertinent to the expression of autonomy. Because of the connection between confidentiality or privacy and autonomy, it may also require nondisclosure of information to specific parties. Because different autonomous individuals have different interests and preferences, the key question is not whether to respect autonomy, but whose autonomy is to be given priority.

Although genetic counselors typically refer to their clients as couples or families, many of those who come for counseling are individual women. For Ross, the dilemma about disclosure of misattributed paternity only arises when both partners are present for counseling. Neither the male partner nor the biological father counts as a client unless a counselor–client relationship is established through a visit. When both partners are present, Ross views them as equally clients, both deserving of the unrequested information. "To argue that only women should be informed," she writes, "is to imply that men are second-class citizens in genetic testing. Non-disclosure shows a lack of respect for the male partner as a person, as a client interested in his own genetic make-up, and as a parent interested in his child's genetic endowment."[33]

Consider, however, an analogy between individuals who are equally patients and those who are equally clients. Equal treatment of patients means respecting their different medical needs in different ways. Similarly, equal disclosure of information to clients in the context of genetic counseling could mean no disclosure to either partner, disclosure only of the information requested to both, or disclosure of all of the information obtained to both. To claim that different individuals are equal clients, however, does not necessarily imply that each should receive precisely the same information. Gender justice in this context could mean different disclosure to different clients. Whether disclosure of misattributed paternity to either or both partners is just depends on the benefits and burdens of disclosure to each, as well as respect for their autonomy.

As indicated earlier, the reasons given by geneticists for protecting a woman's confidentiality by not disclosing misattributed paternity to her partner were preservation of the family unit and the woman's right to decide what to do with the information.[34] If we assume that family disruption is a harm and family preservation is a good, the first reason may be supported by the principles of nonmaleficence or beneficence. Avoidance of potential harm to the woman if her partner is told may also be supported by the principle of nonmaleficence.[35] The second reason, however, gives a priority to the woman's autonomy over the man's, assuming that the autonomy of both cannot be satisfied. The genetic counselors attribute to the woman herself the right not to have this intimate information shared with her partner.[36] Her right to confidentiality is thus associated with her right to privacy, and both are required in the context of respect for her autonomy. In other words, the male partner's right to know is subordinated to her right that he not know. That her autonomy trumps his may be defended on grounds of the other two principles, which require a weighing of the harms and benefits to all of those affected by disclosure to him.

From an egalitarian feminist perspective, the validity of this argument depends on the reliability of our estimates of the harms and benefits of disclosure of misattributed paternity. According to Ross, there is little evidence of harm to women or disruption to families brought on by disclosure.[37] Moreover, preservation of families is not always a good for the individuals involved. Women themselves may exercise the right that the genetic counselors want to preserve for them in these cases, that is, the right to do what they wish with the information. If the information is pertinent to the partner's own treatment or life plan, he has a right to disclosure that the woman has an obligation to respect. However, "respect" does not imply conformity. As already suggested, in complex circumstances, the woman may be morally obliged to subordinate her partner's right to know to the rights of others and her responsibilities to them. Whether or not the woman is obliged to disclose misattributed paternity to her partner, or, for that matter, to the genetic father or to their child, her failure to fulfill that obligation does not imply an obligation on the part of the health professional to do so.

Returning to the case with which we started, the narrative tells us nothing about the risks of disclosure to either partner, the genetic father, Dave's siblings, or the potential child. Neither does it tell us whether any of the pertinent parties would want to be given this information. To some extent, then, we are left with too much vagueness or uncertainty to support a decision by the genetic counselor about disclosure. More details might justifiably sway the decision in one direction rather than another. For example, if Marilyn indicated privately to the counselor that she feared for her life if such information were disclosed to Dave, or if Dave indicated privately to the counselor that he would not want to be told such information—either of these details supports nondisclosure. Dave's siblings may all be childless and planning to remain so, making the information about carrier status irrelevant to their life plans. As for the genetic father, he may be deceased or it may be practically impossible to contact him; quite possibly, he would prefer not to know he had a genetic child that he might be legally called upon to support. While such specifics may not be definitively establishable, their degree of probability is morally relevant.

What kinds of details would support disclosure to Dave? Consider the following possibilities: (*1*) after learning that such information might be obtained through testing, Dave asked explicitly to be told; (2) Marilyn asked that they both be provided with whatever information was obtained through their tests; (3) both partners indicated on their visit to a counselor that their relationship would not be disrupted by such information; or (4) one of Dave's siblings was married to a man with CF, and both were worried about having an affected child. While the details that might lead the genetic counselor to disclose or not disclose are practically limitless, an egalitarian feminist standpoint identifies but one general principle on which the details are to be weighed and a decision made. That of course is the principle of justice, which includes gender equality. Assuming then that both partners are desirous of the information, if disclosure to Dave is likely to be more burdensome to Marilyn than to him, the information should not be disclosed to him, and if the disclosure is likely to be more burdensome to Dave, the information should be disclosed to him. Once one goes beyond the couple to consider disclosure to the genetic father, the potential child, or Dave's siblings, the rationale for disclosure needs to be yet more compelling mainly because these individuals are not clients and disclosure therefore seems intrusive or paternalistic.

In real life, as in the case described, one rarely if ever knows all the details that are pertinent to decisions. The best that we can do is to inform ourselves as fully as possible about the nuances of each situation, and take account of these in formulating decisions that maximize the applicable moral values or principles. In the inevitable absence of some details, we invoke valid generalizations as the only means available by which to approximate the real situation. Here is where the gender generalizations that we have identified throughout this book are necessary even though inadequate. The very fact that disclosure of misattributed paternity becomes problematic only when the one disclosing it is not the female client and when the one to whom it may be disclosed is her male partner illustrates a significant, even if unrecognized, awareness of the gender difference that governs this issue. Clearly, the genetic counselors and medical geneticists who balk at disclosure to the partner are acutely aware of the gender difference in the impact of this information.

That said, another pertinent generalization has been scarcely considered in studies of attitudes about misattributed paternity: the view of clients or potential clients. In the context of genetic counseling, they constitute the nondominant group whose input should be regarded as privileged. To the extent that women are nondominant vis-à-vis their male counterparts, their perspective should be regarded as privileged even within the group of clients and potential clients. Fortunately, Wertz and Fletcher recently gathered data from this crucial source. In 1994, they surveyed 473 first-time genetics patients or their parents as well as 988 members of the adult public in the United States, and they found that their attitudes about disclosure were different from the medical geneticists. In general, they were less concerned about privacy and individual autonomy. In contrast to the geneticists, who mainly opposed disclosure to the man even if he asked, three-quarters of the patients, who were mainly women, thought that the doctor should disclose misattributed paternity to men who asked about it. Most, however, thought the doctor should warn the woman first.[38] Wertz comments wryly on this contrast between the geneticists and the nongeneticists: "Perhaps these patients, as first-time visitors to genetics clinics, rather than more experienced consumers of genetics services, have not yet heard the arguments about genetic privacy that are so prevalent in bioethics circles."[39]

These data constitute an important response to the IOM's recommendation that there be more research and evaluation of current policies and practices regarding disclosure of misattributed paternity. In fact, they suggest that the institute recommendation should be revised to adequately reflect the values of those most affected by such disclosure—women. If women themselves are more likely to support rather than reject disclosure by doctors to their partners, policies which preempt that disclosure are paternalistic. Consistent with this view, they would probably support disclosure by other clinicians, including genetic counselors, in addition to doctors. In advocating that the women be warned, the survey respondents are maximizing respect for their and their partner's autonomy while minimizing potential harms to the women. Women may respond to the warning in whatever way they judge best. If preservation of the family unit appears threatened by the disclosure, the nondominant clients most affected by disclosure apparently don't see this as a worse outcome than nondisclosure.

Unless further details suggest otherwise, therefore, clients would recommend that the genetic counselor contact Marilyn and tell her what the genetic test reveals about Dave's paternity, mentioning that this information will be provided to Dave as well. In light of this "warning" and her anticipation of the consequences of disclosure, Marilyn may then decide for herself what to do. Quite possibly Dave knows already anyway.

Notes

1. Office of Technology Assessment, *Cystic Fibrosis and DNA Tests: Implications of Carrier Testing* (Washington, DC: Government Printing Office, 1992), and Lucille A. Lester, Amy Lemke, Dana Levinson, and Mary B. Mahowald, "The Human Genome Project and Women Cystic Fibrosis: A Case Study," *Journal of Women's Health* 4, 6 (1995): 624.

2. The incidence of CF in African Americans is reported as 1 in 17,000; in U.S. Hispanics, 1 in 30,000; in Native Americans, 1 in 80,000; and in Asian Americans, 1 in 90,000. T. F. Boat, "Cystic Fibrosis," in C. R. Scriver, A. L. Beaudet, W. S. Sly, and D. Valle, eds., *The Metabolic Basis of Inherited Disease* (New York: McGraw-Hill, 1989), p. 2649.

3. R. Wilmott and M. A. Fiedler, "Recent Advances in the Treatment of Cystic Fibrosis," *Pediatric Clinics of North America* 41 (1994): 431.

4. *Cystic Fibrosis Patient Registry Life Table Analysis,* U.S. Affiliated Centers—Patients under Care in 1997, Annual Data Report (September, 1998).

5. Lester et al., p. 624.

6. Lester et al., p. 624.

7. L. M. Taussig, C. C. Lobeck, P. di Sant'Agnese, D. R. Ackerman, and J. Kattwinkel, "Fertility in Males with Cystic Fibrosis," *New England Journal of Medicine* 287 (1972): 586; A. R. L. Penketh, A. Wise, M. B. Mearns, M. E. Hodson, and J. C. Batten, "Cystic Fibrosis in Adolescents and Adults," *Thorax* 42 (1987): 526.

8. S. J. Silber, Z. Nagy, J. Liu, H. Tournaye, W. Lissens, C. Feree, I. Liebaers, P. Devroey, and A. C. Van Steirteghem, "The Use of Epididymal and Testicular Spermatozoa for Intracytoplasmic Sperm Injection: The Genetic Implications for Male Infertility," *Human Reproduction* 10, 8 (1995): 2031–43.

9. L. E. Kopito, H. J. Kosadky, and H. Shwachman, "Water and Electrolytes in Cervical Mucus from Patients with Cystic Fibrosis," *Fertility and Sterility* 24 (1973): 512.

10. R. C. Stern, "Cystic Fibrosis and the Reproductive Systems," in P. B. Davis, ed., *Cystic Fibrosis,* vol. 64; *Lung Biology in Health and Disease* (New York: Marcel Dekker, 1993), p. 381.

11. H. Knothe and G. A. Dette, "Antibiotics in Pregnancy: Toxicity and Teratogenicity," *Obstetric and Gynecologic Surgery* 41 (1985): 31. Fetal well-being may also be compromised by vitamin deficiencies in women with CF.

12. Arturo Anguiano, Robert D. Oates, Jean A. Amos, M. Dean, B. Gerrard, C. Steward, T. A. Maher, M. B. White, and A. Milansky, "Congenital Bilateral Absence of the Vas Deferens: A Primarily Genital Form of Cystic Fibrosis," *Journal of the American Medical Association* 267 (1991): 1794. This condition results from a single mutation in the CFTR gene. Whether it is equivalent to CF depends on how one defines the disease.

13. A website maintained by Lap Chee Tsui, one of the discoverers of the CF gene, reports 862 mutations that have been identified (www.genet.sickkids.on.ca/cftr-cgi-bin/FullTable) as of June 4, 1999.

14. E.g., Genzyme Genetics offers screening for 70 common CF mutations, detecting 97% of mutations in Ashkenazi Jews, 90% in northern European Caucasians, 70% in southern European Caucasians, and 72% in African Americans. *Genzyme Genetics* 1, 1 (1998): 3.

15. Although the term "nonpaternity" is sometimes used for "misattributed paternity," I avoid this usage because it suggests that a child has no father, which is impossible (until and unless human cloning from an adult female occurs). Rick apparently has had two fathers, the one who gave him his genes and the one who raised him. The term "undisclosed paternity" would be an acceptable substitute for "misattributed paternity." "False paternity" is less acceptalbe because it suggests that the man who raises a child is not a true father unless he is genetically related to the child.

16. Sally MacIntyre and Anne Sooman, "Non-paternity and Prenatal Screening," *Lancet* 338 (1991): 869; Marie-Gaelle Le Roux, O. Pascal, M.-T. Andre, O. Herbert, A. David, and J. P. Maison, "Non-paternity and Genetic Counseling," *Lancet* 340 (1992): 607; and Denise Salmon, Jeanine Seger, and Charles Salmon, "Expected and Observed Proportion of Subjects Excluded from Paternity by Blood Phenotypes of a Child and Its Mother in a Sample of 171 Families," *American Journal of Human Genetics* 32 (1980): 432–44.

17. Theoretically, misattributed *maternity* can occur as well, but it is extremely improbable because of the tie between gestation and genetics. While the genetic contribution of the father is provided in private, that of the mother is typically visible to others through her pregnant body.

18. Dorothy C. Wertz, "The 19-Nation Survey: Genetics and Ethics around the World," in Dorothy C. Wertz and John C. Fletcher, eds. *Ethics and Human Genetics* (New York: Springer-Verlag, 1989); Dorothy C. Wertz, John C. Fletcher, and John J. Mulvihill, "Medical Geneticists Confront Ethical Dilemmas: Cross-Cultural Comparisons among 18 Nations," *American Journal of Human Genetics* 46 (1990): 1200–1213; and Deborah F. Pencarinha, Nora K. Bell, Janice G. Edwards, and Robert G. Best, "Ethical Issues in Genetic Counseling: A Comparison of M.S. Counselor and Medical Geneticist Perspectives," *Journal of Genetic Counseling* 1, 1 (1992): 19–30.

19. Wertz, Fletcher, and Mulvihill, p. 1203.

20. These statements are effectively lies because they contradict what the medical geneticist believes is true. The test has virtually proven that the male partner is not the genetic father, and the possibility of a new mutation is about one in a million. Wertz, Fletcher, and Mulvihill, p. 1201.

21. Wertz, Fletcher, and Mulvihill, p. 1201.

22. Dorothy C. Wertz and John C. Fletcher, "Ethics and Medical Genetics in the United States: A National Survey," *American Journal of Medical Genetics* 29 (1988): 821.

23. Pencarinha et al., p. 23.

24. Dorothy C. Wertz, "Society and the Not-so-New Genetics: What Are We Afraid Of? Some Future Predictions from a Social Scientist," *Journal of Contemporary Health Law and Policy* 13 (1997): 314. Wertz indicates in this article that the results of their 37-nation survey of geneticists and patients will be published elsewhere and more fuly elaborated in a book.

25. Institute of Medicine, *Assessing Genetic Risks* (Washington, DC: National Academy Press, 1994), p. 6.

26. Institute of Medicine, p. 127 (parenthetical added to give context).

27. Institute of Medicine, p. 175. Note that the committee's recommendation of further research and evaluation of current policies implies an openness to changing the recommendation to support disclosure to putative fathers—if, for example, the risks of harms to the child or mother were shown to be unfounded.

28. President's Commission for the Study of Ethical Problems in Medicine and Biomedical and Behavioral Research, *Screening and Counseling for Genetic Conditions* (Washington, DC: Government Printing Office, 1983), p. 61.

29. Lainie Friedman Ross, "Disclosing Misattributed Paternity," *Bioethics* 10, 2 (1996): 114–30.

30. Ross, p. 114.

31. F. C. Fraser, "Genetic Counseling," *American Journal of Human Genetics* 26 (1974): 636–59.

32. Cited by Fraser, p. 637.

33. Ross, p. 119.

34. Wertz, Fletcher, and Mulvihill, p. 1201.

35. Wertz, Fletcher, and Mulvihill link preservation of the family unit with protection of the child and mother, interpreting both as based on the principle of nonmaleficence (p. 1203).

36. Pencarinha et al., p. 23.

37. "The dominant theme in the family counseling literature," Ross writes, "is that the woman's behavior has no causal influence on the man's decision to batter, but rather, that the problem lies exclusively in the man" (p. 126). However, even if the woman's welfare were threatened by disclosure to her partner, Ross would oppose a policy of nondisclosure on grounds that "most men do not and would not abuse their partners" (p. 127).

38. Wertz, 1997, p. 314. See n. 24.

39. Wertz, 1997, p. 314.

10

SICKLE CELL DISEASE AND CARRIER TESTING

LIKE cystic fibrosis, sickle cell disease (SCD) is an autosomal recessive disorder associated with a specific genetic mutation found predominantly in people of specific ethnic background. In addition to Africans and their descendants, Greeks, Italians (especially Sicilians), Eti-Turks, Arabs, southern Iranians, and Asian Indians have a high incidence of this condition.[1] The term "sickle" drives from the crescent or sickle-shaped red blood cells that are found in different forms in those who have SCD.[2] In some parts of Africa, the incidence among blacks is 1 in 40 at birth, with a carrier frequency of 1 in 3. The high frequency of the trait is attributed to the selective advantage it provides against a form of malaria.[3]

For those who are affected (i.e., those who have SCD), the severity of symptoms varies considerably. Life span is usually foreshortened, with intermittent morbidity. In general, the sicklelike red blood cells have a reduced survival time, leading to severe anemia and recurrent need for blood transfusions. The abnormal structure of the cells also results in the occlusion of vessels, causing tissue ischemia (lack of oxygen) and severe pain crises.[4] Most emergency room physicians in urban areas are familiar with patients who require urgent care because of their acute pain from SCD. Although any part of the body and any organ may be affected by blockage of the blood supply, the heart, lungs, kidneys, spleen, pelvic bones, and brain are particularly vulnerable to this damage.[5]

As with CF, there are gender differences in the impact of SCD on those affected and on those who are carriers for the condition.

Unlike testing for other genetic conditions, sickle hemoglobin testing for SCD has been available for decades. However, the history of this testing in the United States show gross instances of discrimination. In this chapter, I briefly review this history as a reminder of how current advances in genetics may be utilized to impede rather than promote human equality. I also examine an issue that, like misattributed paternity, may arise in the context of testing for any autosomal recessive disorder: prenatal testing of pregnant women who are carriers, whose partners are either unwilling or unable to be tested.

Gender Differences in the Impact of Sickle Cell Disease

Although the symptoms of SCD are similar for men and women, pregnancy exacerbates the risk of pain crises for affected women. Various studies show that pregnant women with SCD are also at greater risk of spantaneous abortion, hypertension or preeclampsia, anemia, and preterm delivery.[6] Infants born to affected women are more likely to be preterm, small for gestational age, and jaundiced.[7] Notably, one study demonstrates that women with sickle cell trait are at significantly higher risk for the same perinatal complications that are associated with those who have SCD.[8] Nonetheless, most women with SCD (and a fortiori, those who have sickle cell trait) experience normal outcomes to their pregnancies. The good outcomes are attributed to "early aggressive prenatal care, effective counseling, and appropriate intervention by providers with a high index of suspicion for factors that lead to untoward outcomes."[9] Accordingly, a study documenting the pregnancy outcomes of women with SCD in 19 centers concludes that "those caring for women with sickle cell disease should support them if they desire to have children."[10] The desire of women with SCD to have children may thus be based on their expectation that the medical system can and will provide them with effective "aggressive prenatal care." From an egalitarian feminist standpoint, however, the added risks that pregnancies entail not only for them but also for their potential children should be fully and explicitly disclosed to them to ensure that their decisions are as informed and free as possible.

Relevant to caregivers of children with SCD, mainly women, is the fact that affected children face an increased risk of psychosocial as well as physical harms because of their condition. Low self-esteem and learning difficulties, for example, are cited as more prevalent in this group than among their peers.[11] Although one study shows no significant differences in self-perceptions of competence and acceptance between children with SCD and their peers, these data are suspect because the raters included parents of those affected, who consistently scored SCD children higher than did the other raters.[12] It is possible, nonetheless, that the parents' perspectives were more accurate than those of the other raters. Young women with SCD are perceived by their peers as less sociable and less well accepted, and young men with SCD are perceived as less aggressive than their male counterparts.[13] In affected adults, a greater frequency of depression and cognitive deficits is reported.[14] Many adults with SCD are underemployed or unemployed because they lack job skills as a result of sporadic school attendance;[15] single women and their children probably feel the impact of this disadvantage more than their male counterparts.

Not only mothers but grandmothers play pivotal roles in caring for children with SCD, undoubtedly experiencing some of the physical and psychological burdens described for primary informal caregivers in Chapter 8.[16] But perhaps the single most influential gender difference associated with SCD involves the feminization of poverty, which disproportionately affects African-American women and their children. Women's access to prenatal counseling and testing is limited not only by their ability to pay but also by the availability of genetic counselors, distance from clinical centers, child care and transportation needs, and language facility. Even when the costs of genetic counseling and tests are covered, termination of pregnancy is often not covered, negating for some the usefulness of the test itself. Some women who would choose abortion cannot do so because they cannot pay for it; others simply would not terminate a pregnancy to avoid having a child with SCD.[17] For those who continue their pregnancies, give birth, and raise affected children, stressors are apparent on many levels, not the least of which is economic. Increased absences from school, medical visits, and hospitalizations of children with SCD result in missed hours of paid work for their mothers, many of whom are the sole support of their families.

It seems reasonable to assume that the experience and standpoint of a caregiver or carrier is different from that of someone affected by a genetic disease, and that this difference would be evident in their views about prenatal testing. That assumption has been supported by a study of the acceptability of prenatal diagnosis for sickle cell anemia by affected women and by parent carriers in Nigeria.[18] Significantly, while the majority (85%) of those studied would like prenatal diagnosis to be offered, only 35% of those affected would terminate an affected pregnancy. In contrast, 63% of the mothers and 51% of the fathers would terminate a pregnancy in which prenatal diagnosis revealed SCD.[19] Religious convictions and a fear of complications of abortion were the main reasons for opposing abortion; a societal emphasis on perfection and their own experience of caring for children with SCD were the main reasons for choosing it.

Various explanations have been offered for the small number of African-American women who avail themselves of the opportunity for genetic counseling, even when it is offered. These include a general distrust of the medical profession and a fear of eugenics; both factors are reinforced by the knowledge or experience of discrimination on the part of many. Some authors suggest that when adequate education is provided, minority women are as interested in genetic counseling as are other women.[20] An ironic challenge to this view comes from a study of low-income African-American mothers of children with SCD. Finding that 79% of them knew about SCD prior to having a child with the disease and 45% knew that they were carriers of the sickle cell trait, the author suggests that the women refrained from prenatal diagnosis in order to protect "their reproductive autonomy by obfuscating SCD medical knowledge" that may have "threatened their motherhood."[21] Presumably, the women could have known their carrier status through their family histories, but clinicians could know it only through disclosure by the women or by test results. As illustrated in the next section, the obfuscation of medical knowledge can impede rather than promote the autonomy of carriers for disorders such as SCD.

The History of Sickle Cell Disease

For decades, more has been known about the genetics of sickle cell disease than about any other genetic disorder, yet incredibly little progress has been made in the development of effective treatment. In recent years, genetic tests have proliferated as an adjunct to the success of the Human Genome Project, but advances in gene therapy have not matched that progress. The gap between detection and therapy is particularly evident in the history of SCD because a simple means of detection, sickle hemoglobin testing, has been available longer than comparable tests have been available for other conditions.

In the early 1970s, Ortho Pharmaceutical Corporation vigorously marketed a solubility test for sickle hemoglobin, and other pharmaceutical companies soon marketed similar tests. Although the blood tests did not distinguish between sickle cell trait (nonsymptomatic carrier status) and SCD, this crucial uncertainty was at best understated in advertisements and marketing strategies as well as educational activities. In Chicago, for example, the Board of Education approved a screening program by the Black Panthers, by which schoolchildren were given the sickle dex test, a solubility test for sickle hemoglobin which does not delineate between sickle cell trait and SCD.[22] Many health workers, physicians, and community activists used this test to screen for sickle hemoglobin in their communities. They had been told that 10% of black school children have SCD, limiting their life expectancy to about 20 years. According to the Black Panthers, Caucasians knew of these mortality and morbidity data but effectively practiced genocide by doing nothing about it.[23] Some of the educational material distributed by advocates of testing suggested that SCD affects only blacks, ignoring the fact that sickle hemoglobin occurs also in other populations. Influenced by this misinformation, some African-American leaders supported the mandatory screening and encouraged members of their organizations to be screened.

Legislative response to the availability of the test only made matters worse. Mandatory sickle cell screening laws were passed in at least 11 states.[24] In 1972, the U.S. Congress passed the National Sickle Cell Anemia Control Act, which called for screening for sickle cell anemia in all people who were "not of the Caucasian, Indian or Oriental race."[25] The preamble to the act illustrated and reinforced the confusion between the trait and the disease. It falsely estimated that 2 million blacks in the United States had sickle cell anemia. The 2 million figure would have been a good estimate for those who had sickle cell trait; fewer than 100,000 would then have been the estimate for those affected.[26] Presumably, the intent of the legislation was to remedy the longstanding neglect of health care needs among Afican Americans, enabling them to take greater control of their lives.[27] Instead, pervasive ignorance about the distinction between carrier and affected status led to widespread discrimination.

In great numbers, those who tested positive for sickle hemoglobin were stigmatized, regardless of the fact that most were nonsymptomatic carriers. In various contexts (marriage licences, entry to school, athletic competitions, employment), African Americans were subject to selective screening not required of others. On the specious grounds that their red blood cells might sickle at high altitudes, those with sickle cell trait were prohibited from entering the U.S. Air Force Academy; others were restricted to ground jobs by major commercial airlines. Women who tested positive were fired from their roles as flight attendants. Health and life insurance rates for carriers escalated, despite the lack of evidence that their risks were any greater than those of noncarriers. These discriminatory, ignorant behaviors introduced impediments to normal functioning into the lives of normal people, creating for some what James Bowman calls "sickle cell psychological nondisease": a sense that one is sick because society says so.[28]

Soon after the National Sickle Cell Control Act was passed, some black community leaders identified and condemned the link between these programs and the minority status of those they affected, describing the programs, as "racially discriminatory, a form of anti-black eugenics, and even a step towards genocide."[29] Apparently, their voices were not heard by the dominant majority. Had they been granted the privileged status that their standpoint deserved, a great deal of pain and injustice might have been avoided. Eventually, the failure and unfairness of the sickle cell screening programs were recognized, but this took some time. It was not until 1981, for example, that the U.S. Air Force Academy removed its ban on flying for those with sickle cell trait. Gradually, broad social agreement developed that the programs were punitive and that correct and adequate information and counseling should have been provided in conjunction with the offer of screening.

From an egalitarian feminist standpoint, these voices from the past need to be remembered as new tests are introduced for more and more genetic conditions. The shocking history of testing for sickle hemoglobin has a great deal to teach us about the possibilities of genetic discrimination, whether it has its origin in ethnic, class, or gender differences. That these differences may be associated with unequal impact upon members of the same nondominant group is evident in the following case. As we shall see, even within the African-American community, scholars differ in their views on the issues it raises.

A Case and a Pedigree

Susan Jones is 26 years old, 10 weeks pregnant, and recently divorced. Although her mother, her brother, and her nephew all have sickle cell anemia, a form of SCD, she and her sister have no symptoms of the condition. However, because their mother has the disease, Susan and her sister have sickle cell trait, making them carriers for SCD. Susan's former husband is indifferent to whether she continues the pregnancy. She does not know his carrier status, and he is unwilling to be tested for sickle cell trait. Although molecular testing of the fetus for all of the known hemoglobin variants is not routinely available, a definitive diagnosis can be provided if both partners' variants are identified. Susan asks her physician for a referral for prenatal testing, but she is refused on grounds that unless her partner is tested also, the result cannot definitively indicate her risk of having an affected offspring. Pedigree 3 describes her situation.

The pedigree shows a substantial history of SCD on Susan's side, but it is obviously deficient in the information it provides about the family history of her former husband. Such a discrepancy in one partner's family history is not unusual; it may be due to the absence of the partner, adopted status of the part-

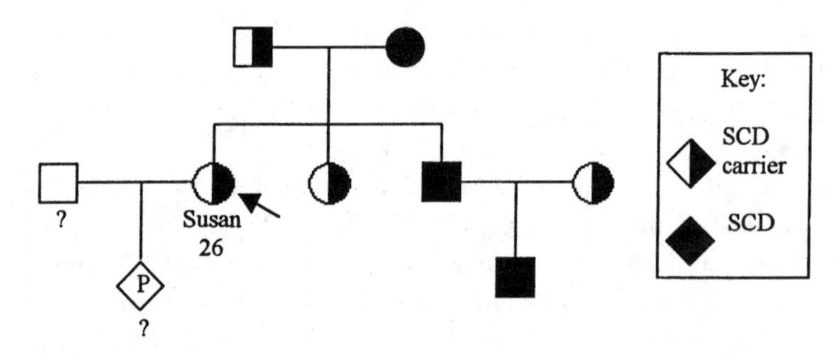

PEDIGREE 3

ner, or the partner's own ignorance of or unwillingness to reveal a family history. If Susan knew that either of her former husband's parents had sickle cell anemia, she would know that he was a carrier without his undergoing testing. Because the risk of SCD to her fetus would then be 1 in 4, she would routinely be offered the option of prenatal testing. However, if the paternal pedigree were fuller but showed no one to be affected with SCD, it still could not exclude the possibility that others are nonsymptomatic carriers for SCD unless genetic tests have ruled that out. Without partner testing, then, Susan is unlikely to obtain a definitive diagnosis of her fetus even if she undergoes prenatal testing.

Prenatal Testing of Carriers without Partner Testing: Pro and Con

Carrier testing for genetic disorders is designed to identify those who may transmit genetic diseases to their offspring but are not symptomatic themselves. Unless they have other disorders, they are healthy individuals. Some of these carriers are women who may transmit X-linked diseases to their sons; others carry a single mutation for an autosomal recessive disorder that will not be expressed in offspring unless their partners also have a mutation for the disorder.

Recently and increasingly, the term "carrier" has been used to identify individuals who are nonsymptomatic but are at risk themselves of developing a specific disease because of a genetic mutation. For some in this group, the onset of the disease is predictable; for others, their carrier status simply indicates susceptibility to the disease. For example, those who are identified through genetic testing as carriers for Huntington disease know that if they live long enough they will develop symptoms, which involve progressive neurological deterioration.[30] In contrast, those who are identified through genetic testing as carriers for breast cancer may be told that they have about an 85% lifetime risk for the disease. As is evident from these examples, possibilities for effective treatment of the diseases for which one may be a carrier vary considerably as well: Huntington disease is as yet incurable; breast cancer is curable if it is detected early enough.

In what follows I examine carrier testing only as it applies to SCD, that is, to individuals who, despite the possibility of transmission to offspring, are expected to remain free of the disease throughout their lifetime. While the history of SCD teaches us that carrier status itself may be stigmatizing, stigmatization presents a moral challenge rather than an ethical dilemma. The moral challenge, to do what one believes is morally right or obligatory, is raised by the fact that there is no ethical dilemma: Stigmatization is clearly wrong. However, a genuine ethical dilemma regarding carrier testing for SCD has been articulated by two experts on the genetics of the disease, James Bowman and Robert Murray, in their book *Genetic Variation and Diseases in People of African Origin.*[31] Despite their collaboration and friendship, Murray and Bowman have decidedly different views on the issue. Murray would agree with the physician who declined to test Susan Jones in the case outlined earlier in the chapter, that is, he would oppose prenatal testing for Susan unless her partner were also tested. In contrast, Bowman believes that Susan's physician should test her regardless of whether her partner is willing to be tested.

Murray's rationale for opposing prenatal testing of African-American SCD carriers unless their partners are also tested for their carrier status is based mainly on two points, the cost effectiveness of the test and support for a traditional image of the family. Prenatal testing alone, he would say, is not cost effective because (*1*) it is not relevant to treatment of the woman herself, and (*2*) the risk of SCD in her fetus cannot be established definitively unless the carrier status of both partners is determined.[32] Moreover, testing pregnant women without testing their partners suggests that men do not play a central role in reproduction and family building, lending support to the high incidence of single woman–headed households in minority communities. In any situation where testing for an autosomal recessive disorder is considered, insistence on testing both partners is a means of upholding the traditional structure of the family.

Although Murray generally supports carrier testing for all individuals at risk (by reason of their ethnicity), prenatal testing of a carrier represents a different situation because of the risk to the fetus that the testing itself involves. This is the same risk of miscarriage that is associated with prenatal tests for other conditions. Bowman believes that this risk to the fetus does not justify refusal of prenatal testing to carriers unless their partners are tested; however, his view does not imply support for prenatal SCD testing of women who are not carriers for the disorder.

Bowman's rationale for disagreeing with Murray is also based on two points, women's autonomy and fairness. If an African-American carrier wishes to undergo prenatal testing for SCD, he would say, she has a right to the test regardless of whether her partner is willing or available to be tested. Respect for the woman's autonomy is buttressed by the fact that this information is relevant to her reproductive plans and by the probability that the impact of having a child with SCD will be greater for her than for her partner. The unfairness of refusing to test a pregnant woman without testing her partner arises from the inconsistency between that practice and the routine availability of prenatal testing for women whose risk is much lower than Susan's, as a known carrier with an African-American partner whose status is unknown. The latter risk is 1 in 40, whereas the risk of fetal abnormality in 35-year-old women who are commonly referred for prenatal testing is approximately 1 in 200.

More reasons and rejoinders can undoubtedly be added to both sides of the issue, and more data on the case of Susan Jones might tilt the disputants in different directions. Murray, for example, might argue that the genetic abnormalities associated with maternal age are more severe than the problems associated with SCD, and that prenatal testing for women over 35 is just as unjustified as, or worse than, prenatal testing of carriers in the absence of partner testing. Alternatively, he might argue that both testing situations are discriminatory or eugenic in intent and in effect. Murray might also suggest that prenatal testing of carriers for SCD, or for any autosomal recessive disease, carries the risk of stigmatizing those tested. The fact that Susan is already subject to that risk does not justify her imposing it on others.

It is possible, of course, that Susan's physician is unaware of her relatively high risk of having an affected fetus if she is a carrier and her partner is an African American. Studies of physicians show that many are woefully deficient in their knowledge of genetics.[33] Patients are frequently more knowledgeable about genetic conditions with which they have experience from their own family histories. Here is a case, then, where imputing a privileged status to the patient could reduce the physician's nearsightedness.

The matter of cost effectiveness needs to be clarified by addressing the question of who pays for the test. If Susan were to pay for it, would Murray still oppose her being tested on that basis? Ordinarily, cost effectiveness is the criterion for determining whether insurance companies or the government will cover specific tests; in that context the test is cost effective so long as its overall economic benefit balances or outstrips its cost. If prenatal testing of SCD carriers resulted in fewer births of children who have costly health care needs to cover, the tests would be cost effective for insurance companies and for the government as well as for individuals who are not insured or covered by government health care policies. Presumably, Murray's rationale is based on a calculation that this criterion would not be met. However, if Susan paid for her own test and its result showed that her fetus was unaffected, the test would incur no cost to others. Alternatively, if she paid for her own test, the result was positive, and she terminated the pregnancy, she would not have an affected child with the concomitant expense of care to the health system and to her.[34] The latter case assumes that abortion of a fetus with SCD is morally acceptable. Without that assumption, Murray's cost effectiveness argument works for him only if Susan does not pay for the test or if she has an affected child whose care must be paid for by others.

Possibly, Murray's position on the requirement of partner testing for pregnant carriers might be influenced by the recent data on increased risk of perinatal complications in women who have sickle cell trait. Those data, which were not available when Murray presented his view on this matter in 1993, support Susan's right to be tested for her own sake, so that she might terminate a pregnancy because of her increased risk. But suppose every African-American woman wanted prenatal testing for SCD regardless of whether she was a carrier, or for that matter, suppose any woman wanted to be tested for one or several autosomal recessive disorders for which they had no family history or ethnic risk: Would Bowman still argue in favor of testing them on grounds of their autonomy? Would he maintain that any woman should have the option of prenatal or carrier testing so long as she can pay for it? Would he argue that genetic testing should be offered to everyone, men as well as women, regardless of their ability to pay? Bowman's support for testing pregnant carriers for SCD would be consistent with opposition to prenatal testing based on maternal age so long as the SCD risk was higher than the maternal age risk. But his patient autonomy argument, ignoring cost effectiveness, would support testing in either case.

In a sense, Bowman's disagreement with Murray represents a realistic rather than idealistic assessment of the African-American family. According to Bowman, the pregnancy rate of single women is so high and their partners are so often unavailable or unwilling to be tested that it is unfair to deprive them of an opportunity for testing, while other women have that opportunity. Moreover, whether single or not, women whose partners are unavailable or unwilling to be tested are likely to find an affected pregnancy more burdensome than those whose partners are tested. While Bowman does not regard support for single women being tested without partner testing to demean the ideal of family that Murray is concerned about, he does insist that single woman–headed families be respected as well.

Despite Murray's probable support for the physician's refusal in the case of Susan Jones, her desire to undergo prenatal testing may in fact be supportive of his ideal of family. She may, in fact, be morally opposed to abortion but want to have this information to facilitate her preparation for the birth of this particular child, whether affected or not. Having been raised by a woman with sickle cell anemia in a family with an affected brother, she may well be influenced in her decision to continue or terminate the pregnancy by that experience. Either decision may be based on "family values." As Carol Gilligan's research illustrates, women's decisions to terminate pregnancy are typically driven by concerns for others to whom they are related.[35]

The "family values" rationale that underlies Murray's position is questionable in its own right because there are diverse meanings of family and different values that may be attributed to those different meanings. I have elsewhere developed a conception of family that is consistent with an egalitarian feminist standpoint: "a set of people who are indefinitely committed to care for each other and for those dependent on them."[36] This definition is open to a wide variety of arrangements, including single or married parents and their children, whether or not the latter are genetically related, and homosexual couples with or without children. As used here, the term "care" suggests emotional attachment as well as supportive action. A commitment involves a decision, and an "indefinite" commitment suggests no limit to the duration of care to which family members as such are committed.

Murray's notion of family seems narrower than the above definition because he insists on involvement of the male partner, at least to the extent of being tested, whether or not he is emotionally attached to or actively supportive of the woman who requests testing. Possibly the role of the potential genetic father figures more significantly in his view. From a feminist point of view, which rejects patriarchal concepts of family, his insistence on the male role is unacceptable even if the male role is not dominant. From an egalitarian feminist point of view, it would also be unacceptable to ignore or preclude the man's involvement.

Bowman's position is consistent with an egalitarian feminist standpoint because it recognizes and responds to the gender inequities that refusal of prenatal testing entails for women who are carriers for SCD. The fact that women are most likely to bear most of the burdens of raising a child with SCD strengthens his argument for testing on grounds of their request, without requiring the partner's test. Both Bowman and Murray would support the offer of SCD carrier testing to African-American men and women, but their rationales would probably differ. Consistent with his view on prenatal testing for SCD, Murray would emphasize the cost effectiveness of testing at-risk individuals, even those who cannot pay for the tests themselves. He might also argue that both men and women should know their carrier status because of its relevance to their family planning. Bowman would probably present a more liberal argument: that individuals at risk have a right to be tested based on respect for their autonomy as well as cost effectiveness. Arguments based solely on respect for autonomy would support the availability of genetic tests, both prenatally and postnatally, for anyone who desires such testing, regardless of their risk status. These represent a libertarian perspective, which may or may not be feminist as well. As an egalitarian feminist, I concur with Bowman's liberal argument but demur from support of carrier testing for anyone, whether pregnant or not, solely on grounds of the individual's desire for the test and ability to pay for it.

Notes

1. James E. Bowman and Robert F. Murray, *Genetic Variation and Disorders in Peoples of African Origin* (Baltimore, MD: Johns Hopkins University Press, 1990), p. 192.

2. Mabel Koshy, "Sickle Cell Disease and Pregnancy," *Blood Review* 9, 3 (1995): 157–64, and Bowman and Murray, p. 198.

3. J. B. S. Haldane, "The Rate of Mutation of Human Genes," *Proceedings of the Seventh International Congress of Genetics Heredity* 35 (1949, suppl.): 267, and A. C. Allison, "Protection Afforded by Sickle-Cell Trait against Subtertian Malarial Infection," *British Medical Journal* 1 (1954): 290–94.

4. J. M. Connor and M. A. Ferguson-Smith, *Essential Medical Genetics,* 4th ed. (London: Blackwell Scientific Publications, 1993), p. 76.

5. Bowman and Murray, p. 196.

6. S. Adams, "Caring for the Pregnant Woman with Sickle Cell Crisis," *Professional Care of Mother and Child* 6, 2 (1996): 34–36; R. J. Howard, S. M. Suck, and T. C. Pearson, "Pregnancy in Sickle Cell Disease in the UK: Results of a Multicentre Survey of the Effect of Prophylactic Blood Transfusion on Maternal and Fetal Outcome," *British Journal of Obstetrics and Gynaecology* 102, 12 (1995): 947–51.

7. A. K. Brown, L. A. Sleeper, C. H. Pegelow, S. T. Miller, F. M. Gill, and M. A. Waclawiw, "The Influence of Infant and Maternal Sickle Cell Disease on Birth Outcome and Neonatal Course," *Archives of Pediatric Adolescent Medicine* 148, 11 (1994): 1156–62.

8. K. D. Larrabee and M. Monga, "Women with Sickle Cell Trait Are at Increased Risk for Preeclampsia," *American Journal of Obstetrics and Gynecology* 177, 2 (1997): 425–28.

9. O. A. Rust and K. G. Perry Jr., "Pregnancy Complicated by Sickle Hemoglobinopathy," *Clinical Obstetrics and Gynecology* 38, 3 (1995): 472–84.

10. J. A. Smith, M. Espeland, R. Bellevue, D. Bonds, A. K. Brown, and M. Koshy, "Pregnancy in Sickle Cell Disease: Experience of the Cooperative Study of Sickle Cell Disease," *Obstetrics and Gynecology* 87, 2 (1996): 199–204.

11. C. Tate Holbrook and George Phillips, "Natural History of Sickle Cell Disease and the Effects on Biopsychosocial Development," *Journal of Health and Social Policy* 5, 3–4 (1994): 7–18; Cary Davis, "Sickle Cell Anemia: An Overview Posing an Employment Quandary," *Vocational Evaluation and Work Adjustment Bulletin* 28, 1 (1995): 20–23; Morris Cohen, Walter Branch, Virgil McKie, and Robert Adams, "Neuropsychological Impairment in Children with Sickle Cell Anemia and Cerebrovascular Accidents," *Clinical Pediatrics* 33, 9 (1994): 517–24. The cognitive deficits are associated with the greater frequency of strokes in children with SCD.

12. Kathleen L. Lemanek, Wendy Horwitz, and Kwaku Ohene-Frempong, "A Multiperspective Investigation of Social Competence in Children with Sickle Cell Disease," *Journal of Pediatric Psychology* 19, 4 (1994): 443–56.

13. Robert Noll, Kathryn Vannatta, Kristine Koontz, Karen Kalinyak, W. M. Bukowski, and W. H. Davies, "Peer Relationships and Emotional Well-Being of Youngsters with Sickle Cell Disease," *Child Development* 67, 2 (1996): 423–36.

14. Mary Sano, Rita Haggerty, Steven Kugler, and Brenda Martin, "Neuropsychological Consequences of Sickle Cell Disease," *Neuropsychiatry, Neuropsychology, and Behavioral Neurology* 9, 4 (1996): 242–47; Jennifer J. Wilson, Karen M. Gil, and Lauren Raezer, "Self-Evaluation, Coping, and Depressive Affect in African American Adults with Sickle Cell Disease," *Cognitive Therapy and Research* 21, 4 (1997): 443–57.

15. Davis, pp. 20–23.

16. Peggye Dilworth-Anderson, "The Importance of Grandparents in Extended-Kin Caregiving to Black Children with Sickle Cell Disease," *Journal of Health and Social Policy* 5, 3–4 (1994): 185–202. The great majority of grandparent caregivers are grandmothers. Some studies suggest that caring for children with SCD is no more stressful than caring for children without the condition; e.g., Robert B. Noll, Eleanor Swiecki, Maria Garstein, Kathryn Vannatta, Karen Kalinyak, W. H. Davies, and William Bukowski, "Parental Distress, Family Conflict and Role of Social Support for Caregivers with or without a Child with Sickle Cell Disease," *Family Systems Medicine* 12, 3 (1994): 281–94.

17. Cultural differences may play a significant role in these decisions as well. In a study of genetic counseling for hemoglobinopathies (thalassemias), for example, Peter Rowley and his colleagues concluded that black women often would not terminate a pregnancy for any reason but Southeast Asians frequently accepted abortion. Peter T. Rowley, S. Loader, C. J. Sutera, M. Walden, and A. Kozyra, "Prenatal Screening for Hemoglobinopathies I: A Prospective Regional Trial," *American Journal of Human Genetics* 48 (1991): 439–46.

18. M. A. Durosinmi, A. I. Odebiyi, I. A. Adediran, N. O. Akinola, D. E. Adegorioye, and M. A. Okunade, "Acceptability of Prenatal Diagnosis of Sickle Cell Anaemia (SCA) by Female Patients and Parents of SCA Patients in Nigeria," *Social Science and Medicine* 41, 3 (1995): 433–36.

19. Presumably, this means that 51% of the men would support their partner's decisions to terminate their pregnancies.

20. E.g., Rayna Rapp, "Women's Responses to Prenatal Diagnosis: A Sociocultural Perspective on Diversity," in Karen H. Rothenberg and Elizabeth J. Thomson, eds., *Women and Prenatal Testing: Facing the Challenges of Genetic Technology* (Columbus: Ohio State University Press, 1994), p. 222. On the basis of her empirical studies of women from different cultural groups at different clinics in New York, Rapp observes that "class-based experiences" are intertwined cultural legacies in shaping women's interest in prenatal testing. A pivotal factor in determining their openness to genetic counseling is whether they feel comfortable and welcome at their first prenatal clinic visit (pp. 222–23).

21. Shirley A. Hill, "Motherhood and the Obfuscation of Medical Knowledge: The Case of Sickle Cell Disease," *Gender and Society* 8, 1 (1994): 29–47.

22. James E. Bowman, "Genetic Screening and Public Policy," *Phylon* 38 (1977): 123. Neither could this test identify hemoglobin variants other than hemoglobin S; potential parents with some hemoglobin variants have a 1 in 4 risk of offspring with SCD if their partners have sickle cell trait.

23. Bowman, p. 124.

24. Bowman, p. 126. The 11 states were Massachusetts, Illinois, Virginia, New York, Georgia, Mississippi, Arizona, Louisiana, New Mexico, Kentucky, and Maryland.

25. Daniel J. Kevles, *In the Name of Eugenics: Genetics and the Uses of Human Heredity* (New York: Alfred A. Knopf, 1985), p. 278. "Sickle cell anemia" generally refers to SCD in individuals who have inherited hemoglobin S (cf. "sickle") from both parents. Other patients with SCD may have the S hemoglobin plus another hemoglobin abnormality or a defect in hemoglobin production. Not all patients with SCD have anemia. Cf. James E. Bowman and Eugene Goldwasser, *Sickle Cell Fundamentals* (Chicago: University of Chicago Press, 1975), p. 9.

26. Kevles, p. 278. Based on the population and risk of African ancestry, Bowman calculates a more accurate estimate as 30,000–50,000. Personal communication, May 26, 1998.

27. According to Bowman, the quest for the African-American vote was a major political motivation for the legislation. Personal communication, October 24, 1998.

28. Bowman, Personal communication, June 2, 1998.

29. Kevles, p. 278.

30. Because the prediction that an individual who tests positive for Huntington disease will become symptomatic is so definitive, the positive test is viewed by some as indictive of having the disease rather than being a carrier for it.

31. Bowman and Murray, see n. 1, this chapter.

32. Because of the impossibility of testing for all of the possible mutations for cystic fibrosis, this argument is more compelling with regard to prenatal tests of women who are carriers for that disorder. To my knowledge, however, no one has maintained that pregnant carriers of cystic fibrosis should be denied testing unless their partners are tested. Given that SCD and cystic fibrosis mainly affect different ethnic groups, it is not unreasonable to suspect that ethnic biases affect attitudes and practices about prenatal testing for these conditions.

33. Karen J. Hofman, Ellen S. Tambor, Gary A. Chase, Gail Geller, Ruth Faden, and Neil Holtzman, "Physicians Knowledge of Genetics and Genetic Tests," *Academic Medicine* 68 (1993): 625–31; Neil A. Holtzman, "Primary Care Physicians as Providers of Frontline Genetic Services," *Fetal Diagnosis and Therapy* 8, suppl 1 (1993): 213–19.

34. A caveat to this conclusion arises from the fact that a partner could falsely represent his carrier status. While unlikely, Susan could eliminate this risk by insisting on seeing her partner's test result.

35. Carol Gilligan, *In a Different Voice: Psychological Theory and Women's Development* (Cambridge: Harvard University Press, 1982).

36. Mary Briody Mahowald, *Women and Children in Health Care: An Unequal Majority* (New York: Oxford University Press, 1993), p. 240.

11

GENETIC TESTING FOR SUSCEPTIBILITY TO BREAST CANCER

IN previous chapters I dealt with conditions that are called genetic diseases because genetic mutations alone trigger their onset; here I consider a disease which is more informatively called "complex" rather than genetic because genetics is only partly "responsible" for its expression, and then only in some cases.[1] Breast cancer (BC) is different from cystic fibrosis and sickle cell disease in other respects: it is multifactorial rather than monogenic, it is not expressed in infancy but only later in life, and it mainly affects women. Because genetic testing for BC cannot definitively establish whether an individual will develop BC, it differs from another late onset disease for which testing is available and which, like cystic fibrosis and sickle cell disease, is monogenic: Huntington disease. Despite these differences, the lessons learned from genetic testing for single-gene disorders may be helpful in determining policies for provision of genetic tests for susceptibility to BC.

In this chapter, I consider the impact of BC on women, noting how this is influenced by gender stereotypes. Despite its gender specificity, issues raised by the availability of genetic testing for BC have become paradigmatic for those raised by susceptibility testing for other disorders. To provide the context for an assessment of options regarding genetic testing for susceptibility to BC, I describe a case that raised questions of confidentiality about disclosure of test results. Because of its relevance to feminist standpoint theory, I also examine a recent effort to reduce the inevitable myopia of BC researchers and reviewers of their research: the inclusion of nonscientists in the evaluation of proposals for funding BC research by the U.S. Department of Defense. A similar strategy, I argue, is needed in the development of procedures for offering or providing genetic tests for BC.

Impact of Breast Cancer on Women

Approximately 1 in 8 women who live to age 85 develop BC at some point during their lives.[2] Throughout the world, BC is the second leading cause of cancer death in women, behind lung cancer. In the United States, the incidence of BC has been increasing by about 2% each year; this is attributable to the increase of older women in the population, earlier onset of menarche, later onset of menopause, delayed childbearing or nulliparity, and decreased breast feeding.[3] Although age is the most important risk factor for BC, 40% of the cases are diagnosed in women less than 60 years of age. BC is the main cause of cancer death among women between 15 and 54 years of age. Additional risk factors include family history, prolonged use of exogenous estrogens, excessive consumption of alcohol, and substantial exposure to radiation.[4] Because African Americans are typically diagnosed at more advanced stages of disease than Caucasians, they have uniformly lower survival rates for BC.[5] Hereditary BC accounts for 5%–10% of all BC and as many as 15% of women under 30 years of age or 25% of early onset cases.[6]

Although knowledge of risk factors often triggers avoidance that may limit the incidence of a disease, this is hardly possible with BC for several reasons. First, over 75% of BC cases are not associated with any major risk factor, and all of the risk factors combined explain less than 30% of its incidence.[7] Second, several of the major risk factors refer to unchangeable features of the individual (family history, race, age at menarche and menopause), and third, preventive interventions such as tamoxifen and prophylactic mastectomy may not be effective.[8]

As with other cancers, the main symptoms of BC are tumors whose unchecked growth may spread to other parts of the body, causing pain, weakness, loss of function, and eventual death. Modes of treatment include radiation, surgery, and chemotherapy. Autologous bone marrow transplantation has increasingly been used in cases of metastatic BC.[9] All of these treatments are iatrogenic in their own right. Although temporary disfigurement through hair loss as a side effect of treatment affects both men and women, this side effect is particularly distressing to women because of societal expectations regarding their appearance. Not only is a woman's baldness jarring to others, as it is not in men, but the experience of hair loss is a greater source of anguish to some women, at least temporarily, than the loss of their breast. As one put it at a meeting in 1994, "To wake up each morning and find my pillow littered with tufts of hair and see my head developing bald spots, felt worse than waking up from surgery to find my breast removed, as had been expected."[10] Acknowledging the educative impact of a similar experience on her own interactions with patients, one physician wrote: "Losing my hair was more upsetting than any of the other physical consequences of cancer therapy."[11]

Although wigs and breast prostheses or reconstruction are broadly utilized means of dealing with the side effects of treatment for BC, the suffering associated with treatment is surely exacerbated by stereotypes regarding women's appearance. For women of reproductive age, it may also be exacerbated by the loss of their capacity to nurse a child. Along with gender identity, sexual interactions are often threatened not only by the disease and its treatment but by the diagnosis itself and by fear of its expression based on family history. A feminist standpoint calls for efforts to reduce the suffering associated with gender stereotypes. This includes rejection of the idealized feminine image popularized by the media, attracting profits for its perpetrators. In a sense, the wigs and prostheses represent acquiescence to a feminine stereotype. Nonetheless, individual women who have already been affected by gender socialization ought not be held hostage to the social critique of feminists who challenge its influence. Egalitarian feminists can consistently support attempts to alleviate the suffering of individual women by helping to restore them to the appearance they had prior to their treatment, even while they do battle with the gender and other group-based stereotypes that exacerbate the suffering of these women.

Surgical options when BC is detected may be radical or conservative. Many studies indicate that lumpectomy patients have a better sense of body image, femininity, and sexual attractiveness than mastectomy patients, but other quality of life factors are apparently the same with either treatment modality.[12] Understandably, the greatest concern of most patients is survival, which explains the interest of some in prophylactic mastectomy. Although the procedure cannot ensure against recurrence or onset of BC, some individuals believe prophylactic mastectomy is the best safeguard available to them. Even before genetic tests for susceptibility to BC were introduced, family histories of the disease led some unaffected women to undergo prophylactic mastectomy. The current availability of tests for susceptibility to BC as well as ovarian cancer is likely to increase the incidence of prophylactic surgery as a means by which to thwart the onset of both diseases.

Less than 1% of all cases of BC occur in men, who are not as likely as women to suffer the anguish associated with hair and breast loss. Still, the disease carries comparable mortality and morbidity rates for both sexes.[13] In fact, BC may carry a particular onus for men precisely because it is generally identified with women, and men are unlikely to have support groups available to them as women do. While women with BC may suffer from the loss of feminine image that treatment involves, men may be embarrassed or feel that their gender identity is threatened by the relationship to feminine image that BC suggests. Both sources of suffering are triggered by gender stereotypes.

Just as women who are unaffected carriers for X-linked diseases may feel guilty for having transmitted a genetic disease to their sons, men who are unaffected carriers of a mutation in a BC susceptibility gene may feel guilty if they transmit the altered gene to their daughters. Preliminary data suggest that men who are carriers of mutations in BC susceptibility genes have an increased risk of prostate cancer.[14] Nonetheless, men are rarely tested to determine whether they are carriers for BC susceptibility. Possibly this is because genetic testing for BC has only recently become available and because most instances of BC are not attributable to family history anyway. In contrast, when a woman gives birth to a son with an X-linked disease, it is clear even without a genetic test that she has transmitted it.

Whether or not genetic risk for BC is transmitted by either parent, unaffected daughters of women with BC apparently face psychological burdens also. In a 1991 study comparing 30 daughters of women who had died from BC or its complications with daughters of women without BC, the former group exhibited significantly less frequent sexual intercourse, lower sexual satisfaction, and greater feelings of vulnerability to BC.[15] Although this study was done before the availability of genetic testing for BC risk, the daughters' fears were probably based on recognition that BC sometimes "runs in families." The pedigree that follows illustrates that possibility for the untested daughters of an untested woman. Negative genetic tests could conceivably alleviate some of these fears, but all of our daughters face the relatively high risk of BC that is applicable to women in general.

A Case and a Pedigree

Beth Brown is a 39-year-old widow who works for a software company. She has two daughters, ages 12 and 14. Beth's grandmother died of ovarian cancer (OC), her mother had a mastectomy for breast cancer (BC) 10 years ago; and her sister was recently diagnosed with BC and treated with a lumpectomy. A genetic counselor would diagram this family history of cancer as in Pedigree 4.

Responding to an offer of free testing for people with a strong family history of cancer, Beth had her blood drawn for testing at the university hospital near her home. On returning to work, she read through her employee health coverage documentation and discovered that she would receive no benefits for conditions that existed prior to her employment. She also learned that her health

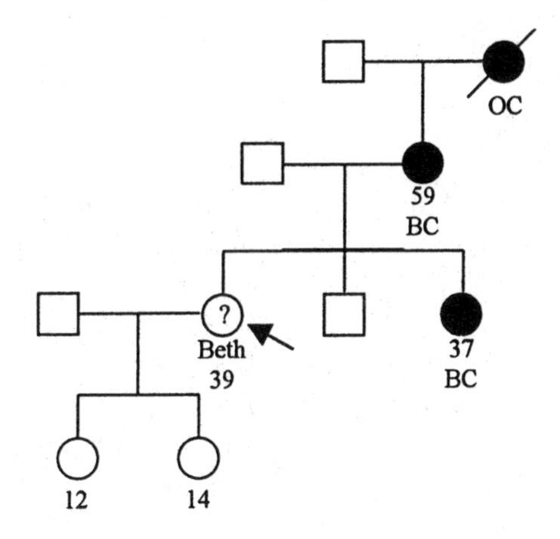

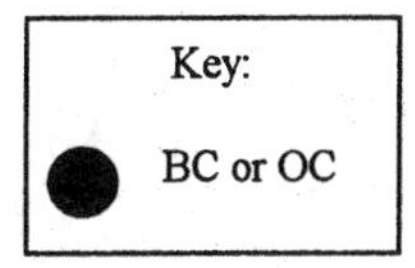

PEDIGREE 4

records were subject to review by the company's insurer, and that if preexisting conditions had not been reported at the time of employment, her entire coverage could be denied.

Concerned about the implications of this information for her health coverage, Beth called the cancer risk clinic where her blood had been drawn and asked that the test not be performed. She was told that the sample had been sent to the lab, and the test had probably been done. Beth indicated that she did not want to be informed of the result, and she did not want her health record to show that she had been tested. By the time her physician learned of her request, he knew the test result: it was negative. The dilemma he then faced was whether to respect her autonomy by refraining from disclosure of the test result or to give her the good news that she had no identifiable genetic risk for BC.

This dilemma is but one of the ethical issues raised by the advent of genetic testing for susceptibility to late onset disorders. Others include the relevance of test results to family members such as Beth's daughters, the possible psychological harm of being told "bad news," and the risk that a negative result might precipitate neglect of preventive behaviors that remain important to the person's health. Beth, for example, might decide to skip her monthly self-examination or regular mammography if she learns that she has not inherited any of the known genetic mutations for susceptibility to BC. Ironically, not informing her of the test result could be defended by opposing points of view: the paternalistic rationale that nondisclosure would prevent her from becoming lax in preventive practices, and the rationale of respect for her autonomy in requesting that she not be told. However, the latter rationale may also support disclosure of the negative test result if the clinician employs the strategy of asking Beth whether she would like to know the result if it is good news. Neither "good news" nor "bad news" is definitive; the former merely connotes a lesser probability than the latter.

The goodness or badness of news obtained from genetic testing for susceptibility to specific conditions is determined by a host of medical as well as psychosocial factors, which may not be identifiable or predictable. With testing for susceptibility to BC, as for susceptibility to other complex disorders, the scientific factors alone present a complex picture.

Genetic Testing for Susceptibility to Breast Cancer

At least four genes are responsible for genetic susceptibility to BC.[16] These genes differ dramatically with regard to the risks of BC that they confer, the incidence of BC that they explain, and the other cancers and phenotypes with which they are associated. Although inherited susceptibility accounts for only a small percentage of BC, these forms of the disease tend to appear earlier in life because the cancer-causing mutation is present in all cells from birth onward, giving the cells an increased susceptibility to other genetic mutations. When the genetically predisposed cells have accumulated multiple genetic mutations within them, the control of cell growth and proliferation is lost and cancer occurs.[17] Women who have this inherited susceptibility to BC face a 50% risk of developing the disease by 50 years of age. However, the odds that women from families with BC alone have a BRCA1 mutation are 7 in 100.[18] Prophylactic mastectomy can reduce but not totally exclude their risk.[19]

The risk of ovarian cancer also escalates for women who have the BRCA1 mutation. Unlike BC, which can be diagnosed early enough for effective treatment, diagnosis of ovarian cancer usually occurs at a much later stage because the symptoms are not manifest until the disease is more advanced. The later detection greatly reduces the possibility of successful treatment. Prophylactic oophorectomy is thus a reasonable option for women in whom a mutation on the gene known as BRCA1 is detected. However, ovarian-type cancers can occur in the peritoneal cavity lining the abdominal wall even after oophorectomy. As with prophylactic mastectomy for BC, prophylactic oophorectomy is not an absolute safeguard against ovarian cancer.

Identification of the susceptibility genes BRCA1 and BRCA2 has led many women with family histories of BC to seek genetic testing to determine their risk. These genes are apparently responsible for 80% of the BC that occurs in families with a high incidence of early onset breast or ovarian cancer.[20] Risk estimates have mainly been based on studies of high-risk or high-penetrance families; they may need to be modified when data are obtained from a broader range of subjects. Even if the estimate is revised downward, however, the overall risk of BC to women will remain high enough to motivate many, including those with no family history at all, to seek testing for genetic susceptibility.

Genetic testing for BC risk is complicated by the fact that the BRCA1 and BRCA2 genes are so large that a huge number of mutations is possible, and not all of these connote susceptibility to BC.[21] Further, many of the mutations occur throughout both genes, with few recurrences.[22] Because of these limitations, genetic testing for susceptibility to BC is relatively uninformative for the majority of women.[23] Until and unless a reliable assay for most or all of the different mutations is developed, genetic tests for BC risk are hardly justifiable on the basis of cost effectiveness or beneficence toward all women. As already suggested, an additional concern is that negative test results may deter women from practices that could ensure early detection. A libertarian version of feminism would nonetheless support the availability of genetic tests for BC risk for all women—at least so long as they can pay for them.

An egalitarian version of feminism would endorse a more complicated approach to testing for this complex genetic disorder. It would consist of two elements:

1. The availability of genetic counseling and tests for susceptibility to BC to all women who are at high risk for the disease.
2. Funding for genetic counseling and tests for BC risk for those women who are at high risk for the disease but have no means of paying for the counseling and test, whether through insurance or out of pocket.

An individual woman is at high risk for hereditary BC if two of her first-degree relatives—for example, her mother and her sister—have breast or ovarian cancer, particularly if the disease has had an early onset in the affected relatives. Early onset usually means prior to menopause. A woman is also at high risk if a germ line mutation (BRCA1 or BRCA2) is detected in an affected member of her family. These factors increase both the risk and the informativeness of a genetic test for susceptibility in individuals, who may be screened for the same mutation found in their affected relatives.[24] If Beth's mother were to test positive for a germ line mutation, that result alone would indicate that Beth has a 50% chance of inheriting the mutation. If her mother were to test negative, Beth's risk is uncertain.

In comparison with genetic screening or testing of all women for BC, limiting the availability of genetic tests to those who are at high risk is more compelling because it is more likely to be cost effective. It may be argued that positive test results would motivate the women tested to engage in early detection practices and life-style practices that may thwart the onset of the disease; in fact, however, there is little evidence that this occurs. Considerations of cost effectiveness also include recognition of the need to improve the specificity and sensitivity of tests for hereditary BC so that eventually they may be available to all women on a cost effective basis. Obviously, this can be done only if genetic testing of some women continues. From an egalitarian feminist standpoint, women at high risk are most deserving of that option, and poor women at high risk are as deserving of the option as are affluent women at high risk. Women at high risk who can pay for genetic counseling and testing should pay for it; if and when it is cost effective, insurance companies will cover these activities. For women at high risk who are not covered by insurance or have no means of their own to pay for genetic counseling and testing for BC, society should cover their expense, just as it provides for other essential health services for the poor.

Because testing is not without its risks, genetic counseling should not be seen as dispensable unless the woman is already fully informed about its implications. Decisions to be tested cannot be autonomous, as they ought to be, unless these risks, along with uncertainties regarding interpretation of the test result, are understood. As the case of Beth illustrates, genetic testing for susceptibility to BC includes not only psychological burdens but also economic risks such as the potential loss of health coverage or employment benefits. Individuals vary considerably in the weight they attribute to these different risks. Had Beth already been aware of her potential for loss of health coverage, she might have declined to be tested.

In a health care system that allows affluent people to buy health services that the poor cannot afford, some individuals can and do buy tests that are not medically indicated, that is, not recommended on medical grounds. Testing women at high risk for BC may be construed as testing for medical indications; testing any woman who wishes to be tested has not been recommended on medical grounds. As with other medical tests and treatment, however, genetic counseling and tests for susceptibility to BC have been offered to those who are not at high risk so long as they can pay for them. In other words, a third element has been added to those listed previously:

3. The permissibility of genetic counseling and tests for BC risk to women not known to be at high risk of the disease so long as they are covered by insurance or pay for the test and counseling themselves.

This element is defensible on grounds that it challenges the paternalism that may be involved in refusing to test those who are not at high risk who nonetheless wish to be tested. From an egalitarian feminist point of view, however, this element is neither desirable nor recommended because it reflects and may even increase the disparity between the health care options that are available to some people as opposed to others. Possibly, the third element could be supported as a compromise, recognizing that within a free enterprise system of health care, the first two elements would be impossible to implement unless the third were allowed. This would add a pragmatic justification to the feminist egalitarian rationale.

While pursuing the ideal of gender justice, most feminists are pragmatists in their recognition that partial fulfillment of the ideal is better than none. A pragmatic orientation is also evident in the integration between theory and practice that feminists affirm.[25] Different versions of feminism support different models of integration, but most if not all concur that participation of women in decisions that affect them is a sine qua non for the development of policies reflective of gender justice. In the next section, I describe a novel and successful mechanism for such participation.

Inclusion of Consumers as a Model for Genetics

As a member of the Integration Panel for the U.S. Department of Defense Breast Cancer Research Program between 1993 until 1997, I took part in a procedural initiative that suggests a means by which to incorporate a feminist standpoint into genetics research: the involvement of consumers in the review process. Initially, the term "consumer" referred to anyone who had survived BC or who had a family member with BC; later, its meaning was limited to survivors. Not surprisingly, this innovation evoked a great deal of skepticism on the part of investigators, who felt that the participation of consumers would compromise the integrity of scientific review, impede its efficiency, and increase its cost.

In 1991, grassroots advocacy and lobbying by BC activists culminated in allocation of $210 million for BC research by the U.S. Congress.[26] Because of budget limitations at the National Institutes of Health, the funds were allocated to the Department of Defense (DOD) appropriations budget. To facilitate the development of a successful research program, the DOD asked the Institute of Medicine (IOM) to provide guidance in constructing a program for scientific and programmatic review of BC research proposals. The IOM recommended that the review process consist of two levels. Initially, the proposals would be assessed for their scientific and technical merit by panels of scientists from different disciplines, career levels, and perspectives. Subsequently, the proposals would be assessed by a single panel for the fit between their scientific and technical merit and the programmatic goals of the BC research initiative. These goals include a reduction in the incidence of BC, escalation of survival rates, and improvement in the quality of life of persons diagnosed with BC, both men and women.

A novel recommendation of the IOM to the DOD was that "consumers"—survivors of BC and their family members—join scientists in the programmatic review process. In accordance with that recommendation, the DOD formed the Integration Panel (IP): a panel of scientists and consumers charged to conduct the programmatic review of proposals that had already been reviewed for the quality of their science. Some of the scientists serving on the IP were also consumers; in fact, our first elected chair was both a BC researcher and a survivor, and our second elected chair was a BC researcher whose sister and mother were (at the time) BC survivors.[27] Because a large proportion of the IP were women, the panel was more representative than other review panels of those who are personally and directly affected by the topic addressed. Each day's deliberations were begun with an explicit reminder of the goals of the program and the privileged standpoint of BC consumers: One among us briefly described her own or another's experience of BC, and this was followed by a moment of silence.

By the end of the first year of the review process for BC research proposals, IP members uniformly supported including consumers as voting members of the panel. In general, it was felt that the insights and input of consumers not only motivated but facilitated decisions about which proposals to fund. Since the charge of the IP was programmatic rather than scientific and technical review, however, the inclusion of consumers at this level was not perceived as threatening the quality of the scientific and technical review which had already been performed by panels composed exclusively of scientists. Our decision to involve consumers at the first level as well was more radical than the recommendation of the IOM. Our plan for implementing our decision to include consumers on the scientific and technical review panels in the 1995 funding cycle included two important components. First, we would prepare both the consumers and the scientists who would serve on these panels through meetings designed to inform them of the background and rationale for inclusion and to address their concerns about it. Second, we introduced a formal evaluation process to assess the impact of consumer inclusion in scientific and technical review.[28]

Prior to the actual inclusion of consumers on scientific and review panels, members of the IP narrowed the meaning of "consumer" applicable to the scientific and technical review panels by excluding family members from that category. Only BC survivors would count as consumers for those panels. The survivors selected were required to be active in a BC advocacy group. Further, those who had been selected for the panels as scientists rather than as survivors would be considered scientists rather than consumers in that context; in other words, their input should be based on their scientific expertise rather than their experience as BC survivors. From an egalitarian feminist standpoint, this narrowing of the basis for consumer representation is problematic. It excludes three standpoints that may in fact deserve privileged positions: close relatives who in some cases are significantly and personally impacted by BC; survivors who are not affiliated with BC advocacy organizations, that is, the majority of BC survivors; and BC researchers who are also survivors, whose experience as both is relevant to the assessment of proposals.[29]

While family members may not occupy as privileged a position as survivors, many are affected significantly by BC, and some, depending on the circumstances, may even be affected more. Since the impact of family history has become more broadly recognized and genetic susceptibility testing is available, the daughters of survivors particularly deserve to participate in decisions about funding for research into hereditary BC, its detection, and treatment. Just as the experience of family members varies considerably, so does that of survivors. For some, BC occurred many years ago, was detected early, and was treated so successfully that they scarcely think of it now; for others, particularly those who have had recurrences and metastases, BC has radically changed their lives and is constantly in their thoughts. Despite the disparity in their experiences, women from both groups are equally survivors.

The evaluation of consumer inclusion on the scientific and technical review panels was undertaken through questionnaires distributed before and after the panels were convened to panel chairs, scientific reviewers, executive secretaries, and consumers. Although the prepanel data showed an overall openness on the part of the scientists to consumer participation, many of them doubted that the consumers would be able to engage meaningfully in discussions of the scientific merit of proposals. Some worried that unpreparedness and emotionality on the part of consumers would slow the process and dilute its scientific rigor. Others felt that consumers would be inclined to support immediate clinical relevance at the expense of basic science, and many indicated that the validity of scoring might be jeopardized.

According to the postpanel questionnaires, none of these concerns materialized in the scientists' experience of consumer participation on the panels. The scientists found the consumers hard working, intelligent, reasonable, open, articulate, and well-prepared. In addition, all of the panels finished before their scheduled time, and consumer judgments generally coincided with those of the scientists. Although it is impossible to tell whether the consumer input influenced the scientists' decisions or vice versa, it is clear that members of both groups found the experience a positive one. A majority indicated that they felt the practice of inclusion should continue.

Although the costs of having consumers and scientists as participants parallel each other, additional costs were incurred by the preparation of potential panelists, chairs, executive secretaries, and staff for inclusion of consumers. These costs were considered reasonable by IP members and DOD personnel. Had adequate orientation of participants to this novel approach not been achieved, fears about compromising the quality of the review process might have been fulfilled. In time, as the rationale for inclusion of consumers is more widely disseminated and its practice spreads, the costs of preparation are likely to diminish. From an egalitarian feminist perspective, the cost incurred may be regarded as an essential expenditure.

At the outset of the DOD BC research initiative, few of the submitted proposals related to the genetics of BC, and fewer of them were funded. Consumers as well as scientists reviewing the proposals generally felt that other areas of research addressed the practical goals of the program more efficiently. A valid rationale for this view was that advances in genetics do not yield cures of BC. However, as understanding of the genetics of BC escalated, the number of proposals related to genetics increased, and the funding of meritorious proposals in genetics increased as well. Interest in the genetics of BC has been heightened by the hope that knowledge of different mutations for specific forms of BC may lead to the development of more effective modes of treatment. Even in the absence of treatment modalities based on genetics, however, genetic tests for susceptibility to BC are increasingly offered to high-risk women and sought by others because of their potential for identifying women for whom earlier and more intensive surveillance or prophylactic surgery may be helpful.

The inclusion of consumers in assessment of research proposals for BC provides a model for the development of genetic testing and treatment protocols. It illustrates feminist standpoint theory because it gives voice to a crucial nondominant perspective that might otherwise not be heard. Ethically, that perspective demands articulation because it represents those most affected by decisions and policies about BC. Epistemologically, their articulation fills a gap in the knowledge of the nondominant group who have never experienced the impact of BC on themselves personally.

As genomic research continues, possibilities for genetic testing not only for susceptibility to BC but for other complex or multifactorial diseases and traits will proliferate. Advances in gene therapy will also increase. For many conditions, groups of individuals who are affected or at risk deserve a privileged position in determination of how the new knowledge or procedures should be applied to them. Although token representation of nondominant standpoints on governmental panels and organizational boards may be required and therefore implemented, the dominant members of these groups are rarely as prepared for that inclusion as the DOD panels were prepared. In fact, the participation of nondominant members is often viewed as a political necessity rather than a source of enlightenment by the dominant members of review panels or policy-making groups.

Tokenism can exacerbate the myopia of the dominant standpoint because the socialization of nondominant individuals sometimes leads to their assimilation of the perspective of the dominant group. Lest their privileged perspective be lost, it is imperative that the rationale underlying the inclusion be understood and accepted by dominant members of the group. In other words, the dominant persons must recognize that their own knowledge base or expertise inevitably involves limitations that can be reduced if not overcome by listening to nondominant others, particularly those most affected by the decisions contemplated. For that to happen, the nondominant group must maintain its own standpoint.

Beth Brown would not have been invited to serve as a consumer on the IP or on the scientific and technical review panels of the DOD BC research initiative. Because it is practically impossible to secure representation of all nondominant perspectives, the criteria that excluded her or others are probably justifiable.[30] Conceivably, however, the university hospital where Beth was tested is developing protocols for genetic testing for susceptibility to BC and other complex disorders. Testing for susceptibility to these disorders may raise some of the same issues about disclosure that Beth faced. She would be an appropriate person to invite to serve on a committee charged with developing these protocols.

The availability of genetic testing for susceptibility to late onset disorders such as BC will undoubtedly increase in years to come. Questions raised in the context of that availability include not only when and to whom the tests may be offered but also what means of testing is morally appropriate. Among the means available, preimplantation genetic diagnosis offers the earliest possible point at which detection may be definitive. As we will see in the next chapter, however, the increasing availability of this means of genetic diagnosis may not avoid the controversies with which other prenatal genetic testing procedures are associated.

Notes

1. Admittedly, a genetic factor may play a part in all diseases, and this leads some authors to classify cancer as a genetic disease. However, environmental factors are reported to account for at least 80% of the incidence of cancer, which means that genetics probably plays a smaller role in cancer that in cardiac, psychiatric, and many rheumatologic and other autoimmune diseases. Walter F. Bodmer, "Cancer Genetics and the Human Genome," *Hospital Practice,* October 15, 1991, p. 101.

2. American Cancer Society, *Cancer Facts and Figures* (Atlanta: American Cancer Society, 1997).

3. Environmental carcinogens may also be responsible for increase in the incidence of BC, but this has not been empirically established.

4. L. A. G. Ries, C. L. Kosary, B. Hankey, A. Harras, B. A. Miller, and B. K. Edwards, eds., "SEER Cancer Statistics Review, 1973–1993: Tables and Graphs," NIH Pub. 96-2789 (Bethesda, MD: National Cancer Institute, 1995).

5. Ries et al.

6. Caryn Lerman and R. Croyle, "Psychological Issues in Genetic Testing for Breast Cancer Susceptibility," *Archives of Internal Medicine* 154 (1994): 609–16.

7. M. P. Madigan, R. G. Ziegler, J. Benichou, C. Byrne, and R. N. Hoover, "Proportion of Breast Cancer Cases in the United States Explained by Well-Established Risk Factors," *Journal of the National Cancer Institute* 87 (1995): 1681–85.

8. C. Mettlin, "Breast Cancer Risk Factors: Contributions to Planning Breast Cancer Control," *Cancer* 69, 7 (1992): 1904–10.

9. B. E. Hillner, T. J. Smith, and C. E. Desch, "Efficacy and Cost-Effectiveness of Autologous Bone Marrow Transplantation in Metastatic Breast Cancer," *Journal of the American Medical Association* 267, 15 (1992): 2055–61.

10. While I do not have the verbatim statement, my colleagues and I heard this sentiment articulated by one of four women with BC who talked about their experience of the disease to our research group. The other three women echoed her sentiment that hair loss was an unexpected source of anguish. Had they been prepared for it as they had been prepared for loss of their breasts through mastectomy, it would probably have been less difficult.

11. Jane Poulson, "Bitter Pills to Swallow," *New England Journal of Medicine* 338, 25 (1998): 1844.

12. C. Pozo, C. S. Carver, V. Noriega, S. D. Harris, D. S. Robinson, A. S. Ketcham, A. Legaspi, F. L. Moffat, and K. C. Clark, "Effects of Mastectomy versus Lumpectomy on Emotional Adjustment to Breast Cancer: A Prospective Study of the First Year Post-surgery," *Journal of Clinical Oncology* 10, 8 (1992): 1292–98; P. A. Ganz, C. A. C. Schag, J. J. Lee, M. L. Polinsky, and S. J. Tan, "Breast Conservation versus Mastectomy: Is There a Difference in Psychological Adjustment or Quality of Life in the Year after Surgery?" *Cancer* 69, 7 (1992): 1729–38.

13. Patrick I. Borgen, George Y. Wong, Vaia Vlamis, Charles Potter, Brian Hoffmann, David W. Kinne, Michael P. Osborne, and William M. P. McKinnon, "Current Management of Male Breast Cancer," *Annals of Surgery* 215, 5 (1992): 451.

14. Olufunmilayo I. Olopade, "The Human Genome Project and Breast Cancer," *Women's Health Issues* 7, 4 (1997): 211.

15. D. K. Wellisch, E. R. Gritz, W. Schain, H. J. Wang, and J. Siau, "Psychological Functioning of Daughters of Breast Cancer Patients. I: Daughters and Comparison Subjects," *Psychosomatics* 32, 3 (1991): 324–36.

16. Douglas Easton, Deborah Ford, and Julian Peto, "Inherited Susceptibility to Breast Cancer," *Cancer Surveys* 18 (1993): 110.

17. Mary-Claire King, S. Rowell, and Susan M. Love, "Inherited Breast and Ovarian Cancer: What Are the Risks? What Are the Choices?" *Journal of the American Medical Association* 269, 15 (1993): 1975–80.

18. F. J. Couch, M. L. DeShano, M. A. Blackwood, K. Calzone, J. Stopfer, L. Campeau, A Ganguly, T. Rebbeck, and B. L. Weber, "BRCA1 Mutations in Women Attending Clinics That Evaluate the Risk of BC," *New England Journal of Medicine* 336, 20 (1997): 1416–21. Editorializing on these data, Bernadine Healy concludes that "Routine screening for BRCA1 mutations, even among women with breast cancer in their families, is wasteful, since more than 9 times out of 10 the test will be negative." "BRCA

Genes: Bookmaking, Fortunetelling, and Medical Care," *New England Journal of Medicine* 336, 20 (1997): 1448.

19. L. C. Hartmann, D. J. Schaid, J. E. Woods, T. P. Crotty, J. L. Meyers, P. G. Arnold, P. M. Petty, T. A. Sellers, J. L. Johnson, S. K. McDonnell, M. H. Frost, and R. B. Jenkins, "Efficacy of Bilateral Prophylactic Mastectomy in Women with a Family History of Breast Cancer," *New England Journal of Medicine* 340, 2 (1999): 77–84.

20. K. F. Hoskins, J. E. Stopfer, K. A. Calzone, S. D. Merajver, T. R. Rebbeck, J. E. Garber, and B. L. Weber, "Assessment and Counseling for Women with a Family History of Breast Cancer: A Guide for Clinicians," *Journal of the American Medical Association* 273 (1995): 577–85. In Askenazi Jewish population studies and high-risk families, the penetrance is 50%–85%. Cf. Jeffrey P. Struewing, Patricia Hartge, Sholom Wacholder, S. M. Baker, M. Berlin, M. McAdams, M. M. Timmerman, L. C. Brody, and M. A. Tucker, "The Risk of Cancer Associated with Specific Mutations of BRCA1 and BRCA2 among Ashkenazi Jews," *New England Journal of Medicine* 336, 20 (1997): 1401–8.

21. As of 1997, 140 mutations were identified in BRCA1 and BRCA2 genes. Struewing et al., p. 1401.

22. Olopade, p. 211.

23. Although linkage studies may increase informativeness regarding risk, they introduce further issues regarding confidentiality and the right of family members not to be tested.

24. Olopade, p. 211.

25. See H. S. Thayer, *Meaning and Action: A Critical History of Pragmatism* (New York: Bobbs-Merrill, 1968), pp. 426–29.

26. An account of how funds were allocated by the U.S. Congress to the U.S. Department of Defense for BC research, and of the Institute of Medicine's recommendations regarding the review of proposals for these funds, see Yvonne Andejeski, Erica Sharp-Breslau, Elizebeth Hart, Ngina Lythcott, Linda Alexander, Irene Rich, Isabelle Bisceglio, Helene Smith, and Fran Vicso, "Evaluation of the Inclusion of Consumers in Scientific Merit Review of Breast Cancer Research," *Journal of Women's Health*, forthcoming.

27. Sadly, our first chair, Helene Smith, subsequently suffered a recurrence and died, and the family members of our second chair, Anna Barker, since died of BC as well.

28. The results of this assessment are reported in Yvonne Andejeski, Isabelle Crawford, Kay Dickersin, Jean Johnson, Helene Smith, Frances Visco, Irene Rich and the U.S. Army Medical Research and Materiel Command Fiscal Year 1995 Breast Cancer Research Program Integration Panel, "Impact of Including Consumers in the Scientific Review of Research Proposals," submitted. A descriptive account of these results appears in Andejeski, et al. Both articles provide documentation for the views expressed by scientists and consumers who responded to the questionnaires.

29. Further criteria for excluding participation of BC survivors as consumers were fluency in English and high school graduation. From an egalitarian feminist standpoint the fluency criterion is problematic because it probably excludes a large number of Hispanic women; the educational requirement is problematic because it may exclude women who have not finished high school for socioeconomic reasons.

30. Beth would have been excluded, as were several BC survivors whom I recommended, because she did not represent a constituency of survivors, e.g., a BC support organization or lobbying group.

12

PREIMPLANTATION GENETIC DIAGNOSIS AND ABORTION

TECHNOLOGIES for genetic diagnosis have been proliferating and improving for decades. In general, they have been developed in the context of prenatal testing, as a means by which to identify fetal abnormalities that will be manifest at birth or shortly thereafter. The main benefit of such testing is to inform potential parents that their fetus is free of the abnormality being investigated. In most cases, learning the test result is good news. However, in the minority of cases in which individuals are given the bad news of a positive test result, they are usually informed as well that there is no cure for the condition identified. At that point, abortion is the only way through which to avoid the birth of an affected offspring.

Because prenatal diagnosis typically occurs after several months of a desired pregnancy, abortion is a particularly distressing option. For some women it is morally objectionable, for some it is economically or legally inaccessible, and for most if not all it is emotionally difficult. Although in most countries women alone have the legal right to end a pregnancy, potential fathers may of course be distressed by the situation also. Occasionally, they disagree with their partners about whether to end or continue an affected pregnancy. A woman may be morally obliged to consider her partner's view on the matter, but her decision has priority because she is the one most affected by it.

Preimplantation genetic diagnosis (PGD) appears to present a means of bypassing the psychological burden and moral controversy of abortion because it occurs before pregnancy is initiated.[1] This technology provides a way by which women and couples can avoid the birth of a genetically anomalous offspring, but whether this constitutes an abortion bypass depends on two factors: the meaning of abortion and the disposition of the affected embryo or preembryo.[2] In this chapter, I examine both factors and provide examples of morally different situations in which PGD may be considered. Preliminarily, I examine what PGD involves.

Methods of Preimplantation Genetic Diagnosis

Preimplantation refers to the period of development that occurs prior to the attachment of a developing embryo to the uterine wall. The implantation process starts at about six days after fertilization and takes about a week to complete. In vivo, fertilization of ova generally takes place in the fallopian tube. Through many cell divisions, sometimes including twinning and recombining, the preimplantation embryo travels to the uterus, where it is implanted for the duration of gestation.

When fertilization occurs in vitro, cell division begins in the laboratory but implantation occurs only after transfer to a woman's body. If the newly fertilized egg is flushed from a woman after fertilization, implantation occurs after it is returned to her or to another woman. In either case, genetic diagnosis can be performed before implantation. Until the organism has divided beyond the eight-cell stage, each cell is totipotent, that is, capable of developing into a complete, mature member of the species.[3] Analysis of single cells can therefore be conducted without affecting development in the remainder of the organism.

The genetic diseases for which PGD has been offered and successfully performed are those for which prenatal tests have already been available, such as X-linked disorders, Tay-Sachs disease, and cystic fibrosis.[4] Potentially, however, PGD can yield whatever genetic information is available through current methods of analysis. This includes information not only about single-gene disorders but also about nonmedical traits, complex diseases, and susceptibility to specific conditions. Completion of the Human Genome Project will eventually allow access to information about the entire genetic makeup of individuals.

Three types of cells may be analyzed in PGD: polar bodies, blastomere cells, and trophectoderm cells.[5] Polar bodies are cells extruded from preovulatory oocytes (egg cells), containing maternal chromosomes. For couples who are carriers for autosomal recessive disorders, an affected polar body may indicate an unaffected complement in the cell nucleus. However, because chromosomal crossing-over may occur, genetic diagnosis of the first polar body cannot yield definitive information about the embryo.[6] So this type of PGD is clinically impractical.[7] Sequential analysis of both first and second polar bodies has been reported to provide definitive information, but analysis of the second polar body takes place after the oocyte has been fertilized.[8] Where this method has been used, its proponents argue that it is more accurate than blastomere analysis.[9]

Blastomeres are cells developed through cleavage of the zygote, each retaining full developmental potential. Until the eight-cell stage, the blastomeres are only loosely associated with one another. As they gradually become compacted, the possibility of survival following genetic analysis is apparently reduced. Trophectoderm cells are the earliest to differentiate, giving rise to extraembryonic tissue that establishes uteroplacental circulation. They thus lack the potential for development into a fetus or newborn.

Unaffected embryos have implanted more successfully when transferred to a woman after blastomere analysis at the four- to eight-cell stage than when transfer occurred after analysis of trophectoderm cells. Polymerase chain reaction (PCR) amplification is used to provide adequate amounts of DNA for analysis.[10] Whether both polar bodies, blastomere, or trophectoderm cells are biopsied, however, the issue of how to dispose of affected embryos is raised. Abortion may be one means of disposal, but this depends, in part at least, on how abortion is defined.

Definitions and Methods of Abortion

Early work on abortion assumed one definition: terminating or ending the life of a fetus or embryo developing within a woman's body. Supporters of a right to abortion argued (and still argue) for their position on grounds that the fetus or embryo is not a person with a right to life. Rather it may be considered part of the pregnant woman's body, or an organism developing parasitically within her. Opponents argued (and still argue) that abortion is morally wrong on grounds that the fetus or embryo is a person whose right to life is not overridable by a pregnant woman's choice to end it. Abortion is thus the moral equivalent of homicide, and sometimes murder.[11]

Both supporters and opponents often use the terms "human life" and "person" synonymously, without defending their usage. Some supporters acknowledge that abortion entails termination of a human life, while arguing that this is not equivalent to ending the life of a person.[12] Whether defending or challenging abortion decisions, both sides have focused on the moral status of the fetus or embryo as determinant of the morality of abortion. In considering murder wrong, both regard the life of a person as a more compelling value than the autonomy of someone who chooses to end another person's life. The definition of abortion assumed in both cases ignores the fact that fetuses cannot exist apart from women's bodies. Arguments in support of both positions illustrate the fallacy of abstraction by ignoring the context that is essential to any adequate understanding of abortion.[13]

From a feminist standpoint, it is not surprising that the first philosopher to articulate an abortion argument based on recognition of the essential tie between women and fetuses was a woman, Judith Jarvis Thomson.[14] Thomson compared an unwanted pregnancy with the situation of an unconscious violinist whose ongoing life support depends on maintenance of his physical connection to a person who never consented to that connection. Without defending or endorsing the view that a fetus is a person, Thomson started with that assumption in order to argue that, even if it were, abortion is still morally permissible. She undertook the more difficult defense, apparently believing that if the fetus were not a person, a woman's right to abortion is adequately upheld on that basis.

Thomson's analogy has been regarded as outlandish, and possibly she chose it because she wanted it to be just that. However, if she wished to accurately represent the uniqueness of pregnancy as a physiological tie between a woman and another living human organism, Thomson could find no comparable human experience.[15] Hence she had to concoct an analogy that is both valid and imaginative. Her operable definition of abortion as the severance of an essential link between a pregnant woman and her fetus avoided the fallacy of abstraction embodied in the prevalent definition.

Interestingly, Thomson's conception of abortion is consistent with definitions of the term found in clinical texts and medical dictionaries. For example, *Williams' Obstetrics,* a classic work in the field, defines abortion as "termination of pregnancy by any means before the fetus is sufficiently developed to survive"; *Stedman's Medical Dictionary* defines it as "giving birth to an embryo or fetus prior to the stage of viability"; and *Dorland's Illustrated Medical Dictionary* defines abortion as "premature expulsion from the uterus of the products of conception."[16] All of these definitions apply to spontaneous as well as induced abortion. Spontaneous abortion is morally unproblematic because there is no agent to whom to impute responsibility.[17] It is not surprising that clinical texts define induced abortion as termination of pregnancy rather than termination of fetal life because physicians generally view their responsibility as sustaining or saving lives, not terminating them. Terminating pregnancy is also a more apt definition of abortion for physicians who view their primary patient as the pregnant woman rather than the embryo or fetus.

The distinction between these definitions is clinically and morally relevant, and the two aspects are inevitably related. Clinical relevance arises from the fact that the procedure chosen can be one by which pregnancy will surely be terminated but the fetus may survive, or one in which there will surely be fetal demise either before or during the pregnancy termination. Obviously, fetal survival can occur only when the fetus is possibly viable, during the second trimester of gestation. *Roe v. Wade* sets viability at 24 weeks; clinical texts generally set it more conservatively at 20 weeks (the midpoint of a full-term gestation) or when the fetus weighs less than 500 grams.[18]

The different definitions of abortion underlie the intention of the pregnant woman and of the clinician who performs PGD. If the clinician's intention is to fulfill the wishes of the pregnant woman, either definition is operable and perceived as morally justifiable in itself or on grounds of respect for her autonomy. But the clinician may view the woman's right to end a pregnancy as distinct from her right to terminate fetal life, regarding the former as justifiable and the latter as not justifiable if the two are separable. The clinician would then be morally obliged to choose a procedure that, while safely ending the woman's pregnancy, maximizes the chance of fetal survival or minimizes the possibility of fetal pain. These two goals are not only different but sometimes at odds. In most areas of health care, the goals of survival and pain relief are simultaneously pursued, but pain is tolerated to the extent that relief of it might reduce the chance of survival.

Dilatation and evacuation is sometimes selected as an abortion method during the second trimester of pregnancy, when most abortions for genetic anomalies occur. At the appropriate threshold of gestation and in the hands of an experienced physician, this method is recommended by the American College of Obstetricians and Gynecologists as faster, less expensive, and less painful or emotionally traumatic than other methods for the pregnant woman.[19] Some physicians inject potassium chloride (KCl) into the fetal heart before performing the procedure. Because the injection constitutes intentional direct killing, it may be compared with fetal euthanasia. Fetal reduction in multiple gestations is also accomplished through this means.

Another abortion method used in second-trimester gestations is infusion of a substance that will induce labor and delivery. This procedure allows confirmation of a prenatal genetic diagnosis through inspection of an intact fetus. The substances used to induce premature labor vary; some (urea and saline) are toxic to the uterine environment of the fetus, whereas others (prostaglandin and oxytocin) are not.[20] The latter may be chosen to promote the possibility of fetal survival. KCl injection may be performed prior to induction as a means of insuring fetal demise.

Both definitions of abortion have long been operable, but a third definition has emerged solely as a result of advances in medical technology. The relevant advances include in vitro fertilization (IVF) and uterine lavage or embryo flushing.[21] IVF refers to the process of fertilizing ova after they are extracted from a woman. Ordinarily, the sperm used for fertilization are obtained from the woman's partner. With uterine lavage or embryo flushing, newly fertilized embryos are removed from a woman so that they are available in the laboratory. Although these procedures are ordinarily used to provide reproductive assistance to infertile couples, they may be used in conjunction with PGD to provide carriers of autosomal recessive or X-linked diseases with a means by which to avoid the birth of an affected child.

Both methods by which embryos may be obtained usually involve drug-induced ovulation stimulation of the woman. The newly fertilized eggs may then be transferred to the woman who provided the eggs or to another woman; alternatively, they may be frozen, used for research, or disposed of in the laboratory. The last alternative brings us to the third definition of abortion: termination of in vitro embryos.

The third definition differs from the others in that a pregnancy has not yet been initiated, and therefore cannot be terminated. In other words, the life of a developing human embryo can be ended without terminating a pregnancy. Those who subscribe to the second definition of abortion do not equate the termination of in vitro embryos with the abortion issue, but those who subscribe to the first definition do. For the former, disposition of in vitro embryos may still be morally problematic but on different grounds than those provided by arguments for and against abortion; for the latter, termination of embryos in vitro is as problematic or unproblematic as termination of embryos or fetuses in vivo.

Different sources of cells that may be analyzed in PGD are relatable to different definitions of abortion. In comparison with implanted embryos and fetuses, the cell sources for PGD represent different possibilities for development. Table 12–1 illustrates these differences.

The potential of an embryo to become a newborn depends not only on the duration of its development but also on where that development occurs (e.g., in utero or in the laboratory). When comparing in vitro embryos, implanted embryos, and fetuses, therefore, the last is most likely to become a child, and the first is least likely to become one. When comparing implanted embryos and fe-

TABLE 12–1. Preimplantation Genetic Diagnosis

CELL SOURCE	NEWBORN POTENTIAL	DEFINITION OF ABORTION RELATED TO DISPOSAL OF AFFECTED EMBRYO (1, 2, OR 3)[a]
First polar bodies	No	None
First and second polar bodies	No	3
Blastomeres	Yes	3
Trophectoderm	No	3
Implanted embryo	Yes	1 or 2 (inseparable)
Fetus	Yes	1 or 2 (separable after viability)

[a] Key: 1 = termination of embryo or fetus; 2 = termination of a pregnancy; 3 = termination of embryo in vitro.

tuses, termination of the in vivo embryo is inseparable from termination of a pregnancy because the embryo is not viable, that is, capable of surviving ex utero; termination of a fetus is separable from termination of a pregnancy if and when the fetus is viable.

The development of technology for PGD has been, in part at least, a response to the desire of many women and couples to avoid pregnancy termination of affected fetuses.[22] From a feminist standpoint, this is surely an appropriate reason for developing the technology. However, an adequate argument for termination of embryos in conjunction with PGD requires an additional premise: denial that the early embryo has moral status, or that if it does, its moral status is sufficient to override the wishes of those who provided the gametes from which it developed.[23] Although feminists may differ on the moral status of the embryo, they generally agree that a woman's legal right to terminate a pregnancy must be preserved.

Even if abortion is defined as termination of in vitro embryos, PGD does not itself entail abortion. In blastomere analysis, the cells examined are embryonic, whereas in polar body and trophectoderm analyses, the cells examined are not embryonic and never will be. However, a link between preimplantation genetic diagnosis and abortion occurs not only in blastomere analysis but also in analysis of sequential polar bodies and trophectoderm cells because a positive diagnosis of the embryo may lead to its disposal. Still, no matter what cell type is examined, PGD merely provides the information on which a woman may base a decision regarding the disposition of the embryo. That disposition may take a variety of forms, some of which are surely not equivalent to abortion.

Methods of Disposing of Affected Embryos

Affected embryos that are not implanted after PGD may be (*a*) stored (frozen), (*b*) used for research, (*c*) killed, or (*d*) allowed to die.[24] These methods are separable but not necessarily exclusive or incompatible. Only (*c*) clearly constitutes termination of the embryo, and is therefore identifiable with the third definition of abortion. However, those who posit a moral equivalence between allowing someone to die and actively terminating someone's life might argue that (*d*) is also the moral equivalent of abortion. In general, the relationship between (*c*) and (*d*) parallels the distinctions between intervention and nonintervention and between active and passive euthanasia.

No matter what definition of abortion is employed, induced abortion constitutes intervention in a process that might otherwise continue. The intervention, for which a competent, informed intervenor is inevitably responsible, may entail surgery or medication, and it may be self-administered (e.g., through RU 486) or other-administered. Certain ways of disposing of in vitro embryos, such as deliberately crushing them in the petri dish, performing lethal experiments on them, or throwing them down the drain, are interventions that may be performed by virtually anyone who has access to them.

But is letting embryos expire in a petri dish an intervention? Isn't it rather like the nonintervention of forgoing life-saving treatment in the case of a dying person whose wishes are unknown or unknowable? Or forgoing futile measures in one for whom necessary interventions are invasive and unlikely to be successful?[25] Given the unlikelihood of successful transfer, implantation, gestation, and birth for a particular embryo, it is not unreasonable to consider it to be dying, or to consider the invasive procedures necessary for it to survive futile. If forgoing treatment of those who are undisputably persons is justified in circumstances of dying and futility, a fortiori it seems justified to allow in vitro embryos to expire. Reinforcing this view is the fact that the treatment required to provide the embryo with any chance of survival[26] necessarily entails considerable risk and discomfort to another whose consent is morally demanded—the woman on whom the embryo would depend for its development. The argument is even more compelling if PGD discloses a genetic condition that would mean neurological devastation or unrelievable pain for a child born with that condition (e.g., Lesch-Nyhan syndrome).[27] In such circumstances, it may be not merely permissible but morally obligatory to let the affected embryo expire in the petri dish.

Careful analyses of the moral relevance of the distinction between intervention and nonintervention have been developed in response to a provocative article by James Rachels on the moral irrelevance of the distinction between active and passive euthanasia.[28] These analyses generally acknowledge responsibility for deeds of omission as well as commission, while pointing to the empirical and psychological differences between nonintervention and intervention, or arguing that there are rule-utilitarian reasons for preserving the killing–letting die distinction.[29] In the United States, laws have consistently upheld this distinction as grounds for the permissibility of letting someone die (even by actively removing life-sustaining technology, which is surely more like an intervention than letting an embryo expire) as distinct from actively intervening to kill her. This last point is supported by legal rulings in many well-known cases: Karen Ann Quinlan, Philip Eichner, Nancy Cruzan, and others.[30] If the distinction provides moral support to these decisions, a fortiori it does so for comparable cases involving embryos.

Beyond the intervention–nonintervention and active–passive distinctions, controversies about the moral status of embryos and fetuses show no signs of abating. Regardless of whether moral status is imputed to embryos, however, one unique feature of PGD is undeniably morally significant from an egalitarian feminist standpoint. Because the procedure is performed in vitro, it eliminates the need for women to undergo abortion to avoid the birth of an affected offspring. That this is no small matter to some women is evident in the reasons they provide for requesting PGD: they have previously had abortions in response to positive results of prenatal testing, and they never want to have that experience again.[31] Others want to avoid a positive prenatal test that requires them to decide whether to undergo abortion. For women who are personally opposed to abortion after pregnancy is established and do not regard disposal of in vitro embryos as morally problematic, PGD followed by implantation of unaffected embryos provides a way of avoiding the conflict that might otherwise be posed by a positive prenatal diagnosis. If PGD were available to women of different cultures and religions, it might be widely embraced as a means through which to avoid both abortion and the birth of a genetically impaired child.

PGD followed by disposal of affected embryos thus bypasses the abortion debate if abortion is defined as termination of a viable pregnancy or as termination of a fetus or embryo in utero. If abortion is defined as termination of an embryo developing in the laboratory, then killing it is abortion. Letting it die in a petri dish is not equivalent to abortion unless intervention in cases where survival is improbable is equated with killing. Regardless of its possible association with abortion, however, the availability of PGD may raise or exacerbate even more complex and troubling issues from a feminist standpoint. The next section illustrates some of these issues.

Different Circumstances, Different Rationales

To appreciate the range of circumstances and rationales that are morally relevant to decisions about use of PGD, consider the following scenarios:

A. After successful IVF, a couple learns that their child has cystic fibrosis. Nine of their embryos are frozen. They ask for PGD before another attempt at pregnancy.

B. The same case as A, but the couple has split, and the woman alone makes the request.

C. The same case as B, but the man makes the request after contracting with a third party ("surrogate") to gestate the embryo(s) after biopsy and transfer.

D. A couple who are carriers for sickle cell disease are opposed to abortion, which they define as termination of an embryo or fetus. As a means of avoiding abortion, they request sequential polar body analysis of the woman's oocytes, intending to pay for the procedure through their savings.

E. The same case as D but the couple cannot pay for the procedure themselves.

F. A couple who already have three daughters ask for IVF and blastocyst biopsy for sex determination. They will cover the cost.
G. A couple who already have three sons ask for IVF and blastocyst biopsy for sex determination. They cannot cover the cost.
H. A couple who have already lost a child to Tay-Sachs disease are opposed to abortion, which they define as termination of a nonviable pregnancy. They are anxious to undergo IVF and blastocyst biopsy to ensure that their next child does not have the same disease. Their insurance will cover prenatal diagnosis and termination, but not IVF and blastocyst biopsy.
I. A single affluent woman requests IVF with donated sperm and blastocyst biopsy that may provide her with whatever genetic information is available about the embryo.
J. A woman with cystic fibrosis requests ova retrieval and IVF with her carrier partner's sperm, blastocyst biopsy, and transfer of nonaffected embryos to her sister for gestation.

All of these scenarios assume a desire on the part of the individual or couple to have a genetic tie to offspring. In some cases, the genetic tie of one parent could be achieved by gamete donation. In all of the cases, the option of adoption could have been pursued.[32]

The collection of cases shows a range of variables, all of which are relevant to a feminist standpoint on the issue of PGD. The distinction between issues and cases is important in its own right: issues are generic; cases are specific or particular. As generic, an issue such as PGD—that is, the question of whether PGD is a morally acceptable procedure for anyone to perform or request—prescinds from the nuances that always accompany actual cases. Cases typically embody a plethora of generic issues, and their particularity sometimes stretches beyond those issues, presenting questions that are unique to the situation. An egalitarian feminist standpoint attends to as many of these nuances as possible, examining the extent, if any, to which they are associated with nondominant or dominant perspectives.

The term "variable" serves as a label for different types of nuances of actual cases. Among the variables associated with PGD are the type of cell to be analyzed, the invasiveness of the procedure, the cost of the procedure, who pays for it, its risk and probability of success, the marital status of the individuals seeking it, and their reasons for doing so. All of these variables are illustrated in the preceding cases. Note, however, that none of the scenarios mentions an additional variable: the disposition of affected embryos. Instead, the focus of the interested parties is on the technology that may afford them the opportunity to avoid having a child who has a specific genetic condition.

Two sets of cases illustrate the fact that a single variable may weight the decision on one side rather than another. In the first set, A–C, case B simply changes the source of the request in case A from the couple to the woman, and case C changes it to the man. From a feminist perspective, the gender difference between cases B and C is relevant not only because the man himself will not be undergoing embryo transfer, gestation, and childbirth, but also because a third party, another woman, is introduced into the process. Obviously, respect for her autonomy as well as concerns about the burdens and benefits of the procedure to her figure significantly in the moral assessment of the particular situation, regardless of whether PGD is generically justifiable.

In the second set, D–E, the couple needs to be informed of the relation between sequential polar body analysis and disposal of affected embryos. The single variable that distinguishes between these cases is the ability of the couple to pay for PGD. From an egalitarian feminist standpoint, if the procedure is available to the couple who can afford it, it ought to be available to the couple who cannot afford it. As with breast cancer testing, however, limiting the availability of an elective procedure to those who can pay for it may be justified by a pragmatic egalitarian argument that consists of two parts: (*1*) it's the best that can be done under the circumstances, and (2) providing PGD for those who can pay now may lead to its availability at lower or no cost to those who cannot pay for it in the future.

Cases F and G illustrate two variables, one involving cost, the other a variable within the variable of reasons for requesting PGD. As discussed in Chapter 6, sex selection for nonmedical reasons is associated with sexism, which makes both cases problematic. But sexism generally entails discrimination against women rather than men, which makes case F more problematic than case G. With respect to the cost variable, however, case G is more problematic than F because unconsenting others (taxpayers or other insurance policyholders) would then have to share the cost of a nontherapeutic or elective procedure. On grounds of both variables, therefore, an egalitarian feminist standpoint would find PGD acceptable in neither case.

Case H shows the importance of attending to the experience of the individuals most affected by specific decisions. A woman who has already undergone prenatal diagnosis and termination of pregnancy for a fetus diagnosed with Tay-Sachs disease knows the burden of that experience better than those who have not had the experience. Studies attest to the greater psychological burden that such women experience through these generally late terminations of desired pregnancies, in comparison with earlier elective terminations for nongenetic reasons. Moreover, the woman's partner knows better than other men what the experience was like for him. Accordingly, a feminist standpoint might impute a more privileged status to the request of this couple than to the request of a couple who had no experiential basis for their request.

Like case D, case H suggests the importance of honoring the religious or cultural values of those who request PGD or a particular method of PGD. In neither case, however, does this imply that clinicians are obliged to perform PGD or to utilize a particular method in doing so. As with provision of other medical tests and treatment, physicians are morally bound not only to respect the patient's autonomy and cultural values but also to determine whether the expected benefits of a requested intervention outweigh, or are at least equal to, its risks. If sequential polar body analysis and blastomere analysis are about equal in cost, risk, and effectiveness, a couple's request for one or the other should be respected. If they are otherwise, the argument for performing the more costly, more risky, or less effective procedure solely to honor a couple's religious or cultural values is considerably weakened. Respect for autonomy, in any of its different cultural manifestations, is not an absolute value for an egalitarian version of feminism.

Like cases B and C, case I illustrates the variable of marital status. A variable on this variable, however, is the fact that the "partner" of the potential single parent is unknown, that is, a (probably anonymous) sperm donor. An egalitarian feminist would argue that single women, single men, and couples have an equal right to PGD—so long as others affected, such as the potential child, do not experience disproportionate burdens. Although it may be argued that children of single mothers start life with a disproportionate burden, there is little evidence to support this position.[33] Despite the fact that very few single parents are men, the same point may be made for those who are. However, the risks and burdens that the woman in case I would experience contrast dramatically with the lack of comparable experience by a man who requests IVF with donor ova to be followed by PGD. This gender difference obviously supports the request of the woman in case I.

Nonetheless, an egalitarian feminist would surely be troubled by the fact that the woman in case I could purchase treatment not available to other single women who might wish to have a child through IVF and donor sperm, let alone one for whom PGD is performed. More troublesome still would be the request for "whatever genetic information is available about the embryo." That request suggests that the woman is not only seeking a child that she knows is free of genetic disease but one who has specific traits. No matter what method of PGD is used, trait selection is hardly an adequate reason from a feminist egalitarian standpoint, even though it would be acceptable to a libertarian feminist.[34]

Case J presents a scenario that is similar to case A with regard to the medical reason for requesting PGD: the avoidance of cystic fibrosis in one's offspring. Another medical reason could underlie the request in case J: the avoidance of a pregnancy that might exacerbate the symptoms of cystic fibrosis through transfer of the nonaffected embryos to the woman's sister. In case A, however, PGD is contemplated at a point where IVF has already been done and the embryos to be analyzed are already available. This means that the variables of cost, invasiveness, and risk are considerably reduced from what they would be for the woman in case J as well as for her sister. Given that reduction and the risk of having an affected child if another pregnancy is attempted (one in four), it may even be argued that failure to provide PGD in case A is irresponsible.

Finally, the involvement of a third party in case J introduces a complexity that has rarely been examined with sufficient care. While commercial "surrogacy" has been condemned as baby selling in some jurisdictions, noncommercial "surrogacy" has been permitted on grounds that it is not baby selling but an autonomous agreement among friends or relatives acting altruistically. Out of concerns about the potential for familial and gender-stereotypic pressures raised by such situations, most feminists would be skeptical about this presumption. Motives are probably mixed in either context, with women acting somewhat altruistically even when they accept payment for their role, and other women acting without remuneration but in anticipation of some other benefit to themselves, such as the favor of their parents or siblings, when they agree to gestate for a relative. An egalitarian feminist would insist on ensuring not only in case C but also in case J that the decision of the woman who agrees to gestate for another is truly informed and autonomous.

The scenario described in case J suggests that the woman with cystic fibrosis should be counted among those for whom genetic ties to offspring are more important than gestational ties. Although the health risk of pregnancy is exacerbated in women with cystic fibrosis, it is not generally considered life threatening and they may in fact conceive, gestate, and give birth in a normal fashion. Still, the hazards of pregnancy could be avoided in this case through a method that, in comparison with the procedures requested, would be less invasive, less costly, and more likely to be successful in terms of producing a healthy newborn: artificial insemination of her sister with her partner's sperm.

It is also possible that the woman in case J requested ova retrieval, IVF, PGD, and "surrogacy" not because of the significance of the genetic tie to her but because that tie was more important to her carrier partner. Several years ago, a woman with cystic fibrosis imputed that sentiment to her husband. When I asked her why—given the failure rate, risk, invasiveness, and expense of ova retrieval, IVF, and "surrogacy"—she preferred that constellation of procedures to artificial insemination of her sister with her husband's sperm, which would be less invasive, less risky, less costly, and more likely to be successful, she replied: "I just wanted to have a child, and would have been happy to adopt one. But my husband wanted a child related to me."

The autonomy of women who pursue or accept medical assistance to have children solely on the basis of their partner's wishes may of course be compromised. Whether in fact that was the case for the woman with cystic fibrosis I do not know, because our conversation revealed nothing about her relationship to her husband or about other possible pressures on her decision making. From an egalitarian feminist standpoint, however, the greater risk and physical burden of one partner implies that the other has an even greater responsibility to respect that partner' s wishes than he would if their risks and physical burdens were equal.

Variables describe not only different circumstances but also different conceptions or interpretations of those circumstances. As the preceding discussion shows, definitions and intentions are variable as well. Taking account of all of the differences or variables applicable to specific cases is probably impossible. Taking account of as many as possible, however, is not only demanded by a feminist egalitarian standpoint; it is an achievable and worthwhile goal from other standpoints, both dominant and nondominant.

Notes

1. One method of PGD, polar body analysis, avoids abortion in that it involves disposal of gametes rather than embryos. As we will see subsequently, however, in practice this method is indirectly related to abortions that occur after pregnancy is established.

2. In the remainder of this chapter, as elsewhere in the book, I use the term "embryo" rather than "preembryo" or "conceptus" to refer to the developing organism from fertilization until implantation. Although some biologists and bioethicists prefer "preembryo," my usage is consistent with that of many clinical texts, many clinicians, and popular understanding of the term "embryo." In using it, however, I am generally referring to the preimplantation embryo, which contains a great deal of extraembryonic material, including the placenta. "Conceptus" would more accurately reflect the fact that the organism contains extraembryonic material, but that term is rarely used by biologists, clinicians, or the public. "Preembryo" may be misleading because it suggests (erroneously) that the genetic material of the implanted embryo is not contained within the organism at that earlier stage. For an excellent, illustrated discussion of this issue, see D. Gareth Jones and Barbara Telfer, "Before I Was an Embryo, I Was a Pre-embryo: Or Was I?" *Bioethics* 9 (1995): 32–49.

3. M. D. Johnson, "Practical Aspects of Preembryo Biopsy and Diagnosis," *Infertility and Reproductive Medicine, Clinics of North America* 5 (1994): 213–31.

4. According to Carson and Buster, indications for PGD are unlikely "to be the same as for chorionic villus sampling or amniocentesis, i.e., advanced maternal age and previous trisomy infant." See Sandra A. Carson and John E. Buster, "Biopsy of Gametes and Preimplantation Embryos in Genetic Diagnosis," *Seminars in Reproductive Endocrinology* 12, 3 (1994): 193. They believe the clearest indications for PGD are situations involving the necessity of gene therapy or metabolic therapy early in gestation, and couples who are at exceptionally high risk for untreatable genetic disorders, such as Huntington chorea.

5. Johnson, pp. 213–31, and Carson and Buster, pp. 184–95.

6. Carson and Buster, p. 185.

7. At least one case of misdiagnosis leading to the birth of an affected infant has been reported through this method. Charles M. Strom and S. Rechitsky, "DNA Analysis of Polar Bodies and Preembryos," in Yuri Verlinsky and Anver Kuliev, eds., *Peimplantation Diagnosis of Genetic Diseases* (New York: Wiley-Liss, 1991), pp. 69–91. The missed diagnosis in this case was cystic fibrosis.

8. Charles M. Strom, Norman Ginsberg, Svetlana Rechitsky, J. Cieslak, V. Ivakhenko, G. Wolf, A Lifchez, J. Moise, J. Valle, B. Kaplan, M. White, J. Barton, A. Kuliev, and Y. Verlinsky, "Three Births after Preimplantation Genetic Diagnosis for Cystic Fibrosis with Sequential First and Second Polar Body Analysis," *American Journal of Obstetrics and Gynecology* 178, 6 (1998): 1298–1303.

9. At the Reproductive Genetics Institute in Chicago, polar body analysis is performed for couples in whom each partner has a different mutation for the same recessive disorder. A flyer distributed by institute personnel to colleagues describes polar body analysis as "the only accurate method to overcome the problems associated with allele specific dropout" (on file with author, www.signetusa.net/RGI).

10. Error rates calculated when PCR is used are higher than for conventional prenatal diagnosis by CVS or amniocentesis: 1.8% for autosomal recessive genes, 15% for autosomal dominant genes, and 7.4% for X-linked recessive genes. As techniques are improved, however, the rates are likely to lower. W. Navidi and N. Arnheim, "Using PCR in Preimplantation Genetic Diagnosis," *Human Reproduction* 6 (1991): 836–49.

11. Mary B. Mahowald, "Concepts of Abortion and Their Relevance to the Abortion Debate," *Southern Journal of Philosophy* 20 (1982): 195–207.

12. A key distinction here is between "a human life" and "a living human organism." It cannot be denied that a developing human fetus is a living human organism, but if a human life is equated only with the life of a human being after birth, than a living human fetus is not a human life.

13. May B. Mahowald, "As If There Were Fetuses without Women: A Remedial Essay," in Joan C. Callahan, ed., *Reproductive Ethics and the Law* (Bloomington: Indiana University Press, 1995), pp. 199–218.

14. Judith Jarvis Thomson, "A Defense of Abortion," *Philosophy and Public Affairs* 1 (1971): 47–66.

15. Inseparable conjoined twins might be proposed as analogous to the interdependence of pregnancy. A difference here, however, is that each party is dependent for life support on the other.

16. F. G. Cunningham, P. C. MacDonald, N. F. Gant, K Leveno, L. C. Gilstrap III, G. Hankins, and S. L. Clark, *Williams' Obstetrics*, 20th ed. (Stamford, CT: Appleton and Lange, 1997), p. 582. *Stedman's Medical Dictionary*, 26th ed. (Baltimore: Williams and Wilkins, 1995), p. 4. *Dorland's Illustrated Medical Dictionary*, 28th ed. (Philadelphia: W. B. Saunders, 1994), p. 4.

17. Suppose, however, a spontaneous abortion occurred because a woman was deliberately negligent, e.g., by not seeking medical assistance when she knew that her pregnancy was threatened. Even spontaneous abortion might then be viewed as morally problematic.

18. *Roe v. Wade*, 410 U.S. 113, 93 S. Ct. 705 (1973). *Stedman's Medical Dictionary*, p. 1936.

19. *ACOG Technical Bulletin* 109 (October 1987): 3–4. This is consistent with more recent documentation by Centers for Disease Control, citing an increase in second-trimester abortions performed by D&E: "The continued reliance on D&E probably has resulted from the lower risk for complications associated with the procedure." Lisa M. Koonin, Jack C. Smith, M. S. Ramick, and Lilo T. Strauss, *Abortion Surveillance: United States, 1995* [July 3, 1998/47 (SS-2)]: 31–68.

20. Cunningham et al., and James W. Knight and Joan C. Callahan, *Preventing Birth* (Salt Lake City: University of Utah Press, 1989), pp. 183–99.

21. Carson and Buster, pp. 184–95, and Diane Bartels, "Built-In Obsolescence:

Women, Embryo Production, and Genetic Engineering," *Reproductive and Genetic Engineering* 1 (1988): 141–52.

22. Ruth S. Cowan, "Women's Roles in the History of Amniocentesis and Chorionic Villi Sampling," in Karen H. Rothenberg and Elizebeth J. Thomson, eds., *Women and Prenatal Testing: Facing the Challenges of Genetic Technology* (Columbus: Ohio State University Press, 1994), pp. 35–48.

23. This position has been strongly defended and refuted by others. See, for example, Brian Johnstone, Helga Kuhse, and Peter Singer, "The Moral Status of the Embryo: Two Viewpoints," in W. Walters and P. Singer, eds., *Test-Tube Babies* (Melbourne, AU: Oxford University Press, 1982), pp. 49–63.

24. Unaffected embryos may be disposed of by the same methods.

25. Futility is admittedly a controversial and unclear concept. For well-developed analyses of its meanings and their moral implications, see Loretta Kopelman, ed., "Moral and Conceptual Disputes about When Treatments Are Medically Futile," *Journal of Medicine and Philosophy* 20 (1995): 109–224.

26. Although fertile couples for whom PGD is performed have a better chance than infertile couples of achieving pregnancy with transferred embryos, the probability of successful transfer, implantation, gestation, and birth is still slim.

27. Lesch-Nyhan syndrome is characterized by self-mutilation, mental retardation, spastic cerebral palsy, and urinary stones. See Victor McKusick, *Online Mendelian Inheritance in Man* (http://www3.ncbi.nlm.nih.gov:8o/omim/).

28. James Rachels, "Active and Passive Euthanasia," *New England Journal of Medicine* 292 (1975): 78–80.

29. E.g., Tom L. Beauchamp, "A Reply to Rachels on Active and Passive Euthanasia," in Tom L. Beauchamp and S. Perlin, eds., *Ethical Issues in Death and Dying* (Englewood Cliffs, NJ: Prentice-Hall, 1978), pp. 246–58.

30. *In re* Karen Quinlan, 70 N.J. 10, 355 A.3d 647 (N.J. Sup. Ct. 1976); *in re* Philip K. Eichner, On Behalf of Joseph C. Fox, 420 N.E., 2d 64 (N.Y. App. Div. 1981); *Nancy Beth Cruzan v. Robert Harmon v. Thad McCanse,* No. 70813 (Supreme Court of Missouri, 1988).

31. Several studies indicate that women who undergo abortions late in their pregnancies and who have previously had a pregnancy in which the fetus was diagnosed with a genetic condition experience more difficult grief reactions than those whose abortions are not associated with these factors. See, for example, Rita Beck Black in Rothenberg and Thomson, pp. 271–90.

32. Given the cost and relative unavailability of PGD, few individuals experience it as a genuine option.

33. Cheryl F. McCartney, "Decision by Single Women to Conceive by Artificial Insemination," *Journal of Psychosomatic Obstetrics and Gynecology* 4 (1985): 321, and Maureen McGuire and Nancy J. Alexander, "Artificial Insemination of Single Women," *Fertility and Sterility* 43 (February 1985): 183.

34. The fact that a desire to promote desired traits in offspring is common and natural does not make it morally adequate, particularly in cases where the desire cannot be implemented without technological assistance.

13

GENOMIC ALTERATIONS AND WOMEN

PREIMPLANTATION genetic diagnosis is not only associated with abortion, as illustrated in the previous chapter; it is also a means by which to identify conditions for which gene therapy may be provided during early development. Performing both procedures for the same condition would constitute what some authors call "preimplantation genetics."[1] Although gene therapy before preimplantation is not yet possible, it could technically be a simpler procedure than gene therapy later in development because it involves a single cell or zygote rather than a more developed organism.[2]

Ordinarily, various types of therapy for specific conditions are acceptable and even commendable. When the target of the therapy is a person's genes, however, philosophical and ethical questions are raised that are probably as controversial as abortion: To what extent do genetic interventions alter personal identity? May they be utilized to improve the abilities or appearances of specific individuals? Should they be provided to individuals even when they affect their posterity, who, obviously, are incapable of consenting to the intervention? All of these issues affect both men and women, albeit not always in the same way. From an egalitarian feminist standpoint, the most worrisome impact that the possibility of altering the genome may have for women is social pressure to undergo risky and costly interventions for the sake of their potential children, who also face risks through the procedures. Although the issue of coercive treatment of pregnant women for the sake of their fetuses is not new, more women are likely to be subjected to overt or covert forms of coercion as possibilities for genetic interventions escalate.

Because some women as well as men and children are likely to benefit from genetic intervention, an egalitarian feminist standpoint would resist the suppression of its development. However, participants in the research that may bring us these benefits face real risks, to which their fully informed and voluntary consent is ethically indispensable. Only when genetic interventions are shown to be safe and effective should they be offered more widely. Anticipating that, the ethical challenge is to weigh the pros and cons of different interventions for individual women and for women as a group, and to develop a workable strategy for distributing their benefits and burdens equitably. In this chapter, therefore, I examine the potential impact on women of the capacity to alter the genome and assess whether these techniques are more or less likely to promote gender justice. Preliminarily, I consider different kinds and methods of genetic intervention.

Cell Types and Methods of Altering the Genome

Two types of cells may be the target of genetic intervention: somatic cells and germ cells. Only the latter are passed on to one's children. Gene therapy has already been performed on somatic cells in a small number of patients, with apparent success.[3] Influencing the germ line is much more complicated both technically and ethically, and has not been attempted in humans. Many have argued that germ line interventions should never be performed, but their number seems to be declining in recent years.

Somatic cell gene therapy has been attempted through removal of affected cells from the patient, adding normal genes to them, growing them in the laboratory, and then returning them to the patient by injection.[4] Although retroviruses (with their harmful sequences deleted) are generally used to deliver the normal genes to the in vitro cells, other modes of delivery may be used if this method is impractical or ineffective. With some conditions, such as genetic brain disease, it would be more damaging than helpful to remove the affected cells; for others, such as hypercholesterolemia, it is impossible to do so because the disease affects many cell types throughout the body. Efforts to develop methods to treat these conditions in vivo have not as yet been successful, but such an approach could provide less invasive and less costly treatments for other conditions also.[5]

Another potential method of somatic cell gene therapy is cell grafting, which involves both in vivo and in vitro procedures.[6] Here, cells capable of metabolic interaction with nonremovable cells are removed from the patient, and a normal gene is added to them. The treated cells are returned to the patient, where they are expected to produce and transmit the desired gene product to the nonremovable cells.

The scientific and technical expertise that underlies developing strategies for somatic cell gene therapy is extensive and impressive. In contrast, the actual experience of the therapy for those directly involved, especially patients, is relatively uneventful; in fact, it is less invasive and less uncomfortable than many routine forms of medical and surgical treatment. Most people find somatic cell gene therapy as acceptable as other forms of medical treatment. Unfortunately, however, its success thus far has been quite limited.[7]

A second form of somatic cell gene therapy has the potential for greater therapeutic effectiveness. This method involves gene "surgery" and gene replacement: the affected gene is excised and a new healthy gene is inserted in its place.[8] Clinically, this has three advantages over gene addition: the new gene is more likely to be appropriately regulated and expressed; the risk of disrupting another essential gene is avoided, and dominant as well as recessive genetic disorders may be effectively treated through this method.[9] Given these advantages, most people would find replacement somatic cell gene therapy not only acceptable but desirable; some, nonetheless, might resist it on grounds that replacement of genes involves changes that are radically different from those produced by other medical and surgical treatments. Excising and replacing one's genes alters one's unique genetic makeup. Gene addition therapy, which seems to involve that also, at least leaves all of one's original genome intact.

Germ line gene therapy is more controversial than either form of somatic cell gene therapy because germ cells are those we transmit to our offspring. However, because some genetic conditions are caused by mutations in the germ cells, effective treatment cannot be provided without simultaneously altering the genomes of the patient's posterity, who are obviously unable to agree to the procedure. Other genetic conditions can be effectively treated only in utero, before implantation, or even before fertilization; inevitably, even though the goal of the treatment is to cure a somatic disorder, the germ line is also affected.

Potentially, germ line gene therapy in humans may be directed toward the pronuclei of oocytes, toward sperm stem cells, or toward preimplantation embryos.[10] Sperm stem cells have been successfully transferred from fertile mice to infertile mice.[11] The recipient mice developed normal spermatogenesis, and their mature spermatozoa yielded offspring that were the genetic match of the donor sperm stem cells. If this method were combined with techniques for genetically modifying sperm stem cells before transferring them, it could be used to perform germ line therapy. Although the method provides the possibility of avoiding a great deal of medical risk, discomfort, and cost for women, with little risk for the men who participate, it has not yet been attempted in humans. Instead, most studies of germ line gene therapy in humans deal with embryos rather than gametes. This is unfortunate for men as well as women because male infertility may also be treatable by this means.

Because men produce sperm throughout their reproductive life span, sperm stem cells are readily available. In contrast, women are born with their full complement of egg cells, or oocytes, and are therefore unable to provide a replenishable gametic source. Women can and do, however, undergo ovulation stimulation and egg retrieval to provide the ova that are fertilized in vitro and become the preimplantation embryos on which germ line gene therapy may be performed. This is true even if the genetic flaw to be corrected has originated in the male partner.

From the standpoint of clinical effectiveness, germ line gene therapy has several advantages over somatic cell gene therapy.[12] First, it provides a means of successfully treating conditions that affect different organs and different cell types, such as cystic fibrosis. Somatic cell gene therapy would require multiple procedures to achieve similar therapeutic success. Second, because germ line gene therapy would be performed before implantation, it could prevent damage that would otherwise occur during fetal development due to a specific genetic condition. Somatic cell gene therapy cannot prevent this damage because it is performed on differentiated cells only. Third, germ line gene therapy may be used as an alternative to in vivo somatic cell gene therapy (if and when both therapies are available) to treat disorders expressed in nonremovable cells, such as Lesch-Nyhan syndrome and other disorders of the nervous system. Fourth, germ line gene therapy is medically and economically more efficient than somatic cell gene therapy in that it obviates the need to treat successive offspring for the same genetic disorder. In doing so, it reduces the incidence of some genetic disorders in the human gene pool, or, to put it positively, increases the incidence of healthy genes in the population.

If genes are replaced rather than added to the gene pool, the last advantage suggests a potential disadvantage: the loss of a capacity for potentially beneficial functions that the deleted genes may confer, such as resistance to malaria in carriers of sickle cell disease. However, this potential loss must be weighed against the actual loss of a genetic cure that might otherwise be forfeited. In general, the clinical advantages of germ line gene therapy seem to outweigh the advantages of somatic cell gene therapy, but only if we exclude consideration of the impact of germ line interventions on women. In light of that impact, even considering the possible benefits of germ line gene therapy to them and their children, women deserve a privileged status in decisions about its use.

Medical therapy or treatment is usually construed as a means of meeting a health need, such as cure of a disease, amelioration of pain, or "correction" of a disability.[13] It is thus intended to overcome a disadvantage in the person treated. However, the same means have increasingly been offered and sought to satisfy desires rather than needs, providing some people with advantages over others. Some forms of reproductive assistance, cosmetic surgery, and growth hormone treatment are examples in this regard.[14] Gene therapy has its counterpart to these dual objectives of medical treatment in the distinction between enhancement and cure. Genetic enhancement is sometimes equated with genetic engineering. Table 13–1 presents LeRoy Walters and Julie Palmer's illustration of the distinction between gene therapy and genetic enhancement as overlapping with the distinction between germ line and somatic cell interventions.

Preempting the use of "therapy" for enhancement, the possible combinations that the two distinctions permit are (1) somatic therapy, (2) germ line therapy, (3) somatic enhancement, and (4) germ line enhancement. Only 1 has been sufficiently developed for use in humans, and for a very limited number of conditions. Because the most prevalent human diseases are complex, the technical possibility of totally effective gene therapy remains remote. This is also true for the capabilities and characteristics to which 3 and 4 refer. Ethically, 1 is least problematic because it is most akin to a wide array of traditional, acceptable medical therapies.[15] In contrast, 4 is most problematic because it affects unconsenting future generations and does not address medical needs. From an egalitarian feminist standpoint, 4 is unacceptable because it increases inequities; but if, as no one anticipates, the enhancements provided to some were available to all, it would be acceptable.

The clinical advantages just outlined provide a strong argument for permitting germ line gene therapy (2), at least in instances where other effective treatment is unavailable. However, this caveat suggests that perhaps another category should be introduced between somatic and germ line therapies: germ line therapy for somatic disorders that are not otherwise curable. Somatic enhancement (3) raises the same problem of inequity as 4, although on a much less troubling scale. Accordingly, both enhancement categories are unacceptable unless available to everyone. Of course, if they were not only available but utilized by everyone, inequities associated with genetic differences would either disappear or reach a point where further enhancement would not provide advantages to some vis-à-vis others. If the enhancement strategies were stripped of their potential for providing a competitive advantage, interest in them would probably decline.[16]

TABLE 13–1. Genetic Alteration Matrix

	SOMATIC	GERM LINE
Prevention, treatment, or cure of disease	1	2
Enhancement of capabilities or characteristics	3	4

Preventive Gene Therapy versus Interventions for Enhancement

Joining prevention to treatment and cure may raise questions about whether Walters and Palmers's distinction between these and enhancement can be sustained. As Eric Juengst observes, prevention may also be viewed as a form of enhancement.[17] Whether either view is correct depends on the feature that is promoted or improved through the intervention. Consider, for example, the possibility of improving an individual's immune system through gene therapy (whether somatic or germ line); this may be viewed as preventive health practice. In contrast, enhancing someone's height, at least in cases where his stature fits within a normal range for age and sex, is hardly defensible as a strategy for forestalling disease. Intelligence is a more complicated category because its enhancement does not seem to be related to preventive health care; yet enhanced intelligence about the implications of inadequate or dangerous health habits motivate behaviors that deter the onset of disease.

Genetic alterations designed to forestall the onset of specific diseases may appropriately be called preventive gene therapies, and these are morally distinguishable from curative (or ameliorative) gene therapies.[18] Curative therapies differ from preventive therapies in that the need for cure is typically more evident and more immediate than the need for prevention. The latter need is speculative rather than actual because the disease to be prevented may in fact never occur. The patient may, unfortunately, die of other causes before its onset or, fortunately, fall within the group of those who are never affected by the probability that the preventive therapy addresses (e.g., the percentage of women who test positive for genetic susceptibility to breast cancer but do not develop the disease).

Genetic interventions intended to promote a person's well being beyond its normal range for her age and sex may be more accurately construed as enhancement rather than therapy. Walters and Palmer consider three categories of potential genetic enhancements: physical, intellectual, and moral.[19] Physical enhancements are divided between those intended to promote health and those intended to promote other assets. Their only example of a health-oriented "enhancement" is the one that I have suggested properly belongs to the preventive category: genetic intervention that fortifies the entire immune system. Their examples of non–health-related physical enhancements include a more muscular physique, wrinkle-free skin, and increased energy and endurance.[20] In addition, they consider physical enhancements that may or may not be health-related: size, the need for sleep, and aging.

Among intellectual enhancements Walters and Palmer consider memory and cognitive ability. If memory enhancement is proposed for treatment of a late onset disorder such as Alzheimer disease or senile dementia, it may more appropriately be considered therapy rather than enhancement. With regard to cognitive ability, Walters and Palmer cite the potential benefit of genetic enhancement to people who suffer from fragile-X syndrome, the most common genetic cause of mental retardation.[21] Here again, a genetic intervention that restores a person with this disorder to a normal range of intellectual function should be counted as therapy rather than enhancement.[22]

Walters and Palmer acknowledge that genetic enhancement of moral characteristics, which they define as "attitudes towards, and behavior in relation to, one's fellow human beings," is even more controversial than other types of enhancement.[23] For them, impulsive, aggressive, and anti-social behaviors exemplify moral traits for which genetic enhancement may be justified. A plethora of other traits, such as shyness, talkativeness, or audaciousness, would also be candidates. Characteristics such as these apparently illustrate the authors' broad conception of "moral," but they would hardly conform to the stricter sense of "moral" employed by those who equate ethics with morality (i.e., as involving obligations to others).[24] Potential interventions to alter such basic human attitudes or behaviors are not only ethically and socially problematic; they raise yet more fundamental questions about the meaning and integrity of individuals.[25]

Under the aegis of enhancement, Walters and Palmer explicitly endorse health-related physical genetic alterations and intellectual genetic alterations that are remedial, that is, interventions whose effect is to bring recipients into a normal range of physical or intellectual function. As already suggested, both types of genetic intervention may more appropriately be described as therapies. The authors also support "moral enhancement for violent sociopaths—provided that such sociopaths freely consent to the intervention."[26] But, to the extent that the sociopathology of an individual is a disease, the genetic intervention may again be considered therapy rather than enhancement. Moreover, the intervention may be justified as a necessary means of protecting others.

Although Walters and Palmer view other modes of genetic alterations for enhancement as problematic, they seem open to these means once the safety of their utilization is established. Nonetheless, the authors express reservations about genetic alterations in children, in competitive sports, and in the germ line. They themselves disagree about whether individual liberty or distributive justice is the more important value to be promoted in the allocation of resources for genetic enhancement—an issue that is of central importance from an egalitarian feminist standpoint. Palmer avers that "individual liberty is such an important feature of both morality and social and political life that it should only be interfered with to protect the defenseless—for example, children—from serious harm." Walters maintains that "the long-term goal of reducing the gap between the best and worst-off members of society is preeminently important, both as a sign of respect for the dignity of all human beings and as a means for reducing social conflict."[27] Palmer's priority is defensible from a libertarian or liberal feminist standpoint. Walters's exemplifies that of an egalitarian feminist.

A More Adequate Framework

The preceding account illustrates a range of differences in gene therapy that cannot be accommodated by Walters and Palmer's outline (Table 13–1). Their taxonomy misses therapies whose goal is to cure the individual, but in doing so, affect the germ line; it also misses the distinct role that prevention plays, which is likely to increase with the expansion of genetic testing for susceptibility to specific disorders. Table 13–2 accommodates these additional distinctions

While it is still true that somatic cell gene therapy (1) is least problematic and germ line enhancement (9) is most problematic, this expanded taxonomy is a means by which to illustrate other morally relevant features of different types of genetic alteration. For example, if other relevant features of the comparison are equal, 2 is more readily justifiable than 3 because it purports to cure an actual genetic disorder in a person already born; but 2 is less justifiable than 1 because it affects unconsenting future generations. The same rationale could apply to the relationships between 8 and 9, 8 and 7, 5 and 6, and 5 and 4. In other words, other factors being equal, the types of interventions listed in the middle column are more ethically acceptable than their counterparts in the column at the right, and vice versa for the column at the left.

Considering the relationships among therapy, prevention, and enhancement, the priority that an egalitarian feminist standpoint would support is illustrated by the order in which they are listed: therapy is usually more compelling than prevention, and prevention more compelling than enhancement. Therapy is more compelling than prevention if both apply to the same need because the need is more immediate in one case than in the other. Prevention, moreover, involves a speculative element, based on the fact that other unknown or unpredictable elements may intervene to annul its effectiveness. Conditions to be prevented are those that count as harms or disadvantages to individuals, whereas enhancements count as advantages to them. Accordingly, so long as there is reasonable expectation that prevention will be effective, it is more likely to promote equality than enhancement.

Table 13–2 represents similar ordering on the vertical and on the horizontal planes: other factors being equal, the different types of genetic interventions listed across the middle are more ethically acceptable than their counterparts

TABLE 13–2. Expanded Genetic Alteration Matrix

	SOMATIC	SOMATIC THROUGH GERM LINE	GERM LINE
Therapy	1	2	3
Prevention	4	5	6
Enhancement	7	8	9

on the bottom row and less acceptable than those on the top row. In all of these comparisons, the "more" and "less" may be modified if other variables are introduced into the different categories.

Other variables include the availability of nongenetic modes of intervention, the severity of the disease to be treated or prevented, the impact on others of the trait to be enhanced, the risk or invasiveness of the intervention, and its prospect of success. The relationships outlined hold only if the other variables do not distort the comparison of the different types of interventions as such. While the expanded diagram thus constitutes a guide to moral assessment of different types of genetic alteration vis-à-vis each other, many more factors need to be considered if policies and decisions are to serve the "long-term goal of reducing the gap between the best- and worst-off members of society." Gender is of course one of the major variables that may be superimposed on different types of genetic interventions. In the next section, therefore, I review the major arguments for and against gene therapy from a feminist perspective.

Arguments Pro and Con Genetic Intervention

To its supporters, somatic cell gene therapy, whether by addition or replacement of genes, is as morally and medically justifiable as any other mode of treatment for disease or disability. Opponents challenge this comparison, arguing that tampering with people's genetic make-up, even when it may cure or prevent illness, is wrong because it alters what is yet more fundamental than their health, their identity.

Three lines of argument may be offered in response to concerns about identity: one extending the comparison with other medical treatments, another based on the multifactoriality of most genetic conditions, and a third which critiques the notion of genetic identity.[28] The first argument stems from recognition that the uniqueness of the individual involves constant changes, some drastic, some trivial. Many medical therapies run a much greater risk than gene therapy of changing a person's so-called "identity." Consider, for example, someone whose affect or behavior is so altered by medication that friends and family are no longer recognized, or someone whose appearance is radically transformed through extensive cosmetic surgery. Diseases such as Alzheimer, Huntington or other neurological disorders also seem to influence a person's identity more than somatic cell gene therapy. Even nonmedical events can cause such drastic changes that an individual is no longer recognizable as his or her former self, as when a tragic accident results in the victim's permanent loss of cognition or previous level of functioning.

The second argument suggests that even if one's genome were altered by genetic intervention, the change is hardly substantial even from the standpoint of genetics. The multifactoriality of most genetic conditions means that their expression or phenotype is governed not simply by one gene but by the interaction of different genes and by the interaction between genes and nongenetic factors, both internal and external. Because of these potential interactions, the genome alone does not and cannot determine the uniqueness of the individual. Even identical twins, after all, are unique individuals, as any parent of them will attest.

A third argument debunks the claim that genes define the individual on grounds that it ignores the relationships to other persons without which individuality can be neither developed nor sustained. Feminists are particularly committed to a social rather than genetic conception of identity. Annette Baier, for instance, describes a person as someone who comes into being through the experience of dependence on other persons. "Persons," she says, "come after and before other persons."[29] Moreover, the identity of a person who thus comes into being does not remain static; it changes through ongoing interactions with other persons and other biological and environmental influences.

If the preceding arguments are persuasive, somatic cell gene therapy, whether by addition or replacement, is not ethically problematic so long as the usual ethical requirements for medical treatment are observed, that is, it is shown to be therapeutically effective, and patients or their surrogates provide adequate informed consent for their treatment. Germ line gene therapy has generated much more controversy because even surrogate consent is impossible for some of those affected.[30] It was not surprising, therefore, that germ line gene therapy was virtually excluded from consideration by the Working Group of the Recombinant DNA Committee of the National Institutes of Health, which developed the first federal guidelines for use of gene therapy. The advisory document that this group prepared was entitled "Points to Consider in the Design and Submission of Human Somatic-Cell Gene Therapy Protocols."[31] Narrowing the scope of their consideration to somatic cell gene therapy undoubtedly expedited approval of the first gene therapy protocols. So long as researchers proposed only to introduce therapies that might cure specific genetic conditions in specific individuals, gene therapy could be regarded as the moral equivalent of any other medical therapy which they sought support to investigate.

In the years since the U.S. National Institutes of Health authorized the first somatic cell gene therapy protocols, support for germ line gene therapy has grown. Arguments offered in its favor include the duty of nonmaleficence toward fetuses as well as future generations, cost effectiveness, beneficence toward parents, and respect for parental autonomy.[32] The duty of nonmaleficence is fulfilled and the costs of treatment are reduced through germ line gene therapy because it avoids having to treat affected individuals in successive generations. However, for somatic genetic conditions that can be effectively treated only in utero, the duty of nonmaleficence toward the fetus as a potential child is more compelling than the duty of nonmaleficence toward children who have not yet been conceived, and may never be.

Germ line gene therapy could benefit parents who are carriers for dominant, autosomal recessive, or X-linked disorders by providing them with a means of ensuring that their children will neither be affected by these disorders nor be carriers for them. In most cases, this advantage is more significant for women than for men because women are so much more likely to be principal caregivers for the affected children. For the same reason, while "respect for parental autonomy" provides a rationale for germ line gene therapy, a feminist standpoint reminds us that parents might disagree about whether to employ the procedure; where that occurs, the woman's decision should ordinarily prevail.

An even more convincing rationale for subordinating men's decisions to women's with regard to germ line gene therapy is the fact that women's bodies are directly affected by the procedure. Until and unless germ line gene therapy is performed on sperm stem cells, the treatment will require women to undergo the risks, invasiveness, and discomfort of either fetal therapy, which can only be undertaken through their bodies, or ovulation stimulation, egg retrieval, and embryo transfer for the sake of a potential child. The argument for giving priority to the woman's autonomy in decisions about these procedures is based on the obvious difference between the risks, invasiveness, and discomfort that the interventions mean for women in contrast with the lack thereof for the men responsible for the women's pregnancies.

Giving priority to women's autonomy is easier said than done because of the impact of socialization on women with regard to their responsibility for children and potential children. Just as women may be pressured by the expectations of others, including clinicians and family members, to undergo prenatal testing, they may feel obliged to undergo surgery for the sake of fetuses shown through genetic testing to have a condition that is correctable in utero.[33] Some bioethicists believe women are obligated to undergo such treatment, despite its risk and lack of benefit to them. John Robertson, for example, supports this view on grounds of a link between postnatal and prenatal responsibility for children. Ignoring the gender difference in the impact of prenatal intervention, he writes:

> Parents have a moral and legal duty after a child is born to provide treatment when necessary for its health. It should follow that they have a moral duty to provide the treatment before birth if postbirth treatments are not feasible and if there is a safe, effective, and minimally intrusive prenatal treatment available.[34]

Possibly Robertson might acknowledge that fetal surgery is neither safe nor minimally intrusive for the pregnant woman. Further, while it has been effective in a few cases, it is still mainly experimental. In a note to the quoted passage, however, Robertson extends his understanding of parental obligation to the duty of parents "not to engage in prenatal behaviors that would cause a child who would have been born healthy to be born with disability," and he identifies as a related issue the question of "whether to punish mothers whose babies are born drug-addicted."[35]

In addition to concerns about coerciveness and risks to women, arguments against germ line gene therapy may also be based on its potential for reducing the variety of the gene pool and foreclosing the possibility of some as-yet-undiscovered benefits from deleted or unrepaired genes. Like concerns about affecting nonconsenting future generations, these worries are largely speculative. Mutations will continue to occur, precipitating possible genetic advantages as well as disadvantages, and future generations are more likely than not to consent to interventions that preempt a genetic disease or disability that they might otherwise experience.

From a feminist standpoint, risks to women and potential pressures on them are the most persuasive reasons for opposing germ line gene therapy. However, banning the therapy entirely might deny its advantages for some women. What is crucial in order to minimize its potential for gender injustice is to maximize the autonomy of the women for whom the procedure may be relevant.

In addition to the concerns that apply to germ line gene therapy as distinct from somatic cell gene therapy, genetic interventions for enhancement raise important issues regardless of whether somatic cells or germ cells are affected. From a libertarian feminist standpoint, so long as women freely consent to enhancement procedures, most of them are probably acceptable. From an egalitarian feminist standpoint, many are not.

Although not a feminist, Robertson exemplifies a libertarian point of view in his arguments in support of enhancement. His position draws on his notion of procreative liberty or the right to reproduce, from which he extrapolates a right to control the characteristics of offspring. The extrapolation depends on two factors: whether the specific enhancement determines whether reproduction will occur, and whether harms associated with the enhancement outweigh its benefits.[36]

Robertson acknowledges that people attribute different degrees of importance to the characteristics they desire for their offspring. They also differ in the lengths they will go to procure those characteristics in their children or, conversely, to avoid having children who lack those characteristics. For some, the desire is a preference whose fulfillment they are willing to forgo; for others, its fulfillment is essential to their reproductive plans. According to Robertson, for genetic enhancement to fall within the scope of procreative liberty, a couple would have to claim that they only want offspring with the greatest possible chance to excel, be successful, have a happy life, and thus that they would not reproduce unless they could engage in the enhancement activities. If they would have the child anyway, then prebirth enhancement would not be part of procreative liberty.[37]

In cases where procreative liberty would not support genetic alteration for enhancement of offspring, Robertson proposes an additional argument for the couple's right to the intervention: that enhancement prior to birth through genetic technology is part and parcel of the parents' right to shape specific characteristics of their child after birth, for example, "through special tutors, music camps, orthodontia, rhinoplasty, and even the administration of exogenous human growth hormone to increase stature."[38]

Robertson then examines the possibility of harms to those affected by enhancement strategies: embryos and fetuses, children, people with disabilities, and women. "Symbolic moral considerations," he says, may prompt some people to oppose prenatal enhancement, but the potential for harm through their use is negligible, and enhancement as distinct from therapy is consistent with the legal permissibility of abortion before viability for any reason.[39] Rather than suffer harm, children born as a result of genetic enhancement and others who are genetically enhanced subsequent to birth are likely to benefit by the procedures. Further, just as abortions based on genetic impairment do not imply discrimination against people who are disabled, neither would enhancements of some people lead to discrimination against others. Robertson argues that neither sex selection nor selection of traits such as hair and eye color is likely to harm others, particularly if the means of selection does not involve termination of embryos or fetuses that do not meet the desired specifications. On grounds of the procreative liberty of couples and possible harms to those affected, he concludes that "Prebirth selection of offspring characteristics is a basic right."[40]

If Robertson were a libertarian feminist, his consideration of the principle of procreative liberty would have to be developed in a manner that respects gender differences within a couple. Unfortunately, even when he adverts to the possible harms of prenatal tests, he ignores their disparate impact on women. Such tests, he writes, may "be physically intrusive or have untoward social and psychological effects on *the couple*."[41] If Robertson were to utilize a feminist standpoint to reduce his apparent myopia, he would acknowledge explicitly not only that women face risks through genetic interventions that men do not face but also that couples are not a single autonomous entity.[42] Rather, they are comprised of separate individuals who may or may not agree on whether genetic interventions should be performed on their potential offspring or their children. He would also acknowledge that women, because of their more extensive role in caregiving, are more affected than men by postbirth genetic interventions. While such interventions entail risks and costs, they may of course be advantageous to caregivers as well as those for whom they care.

To an egalitarian feminist, even if the principle of procreative liberty took account of gender differences in couples, it would not suffice as a criterion by which to assess whether genetic technologies should be employed for enhancement. Neither would the argument that a right to enhance children after birth implies a right to enhance them before birth. Strategies for enhancement are generally problematic because they provide a means by which some people may obtain or increase their advantages over others. In other words, enhancements are at odds with, or not conducive to, social equality unless they are accessible to everyone.

Admittedly, individuals not only have a natural drive to enhance their abilities and characteristics; they probably have a right and even an obligation to do so. The same drive, right, and obligation apply to parents vis-à-vis their children. In the competitive world in which we live, not only are efforts to enhance oneself or one's children reinforced and often rewarded, but social progress seems to depend on those efforts. To the extent that an egalitarian view opposes such progress, it is unlikely to draw followers. Perhaps this explains why W. French Anderson, a pioneer in gene therapy, found himself the lone dissident at a conference on germ line gene therapy at Cold Spring Harbor in 1998. Unlike his compatriots, Anderson argued that researchers have a duty "to use this powerful technology [only] for the treatment of disease and not for any other purpose."[43]

Equal access makes possibilities for enhancement, whether through genetics or through other means, compatible with an egalitarian framework. Libertarian thinking subordinates equal access to individual liberty; egalitarian thinking does the opposite but is not opposed to enhancement or social progress as such. If universal access is a goal that cannot (yet or ever) be achieved but can be best approximated by permitting partial access at this point in time, then the latter is acceptable at least to some egalitarian feminists.

An egalitarian standpoint differs from a libertarian standpoint in another important respect: the meaning of liberty, freedom, or autonomy. The egalitarian feminist is likely to be distrustful of the meaning that Robertson has in mind when he champions procreative freedom and parental autonomy. His tendency to treat individual choice uncritically is characteristic of many contemporary bioethicists, who seldom attend to the impact of socialization on individuals from whom "informed consent" is elicited and obtained.[44] For feminists in general, and egalitarian feminists in particular, women's "autonomy" is often compromised by the circumstances and relationships in which they are enmeshed.[45] These factors have special impact on decisions associated with stereotypic expectations of women, such as reproductive and caregiving behaviors.

From an egalitarian feminist standpoint, respect for women's autonomy, contextually understood, is crucial to determination of whether genetic alterations for enhancement should be utilized even if accessible to all. As for access by anyone, it is doubtful that genetic interventions for enhancement will be available soon because so little is known of the multifactorial influences on their expression. The conditions for which enhancement may be desired are so complex that they may never be producible through genetic interventions.

Whether or not enhancement strategies become available, other ways in which the genome may be altered entail possibilities for harming as well as helping women. Fair distribution of the potential harms and benefits requires assessment not only of each method that is developed but also of the context in which it may be used. Understanding that context and appreciating its impact on women's lives requires input from women themselves. Without imputing a privileged status to that input, decisions and policies about genetic alterations are unlikely to satisfy the criterion of gender justice.

Notes

1. Eugene Pergament and Andrea Bonnicksen, "Preimplantation Genetics: A Case for Prospective Action," *American Journal of Medical Genetics* 52 (1994): 152.

2. Meredith Wadman, "Germline Gene Therapy 'Must be Spared Excessive Regulation,'" *Nature* 392 (March 26, 1988): 317.

3. The term "apparent" is significant because the patients on whom somatic cell gene therapy has been performed received traditional treatment as well; the fact that their condition improved is therefore not definitively attributable to gene therapy. These first patients were two children with adenosine deaminase (ADA) deficiency, a condition caused by a mutation on the twentieth chromosome, which is usually fatal because the body lacks immunological resistance to infections. For a clear and succinct account of ADA deficiency and the use of somatic cell gene therapy for these patients, see LeRoy Walters and Julie Gage Palmer, *The Ethics of Human Gene Therapy* (New York: Oxford University Press, 1997), pp. 17–20. For a fuller account of the patient for whom the treatment was apparently successful and of the researchers who developed and performed the therapy, see Larry Thompson, *Correcting the Code: Inventing the Genetic Cure for the Human Body* (New York: Simon and Schuster, 1994), pp. 13–52.

4. Walters and Palmer, pp. 20–25. The first approved somatic cell gene therapy in the United States was performed on a four-year-old in 1990. W. French Anderson and Theodore Friedmann, "Gene Therapy: Strategies for Gene Therapy," in Warren Reich, ed., *Encyclopedia of Bioethics* (New York: Macmillan, 1995), p. 909.

5. Walters and Palmer, pp. 167–68. Although germ line gene therapy is more controversial and complicated, it may also be used to treat these conditions.

6. Walters and Palmer, pp. 168–69.

7. Wadman, p. 317.

8. Walters and Palmer, pp. 72–74, 186–96.

9. Walters and Palmer, pp. 72–73.

10. Pergament and Bonnicksen, p. 153.

11. Ralph L. Brinster and Mary R. Avarbock, "Germline Transmission of Donor Haplotype following Spermatogonial Transplantation," *Proceedings of the National Academy of Sciences* 91, 24 (1994): 11301–7, and Ralph L. Brinster and James W. Zimmerman, "Spermatogenesis following Male Germ-Cell Transplantation," *Proceedings of the National Academy of Sciences* 91, 24 (1994): 11298–302.

12. Walters and Palmer, pp. 62–63.

13. Although some persons with disabilities would probably object to my use of the term "correction," those who seek the therapy are likely to agree.

14. For individuals who are short of stature due to normal heredity ("constitutional shortness of stature"), the advantage provided by growth hormone therapy is apparently only temporary. Although the growth rate is accelerated, final height is within the previously expected range.

15. This does not imply that traditional, acceptable medical therapies are always or necessarily justified. But the same criteria required for their justification should be applied to both situations (e.g., expectation that the benefit of therapy is greater than, or at least equal to, its expected burden to the patient, and fully informed and voluntary consent to treatment on the part of the patient).

16. Some "enhancements" would probably be valued by some individuals regardless of whether they were similarly valued by others. But if they were not valued by the others, neither would they be identified as enhancements to them.

17. Eric T. Juengst, "Can Enhancement Be Distinguished from Prevention in Genetic Medicine?" *Journal of Medicine and Philosophy* 22 (1997): 126. Juengst's critique of this view supports my interpretation of prevention as health-related.

18. Ameliorative therapies may be interpreted as curing some aspects of a disease, at least temporarily. The removal of all symptoms on a permanent basis would be a total cure.

19. Walters and Palmer, pp. 101–33.

20. Because they facilitate healthful exercise, increased energy and endurance may also be regarded as health-related enhancements.

21. Walters and Palmer, p. 121.

22. Although some philosophers support a standard of "normal species functioning," others critique that notion. Cf. Erik Parens, "Is Better Always Good? The Enhancement Project," in Erik Parens, ed., *Enhancing Human Traits: Ethical and Social Implications* (Washington, DC: Georgetown University Press, 1998), pp. 3–7; Eric T. Juengst, "What Does Enhancement Mean?" in Parens, pp. 35–37; and Anita Silvers, "A Fatal Attraction to Normalizing," in Parens, pp. 95–121. As used here, the term "normal" is intended to refer to a range of capability rather than to a range of human worth. As described in Chapter 4, equality means equal valuing of people regardless of their differences. A social ideal of equality entails efforts to reduce unequal advantages—not by reducing the capabilities of those who are advantaged but by increasing the capabilities of those who are disadvantaged.

23. Walters and Palmer, p. 108.

24. It seems strange to describe personality traits such as shyness and talkativeness as "moral." Even if ethics and morality are contrasted, with ethics defined as an intellectual enterprise (moral philosophy) and morality defined as practical behavior, the term "moral" is typically construed more narrowly than Walters and Palmer use it.

25. Attempts to alter or influence human attitudes and behavior are surely not new, nor are they necessarily wrong. If the integrity of individuals refers in some cases to behaviors that are harmful to others, alteration may be not only justified but commendable on utilitarian grounds. However, coerciveness always carries a moral onus, which is exacerbated by the possibility that its effect is permanent.

26. Walters and Palmer, p. 131.

27. Walters and Palmer, p. 132.

28. For more extended discussion of the problem of identity, see David Heyd, *Genetics: Moral Issues in the Creation of People* (Berkeley: University of California Press, 1992), pp. 160–90, and Dan W. Brock, "Genetic Identity and Self-Knowledge," in Robert F. Weir, Susan C. Lawrence, and Evan Fales, eds., *Genes and Human Self-*

Knowledge: Historical and Philosophical Reflections on Modern Genetics (Iowa City: University of Iowa Press, 1994), pp. 18–33. While arguing for the responsibility to avoid the birth of people with severe disabilities, Laura M. Purdy criticizes a genetic conception of identity in *Reproducing Persons: Issues in Feminist Bioethics* (Ithaca, NY: Cornell University Press, 1996), pp. 69–71.

29. Annette C. Baier, *Postures of the Mind: Essays on Mind and Morals* (Minneapolis: University of Minnesota Press, 1985), p. 85.

30. The impossibility of consent by future generations of individuals affected by germ line gene therapy arises also with other treatment modalities, such as radiation therapy.

31. LeRoy Walters chaired the Working Group, and Julie Gage Palmer was a research assistant working with the group. For an account of how the committee came into being, its early activities, and the "Points to Consider" that it developed, see Walters and Palmer, pp. 148–51.

32. David Perlman, "The Ethics of Germ-Line Gene Therapy: Challenges to Mainstream Approaches by a Feminist Critique," *Trends in Health Care, Law & Ethics* 8, 4 (1993): 36–38. Perlman critiques these arguments from a feminist perspective.

33. Feelings of obligation are not necessarily wrong; in fact, they are often appropriate. However, such feelings may be the result of unjustifiable pressure or coercion from others to act in a manner contrary to one's own interest.

34. John A. Robertson, "Genetic Selection of Offspring Characteristics," *Boston University Law Review* 76, 3 (1996): 470.

35. Robertson, p. 470, n. 200. Would that Robertson's concerns about harms to potential children extended to advocacy of prenatal care and drug rehabilitation programs for poor women.

36. Robertson, p. 429.

37. Robertson, p. 436.

38. Robertson, p. 436.

39. Robertson, p. 448. In this article as in his other writing, Robertson equates "symbolic" with "moral" and "moralistic." Cf. pp. 445, 463.

40. Robertson, p. 479.

41. Robertson, p. 440 (italics added).

42. An apparent exception to this emphasis on *the couple* is Robertson's support for a woman's right to abortion, which appears at odds with his advocacy of coercive treatment of pregnant women for the sake of their fetuses. See John A. Robertson, *Children of Choice: Freedom and the New Reproductive Technologies* (Princeton, NJ: Princeton University Press, 1994), pp. 66–58, and n. 22 above. To his credit, however, and despite his support of the woman's right to abortion, Robertson also argues for postnatal and prenatal responsibilities of fathers. See, e.g., *Children of Choice,* pp. 190–93.

43. Wadman, p. 317.

44. An exception to Robertson's uncritical tendency is his position on the moral responsibility of parents to provide treatment for children before birth. See also n. 42 above.

45. Perlman, pp. 37–, and Susan Sherwin, *The Politics of Women's Health: Exploring Agency and Autonomy* (Philadelphia: Temple University Press, 1998), pp. 19–45.

14

BEHAVIORAL GENETICS AND ALCOHOL CONSUMPTION IN WOMEN

AS we saw in the last chapter, the distinction between enhancement and therapy is sometimes difficult to establish, despite the fact that one is relatively uncontroversial in comparison with the other. Behavioral genetics presents a similar and overlapping contrast. Some conditions are identified as diseases; others involve traits or tendencies that are unrelated to health; and the vast majority of conditions are polygenic or multifactorial. As with the enhancement category of genomic alterations, some behavioral conditions have been categorized as moral or immoral,[1] while others are considered morally neutral or amoral. Unlike genetic enhancement strategies, behavioral genetics refers to a discipline within genetics, embracing both basic and clinical research as well as clinical testing, diagnosis, and interventions.

Testing for behavioral conditions may occur before conception or implantation, prenatally, or postnatally, and interventions may be genetic or nongenetic, as well as preventive, therapeutic, or enhancing. All of these variables are relevant to assessment of whether the intervention ought to be undertaken, but conceptual factors are relevant also. In this chapter, I discuss some of the empirical variables before considering implications of behavioral genetics for concepts of autonomy and assignment of responsibility for behaviors that are influenced by each individual's genome. While highlighting various examples of gender differences in behavioral traits and disorders, I target alcohol consumption as a behavioral trait with specific implications for women and examine a case that involves probable hereditary alcoholism in a pregnant woman.

The Meaning and Scope of Behavioral Genetics

As a discipline, behavioral genetics studies specific characteristics of individuals as shaped by genetic factors;[2] characteristics that are related to appearance only, such as hair or eye color, do not belong to this domain. In humans, behavioral genetics has typically involved twin, family, and adoption studies by which investigators attempt to determine the degree of interplay between environmental and genetic influences on behavior. The focus on individual differences distinguishes this field from those that are mainly concerned with characteristics shared by different members of the same species, such as sociobiology and evolutionary psychology.

In the late 1980s, a study of twins reared apart estimated the extent to which some behavioral traits are determined by heredity: conformity, 60%; tendency to worry, 55%, aggressiveness, 48%; creativity, 55%; extroversion, 61%.[3] Other characteristics of individuals that have been attributed in part to genetics are mental illness, intelligence, memory, novelty-seeking, shyness, sociability, homosexuality, dyslexia, addiction, zest for life, perfect pitch, and the tendencies to tease, take risks, giggle, and use hurtful words.[4]

Although scientists once viewed many behavioral characteristics as caused predominantly by environmental factors, they have increasingly placed greater weight on genetics as their determinants. The impact of many genetic traits is augmented rather than diminished as children grow older; this reinforces the emphasis on genetics.[5] From the standpoint of most moral philosophers, what is notable on either account of human behavior is the absence of any reference to the freedom or autonomy of the individual. Whether separately or together, if environment and genetics are viewed as (totally) determining human behavior, there is no room for autonomy or for ethics.

Philosophers of different persuasions regard autonomy as essential to moral decision making.[6] Consider, for example, Thomas Aquinas, for whom a virtuous or moral life consists of good habits formed from the repetition of human acts as a subset of "acts of man."[7] Anything a person does is an "act of man"; human acts are those "acts of man" that arise from what is essentially human, that is, reason and free will. Immanuel Kant argues that certain knowledge of freedom, as nonempirical, is unattainable. Nonetheless, he claims that we can know *that* freedom is without knowing *what* it is, and we can *know* that it is through the experience of obligation vis-à-vis present or past decisions.[8] A necessary condition for this experience is that individuals are capable of choosing among alternatives. Freedom is thus essential to moral agency. While consistent with Kant's account, Jean-Paul Sartre's notion of freedom is more demanding: to be free *is* to be human. Freedom rather than nature or nurture determines not only the humanity but the morality of the individual. Immorality is defined as a refusal to acknowledge the total responsibility that arises from freedom. As Sartre puts it, "I am, without excuse."[9]

Despite these views of philosophers and the emphasis on individual liberty within various legal and health care systems, support for determinism is undoubtedly buttressed by advances in behavioral genetics. The nature versus nurture debate[10] is by no means settled in favor of nature, yet the very continuation of the debate without introducing the capacity for choice as a third element shows the strength of the determinist thesis as a denial of freedom. Obviously, a libertarian version of feminism is incompatible with this denial, but egalitarian feminists who consider autonomy an important, although not absolute value challenge it as well.[11]

Decades ago, when social determinism was in the ascendancy, B. F. Skinner wrote *Beyond Freedom and Dignity*,[12] in which he argued that if we knew all of the social factors that conspire together in human decision making, we would recognize that they collectively determine those decisions, despite our thinking that we decide freely. In other words, freedom is a myth; we may be determined to believe ourselves free and may therefore persist in the belief, but it is nonetheless a fiction. Skinner denied that he had attempted "to prove that there is a science of behavior" and said he had only asked the reader to take his word for it. However, he apparently anticipated that proof of social determinism would someday be provided. "All aspects of human behavior," he wrote, "will eventually be submitted to this kind of analysis."[13]

Years of scrutiny by social scientists have yet to fulfill Skinner's expectation. Instead, advances in genetics have introduced a new kind of determinism, biological rather than social. Media promulgation and embellishment of these advances have influenced large segments of the public to subscribe to the belief that biology is destiny or, more narrowly, that genes define us. As the genetic revolution continues, all aspects of human behavior may be submitted to the analysis that Skinner anticipated, increasing the evidence in support of genetic determinism. However, just as expanded knowledge of environmental influences on behavior have still not proved Skinner's claim, increased knowledge of the genetic influences is unlikely to provide definitive proof of genetic determinism.

In many quarters the nature–nurture debate has been settled as a draw through acknowledgment that genetics and environment are interactively influential in human behavior. Taking both factors into consideration strengthens rather than weakens the determinist thesis because it augments their explanatory power. Nonetheless, in the absence of definitive proof that nature, nurture, or both together *determine* human behavior, insistence on that third "determinant," the capacity to transcend genetic and social influences through freedom, is logically supportable.

Although most feminists reject determinism, some seem to deny the impact of biology entirely while critiquing the environmental or social forces that constrain women's autonomy. Sexism, they maintain, is the product of an inequitable double standard that prevails in society. Only when social practices are transformed so that men's and women's capabilities are equal will it be possible for women to make truly autonomous choices. As we saw in Chapter 3, however, biological sex differences related to reproduction are virtually unchangeable and disadvantageous for women. Studies in behavioral genetics show that unchangeable biological sex differences are also related to many other types of human behavior. Hence, while it is clear that a social double standard with regard to men and women should be eliminated, it is also clear that this is not enough to maximize gender justice. For that to occur, the inequitable impact of some unchangeable biological differences that affect human behavior also needs to be addressed through policies or practices that, while not changing the differences, reduce their inequitable impact.

Some behavioral conditions associated with inequitable gender impact are

TABLE 14–1. Behavioral Conditions Related to Genetics

Health-Related Conditions

Disease states (e.g., mental illnesses, neuropathologies)[a]
Disease risks (e.g., tendency to alcoholism, obesity)

Non–health-related Conditions

Moral or immoral tendencies (e.g., to violence,[b] arson, altruism)
Cognitive ability (e.g., intelligence, memory, dyslexia)
Amoral
  Sexual orientation[c]
  Personality (timidity, emotional stability)[d]
  Physical skills and talent (athleticism, perfect pitch)
  Creativity (also associated with manic depressive illness)

[a]To the extent that an individual with a genetic predisposition for a behavioral disease has not (and may not) manifest its phenotype, it should be considered a disease risk rather than a disease state

[b]Walters and Palmer consider "violent aggression" to be a "moral trait" worthy of genetic intervention for enhancement. However, because violent aggression is socially endorsed in some circumstances (e.g., war and sports such as football and boxing), it may also be considered amoral. Walters and Palmer (n.1 above), pp. 123–128.

[c]Homosexuality was once considered a psychiatric disorder, but it has not been recognized as such in successive editions of the *Diagnostic and Statistical Manual.* As a colleague recurrently tells medical students, "Defining homosexuality as a disorder is like diagnosing men as avaginal."

[d]Sherman and her colleagues characterize emotional stability as "a trait based on normal variation," contrasting it with schizophrenia, "a trait falling within the pathological range." Sherman et al. (n. 2 above), p. 1266.

health-related, many are not, and some are only indirectly health-related. Similarly, some conditions have little to do with ethical conduct, while others clearly do, and some are probably related to morality only indirectly. Table 14–1 illustrates some of these possibilities, but none of the categories listed are necessarily exclusive of others. Moreover, many of the conditions that various authors claim to be influenced by genetics could reasonably be assigned to other categories also.

Gender Differences in Behavioral Conditions

Mental illnesses, some of which occur more prevalently in one gender than the other, are generally recognized through their behavioral manifestations. However, the extent to which the behavioral manifestations are influenced by genetics is in most cases unclear. Women are more prone to affective and anxiety disorders, whereas men are more likely to develop substance abuse and antisocial personality disorders.[14] Although the reported incidence of depression in women is greater than in men, men may underreport depressive symptoms and "self-medicate" mood disorders through alcohol and violence. Rett disorder, a rare syndrome similar at some ages to autism, has been diagnosed only in girls,[15] and premenstrual dysphoric disorder obviously occurs in women only. Psychiatric conditions such as histrionic personality and borderline personality are diagnosed more often in women than in men, but these disorders may result entirely from environmental rather than genetic influences, for example, gender bias and cultural factors that encourage a dependent role for women.[16] Eating disorders, which principally affect young women, are also influenced by environmental factors such as gender socialization and family relationships, although evidence has been mounting that neurobiological factors increase the probability that a particular young woman will develop one of these disorders.

Two of the most devastating mental illnesses, bipolar disorder and schizophrenia, are about as likely to occur in men as in women; for both of these, genetic susceptibility has been established.[17] Bipolar disorder raises important questions because of its association with a high degree of creativity in the manic phase. Kay Redfield Jameson has elegantly documented the fact that many of the most creative individuals in history had manic depressive illness.[18] Treatment through drugs, or potentially through genetic alteration, may not only reduce this creativity for some individuals but, arguably, may affect the individual's identity or conception of the self. For such treatment, the moral requirement of respecting individual autonomy may be impossible to meet definitively because the individual's capacity for autonomous decision making is already compromised by her underlying mental disorder. From an egalitarian feminist standpoint, however, an individual should not be required to suffer the depths of depression, which puts some women at risk for sexual exploitation or financial manipulation, solely to provide others with the benefits of the hypomanic creative phase.

In contrast with bipolar disorder, unipolar disorder is more prevalent in the general population, affecting about twice as many women as men.[19] Unipolar depression is associated with excessive motor activity and a feeling of inner tension, whereas bipolar depression is associated with psychomotor retardation. Unipolar patients are more likely to experience somatic problems, to express anger, and to experience insomnia. Their symptoms are also more heavily influenced by environmental factors than those of patients with bipolar disorder. Consistent with this finding is the fact that major depression in women has been attributed to four sources: genetics, trauma, temperament, and interpersonal relationships. Among these factors, stressful life events is the strongest predictor of depression.

Schizophrenia, whose worldwide incidence stands uniformly at about 1%,[20] is a challenging behavioral condition in part because of the different ways in which different cultures respond to it. In some third-world countries, for example, people with schizophrenia are cared for in their homes by their relatives without benefit or burden of medication. In contrast, in the United States, schizophrenia is prevalently treated with drugs of variable efficacy, and many of those not treated or treated unsuccessfully for schizophrenia and other mental disorders are found among the homeless of our urban centers. Little support is available to the many women who care for schizophrenic relatives.

Some behavioral genetic conditions involve gender stereotypes that are particularly problematic for women. Aggressiveness, for example, is often admired in men but condemned in women. Despite the evidence that violence is much more prevalently manifest in men, some studies show that women relatives of violent individuals often have a somatization disorder that may be interpreted as the female equivalent of male aggressiveness, that is, as a gender-defined aggression syndrome that entails relatively high cost to themselves and their families.[21] Briquet disease, for example, occurs primarily in women whose first-degree relatives carry diagnoses of antisocial personality or alcoholism.[22]

Timidity and altruism are sometimes expected and desired in women, but at the cost of their own social or professional advancement; the opposite tends to be true for men. Lack of emotional stability is frequently and pejoratively attributed to women, whereas intelligence, especially in content areas such as math and science, is more likely to be attributed to, esteemed, and rewarded in men. The same sexual double standard applies to physical traits such as athletic ability. Even a cursory comparison between the level of support for athletically talented women and support for their male counterparts, some of whom are less athletically talented, offers compelling evidence in this regard.

Alcoholism, a form of addiction involving genetic susceptibility, occurs in both men and women, but has been studied much more prevalently in men.[23] In the next section, therefore, I concentrate on its impact on women. Although alcohol consumption poses health and social hazards to both sexes regardless of whether it is addictive, a significant gender difference arises because of its potential impact on pregnancy. Women are expected to abstain from alcohol during pregnancy in order to avoid fetal alcohol syndrome in their potential children. In some cases, this expectation has led to coercive treatment of women that their male counterparts do not face, although they obviously share responsibility for the pregnancy.

Alcoholism and Women[24]

Approximately 60% of adult women in the United States drink alcohol at least occasionally. While many of these are light drinkers, 12% of adult women are moderate drinkers (4 to 13 drinks per week) and 3% drink heavily (14 or more drinks per week).[25] About half the women who drink are considered non–problem drinkers, whereas 39.6 % of men who drink are considered problem drinkers.[26] Like their male counterparts, women may compromise their health and the welfare of others through excessive alcohol consumption. However, even if their drinking is not excessive, women face risks to their potential children if they drink during pregnancy, and they often experience gender-related social stigmas related to alcohol consumption when they are not pregnant.[27]

Although no single study has definitively demonstrated the influence of genes on alcohol dependence, a large body of evidence from multiple studies points powerfully in that direction.[28] Some studies suggest that maternal transmission to daughters is more prevalent than paternal transmission to them.[29] The genetic risk for alcoholism apparently varies according to sex with women affected more modestly than men.[30] As already mentioned, however, the data on alcoholism in women are extremely limited in comparison with comparable studies of men.

Adoption studies in the United States and in Scandinavia have led researchers to postulate two independently transmissible forms of the disease.[31] Type I has been described as milieu-limited and Type II as male-limited.[32] The former is characterized by psychological dependence and an emotional component of guilt and fear regarding alcoholism; its usual age of onset is about 25 years, and it manifestation ranges from mild to severe. The latter, whose onset is earlier, is more likely in men; its moderately severe impact is associated with a tendency to pugnaciousness and low-impulse control. Type II appears to be only weakly influenced by environmental factors.[33] Two additional types of alcoholism have been described as specific to women: an early onset type that often develops before age 21 and occurs in families with a particularly high frequency of alcoholism, and a late onset type that is more strongly influenced by environmental variables. As with other diseases, early onset typically represents a severe form of the disorder.[34]

In general, environmental factors are more predictive of alcoholism in women than in men.[35] The sociocultural factors associated with women's drinking behavior include age, ethnicity, marital status, and employment. Women between 21 and 34 years of age are more likely than other women both to drink heavily and to discontinue problem drinking; their behavioral shifts are attributed to the multiple changes in women's employment, marital status, and parental status during these years.[36] Comparing non-Hispanic white women with Hispanic women and African-American women, the non-Hispanic white women are most likely and the African-American women are least likely to consume alcohol.[37] The highest rates of heavy drinking occur among single, divorced, or separated women, for whom alcohol consumption may be more culturally acceptable than it is for married women or mothers.[38] Not surprisingly, women employed outside the home, particularly those who work in traditionally male occupations, are more likely to drink than other women.[39]

Gender differences are apparent not only in phenotypic expressions of alcoholism but also in the psychosocial circumstances that make women vulnerable to it. For example, adolescent girls with low self-esteem and impaired coping ability are more likely to develop alcohol problems later in life than their male counterparts.[40] Domestic abuse, whether experienced as children or as adults, also makes women vulnerable to alcoholism.[41] In treatment programs, alcoholic women are more likely than alcoholic men to report anxiety, depression, eating disorders, and low self-esteem. Most women enter these programs in response to health and family problems, whereas men enter because of job and legal problems.[42]

Throughout the history of Western culture, women have been held to a different standard than men with regard to alcohol consumption. In ancient Rome, for example, women were prohibited from drinking and could be put to death for the offense.[43] A rationale for the prohibition was the prevention of adultery: alcohol consumption was thought to make women sexually promiscuous.[44] Interestingly, the phenotype of Type I alcoholism, which occurs equally in men and women, does not support that expectation, whereas the phenotype of Type II alcoholism, prevalent in males, does support it. In fact, alcohol consumption usually depletes sexual desire in both sexes.

The sexual double standard persists in stereotypic views of feminine nurturance and compliance as distinct from masculine assertiveness and dominance. As one author puts it, our culture interprets drinking by women as deviant behavior, or at least as more deviant than drinking by men; women who become alcoholics, he says, are considered "fallen angels."[45] Despite longstanding recognition of alcoholism as a disease and more recent recognition of its association with genetics, alcoholics of both sexes are frequently blamed for their behavior. Women who drink are further stigmatized because of the higher moral standard demanded of them, especially with regard to sexuality. The wrongness of this stigma stems from that fact that it is much more likely that women who drink become victims of male sexual aggressiveness than vice versa.[46]

While providing useful knowledge, advances in genetics, obstetrics, and developmental pediatrics have exacerbated social antagonism toward women who drink during pregnancy. In a restaurant in Washington, for example, a woman who had come to dine with her husband during the eighth month of her pregnancy was refused a drink by the waiter, who felt that he was imperiling the fetus. Admittedly, there are legitimate concerns about the risk of fetal alcohol syndrome, which is associated with drinking during pregnancy. From an egalitarian feminist perspective, however, those concerns must be balanced against the need to minimize burdens to the pregnant woman and to respect her autonomy. On the latter point, the impact of genetics as well as environmental determinants of behavior surfaces again. The following case illustrates how these factors are relevant to policies and practices regarding women and alcohol.

A Case Involving Probable Hereditary Alcoholism

Jill O'Mara is a 29-year-old Caucasian with a history of drunkenness, that is, she has been arrested and convicted for drunk driving. Because her mother is a known alcoholic, Jill's teachers in junior high wondered whether her learning difficulties were due to fetal alcohol syndrome. She left high school in her junior year and has worked intermittently since then. Jill married at 19 and had a child at 20; the infant, Jake, tested positive for cocaine and was placed in foster care. Although the social worker has told Jill that Jake is healthy and doing well in school, she has not been in touch with him or with his foster family. Jill has been separated from her husband, Jim, for the past two years. Like Jill's father, Jim was a wife-batterer. Jill drinks heavily when she is depressed, which happens especially on weekends, but she rarely drinks during the week when she is working.

Two months ago, Jim returned to town and spent the night with Jill. Some time later, when she realized she was pregnant, she had just been fired from her job. She called Jim to tell him about the pregnancy. Jim said he hoped Jill would get an abortion, but Jill wanted to continue the pregnancy. While searching for a new job, she became increasingly depressed and started drinking heavily. Jim returned and reported her behavior to the police, alleging that she placed her fetus in jeopardy.

This case presents a classic description of the interplay between genetic and environmental factors in the etiology of alcoholism. Jill's family history suggests that she may well have inherited a susceptibility to Type I alcoholism, but as yet no test is available to confirm this. Even if it were, alcoholism is unlike many other disorders in that, in theory at least, its manifestation is entirely preventable by controlling the environment so as not to permit alcohol intake. Assuming that the genetically susceptible person is autonomous enough to forgo alcohol consumption, the alcoholic phenotype may be avoided voluntarily. If she is so shaped by genes and social factors that she lacks such autonomy, "coerced" abstinence is of course possible even while ethically and legally questionable.

The social factors in Jill's life robustly support a diagnosis of alcoholism: a battered alcoholic mother and a battering father, her battering as a wife, her age, unemployment history, ethnicity, and single status. Given these factors, it is no surprise that her medical history includes depression, which is often associated with alcoholism.[47] However, because some individuals with comparable family, social, and medical histories are not alcoholics, there is no way of determining with certainty that the sum of genetic and environmental factors affecting Jill have made her an alcoholic. Absent that determination, we may still credit her with some semblance of autonomy to affect her fate.

Libertarian feminists would give more credit to that semblance of autonomy in Jill than would egalitarian feminists because they are less likely to acknowledge constraints on her autonomy. Consistent with their resistance to any impediment to individual choice, libertarian feminists would also be more likely to deny any responsibility for the (nonautonomous) fetus. From an egalitarian feminist standpoint, however, not only the possibility of Jill's autonomy but the probability of extreme constraints on her autonomy, from both genetic and social factors, must be considered. Moreover, even though the fetus is not a moral agent, its status as a developing human entity and potential child is morally relevant to decisions about Jill's alcohol consumption. To egalitarian feminists, therefore, this case is more complicated than it is to libertarian feminists.

Her probable genetic predisposition to alcoholism and the predisposing social circumstances that she has already experienced are not changeable for Jill. However, her current circumstances could be changed to forestall the phenotypic expression of the disease that threatens her health as well as that of her fetus. Changing her current circumstances could also allow her to make maximally autonomous decisions about her pregnancy. Unfortunately, if Jill continues her pregnancy, she is highly unlikely to find herself in such health and autonomy-promoting circumstances. Therapeutic modalities for alcoholism have mainly been designed for men, for whom separation from family and confrontational techniques have proved the most effective form of treatment. For alcoholic women, who often have major or sole responsibility for children and lose more self-esteem through confrontational techniques, these measures are less effective. Even if they were effective, only 20% of the available treatment programs offer services to women, and only 8% offer child care services to mothers or pregnant alcoholics.[48]

Like maternal phenylketonuria, fetal alcohol syndrome (FAS) is a result of a maternal condition rather than a genetic condition in its own right. Symptoms of FAS include growth retardation, cognitive and behavioral impairment, and facial abnormalities.[49] FAS is considered the leading cause of preventable mental retardation in the United States, occurring in about 0.7 cases per 1000 live births.[50] In addition to the psychosocial costs to those affected and their families, the economic costs of FAS-related abnormalities have been estimated at $250 million annually in the United States.[51]

The probability that a particular infant whose mother consumes alcohol will have FAS is considerably less than the risk that a woman who does not return to a phenylalanine diet during pregnancy will have maternal PKU. Although the majority of women in the United States dramatically reduce their alcohol intake during pregnancy, from 5% to 10% of pregnant women may drink sufficient alcohol to produce FAS. Many alcoholic pregnant women attempt to exert their autonomy to stop their alcohol intake but fail because of their dependence, social influences, and lack of resources; these women face a 35% risk of FAS in their offspring.[52] The alcohol intake of a woman's partner may present an additional risk of FAS. One study of nonhuman animals suggests that alcohol is a direct toxicant to sperm; if such data were applicable to humans, paternal alcohol consumption would introduce a risk to the fetus even if the pregnant woman totally refrained from alcohol consumption.[53]

Jill probably has a 35% risk of FAS in her potential child. Obviously, this means that it is more likely than not that her offspring will be free of the syndrome. Even for children without FAS, however, alcohol consumption during pregnancy increases the risk of neurodevelopmental disorders.[54] Moreover, although the case tells us nothing of Jim's drinking habits, they may increase fetal risk regardless of the risk that Jill's behavior imparts. Not only is there a possibility that the animal study cited above is applicable to this pregnancy, but it is probable that Jill's alcohol consumption has been influenced—even reinforced—by her complicated and battered relationship to Jim. From an egalitarian standpoint, then, Jim's apparent denial of his own responsibility for placing their fetus in jeopardy is misleading and unfair.

If Jim is partly responsible either for Jill's drinking or for risk to the fetus from his own alcohol consumption, surely the allegation he made to the police should be interpreted as applicable to him as well. How should the police respond to his allegation? As with the case of Julia in Chapter 1, the question raised is whether "coercion" is justified for the sake of the fetus. Because of the probable genetic component of Jill's drinking behavior, she is not as autonomous as those not as susceptible to alcoholism as she. Nor is she as autonomous as those who have not been as socially influenced in the direction of alcoholism. To the extent that she is not autonomous, moral coerciveness is impossible.

To the extent that Jill is autonomous, coerciveness is unjust unless some rather demanding moral requirements are met. Possible justifying conditions include the following: (*a*) the interests of the fetus or potential child outweigh respect for her autonomy; (*b*) the costs to society of a child with FAS or some other alcohol-related disorder outweigh respect for her autonomy; (*c*) the chance that her child will have FAS or another alcohol-related disorder outweighs the probability that her child will not have it; and (*d*) the birth of a child with FAS or some other alcohol-related disorder is worse than that Jill be coercively treated. If any or all of these conditions justify coercion, other behaviors commonly permitted by law and social custom should also be treated coercively. Condition (*a*) is inconsistent with current U.S. abortion law, which permits women to terminate pregnancies for any reason until the fetus is viable.[55] The rationale of condition (*b*) would also justify coercive termination of pregnancies for a wide range of fetal abnormalities, some of which would entail even greater social costs if the affected children are born. Similarly, regarding (*c*), even if a woman is more likely to have a healthy child, substantial risk of not having one would justify coercive treatment of her. Condition (*d*) has implications regarding social attitudes toward the disabled such as we discussed in Chapter 8. So long as society permits abortion for nontherapeutic as well as therapeutic reasons, consistency demands that a woman be free to continue her pregnancy while knowing her fetus is at risk of an anomaly.

Presumably, if the police were responding from an egalitarian standpoint to Jim's allegation about Jill, they would consider some of the foregoing factors. They would realize, for example, that neither men nor nonpregnant women in our society can justifiably be constrained by the law for consuming alcohol unless their behavior harms or imposes grave risk to others who are undeniably persons. If they recognize as well that alcoholism is a disease, typically triggered by a combination of genetic susceptibility and social determinants, they may be less likely to blame Jill for her drinking behavior. They may even suspect that what Jill needs is not legal coercion but a treatment program and social reinforcement that make it possible for her to be healed of her disease and free of its constraints. Even if she were fully autonomous and persisted in drinking, coerciveness is not justified on that basis alone.

If the legal system held Jill responsible for placing her fetus in jeopardy, it would thereby assume the inadequacy of genetics and social determinism in explaining the behavior of an individual. By thus affirming the autonomy of the individual, it would, like Jim, neglect to acknowledge its own responsibility for the situation in which Jill found herself. From an egalitarian standpoint, such acknowledgment is crucial because societal conditions are generally changeable, and if they entail inequity by compromising the autonomy of some individuals, they should be altered.

In Jill's case, as in other cases involving human behavior, the standpoints of genetics and the environment provide inadequate accounts, whether taken separately or together. But the same is true for any account of behavior based solely on autonomy. The nature–nurture debate is settled with recognition that neither side wins, not only because both are inextricably intertwined, but also because a third invisible but real element—the capacity to choose, which allows for moral as well as immoral human behavior is intertwined with both.

Although the tendency to take risks is probably influenced by genetics, the capacity to choose allows individuals to counter this tendency or to acquiesce to it. As we have seen, it is difficult to determine the extent to which risk-taking behavior is autonomous. Regardless of whether it is autonomous, however, employers and insurance companies are interested in ascertaining whether their workers or customers engage in risk-taking behavior. Accordingly, the next chapter considers insurance and employment practices as major ways in which the social environment influences the impact of genetics on women.

Notes

1. E.g., LeRoy Walters and Julie Gage Palmer, *The Ethics of Human Gene Therapy* (New York: Oxford University Press, 1997), p. 108.
2. Stephanie L. Sherman, John C. DeFries, Irvin I. Gottesman, J. C. Loehlin, J. M. Meyer, M. Z. Pelias, J. Rice, and I. Waldman, "Behavioral Genetics '97: ASHG Statement Recent Developments in Human Behavioral Genetics: Past Accomplishments and Future Directions," *American Journal of Human Genetics* 60 (1997): 1265.
3. Thomas J. Bouchard Jr., David T. Lykken, Matthew McGue, N. L. Segal, and A. Tellegen, "Sources of Human Psychological Differences: The Minnesota Study of Twins Reared Apart," *Science* 250 (October 12, 1990): 223.
4. Sherman et al., p. 1265; Dorothy Nelkin and M. Susan Lindee, *The DNA Mystique: The Gene as a Cultural Icon* (New York: W. H. Freeman and Company, 1995), p. 82; and "Perfect Pitch Is Linked to Training before Age 6," *New York Times,* February 3, 1998, p. B12, citing research from the University of California at San Francisco and published in the February issue of the *American Journal of Human Genetics.*
5. K. McCartney, M. J. Harris, and F. Bernieri, "Growing Up and Growing Apart: A Developmental Meta-Analysis of Twin Studies," *Psychology Bulletin* 107 (1990): 226–37.
6. Mary B. Mahowald, "Beyond Skinner: A Chance to Be Moral," *Journal of Social Philosophy* 4 (1973): 1–4.
7. *Basic Writings of Saint Thomas Aquinas,* ed. Anton C. Pegis (New York: Random House, 1945), vol. 2, pp. 225–38, 412–18. Although "man" is intended to be generic, "woman," for Aquinas as in Aristotle, is "defective and misbegotten" in her "individual nature," and "naturally subject to man, because in man the discernment of reason predominates." Vol. 1, pp. 880–81.

8. Freedom, for Kant, is a transcendental idea which is noumenal, and therefore unknowable. It is a necessary condition of morality as expressed in the universal experience of "oughtness" or obligation. Immanuel Kant, *Critique of Pure Reason,* trans. F. Max Muller (Garden City, NY: Doubleday, 1966), pp. 371–80, and *The Essential Kant,* ed. Arnulf Zweig (New York: New American Library, 1970), pp. 361–77.

9. Jean-Paul Sartre, *Existentialism and Human Emotions* (New York: Philosophical Library, 1957), p. 56.

10. The term "nature," as used here, does not refer to the nature of the human species but to individual differences triggered by inheritance, i.e., DNA differences transmitted from generation to generation. In contrast, the term "nurture" is used broadly to refer to "any affects on individual differences that are not inherited." See Robert Plomin, "Beyond Nature versus Nurture," in Laura Lee Hall, ed., *Genetics and Mental Illness: Evolving Issues for Research and Society* (New York: Plenum, 1996), pp. 30–31. Although so broad a definition of nurture could include the individual's capacity for autonomous decision making, participants in the nature–nurture debate rarely if ever concern themselves with that possibility.

11. E.g., Susan Sherwin, coordinator, *The Politics of Women's Health: Exploring Agency and Autonomy* (Philadelphia: Temple University Press, 1998), pp. 19–45.

12. B. F. Skinner, *Beyond Freedom and Dignity* (New York: Alfred A. Knopf, 1971).

13. B. F. Skinner, "'I have been misunderstood. . . .' An Interview with B. F. Skinner," *Center Magazine,* March/April, 1972, pp. 63, 65.

14. R. C. Kessler, K. A. McGonagle, S. Zhao, C. B. Nelson, M. Hughes, S. Eshleman, H. U. Wittchen, and K. S. Kendler, "Lifetime and 12-Month Prevalence of DSM-III-R Psychiatric Disorders in the United States. Results from the National Cormorbidity Survey," *Archives of General Psychiatry* 51 (January 1994): 8–19.

15. Michael B. First, Allen Frances, and Harold Alan Pincus, "Psychiatric Classification," in Allan Tasman, Jerald Kay, and Jeffrey A. Lieberman, eds., *Psychiatry* (Philadelphia: W. B. Saunders Company, 1997), p. 575.

16. At least two-thirds of those with histrionic personality disorder are women, and about three-fourths of those with borderline personality disorder are women. See Thomas A. Widiger and Cynthia J. Sanderson, "Personality Disorders," in Tasman, Kay, and Lieberman, pp. 1302, 1305.

17. Debra A. Pinais and Alan Breier, "Schizophrenia," and Mark S. Bauer, "Bipolar Disorders," both in Tasman, Kay, and Lieberman, pp. 927–61, 969.

18. Kay Redfield Jameson, *Touched with Fire: Manic-Depressive Illness and the Artistic Temperament* (New York: Free Press, 1993). Among the highly creative and successful people who suffered from manic depressive illness, cited by Jameson, are William Blake, Lord Byron, Samuel Taylor Coleridge, Gerard Manley Hopkins, Herman Melville, Edgar Allen Poe, Dante Gabriel Rossetti, Percy Bysshe Shelley, Alfred Lord Tennyson, Robert Lowell, and Anne Sexton. Composers who had significant mood disorders include George Frederick Handel, Robert Schumann, Hector Berlioz, Gustav Mahler, Gioacchino Rossini, Peter Ilyich Tchaikovsky, and Sergey Rachmaninoff. See Hall, p. 115. The fact that the great majority of these well-known creative individuals were male does not necessarily imply lesser creativity, with or without manic depressive illness, on the part of women. Factors such as their more limited educational and social opportunities undoubtedly influenced their disproportionate representation.

19. Information on unipolar disorder in this paragraph is from Ming T. Tsuang and Stephen V. Faraone, "The Inheritance of Mood Disorders," in Hill, p. 80, 81, 100, 90.

20. Irving I. Gottesman, "Blind Men and Elephants: Genetic and Other Perspectives on Schizophrenia," in Hall, pp. 53, 54.

21. Soren Sigvardsson, Anne-Liis von Knorring, Michael Bohman, and Robert Cloninger, "An Adoption Study of Somatiform Disorders," *Archives of General Psychiatry* 41 (September 1984): 853–59.

22. Samuel B. Guze, "Genetics of Briquet's Syndrome and Somatization Disorder," *Annals of Clinical Psychiatry* 5 (1993): 225–29.

23. M. Vanicelli and L. Nash, "Effect of Sex Bias on Women's Studies on Alcoholism," *Alcoholism: Clinical and Experimental Research* 8, 3 (1984): 334–36.

24. Material in this section is drawn from Cathleen M. Harris and Mary B. Mahowald, "Women and Alcohol Abuse," in Wayne Shelton and Rem Edwards, eds., *Advances in Bioethics: Values, Ethics and Alcoholism* (Greenwich, CT: JAI Press, 1997), pp. 153–170.

25. K. Stratton, C. Howe, and F. Battaglia, eds. *Fetal Alcohol Syndrome: Diagnosis, Epidemiology, Prevention and Treatment* (Washington, DC: National Academy Press, 1996), and S. C. Wilsnack, R. W. Wilsnack, and S. Hiller-Sturmhofel, "How Women Drink: Epidemiology of Women's Drinking and Problem Drinking," *Alcohol Health & Research World* 18 (1994): 173–84.

26. K. K. Bucholz, A. C. Health, T. Reich, V. M. Hesselbrock, J. R. Kramer, J. I. Nurnberger Jr., and M. A. Schuckit, "Can We Subtype Alcoholism? A Latent Class Analysis of Data from Relatives of Alcoholics in a Multicenter Family Study of Alcoholism," *Alcoholism: Clinical and Experimental Research* 20, 8 (1996): 1462–71. Although there is no sharp demarcation between "social" or "moderate" drinking and "problem" drinking, the latter is usually associated with harm to oneself or others. Cf. Henry R. Kranzier, Thomas F. Babor, Pamela Moore," Alcohol Use Disorders," in Tasman, Kay, Lieberman, p. 755.

27. P. Morgan "Women and Alcohol: The Disinhibition Rhetoric in an Analysis of Domination," *Journal of Psychoactive Drugs* 19, 2 (1987): 129–33.

28. Victor M. Hesselbrock, "The Genetic Epidemiology of Alcoholism," in Henri Begleiter and Benjamin Kissin, eds., *The Genetics of Alcoholism* (New York: Oxford University Press, 1995), p. 33.

29. Hesselbrock, p. 28.

30. Robert Plomin, John C. DeFries, Gerald E. McClearn, and Michael Rutter, *Behavioral Genetics* 3rd ed. (New York: W. H. Freeman and Company, 1997), p. 228.

31. Kimberly Quaid, Stephen H. Dinwiddie, P. Michael Conneally, and John N. Nurnberger Jr., "Issues in Genetic Testing for Susceptibility to Alcoholism: Lessons from Alzheimer's Disease and Huntington's Disease," *Alcoholism: Clinical and Experimental Research* 20, 8 (1996): 1430.

32. Michael Bohman, Robert Cloninger, Anne-Liis von Knorring, and Soren Sigvardsson, "An Adoption Study of Somatoform Disorders. III: Cross-Fostering Analysis and Genetic Relationship to Alcoholism and Criminality," *Archives of General Psychiatry* 41 (September 1984): 872–78.

33. Quaid et al., p. 1430, and C. Robert Cloninger, Soren Sigvardsson, and Michael Bohman, "Type I and Type II Alcoholism: An Update," *Alcohol Health and Research World* 20, 1 (1996): 18–23. The distinction between Type I and Type II alcoholism has been a matter of debate among experts. See, for example, George E. Vaillant, "Evidence That the Type I and Type 2 Dichotomy in Alcoholism Must Be Re-examined," and "Let the Splitters Lump the Lumpers," *Addiction* 89, 9 (1994): 1049–57, 1070; Vijoy K. Varma, "Type 1/Type 2 Dichotomy in Alcoholism: The Controversy Continues," *Addic-*

tion 89, 9 (1994): 1064–66; Kenneth J. Sher, "There Are Two Types of Alcoholism Researchers: Those Who Believe in Two Types of Alcoholism and Those Who Don't," *Addiction* 89, 9 (1994): 1108–15.

34. Shirley Y. Hill, "Neurobiological and Clinical Markers for a Severe Form of Alcoholism in Women," *Alcohol Health and Research World* 19, 3 (1995): 249–56.

35. Hesselbrock, p. 34.

36. S. C. Wilsnack and R. W. Wilsnack, "Drinking and Problem Drinking in U.S. Women: Patterns and Recent Trends," in M. Galanter, ed., *Recent Developments in Alcoholism* 12 (1995): 29–60; and S. C. Wilsnack, A. D. Klassen, B. E. Schur, and R. W. Wilsnack, "Predicting Onset and Chronicity of Women's Problem Drinking: A Five-Year Longitudinal Analysis," *American Journal of Public Health* 81, 3 (1991): 305–18.

37. Wilsnack and Wilsnack, 29–60 and D. Herd, "Sex Ratios of Drinking Patterns and Problems among Blacks and Whites: Results from a National Survey, *Journal of Study of Alcohol* 58, 1 (1997): 75–82.

38. Wilsnack and Wilsnack.

39. E. R. Shore, "Drinking Patterns and Problems among Women in Paid Employment, *Alcohol Health Research World* 16 (1992): 160–64.

40. M. C. Jones, "Personality Antecedents and Correlates of Drinking Patterns in Women," *Journal of Consultation Clinical Psychiatry* 36, 1 (1971): 61–69; cf. M. C. Jones, "Personality Correlates and Antecedents of Drinking Patterns in Adult Males," *Journal of Consultation Clinical Psychiatry* 32 (1968): 2–12.

41. Stratton et al., p. 107.

42. S. B. Blume, "Women, Alcohol and Drugs," in N. S. Miller, ed., *Comprehensive Handbook of Drug and Alcohol Addiction* (New York: Marcel Dekker, 1991), pp. 147–77; E. S. L. Gomberg and R. D. Nirenberg, "Antecedents and Consequences," in E. S. L. Gomberg and R. D. Nirenberg, eds., *Women and Substances Abuse* (Norwood, NJ: Ablex Press, 1993), p. 107.

43. A. P. McKinlay, "The Roman Attitude towards Women's Drinking," in R. G. McCarthy, ed., *Drinking and Intoxication* (Glencoe, IL: Free Press, 1959), pp. 58–61.

44. Blume. 147–77.

45. K. M. Fillmore, "'When Angels Fall': Women's Drinking as Cultural Preoccupation and as Reality," in S. C. Wilsnack and L. J. Beckman, eds., *Alcohol Problems in Women* (New York: Guilford Press, 1984), pp. 7–36.

46. Fillmore. 7–36.

47. Plomin et al., p. 224.

48. Sue V. Rosser, *Women's Health: Missing from U.S. Medicine* (Bloomington: Indiana University Press, 1994), p. 43.

49. Nancy L. Day, Dorcie Jasperse, Gail Richardson, Nadine Robies, Usha Sambamoorthi, Paul Taylor, Mark Scher, David Stoffer, and Marie Cornelius, "Prenatal Exposure to Alcohol: Effect on Infant Growth and Morphologic Characteristics," *Pediatrics* 84, 3 (1989): 536–41.

50. E. L. Abel and R. J. Sokol, "Incidence of Fetal Alcohol Syndrome and Economic Impact of FAS-related Anomalies," *Drug Alcohol Dependence* 19 (1987): 51–70, and Centers for Disease Control, "Update: Trends in Fetal Alcohol Syndrome: United States 1979–1993," *Morbidity and Mortality Weekly Report* (MMWR) 44, 13 (1995): 249–251.

51. Abel and Sokol. 51–70.

52. C. D. Coles, "Impact of Prenatal Alcohol Exposure on the Newborn and the Child," *Clinical Obstetrics and Gynecology* 36, 2 (1993): 255–66.

53. Theodore J. Cicero, "Effects of Paternal Exposure to Alcohol on Offspring Development," *Alcohol Health and Research World* 18, 1 (1994): 37–41.

54. The combined incidence rate of FAS and alcohol-related neurodevelopmental disorders is 9.1 in 1000 births. See Paul D. Sampson, Ann P. Streissguth, Fred L. Bookstein, Ruth E. Little, Sterling K. Clarren, Philippe Dehaene, James W. Hanson, and John M. Graham Jr., "Incidence of Fetal Alcohol Syndrome and Prevalence of Alcohol-Related Neurodevelopmental Disorder," *Teratology* 56 (1997): 317.

55. Inconsistency with the law does not imply that an action is immoral; in this case, however, the rationale of the law supports a moral judgment that the woman's decision has priority.

15

EMPLOYMENT, HEALTH INSURANCE, AND THE PUBLIC–PRIVATE DISTINCTION

WOMEN have long faced employment discrimination based on their distinctive reproductive roles. For example, they are less likely than men to be offered common non–wage benefits such as health and disability coverage. Insurance discrimination has been practiced toward both sexes, but there is little documentation of gender-related *genetic* discrimination in either employment or health insurance, and little court litigation to date has focused on the burden of genetic testing on women. From an egalitarian feminist standpoint, discrimination against either sex is obviously unacceptable.

Unless respect for privacy and confidentiality is strictly observed, the proliferation of genetic tests and consequent availability of genetic information multiplies the possibilities for genetic discrimination in employment and insurance. In the United States, most people have their health insurance through their employers, making threats to privacy and confidentiality in one context applicable to the other. This chapter examines the public–private distinction on which claims of a right to privacy and confidentiality are based, critiquing that distinction while arguing against the right of employers or insurance companies to have access to genetic information concerning their employees or customers. First, however, I review some of the ways in which genetic and gender discrimination in employment or insurance has occurred.

Genetic and Gender Discrimination in Employment

Genetic discrimination has been defined as "the denial of rights, privileges or opportunities on the basis of information obtained from genetically-based diagnostic and prognostic tests."[1] Employers are interested in such information because of its potential impact on job performance and on the cost of insuring workers. Consider, for example, a 30 year old who has tested positive for Huntington disease; he applies for a position that requires years of training and experience to reach the level of productivity that the company desires. Knowing the limited years of working life that remain to someone so affected, the employer is highly unlikely to hire him rather than a 30 year old with equal qualifications and a normal life expectancy.

Although a positive genetic diagnosis of Huntington disease is virtually definitive in its prediction that an individual will eventually become symptomatic, the time of onset is uncertain. Even when genetic diagnosis is not definitive, however, genetic information regarding susceptibility to specific conditions has been grounds for employment discrimination. Women have been disproportionately represented among those who experience discrimination in the workplace because of their role in reproduction. Whereas in the past employers cited concerns about women's health as grounds for excluding them from traditionally male, high-paying jobs, their concern has recently shifted to a focus on fetal health as the basis for exclusion.

In 1991, the tendency of employers to exclude women from jobs that might place their fetuses at risk was addressed by the U.S. Supreme Court in its ruling in the *International Union* v. *Johnson Controls* case.[2] In a unanimous decision, the justices held that the "fetal protection policy" adopted by Johnson Controls, Inc, unjustly excluded fertile women from jobs involving the manufacture of batteries. The rationale for the exclusion was that the women would thereby be exposed to lead, which could compromise fetal development. Addressing the risk to fetuses, the Court maintained that decisions "about the welfare of future children must be left to parents who conceive, bear, support, and raise them rather than to the employers who hire the parents."[3] This gender-neutral rationale appropriately emphasizes the rights and responsibility of parents, but it neglects a morally relevant sex-based difference between them: only one of the two conceives and bears the child. What happens if potential parents disagree about decisions affecting their potential children? An egalitarian feminist standpoint offers guidance not found in the Court's ruling: the woman's decision should prevail because she faces risks and discomforts that her partner does not face.

The ruling in the Johnson Controls case is clearly based on a notion of gender justice. However, the very fact that the case was adjudicated by the courts demonstrates that women may face discrimination because of their reproductive capacity, regardless of whether they are or intend to be pregnant. Male exposure to lead may also cause genetic anomalies in fetuses, but only women were targeted by the policy. In addition to Johnson Controls, General Motors, DuPont, Union Carbide, and other major corporations have prohibited fertile women from working in high-level high-paying positions that involve substantial exposure to lead. In fact, such fetal protection policies have barred women from as many as 20 million jobs.[4] As knowledge of genetic risks accelerates, employment opportunities may increasingly be withheld from people in general and fertile women in particular unless laws are introduced to prevent employers from obtaining genetic information that they may utilize in discriminating against employees.

In general, policies involving genetic prognosis in employment decisions are gender- and race-neutral. For example, Title VII of the 1964 Civil Rights Act in the United States prohibits wage discrimination based on sex or race. The rationale for the prohibition is disparate impact theory, that is, a rationale which requires employers to show "business necessity" to justify practices that affect their employees unequally.[5] "Disparate impact" is considered discriminatory if it entails exclusion of certain groups on grounds unrelated to their "bona fide occupational qualifications" (BFOQs). Most genetic differences are irrelevant to that criterion. The Americans with Disabilities Act, passed in 1991, requires employers to make "reasonable accommodations" for people with disabilities in their work environment.[6] Although both laws probably reduce employment discrimination, the meanings of "business necessity," "disparate impact," "BFOQ," and "reasonable accommodation" are subject to interpretations that allow discrimination to continue. Whether advertently or not, employers who are dominant on the basis of their race, sex, ability, appearance, and age may legally make decisions that limit the opportunities of nondominant individuals who work for them.

Not surprisingly, employers have focused their concerns on reproductive risks to women while neglecting other hazards that women face. As we saw in the previous chapter, various features of the environment are likely to determine whether and how genetic predispositions to multifactorial genetic diseases and behavior traits are expressed. Sexist practices in the workplace, whether advertent or not, can escalate the risks of becoming symptomatic for complex genetic disorders. Consider, for example, the tendency of mainly male employers and builders to ignore gender differences in the design of workplaces and workplace protections. As Naomi Swanson and Ami Becker put it, "With respect to many physical hazards, women are regarded as small men who differ only with respect to their reproductive systems."[7] For many women, workstations are too high, reaches are too great, and chair seats cannot be adjusted low enough: deficiencies such as these necessitate poor posture that often leads to pain and injury that can be both permanent and costly. Another example of myopia regarding gender differences is a male-based standard regarding permissible levels of carcinogens in the work environment. Because male hormones are predominantly anabolic, whereas female hormones tend to inhibit anabolism, women in these environments are more likely to develop the related cancers than their male counterparts.[8] Other complex disorders are probably induced or exacerbated by failure to take account of sex differences in the workplace.

Occupations in which women predominate, such as dry cleaning and textile production, often expose them to mutation risks not only with regard to potential fetuses but also for themselves. In the meat industry, for example, where over 90% of the workers who wrap and label meat are women, employees are heavily exposed to fumes emitted from the thermal decomposition of the plastic, which can result in an acute form of asthma.[9] Several studies suggest a link between long-term exposure to these fumes and an increase in myeloid leukemia, non-Hodgkin's lymphomas, and lung cancer.[10] Workers involved in meat curing or smoking are also exposed to smoke, nitrosamines, and antioxidants that have been associated with tumor production in animals.[11]

As indicated in Chapter 3, women also predominate in the lower ranks of health care occupations, where risks of mutation are greater than those faced by their counterparts whose work is more prestigious and better remunerated. For example, formaldehyde, which can compromise pulmonary function, is heavily used by "low-level" workers in pathology, renal hemodialysis, and histology.[12] "Low-level" employees are also more frequently and heavily involved in hospital wet work (e.g., cleaning patient units and kitchen jobs), which commonly leads to various forms of dermatological disorders.[13] Many hospital workers are exposed to radiation, anesthetic gases, infectious diseases, chemicals, and other toxic substances, all of which accentuate the risk of complex genetic disorders.[14] Obviously, these class-related health risks should be eliminated or reduced as much as possible for men as well as women.

Despite the applicability of workplace hazards to both sexes, differences in their impact on each sex need to be identified and addressed so as to maximize gender justice. Unfortunately, the differential impact has seldom been considered with regard to women themselves, apart from the risk to potential children, for whom liability concerns are often central. These concerns have apparently been the chief basis for excluding women from jobs that might be more satisfying or remunerative for them. As the Johnson Controls case recognized, men of reproductive age have not been similarly treated, but they should be.

Beyond gender differences associated with health risks in the workplace, sexist practices are evident in salary differentials between women and men, in sex role stereotypes associated with hiring and assignment of tasks, and in response to sexual harassment, another form of discrimination.[15] Despite laws against sexual discrimination and harassment, many women are loath to pursue charges against the perpetrators because of the psychological or economic costs that these entail. Although these practices are not directly related to genetic risks (except for the relative immunity that the Y chromosome confers), they introduce a disproportionate degree of tension on the job. Such stressors, often associated with depression, may be intensified for women who, on leaving their remunerated employment, are likely to sustain the additional stress of having primary responsibility for child care and housework.[16]

Gender discrimination in the workplace has contributed to the phenomenon described in Chapter 5 as the feminization of poverty as well as to a situation that some regard as perpetuation of a "glass ceiling." The term "glass ceiling" refers to "employment practices that effectively keep working women out of top ranking positions."[17] For example, one study of managers reports the underrepresentation of women in middle management and their virtual absence in the top positions.[18] The top managers tend to promote their own kind, a nearsighted phenomenon that feminist standpoint theory obviously opposes. If more top managers were women, they might hire and promote more women, thereby reducing the number of women who subsist below the poverty level, with or without government assistance. This practice may of course be nearsighted too. But given the tendency of those in power to remain in power, it is extremely improbable that the numerical dominance of men in managerial positions would be overturned by an influx of women into management. Rather than reverse discrimination, the situation would be remedial. Factors that will continue to impede the advancement of women in professional as well as blue-collar settings include sex role biases, underutilization of their skills, denial of decision-making authority, and restriction of access to people or information conducive to their job success.[19]

Genetic and Gender Discrimination in Health Insurance

In the United States, more than 15 million women of childbearing age are without health insurance, and an additional 5 million have minimal coverage.[20] Although women are three times more likely to suffer from chronic conditions than men are, their most significant insurer, Medicare, provides more acute than chronic care coverage.[21] In general, women pay higher premiums for coverage than men and receive less reimbursement. Because of disruptions in employment during pregnancy or serious illness, women are also more likely to lose insurance than men are. When they are ready to return to work, they have greater difficulty finding jobs and obtaining insurance.[22] Working poor women and their families are less likely to have access to basic health care services than are women who receive government assistance.[23] But the health assistance provided through government programs is often inferior to that which is provided for patients who are privately insured. In teaching hospitals throughout the country, care for the poor is mainly provided by physicians who have not completed their residency training. The poor are also more likely to be hindered in communicating with clinicians by a limited understanding of English, whether on their own part or on the part of clinicians trained in non–English speaking countries.

A particularly troublesome example of gender and ethnic discrimination in health insurance is the situation of Latina or Hispanic women. In 1990, some 35% of all Hispanics and 52% of working Hispanic women below the poverty level in the United States had no health insurance.[24] Apparently, the occupations in which Hispanics predominate, such as construction and agriculture, are less likely to offer insurance than the occupations in which Caucasians and African Americans, who have a higher level of coverage, tend to predominate.[25] Even for those who are insured, the benefits packages most needed by Hispanic families, such as prenatal and postnatal care, are often limited by employers.[26] Among different Hispanic groups, the high number of female-headed households in Puerto Rican neighborhoods has made them more likely candidates for Medicaid coverage, while Mexicans and Mexican Americans are less likely to be covered because two-parent households are more common. In many states, families with two parents are excluded from Medicaid regardless of whether they meet the income requirements.[27]

Beyond these gender-based, class-based, and ethnic-based discrepancies in health insurance coverage, advances in genetics have introduced further risks to the poor and women. For example, the escalating availability of genetic tests has precipitated the development of commercial testing companies and private institutes who advertise and offer their services for a fee even to those who are not at risk, that is, those whose insurance plan would not cover the test because it is not cost-effective. Researchers may join those who have embraced genetic testing as a business through an additional "profit" motive—the expansion of the data base through which to pursue their research. The availability of breast cancer testing for women who can afford it but have no family history of the disease is but one example of this questionable service.

In contrast to women who can and do pay for unneeded genetic tests, poor and uninsured women may be coopted to become unpaid tests subjects in research projects that carry no expected benefit for them. The fact that they may thereby receive health care they would not otherwise receive serves as an incentive to their participation, as does, in some cases, a desire to conform to the wishes of the practitioners on whom they depend for care. The history of disease, or other preexisting condition, has been used as a reason to deny health insurance to many individuals of both sexes, and genetic disease as well as susceptibility may be considered "preexisting conditions." Whether this practice affects women more often than men or whether the loss of health insurance is generally more disastrous for women as individuals than for men is unclear.

However, the increasing number of female-headed households strongly suggests that a greater number of women are responsible for coverage of affected relatives.

In general, the principal health and economic risk associated with advances in genetic testing for men and women alike is the denial or loss of insurance coverage based on the increased availability of diagnostic and prognostic genetic information. It is a health risk because it may lead to avoidance of detection procedures or other routine preventive care; it is an economic risk because the costs that may be incurred by the uninsured through unexpected health crises are astronomical. So long as employers cover the majority of the insured, genetic information entails risks of discrimination in hiring, firing, advancement, and employment practices in general. In a free enterprise system, insurance companies and employers have legitimate grounds for arguing that statistical risks, as calculated by actuarial data, justify their selective practices toward customers and workers. Unless laws restrict these practices, individuals are likely not only to resist disclosure of identified genetic conditions, but also to resist testing that might otherwise yield information they would like to have. Negative test results are usually a source of relief and reassurance. But even positive results, whether they identify "disease-conferring" or "susceptibility-conferring" genetic mutations, are useful to and desired by some individuals.[28] Individuals at risk for Huntington disease, for example, might consider this information crucial to their reproductive plans; those at risk of familial breast or ovarian cancer would surely find it relevant in deciding whether to undergo prophylactic surgery.

Information regarding an individual's genome is obviously very personal, despite its implications regarding the genomes of related others. Accordingly, respect for the privacy and confidentiality of genetic information has been emphasized in discussions of genetic stigmatization and discrimination. The Institute of Medicine, for example, cites privacy and confidentiality, along with autonomy and equity, as the foremost ethical principles to be observed in law and policies regarding genetic testing.[29] As with reproductive issues and health care information in general, the distinction between the public and private is often invoked to justify the observance of confidentiality through nondisclosure of genetic information to anyone other than those who are tested. From an egalitarian feminist standpoint, however, the public–private distinction has been attacked in recent years. In the next section, therefore, I examine this distinction in the context of its applicability to disclosure of genetic information.

Genetic Information and the Public–Private Distinction

Madison Powers discusses genetic information as a type of information that entails a special obligation to respect privacy because of its unique constellation of characteristics, which include the following:

1. The information is personal in that it relates to one's genetic identity.
2. It is predictive of one's medical future.
3. It has impact throughout one's lifetime.
4. It may have adverse financial, emotional, and social consequences.
5. It has potential for later revelations.
6. It is subject to misleading or incorrect interpretation.
7. Its disclosure is relevant to other family members.[30]

These characteristics generally support the call for privacy with respect to genetic information. However, they also suggest a basis for challenging that respect with regard to the individual: the potential impact of the information on other parties.

Conflicts between the right to privacy and the right to know in genetics are, in a sense, a new incarnation of ancient disputes about the public–private distinction. Plato, for example, idealized a state in which the distinction was virtually dissolved, yet he lived and thrived under its influence. The dissolution that he advocated in the *Republic* would in fact be a victory for the public domain. One means of achieving the ideal society, for Plato, was to limit the ties between monogamous sex partners, and between parents and their children, by promoting a community of wives and children.[31] Privacy thus gave way to social betterment.

Aristotle, like many philosophers since his time, explicitly distinguished between the two domains, giving priority to the public over the private through his emphasis on "the common good." It is consistent with the natural order of things, according to Aristotle, that the state's interests take precedence over the interests of individuals and of families. As he put it in the *Politics,* "The state is by nature clearly prior to the family and to the individual, since the whole is of necessity prior to the part." The evidence for this priority, he claimed, is that "the individual, when isolated, is not self-sufficing" but depends on the state.[32] Thus neither Plato nor Aristotle would have supported the emphasis on individual rights and privacy to which we have become accustomed in our own day and culture.

More recent thinkers would have fostered the emphasis while maintaining the public–private distinction. Foremost among these are John Locke and John Stuart Mill. Locke extended the Aristotelian emphasis on nature and natural law to the natural rights of individuals. The right to private property, broadly defined to include lives and liberties as well as estates, derives from the relationship between nature and labor. Using the feminine pronoun for nature and the masculine for human, Locke wrote: "His labour hath taken it [i.e., property] out of the hands of nature, where it was common and belonged equally to all her children, and hath thereby appropriated it to himself."[33] The role of the state, as he defined it, is to ensure that private property is protected. In a sense, this view reverses the subordination of the private to the public that Aristotle and others affirm. If Locke were to comment on the privacy of genetic information, as personal property, doubtless he would strenuously object to the right of employers or insurance companies to obtain such information without the employee's or customer's consent.

Mill would have concurred in that opposition except for a utilitarian caveat: that privacy should be respected so long as it does not interfere disproportionately with the welfare of others. This would of course give employers and insurance companies room to argue, but their argument would be persuasive only if they could show that the havoc wreaked on a single individual through revelation of his or her personal genetic information was outweighed by the havoc wreaked on other individuals if the information were not disclosed to them. In many cases, that is highly unlikely.

As already suggested, the emphasis on individual rights, including the right to privacy, embodied in the liberal tradition of Locke and Mill has been critiqued in recent years. Typically, the criticisms stem from concerns about the possible excesses of individualism and its implications regarding the just treatment of *all* individuals. Feminists, communitarians, and socialists have joined in this critique, often pointing to the potential for neglect or exploitation of nondominant interests by those in power. Those in power are most likely to be currently able, heterosexual, socioeconomically advantaged, Caucasian, and male.

Feminist critics offer different political perspectives on the public–private distinction. Iris Marion Young, for example, targets the ideal of impartiality embodied in the liberal tradition. Her critique addresses liberal versions of feminism as well as other theories that assume a clear separation between the public and the private:

> The feminist critiques of traditional moral theory retain a distinction between public, impersonal institutional roles in which the ideal of impartiality and formal reason applies, on the one hand, and private, personal relations which have a different moral structure. Instead of retaining this public/private dichotomy, these criticisms of an ethic of rights should lead us to question the ideal of impartiality itself, as an appropriate ideal for any concrete moral context.[34]

Young maintains that the ideal of impartiality attempts to deny the reality and relevance of differences. This ideal is presumed to be achievable from a detached and dispassionate perspective, that is, the standpoint that the dominant group believes itself to have achieved. In fact, however, the ideal generates a dichotomy not only between the public and the private but also between the universal and the particular, and between reason and passion. None of these dichotomies is feasible or desirable because they ignore the actual circumstances in which people live their lives and make their choices, "the particularities of context and affiliation "cannot and should not be removed from moral reasoning."[35]

To Young, the ideal of impartiality that underlies the public–private distinction is especially problematic because it serves ideological goals. Its presumption of detachment "masks the ways in which the particular perspectives of dominant groups claim universality, and helps justify hierarchical decision making structures."[36] Throughout history, the public–private dichotomy has been invoked as a principle of exclusion of nondominant groups from public participation. As a corrective, Young proposes a reconceptualization of the realm of the private, based on the right to exclude others from certain aspects of one's own life or activity. "The private in this sense," she writes, "is not what public institutions exclude, but what the individual chooses to withdraw from public view."[37] In other words, Young would have us keep the distinction but reject the dichotomy, letting individuals themselves draw the line between the two. Judged in this light, the right to disclose genetic information belongs a priori to those whose genome has provided the information.

Both Young and Susan Moller Okin cite a feminist slogan, "The personal is political," to support their critiques of the public–private distinction in the liberal tradition. Okin draws heavily on the work of John Rawls and focuses more on gender differences than does Young. The context in which she focuses on these differences is also more limited, that of the family.[38]

Okin credits Rawls with having acknowledged at the outset of *A Theory of Justice* that the family is a social institution, but she faults him for ignoring the family in the rest of his work. Her critique delineates four respects in which the personal is political. First, she observes that "what happens in domestic and personal life is not immune from the dynamic of *power*, which has typically been seen as the distinguishing feature of the political."[39] For women and children in particular, the privacy of the home can be a dangerous place because of that power.

Second, according to Okin, political decisions define the acceptability of behaviors within the private sphere. Marriage, divorce, and child custody laws, for example, show the involvement of government in domestic life. A third respect in which the personal is political is the socialization process by which individuals are steered in one direction as opposed to another. Because of sex role stereotypes in the home, for example, girls are more likely to be drawn to the private sphere, where their mothers concentrate; boys, on the other hand, are more likely to be drawn to the public sphere, where their fathers concentrate. Finally, Okin points to the division of labor which, within most families, introduces psychological as well as practical barriers against women in other spheres. Women's public and private personae, she maintains, "are inextricably linked in the minds of many men,"[40] and this leads to women's being represented only in token numbers in influential positions and authoritative bodies:

> Sometimes women in the public sphere are simply not seen or heard. Sometimes we are seen and heard only insofar as we make ourselves seem as much as possible like men. Sometimes we are silenced by being demeaned or sexually harassed. And sometimes what we say is silenced or distorted because we have projected onto us the personae of particularly important women (especially their mothers) in the intrapsychic lives of men.[41]

For women in particular, then, the public–private dichotomy exacts a toll. In many ways, women do not experience the public and domestic spheres of their lives as separate or distinct. The perception of a sharp dichotomy between these spheres comes from "a traditional male perspective," one that tacitly assumes different natures, roles, and domains for men and women. Practices and attitudes that assume the separability of the domains and male dominance in the public sphere are thus at odds with the experience of many women. Okin views such practices and attitudes as an impediment to the participation that is essential to "a truly humanist theory of justice."[42]

To both Okin and Young, the public–private distinction is a false dichotomy. Neither advocates dissolution of the distinction itself, but both eschew its rigidity and are wary of its potential for exploitation or oppression of nondominant groups. Okin offers a nice summary:

> Challenging the dichotomy does not necessarily mean denying the usefulness of a concept of privacy or the value of privacy itself in human life. Nor does it mean denying that there are *any* reasonable distinctions to be made between the public and domestic spheres. It does not mean . . . a simple or a total *identification* of the personal and the political. . . . Both the concept of privacy and the existence of a personal sphere of life . . . are essential. However, such a sphere can be just and secure only if its members are equals.[43]

Okin's critique of the public–private distinction exemplifies a liberal version of feminism that draws on Rawls even while correcting him. In contrast, Young rejects the liberal tradition in its entirety, not only because of its gender injustice but also because of its classism, racism, heterosexism, and ableism. Young's account is thus more consistent with an egalitarian version of feminism. To better illustrate the relevance of their critique, consider a case that raises issues of privacy and family responsibility as well as social conflict.

Familial Risk for Huntington Disease: Insurance and Family Issues

---

When Joe Burns, now 25, was married 4 years ago to Joann, both fully intended to have children. Since then Joe has learned that two of his great uncles, whom he never met, had Huntington disease (HD) sometimes called Huntington chorea—a progressive, incurable, devastating neurological condition that tends to be nonsymptomatic until one's middle years. Joe's father, now 50, has recently been diagnosed with HD, which means that Joe has a one in two chance of having the disease himself. Although a newly available genetic test would reveal to Joe whether he does in fact carry the genetic mutation for HD, he does not want to be tested. He says his job and health insurance would both be jeopardized by a positive test result. Joann wants him to be tested because she would like to have children but would choose not to do so if Joe is positive. Joe maintains that they should go ahead and have children without that determination.

Obviously, the information about Joe's susceptibility to HD is relevant to Joann as well as Joe. His employer and insurance company might well claim it is relevant to them also. While their claim is disputable on grounds of the public–private distinction, information about the health status of their employees and customers is commonly and legitimately asked and received by employers and insurance companies. Typically, this information includes family history, which could establish Joe's susceptibility even without a genetic test. Presumably, in this case Joe's employer and insurance company are unaware that he has a family history of HD because he did not know about it himself until recently. He is unlikely to volunteer the information to avoid its economic implications. Had he listed a family history of HD in his employment application, he might not have been hired on that basis alone; or he might have been asked to undergo the genetic test for HD to determine whether he was affected, in which case he might not have been hired on that basis.

Given Joe's age, even if he has the genetic mutation for HD, he could have a decade or more of nonsymptomatic work life remaining if the disease is manifest at its average age of onset (38).[44] Workers who have neither disabling conditions nor genetic susceptibility often change jobs in less time than that, sometimes after years of training by company management. From the employer's point of view, then, the risk of not knowing Joe's family history, and therefore being unable to act on it, hardly justifies a requirement of such disclosure. If he were a decade or more older, however, the case for an employer's right to know his family history or to require a genetic test in light of that history is stronger, and it is stronger still if symptoms of the disease have begun to appear. In the latter case, the employer has grounds based on a BFOQ, which inhibits an employee from successfully carrying out his or her job responsibilities.[45] However, whether this legally permissible exclusion suffices as a moral warrant for the practice is another matter. An egalitarian ethic demands consideration not only of the employer's right to hire workers on the basis of their productivity but also of the right of people to find work that allows them to support themselves and their families. Beyond their legal right to profit, employers have a moral responsibility as members of society to facilitate employment even by those who will not maximize their profits.

Ruth Faden and Nancy Kass identify three potential applications of genetic testing in the workplace: the monitoring of workers for evidence of genetic damage from workplace exposures; the screening of workers for genetic predisposition or susceptibility to harm from the work environment; and the screening of workers for susceptibility to conditions that are not related to their work.[46] These illustrate grounds for intruding on the private domain of an individual's genome for public reasons. From an egalitarian standpoint, the first application is demanded for the sake of all of the employees whose health might be threatened by a toxic exposure. A company that did not conduct appropriate monitoring would be both legally and morally delinquent for not doing so.

From that same standpoint, the second application is defensible as a means of protecting susceptible workers as well as the employer. An employee who is shown to be at risk in a specific environment may be transferred to another, avoiding liability for the employer without having to change the environment itself. But this application is surely contestable because it may be both paternalistic and irresponsible: paternalistic by not allowing employees to determine for themselves what risks they wish to sustain for the sake of their preferred employment, and irresponsible by permitting employers not to optimize the work environment for all employees.

Screening potential workers for genetic conditions unrelated to their work is as problematic as screening them for gender, race, class, age, sex, or sexuality. A condition predictive or indicative of an employee's ability to perform his or her job over a reasonable spate of time is legitimately viewed as work-related. If an employer wanted to train someone for a new job function, for example, he or she would want to know, and may well have a right to be informed, of an employee's anticipated inability to do the job. The situation is analogous to an employer's decision not to hire an applicant who is only available to work during the summer or for a stretch of time that would make training and paperwork on the part of the company cost ineffective.

Joe's situation does not match the above analogy. Although his family history of HD reveals risk of inability to work in the future, his current age argues that he can still be a productive employee for many years. For the present, then, the argument for Joe's disclosure of his risk status to his employer is weak. However, if Joe were asked about his family history of genetic disease when applying for a new position, or if he were asked about it at the annual physical examination by the company's physician, honesty would demand an honest answer, and Joe would therefore have a prima facie obligation to tell the truth about his history. The company has a prima facie obligation as well: not to fire Joe on grounds of his genetic susceptibility so long as he can adequately fulfill the terms of his employment. Its obligation to hire him may be less compelling if there are other qualified candidates without a family history of genetic disease.[47] Beyond truthfulness, the principle of fairness is applicable to employees as well as employers.

Joe's family history of HD would probably preclude his getting health insurance if he were to apply for it now that he knows that history, except perhaps at exorbitant rates or if he subjected himself to the genetic test and obtained a negative result of his risk of HD. By actuarial standards, coverage may be refused even without the test because the risk is already so high (50%). By egalitarian feminist standards, however, the most compelling argument for Joe's being tested is Joann's desire to know (*1*) whether Joe has in fact inherited the genetic mutation for HD, and (2) whether a child that she might have with Joe would carry the same 50% risk.[48] Her personal future is so intimately and deeply affected by this information that it surely is unfair of Joe not to be tested.

The unfairness of denying Joann this information is based in part on the inadequacy of the public–private distinction, which, as Okin recognized, sometimes masks family injustice. Because the test itself involves mild bodily intrusion, yielding information that is private about one's own genome, Joe has a prima face right to refuse testing. But Joann's relationship to Joe occurs entirely within that same private domain; her right to the information is thus quite separable from the public right to know that an insurance company or an employer might claim.

From an egalitarian feminist standpoint, Joann's right to the information is supportable for reasons beyond those that might apply to Joe if their situations were reversed (i.e., if Joann had the family history and Joe did not). Joann, after all, is the person whose decision about whether to become pregnant will be determined by that information or lack thereof; it is she who would be the principal caregiver of Joe if he is affected, and she who would probably be the primary caregiver of a child born to them, whether affected or not. If Joe is tested and the result is positive, Joann is the one who might then choose to undergo prenatal testing for HD and base a decision to continue or discontinue the pregnancy on that result.[49]

That said, is the unfairness to Joann of Joe's refusal to be tested so morally wrong that Joe might be coercively tested? On egalitarian feminist grounds, I think not; this view is not based on a right to personal or family privacy but on a right to resist bodily intrusion, even where it is as minor as it would be in Joe's case. The egalitarian aspect of this argument stems from the inconsistency between such coerciveness and other situations in which refusal of treatment or testing is honored, despite its being medically indicated or desirable for the one tested or treated or for others. Until and unless society requires procedures as invasive as blood or bone marrow donation from one person in order to treat another, coercive genetic testing is unfair. This conclusion is of course open to revision if we alter current policies of noncoerciveness with regard to treatment or testing for the sake of others.

If and when genetic testing is so exhaustive that it identifies all of the genetic mutations present in each individual, the concept of risk on which actuarial data regarding genetic information are based will, in a sense, no longer be applicable to insurance coverage. Fortunately or unfortunately, however, real risk will remain because most of the genetic information available will be less definitive than it is in the case of HD and other monogenetic disorders. Even if genetic testing revealed all of the polygenic factors that conspire in specific conditions, the interaction between genes and environment would make it impossible to go beyond risk to certainty regarding the manifestation of specific conditions.

Genetic information remains relevant to employers and insurers as well as family members, despite the private or personal nature of such information. From both liberal and egalitarian feminist perspectives, confidentiality regarding this information should be respected, but that confidentiality is not absolute. As we saw in Chapter 11, a free enterprise system offers legitimacy to those who seek genetic information so as to reduce their financial or personal risks. Ironically, for egalitarian feminists, it also supports the challenge to the public–private distinction that Okin and Young articulate. But perhaps the strongest argument against the privacy of genomic information has been developed by nature itself, and abetted recently by technology, through genetic copies of individual organisms. In the next chapter, therefore, we consider both nature's practice of, and technology's attempts to obliterate, genetic uniqueness through human cloning.

Notes

1. Larry Gostin, "Genetic Discrimination: The Use of Genetically-Based Diagnostic and Prognostic Tests by Employers and Insurers," *American Journal of Law and Medicine* 17, 1 and 2 (1991): 110. Problems of confidentiality may also arise from the genetic information obtained by employers and insurance companies through family histories.
2. *International Union v. Johnson Controls,* 111 S. Ct. 1196 (1991).
3. *Johnson Controls,* 1991 US LEXIS 1715, cited in Gostin, p. 140.
4. Cf. Mary E. Becker, "From *Muller v. Oregon* to Fetal Vulnerability Policies," *University of Chicago Law Review* 53 (1986): 1219.
5. This act has been interpreted as requiring "that women—like Blacks, Hispanics and Jews or other racial, ethnic or religious minorities—cannot be paid less for the work they do simply because they are women." W. Newman and C. Owens, "Race and Sex Based Wage Discrimination Is Illegal," in U.S. Commission on Civil Rights, *Comparable Worth: Issues for the 80's* (Washington, DC: Government Printing Office, 1984), pp. 131–37, cited by Carolyn R. Payton, "Every Work into Judgment," in Georgine M. Vroman, Dorothy Burnham, and Susan G. Gordon, eds., *Genes and Gender, vol. 5: Women at Work* (New York: Gordian Press, 1988), p. 197.
6. To counter the possible ambiguity of the Americans with Disabilities Act regarding presymptomatic genetic conditions and carrier status, the Institute of Medicine has recommended that the U.S. Equal Employment Opportunity Commission interpret its language to require "protection for presymptomatic people with a genetic profile for late-

onset disorders, unaffected carriers of disorders that might affect their children, and people with genetic profiles indicating the possibility of increased risk of a multifactorial disorder." See Institute of Medicine, *Assessing Genetic Risks: Implications for Health and Social Policy* (Washington, DC: National Academy Press, 1994), p. 282.

7. Naomi G. Swanson and Ami B. Becker, "Women's Health in the Workplace," in Karen Moses Allen and Janice Mitchell Phillips, eds., *Women's Health: Across the Lifespan* (Philadelphia: Lippincott-Raven, 1997), p. 490. Short men, of course, are a nondominant group vis-à-vis their taller counterparts; as such, they are as likely as women to be deleteriously affected by a workplace designed by and for the dominant group.

8. Swanson and Becker, p. 490. Anabolism is the process by which nutritive matter is assimilated and converted into living substance; the process requires both syntheses and energy. Cf. *Illustrated Stedman's Medical Dictionary*, 24th ed. (Baltimore, MD: Williams and Wilkins, 1982).

9. Swanson and Becker, p. 494.

10. E. S. Johnson, H. R. Fischman, G. M. Matanoski, and E. Diamond, "Occurrence of Cancer in Women in the Meat Industry," *British Journal of Industrial Medicine* 43 (1986): 597–604.

11. Swanson and Becker, p. 494.

12. K. H. Kilburn, R. Warshaw, and J. C. Thornton, "Pulmonary Function in Histology Technicians Compared with Women from Michigan: Effects of Chronic Low Dose Formaldehyde on a National Sample of Women," *British Journal of Industrial Medicine* 46 (1989): 468–72. The "lowness" of "low level" refers solely to the lack of prestige and low wages that attach to particular positions.

13. K. S. Hansen, "Occupational Dermatoses in Hospital Cleaning Women," *Contact Dermatitis* 9 (1983): 343–51.

14. Swanson and Becker, p. 495.

15. Swanson and Becker, pp. 496, 499–500.

16. S. L. Sauter, L. R. Murphy, and J. J. Hurrell Jr., "Prevention of Work-Related Psychological Disorders: A National Strategy Proposed by the National Institute for Occupational Safety and Health," *American Psychologist* 45 (1990): 1146–58.

17. Swanson and Becker, p. 497.

18. B. F. Reskin and C. E. Ross, "Jobs, Authority, and Earnings among Managers: The Continuing Significance of Sex," *Work and Occupations* 19 (1992): 342–65.

19. B. A. Metcalfe, "Male and Female Managers: An Analysis of Biographical and Self-Concept Data," *Work and Stress* 1 (1987): 207–19.

20. E. Abel and S. Sofaer, "Older Women's Health and Financial Vulnerability: Implications for the Medicare Benefit Structure," *Women's Health* 16 (1990): 47–67. Because the total number of medically uninsured in the United States has escalated to about 43.4 million, this number has probably increased considerably since 1990. Robert Pear, "Americans Lacking Health Insurance Put at 16%," *New York Times,* September 26, 1998, p. A1.

21. National Center for Health Statistics, *Measuring the Health of Women in America. National Health Interview Survey* (Hyattsville, MD: U.S. Department of Health and Human Services, 1995).

22. Linda Burnes Bolton, "Poverty," in Karen Moses Allen and Janice Mitchell Phillips, eds., *Women's Health Across the Lifespan: A Comprehensive Perspective* (Philadelphia: Lippincott, 1997), p. 483.

23. B. Weitzman and C. Berry, "Health Status and Health Care Utilization," *Women and Health* 19, 2–3 (1992): 87–105.

24. National Council of La Raza, *Health Promotion Fact Sheet: Hispanic Women's Health Status* (Washington, DC: National Council of La Raza, 1992); National Council of La Raza, Policy Analysis Center, Office of Research, Advocacy, and Legislation, *State of Hispanic America 1993: Toward a Latino Anti-Poverty Agenda* (Washington, DC: National Council of La Raza, 1993), and Aida L. Giachello, "Issues of Access and Use," in C. W. Molina and M. Aguirre-Molina, eds., *Latino Health in the U.S.: A Growing Challenge* (Washington, DC: American Public Health Association, 1994).

25. U.S. General Accounting Office, *Hispanic Access to Health Care: Significant Gaps Exist* (GAO/PEMD 92–6) (Washington, DC: Government Printing Office, 1992); R. B. Valdez, H. Morganstern, R. Brown, R. Wyn, C. Wang, and W. Cumberland, "Insuring Latinos against Cost of Illness," *Journal of the American Medical Association* 269, 7 (1993): 889–94.

26. National Coalition of Hispanic Mental Health and Human Services Organizations, *The State of Hispanic Health* (Washington, DC: National Coalition of Hispanic Mental Health and Human Services Organizations, 1992); Valdez et al., 1991.

27. Aida Giachello, "Latino/Hispanic Women," in Allen and Phillips, pp. 391–92.

28. Ruth R. Faden and Nancy E. Kass, "Genetic Screening Technology: Ethical Issues in Access to Tests by Employers and Health Insurance Companies," *Journal of Social Issues* 49, 2 (1993): 76.

29. Institute of Medicine, p. 247.

30. Madison Powers, "Privacy and the Control of Genetic Information," in Mark S. Frankel and Albert Teich, eds., *The Genetic Frontier* (Washington, DC: American Association for the Advancement of Science, 1994), pp. 78–79.

31. Cf. *Republic* V.457d–e.

32. *The Pocket Aristotle,* trans. W. D. Ross (New York: Washington Square Press, 1958), p. 281.

33. John Locke, *An Essay concerning Human Understanding,* ed. A. C. Fraser (Oxford, UK, 1984), vol. 1, p. 56.

34. Iris Marion Young, *Justice and the Politics of Difference* (Princeton, NJ: Princeton University Press, 1990), p. 97.

35. Young, p. 97.

36. Young, p. 97.

37. Young, p. 120.

38. Susan Moller Okin, *Justice, Gender, and the Family* (New York: Basic Books, 1989).

39. Okin, p. 128.

40. Okin, p. 133.

41. Okin, p. 133.

42. Okin, p. 133.

43. Okin, pp. 127–28.

44. Although HD is mainly expressed in one's middle years, it may become symptomatic as early as 2 and as late as 70 years of age. See I. A. Farrar and P. M. Conneally, "A Genetic Model for Age of Onset in Huntington's Disease," *American Journal of Human Genetics* 37 (1985): 350–57.

45. In the United States, Title VII of the Civil Rights Act of 1964 provides that it is not unlawful for employers to hire on the basis of religion, sex, or national origin if the decision is based on BFOQ reasonably necessary to the normal operation of the business. Kathleen Zeitz, "Employer Genetic Testing: A Legitimate Screening Device or Another Method of Discrimination?" *Labor Law Journal* 42, 4 (1991): 232. The Ameri-

cans with Disabilities Act makes it illegal to fire or refuse to hire an employee based on susceptibility to a genetic condition or on genetic conditions that do not constitute BFOQs. Institute of Medicine, pp. 272–73. 281–82.

46. Ruth R. Faden and Nancy E. Kass, "Genetic Screening Technology: Ethical Issues in Access to Tests by Employers and Health Insurance Companies," *Journal of Social Issues* 49, 2 (1993): 77.

47. Employers' options in hiring may be broader than those they have for firing because the employment agreement involves a commitment to workers. Legally, Joe could challenge denial of a job on grounds of genetic risk, whether the information about his risk is generated by family history of HD or by genetic test results. However, employers are often able to argue successfully that job applicants are not equally qualified and use that as grounds for acceptance or rejection, even when the actual grounds are not job-related.

48. Other ethical considerations are broadly applicable to the case: the value of the life lived prior to the onset of HD and the compatibility of advocacy for the disabled with a decision to forgo pregnancy to avoid having a child for whom adult onset of HD is predictable. I have discussed the latter point in more general terms in Chapter 8. On the first point, my egalitarian feminist view is that a life lived before the onset of HD is of equal value to life lived after the onset of symptoms, and both are of equal value to a life lived without either HD or susceptibility to HD.

49. Even if Joe is not tested, Joann has alternative ways of avoiding the risk of a child affected with HD: donor insemination, adoption, and childlessness. Although these are reasonable options in light of the risk of HD already known through Joe's family history, Joann may have ethical, religious, or cultural reasons for declining to consider them.

16

Human Cloning, Women, and Parenthood

NEVER before had the birth of a little lamb evoked such clamor as did the belated announcement of the birth of "Dolly" in February 1997.[1] Scientists were shocked because they had long believed it impossible to clone a whole organism from an adult cell. The public—at least a large portion of it—were horrified at the thought that humans might soon be cloned from adult cells. Responding to the public outcry, various governments scurried to curtail the prospect of human cloning.[2]

In the months that followed, other clones of nonhuman animals appeared but generated less publicity.[3] Most were generated from embryonic or fetal rather than adult cells, but clones from female adult mice and from a cow have now been reported as well.[4] One year after the announcement of Dolly's birth, Ian Wilmut, the scientist who led the team that cloned her, acknowledged the possibility that the lamb was formed from fetal rather than adult cells.[5] However, in July 1998, DNA analysis confirmed that Dolly was in fact the genetic match of the ewe whose mammary tissue had been used to clone her.[6]

In December 1998, researchers in South Korea announced that they had produced a human embryo cloned from an infertile woman; the embryo developed into four cells before the experiment was halted.[7] This work has not yet been published in the scientific literature. Although cloning from mature human cells has not yet produced a newborn, and cloning from adult males of other species has not yet been reported, most scientists believe that these possibilities will be realized in due time.[8]

Until and unless cloning of adult humans leads to the birth of children, some of the issues addressed in this chapter are speculative. From a feminist standpoint, however, it seems worthwhile to consider them now because the issues arise, in part at least, from ongoing gender inequities. Identifying such inequities in the context of cloning may highlight their occurrence in other circumstances, facilitating their avoidance.

Preliminarily, it should be acknowledged that human cloning has occurred in nature throughout human history, and in laboratory science for decades.[9] Nature's cloning occurs through identical twinning in vivo before implantation; scientific cloning occurs through the replication of genetically identical DNA, cells, bacteria, viruses, or whole organisms. Replication of genes through recombinant DNA technology[10] has led to the development of treatments such as insulin for diabetes and erythropoietin for anemia. Somatic cells are replicated by retrieving them from people and growing them in culture in the laboratory; like DNA clones, these cell lines are used for experimental purposes that may lead to clinical applications.

Recombinant DNA technology was controversial when first proposed, but it is now widely accepted on moral as well as scientific grounds.[11] Although the other methods listed above are also noncontroversial, two forms of human cloning continue to be debated: cloning from embryonic or fetal cells and somatic cell nuclear transfer from humans already born. These methods differ from natural twinning because they are induced by scientific technology; they differ from DNA and somatic cell replication because they may produce a genetic duplicate of the entire human organism. In what follows, therefore, I examine these methods of cloning, evaluating arguments for and against them.

Human Embryo Cloning

Three types of embryo cloning have already been performed in nonhuman animals: blastomere separation, embryo splitting, and nuclear transplantation. Blastomere separation occurs through the isolation of individual cells, or blastomeres, each of which is totipotent, at the two- or four-cell stage of development.[12] Although the process is expensive and rarely successful, nonhuman animals have been produced from each of the four cells of a four-celled embryo of the corresponding organism. In humans, blastomere separation has been used successfully in preimplantation genetic diagnosis. As we saw in Chapter 12, this process is experimental, invasive, and costly. Nonetheless, blastomere separation and analysis provides a means by which women who are carriers for autosomal recessive or X-linked conditions may avoid prenatal diagnosis while obtaining definitive information about the genetic status of their in vitro embryos.

Embryo splitting is a bisection technique used in the cattle industry to increase the production of prize calves. The method calls for blastocysts obtained commercially by flushing them from the uterus after the cow has been artificially inseminated. On average, bisection of the blastocyst produces 1.5 times more calves per blastocyst than would otherwise be obtained. In humans, however, this method has not been successful, apparently because acquisition of blastocysts by uterine flushing usually fails, and oocytes fertilized in vitro seldom reach the blastocyst stage with present culture systems. Howard Jones and his colleagues claim that blastocyst transfer "has itself not been found to offer any advantages over the transfer of cleaving preembryos."[13]

Human blastocyst splitting has nonetheless been proposed as a means by which treatment of infertility may be enhanced. To that end, a prize-winning paper was presented at the Conjoint Annual Meeting of the American Fertility Society and the Canadian Fertility and Andrology Society in 1993. The paper, "Experimental Cloning of Human Polyploid Embryos Using an Artificial Zona Pellucida," by a team of researchers from George Washington University in Washington, D.C., precipitated a brief but intense media frenzy concerning the possibility of human cloning.[14] Although the authors claimed that their results pointed the way to improved treatment of infertility, their research had not been conducted on normal human embryos of either fertile or infertile couples. Because all of the 17 embryos utilized in their experiment were abnormal, none of the separated blastocysts that developed in vitro was considered suitable for transfer to potential mothers. Even if they had been suitable, Jones and his colleagues doubt that the method would be therapeutically effective or efficient.

From an ethical point of view, the public discussion of the social implications of human cloning provoked by the work of the George Washington University investigators was probably valuable. As is their wont, bioethicists positioned themselves on different sides of the issue, some arguing that the technique simply adds another reproductive option to the mix to which couples already are entitled, so long as they are aware of, and have freely consented to, its risks to themselves and their potential offspring. Others argued that cloning marks a point beyond the morally acceptable scope of medical assistance in reproduction; for them, issues such as the loss of genetic uniqueness across generations was particularly problematic. Still others addressed the issue as one more illustration of the human arrogance involved in medical manipulation of the normal and natural reproductive process.[15]

Interestingly, while some bioethicists expressed concerns about the impact of human cloning on cloned individuals, none, to my knowledge, indicated that there were gender differences to worry about as well. In fact, however, as with medical technologies already available to assist infertile men or women, human cloning from embryos entails disproportionate burdens for women. More women than men are affected by the process because of the separability of gestation and genetics and because sperm are so much more numerous and accessible than ova. Even if an equal number of men and women participated in the process, women alone would be undergoing the risks, pain, and discomfort of ova stimulation, ova retrieval, embryo transfer, gestation, and childbirth.

The third method of embryo cloning is nuclear transplantation. This involves the transfer of the nucleus of an embryo into an egg from which the nucleus has been removed. Extensive studies show that 60%–70% of calves cloned through this method from very early embryos are completely normal morphologically and genetically. If this method were applied to humans, it could introduce an extra risk for women because 20%–30% of the cloned calves are transiently much larger than normal, requiring cesarean section delivery.[16] Until the birth of Dolly, there were no reports of successful cloning of mammals from nonembryonic nuclei.

Nuclear Transfer from Mature Somatic Cells

The belief that cloning from adult cells was impossible was based on evidence that irreversible nuclear changes have occurred through differentiation. In amphibia, some development from differentiated cells had been induced in the past, but the resultant organisms never progressed to maturity. Researchers who wished to clone animals from the nuclei of mature cells attempted to reverse differentiation and to reprogram development. By establishing a state of quiescence in the nuclei of the donor cells obtained, they induced the nucleus to respond to the cytoplasmic environment of the zygote, triggering development into a whole "new" organism. This whole new organism is in fact genetically identical to the adult that provided the mature cells. Although its developmental stage is earlier, the age of the DNA in the younger individual or clone is the same as that of the adult donor. This has led to concerns about possible acquired mutations in the tissue that is cloned.

In their letter to *Nature* early in 1997, Ian Wilmut and his colleagues reported that they had induced quiescence in the nuclei of cells taken from sheep at different stages of development, all of which involved some differentiation: a 9-day embryo, a 26-day fetus, and a 6-year-old ewe in the last trimester of pregnancy.[17] From 277 attempts to clone adult (mammary gland) tissue, 172 attempts from the fetal (fibroblast) tissue and 385 attempts from the embryonic tissue, 8 live lambs were produced: 1 from the adult cells, 3 from the fetal cells, and 4 from the embryonic cells. One of the lambs developed from fetal cells died within a few minutes of birth. Since the birth announcement of Dolly, however, the low success rate has improved significantly because many more clones have been produced from fetal bovine cells of males and females and from mature female cells of other nonhuman animals.[18] In comparison with clones of sheep and cattle, the clones of mice are particularly useful to investigators because of their shorter life cycle and the relative ease with which they can be maintained and studied in laboratories.

Although clones from adult male cells have been attempted, none has as yet been successful.[19] With Dolly, for example, multiple ewes, but no male sheep, were directly involved in her production. Her entire set of genes came from the mammary gland of one ewe, who may therefore be called her genetic mother and father. R. C. Lewontin alleges that her genetic mother and father were the genetic parents of her immediate progenitor, but those sheep were obviously not directly involved in Dolly's development.[20] Dolly may be viewed as both the identical twin and daughter of the ewe from whose tissue she was formed; the parents of that ewe might also be described as her grandparents.

Dolly had two additional biological mothers: the ewe whose egg was enucleated to make room for the DNA obtained from the progenitor ewe and the ewe to which the renucleated egg was transferred after development commenced. Moreover, Dolly might have had a fourth biological mother. After the gestating ewe gave birth to her, she might have been nursed by another ewe still, as happens with women who serve as "wet nurses" for other women's offspring. Whichever ewe nursed Dolly, whether gestationally or genetically related to her or not, is probably the one that Dolly herself would have regarded as her mother.

Cloning through somatic cell nuclear transplantation from adults not only involves multiple females in reproductive roles, but it may involve no males at all. Although strictly speaking this is not equivalent to parthenogenesis because the progenitor ewe was derived from male and female gametes, the process could continue in a parthenogenetic manner—through females alone. If and when male clones are produced from the DNA of adult males, females will still be required to provide ova, gestation, and lactation. These disparate biological roles of females are not without risk, discomfort, and invasiveness. While raising questions about the meaning of parenthood in general and motherhood in particular, the production of Dolly also illustrates a social tendency that the Human Genome Project has accentuated: a genetic bias.

The Genetic Bias of Human Cloning and Infertility Treatment

The goals of nonhuman cloning include the improvement of food production and development of therapeutic modalities for use in humans. These goals parallel those that have long been pursued in plant genetics.[21] In contrast, the principal goal of human embryo cloning, as it has developed thus far, is more effective treatment of infertility. In conjunction with that goal, cloning is a means by which women may avoid invasive procedures that they would otherwise undergo for treatment of their own or their partner's infertility. For example, the cloning of embryos already retrieved eliminates the need for further ovulation stimulation and ova retrievals in subsequent attempts to achieve pregnancy. In time, embryo cloning could also be more cost effective in treating infertility. From an egalitarian feminist standpoint, these advantages of embryo cloning for some women and for society at large are desirable and justifiable so long as they are not purchased at the cost of greater disadvantages for women or others who are already disadvantaged.

From that same standpoint, another projected goal of human cloning is problematic: cloning one individual to provide treatment for another, for example, through organ or tissue donation.[22] In Kantian language, the obvious moral problem raised by such a situation is that a person is treated as a means rather than an end. Years ago, that question was considered by Mary and Abe Ayala, whose teenage daughter, Anissa, was suffering from chronic myelogenous leukemia, which required bone marrow donation for effective treatment.[23] Because neither they nor their son was a tissue match for Anissa and no other compatible donor could be found, the parents decided to try to have another child, hoping that he or she would provide the desired match. The attempt required a reversal of Abe's vasectomy.[24] Even if the reversal were successfully performed, the couple realized the probability that their newborn would be a match was only one in four. Regardless of whether the infant was a tissue match for their daughter, however, they said they would love and care for the child as fully as they loved and cared for Anissa. In other words, their motives were mixed, as is true of most people most of the time. In time, their hope was fulfilled: their second daughter, Marissa, was a match to Anissa and became a donor to her sister when she was 14 months old. About a year later, Anissa was healthy enough to walk down the aisle at her wedding, with Marissa serving as flower girl.[25]

If the Ayala family could have cloned Anissa to produce another child, they would have thereby ensured a match for bone marrow donation to her. Just as in the actual case, they probably would have indicated their intention to love and care for Anissa's identical twin as they did for her. They might wonder, however, whether in time the identical twin might develop the same condition as Anissa, needing donation from another identical twin who might be cloned, need donation for another, and so on, for each cloned generation. Moreover, Anissa's own consent to provide her DNA for insertion into her mother's enucleated egg would be ethically required. The cloning process would be accomplished through somatic cell nuclear transplantation unless Anissa herself had been generated from an embryo formed through embryo splicing and the untransferred genetically identical embryos had been frozen for future use.

If Anissa's bone marrow donor had been produced by cloning Anissa and by having Anissa's mother gestate and give birth to her, the question of who is the mother is complicated not only by biology but also by psychology, that is, by the set of relationships already formed between mother and daughter. Moreover, the rationale for cloning in this case is morally different from that of those who support the procedure solely on grounds of reproductive choice.[26] The desire of the Ayalas to have a genetically related offspring was based on their desire to cure another offspring rather than the desire to replicate their own genes. In fact, if they had found a nonrelated donor who matched Anissa's cell type, they probably would not have had another child.

Two cases mentioned in the President's Commission Report on Human Cloning provide better examples than the preceding case of a genetic bias (i.e., a tendency to prefer offspring who are genetically related to oneself).

1. "A couple wishes to have children, but both adults are carriers of a lethal recessive gene. Rather than risk the one in four chance of conceiving a child who will suffer a short and painful existence, the couple considers the alternatives: to forgo rearing children; to adopt; to use prenatal diagnosis and selective abortion; to use donor gametes free of the recessive trait; or to use the cells of one of the adults and attempt to clone a child. To avoid donor gametes and selective abortion, while maintaining a genetic tie to their child, they opt for cloning."[27]
2. "A family is in a terrible accident. The father is killed, and the only child, an infant, is dying. The mother decides to use some cells from the dying infant in an attempt to use somatic cell nuclear transfer to create a new child. It is the only way she can raise a child who is the biological offspring of her late husband."[28]

In case 1, the couple clearly desires to have a child genetically related to both of them, while free of a genetic disease; they also desire to avoid prenatal testing and abortion. But another desire is suggested by the case description: avoidance of a short and painful existence on the part of an affected child. Shortness of life span does not necessarily limit the quality of someone's life, but the shortness of a child's life is likely to cause suffering for the parents, thereby limiting their quality of life.

Unfortunately, the commission does not indicate the nature of the recessive disorder for which the parents are both carriers, nor does it define the type of condition it considers "lethal." Sickle cell anemia and cystic fibrosis are the most common recessive conditions in African Americans and Caucasians, respectively, but affected individuals typically survive to adulthood and beyond.

Tay-Sachs disease, a recessive, progressive, neurological disorder that particularly affects Ashkenazi Jews, is considered lethal because those who are affected die in early childhood. Whether the experience of the disease is painful to the child, however, depends on the systems affected, the treatments administered, and whether adequate palliation is provided. In light of these variables, the possibility that even the most severe genetic disease *necessarily* entails pain for the person affected is questionable. Parents, however, surely experience a great deal of anguish or suffering in the course of caring for an affected child.

The desire to be a parent is as natural and good as the desire to have a genetically related child, but the two desires are not the same, and their fulfillment is not essential to one's health or life. Choosing to remain childless in a situation such as case 1 may not only be morally permissible but commendable, depending on its rationale. Adoption is also a morally commendable option. Neither childlessness nor adoption illustrates the genetic bias that supposedly motivates the couple's desire for cloning. In contrast, case 1 suggests a gender-based genetic bias on the part of the President's Commission. The commission represents the genetic tie as the most important one for the potential parents, ignoring the nongenetic biological tie that the woman may have through gestation and childbirth. Egg donation in this case would allow both partners to avoid the risk of transmitting the genetic condition for which they are carriers.

Case 2 illustrates cloning itself as the objective of reproductive assistance. Presumably, the woman could have another child through adoption, artificial insemination by a donor, or sexual intercourse with a new partner, but she apparently desires not only to raise a child who is genetically related to her but to ensure that the child be the genetic duplicate of her son. Of course, the genetic duplicate would not be the same person as the son who is dying; rather, he would be the son's identical twin, born several years later and genetically related to her dead husband and to her.[29] Interestingly, the woman's genetic bias in this case is mainly oriented toward propagating another's genes rather than her own. She could, after all, replicate the entirety of her own genome by cloning herself, or she could be as genetically related to a new child as to her dying son by simply repeating the process through which the latter had been conceived.

While libertarian-minded feminists might support cloning in this instance, egalitarian feminists would not. The woman's desire to have her son cloned is an understandable instance of genetic bias, but it cannot be justified on that basis alone. Unlike the Ayala case, which involved the goal of effective treatment for a child already born, this case involves no effective treatment for anyone. In fact, the woman's recovery from the loss of her husband and son might be impeded by the attempt to replicate the genetic contribution of one and the genome of the other. Although the Ayala case also raises the question of treating a child as a means rather than an end, this case raises that question yet more problematically because the clone is apparently desired for more individualistic than therapeutic reasons.

As we saw in Chapter 7, the desire for a genetic tie to offspring is natural and prevalent, but it is less strong in many women than in men. While both men and women prefer to have children biologically rather than through adoption, the gestational tie established through pregnancy may be at least as important as the genetic tie for women. To the extent that the genetic tie induces individuals to stay together and to protect and nurture one another, it is surely a good thing. Interestingly, however, the origin of families is precisely *not* a genetic tie between parents themselves. Despite the high incidence of divorce in contemporary society, the fact that so many couples do stay together and protect and nurture each other argues for the enduring significance of nongenetic ties. The nongenetic tie between partners is reinforced, in most societies, by their having chosen each other as mature individuals who were aware, to some degree at least, of each other's strengths and weaknesses.

The lack of a genetic link between stepchildren and one of their social parents has been associated with a higher incidence of violence in their families compared with the families of adoptive children and families in which all of the children are genetically related to both parents.[30] Adoption represents the desire of both parents to have a child who is not genetically related to either of them; egg or sperm donation represents a desire to have a child genetically related to one but not both; a couple's decision to initiate or continue a pregnancy to which both have contributed their gametes represents a desire to have a child who is genetically related to both parents. Each of these scenarios involves a specific decision on the part of both partners to be parents. In contrast, stepfamilies are formed by partners' choosing each other, but not necessarily choosing to be parents of children produced through previous relationships. The fact that ties between children and their adoptive parents tend to be stronger than ties between stepparents and their stepchildren suggests the importance not only of nongenetic ties but also of the autonomy of both partners in decisions to have children. Children themselves, whether adopted or not, do not have that opportunity. Another factor that may contribute to successful parenting by adoptive couples is the fact that they are usually screened by professionals for their suitability to be parents.

A genetic bias is natural, prevalent, and good in most instances, but it can lead to social inequities as well. Consider, for example, the fact that medical and technological assistance in acquiring genetically related offspring is a growth industry whose benefits are virtually unavailable to the poor, who are just as likely, or more likely, than the affluent to be infertile. Consider also the economic disparity that usually prevails between gamete donors and their recipients. In a sense, the former sell their genes to allow others to (re)produce their partners' genes. The greater reluctance of women to be egg donors than of men to be sperm donors is undoubtedly influenced by the greater invasiveness and risk of egg donation.[31] Women's reluctance may also be influenced by their limited number of eggs and a desire to ensure their own capability for pregnancy and childbirth. Commercial surrogacy is perhaps a clearer illustration of social inequity associated with a genetic bias. When the surrogate is both gestationally and genetically related to the offspring, she, like an egg donor, sells her genes so that someone can fulfill his genetic bias. If she is not genetically related, she contributes to the genetic bias of both partners whose embryo she gestates.

Human somatic cell nuclear transfer offers the prospect of extreme and unnatural genetic bias. It is extreme because it entails the contribution of not only half but all of one's genetic material. It is unnatural because this never occurs in nature. Both factors make human somatic cell nuclear transfer radically different from other modes of reproductive assistance. The other modes conform to the model of combining gametes from a male and female to produce genetically new offspring related to both of the contributing partners. Human somatic cell nuclear transfer might be more accurately described as replicative assistance than reproductive assistance. Replicative assistance might be further characterized as radically conservative because it attempts to preserve a phenotype that has already been expressed, forgoing not only the risk of a new genetic combination but also the possibility of a superior phenotype.

Beyond the priority that some women impute to the gestational, rather than genetic, link to their offspring, a genetic bias has historically been associated more with men than with women. Without recognizing that infertility in couples is as likely due to the male partner as the female partner, women have in fact been blamed for childlessness. In biblical times, the "barrenness" of a woman was grounds for her husband's "lying" with another woman in order to have a child, or, if his wife had only had daughters, to have a son.[32] The practice of women taking their husbands' surnames is a way of indicating the male's genetic lineage only. Although sperm "donation" is mainly undertaken for money, the keener interest of men in sperm "donation" than women in egg donation suggests that men may also be motivated by a desire to propagate their own genetic endowment. Women are sometimes prone to support that motivation on the part of their partners, resorting to extreme measures to have children genetically related to their husbands. In postmenopausal gestation, for example, women undergo hormonal stimulation, embryo transfer, and gestation after in vitro fertilization of donor eggs with their husband's sperm, in order to give birth to children who are genetically unrelated to them.

The language in which adoptive parents and biological parents are sometimes described also connotes a genetic bias. The latter, for example, are sometimes called "real" parents, even if they have never been involved in parental nurturance. In Chicago, for example, in the early 1990s a child known as Baby Richard was adopted by a couple who cared for him from his fourth day of life until he was nearly four years of age. At that point, the couple was ordered by a judge to surrender the child to his genetic father.[33] The child had been conceived in the course of an affair after which the genetic father went abroad and developed another sexual liaison. On giving birth, Richard's biological (gestational and genetic) mother legally surrendered the child to the couple who became his adoptive parents. When the genetic father learned of the boy's birth he initiated a legal effort to take him from his adoptive home, claiming he had a right to do so because he was the child's "real" father.[34] Although the genetic father married the biological mother while engaged in his effort to take Richard from his adoptive family, her "real" motherhood status was neither acknowledged nor legally restored, even after her husband separated from her and Richard several years later.[35]

Real Parents, Real Mothers

Was Baby Richard's genetic father his real father? Genetically, he was as really the boy's father as a sperm donor is the real father of a child he never intended to see or nurture. Comparing the two, the sperm donor is intentionally a genetic parent, whereas Baby Richard's genetic father was not, at least until sometime after the child was born. Sperm donors never become legal parents; in most states, the husband of a woman who is artificially inseminated with donor sperm is considered the child's legal father.[36] Richard's genetic father became his legal father only after a lengthy court battle and a controversial judicial decision.[37] He was the child's only legal parent even after he left the family, while Richard's biological mother remained to care for him even though she was not legally his parent. Once removed from his adoptive family, Richard had no legal mother.

A different view of what constitutes a real parent was articulated by a sperm donor in a letter to his potential genetic offspring. "I am not your parent," he wrote, even though I am your (genetic) father because I never gave you anything. I never held you or cared for you. The man who did those things for you is your real parent."[38] From an egalitarian feminist perspective, something similar might be said by an egg donor. Because of the physical demands and risk of egg "donation," however, it is less likely that a woman who provides gametes would say that she gave her genetic progeny "nothing" even though she is paid more than a sperm "donor."[39] What sperm donors and egg donors do have in common is that neither intends to be a parent. For a woman, that intention tends to be more encompassing than for a man because it necessarily entails the negation of a greater degree of involvement through gestation and childbirth, and it usually entails negation of a greater degree of responsibility for child care or nurturance.

If and when human somatic cell nuclear transfer becomes available, both men and women may donate their DNA with much less discomfort or risk than a woman undergoes in providing ova. Female recipients would still be required to gestate and give birth. Because DNA is so easily obtainable from donors, its value would be negligible unless the donor were a particularly prized tissue source. Even then, it would be difficult for such a donor to prevent others from freely obtaining DNA traces from cells left through routine touching. According to Davor Solter, a molecular geneticist at the Max-Planck Institute, the unique role of women in human somatic cell nuclear transfer suggests an advantage for them that feminists would support. Whether the procedure is used to generate whole organisms or specific organs or tissue, women's eggs are necessary to that generation, and "women hold all the eggs." Solter observes that a woman, therefore, "could use one of her own eggs to create an organ she needs. But a man would have to buy eggs from a woman, if he could find a woman to provide them and if he could afford them."[40] Although Solter seems to think that their egg producing capacity might make women all-powerful in society, feminists are unlikely to agree with that assessment. Rather, most of us see the fact that we already hold all the eggs as disempowering, although not necessarily so. Men, after all, have always depended on women not only to provide their eggs but also their DNA and their uterine environment to produce their offspring. So long as men hold more economic power than women, further dependence on women for enucleated eggs is hardly likely to result in reverse sexism.

In its dependence on use of enucleated eggs, somatic cell nuclear transfer introduces a new way in which women may be biologically related to offspring. Even if men provide the entire genetic complement to an embryo, they remain biologically related to the eventual offspring through that mode alone. They may in fact be described as genetic mother and genetic father. But women may be related biologically through (enucleated) egg provision, through gestation, and through lactation. Even the enucleated egg contains mitochondrial DNA, which influences the health of the developing embryo or fetus, regardless of whether the nuclear DNA transferred into it comes from a male or female progenitor. Through use of one woman's nuclear DNA and another woman's enucleated egg, a lesbian couple may have a child who is biologically related to both without requiring sperm donation.

All of these biological roles for women may be viewed as grounds for calling them mothers. But if women serve only as DNA providers, egg providers, gestation providers, or lactation providers, are they *real* mothers? Certainly they may all be called biological mothers because they all fulfill biologically determined maternal roles. But are all biological mothers real mothers or real parents? Traditionally, mothers have been defined as those who give birth. This definition implies that gene providers (whether they contribute all or only half the recipient's DNA) and enucleated egg providers are not mothers unless they also gestate and give birth. But the traditional definition was formulated in the absence of the technical possibility of separating genes from gestation. Probably it was also formulated with the assumption that one who gives birth goes on to nurse the child, as gestation and childbirth prepare her to do; in other words, continuity between natural and nurturant roles of a mother was presumed. Once nurturance is introduced as a maternal function, we need to recognize that men as well as women can and do nurture infants. Women alone of course can fulfill the nurturant function of breast feeding, but men are fully capable of bottle feeding, which many women choose as well. Essential nurturance of infants is thus a parental function fulfillable by either mothers or fathers. Moreover, it is fulfillable by men or women who are not biological parents but who are committed to the child's nurturance,—that is, by adoptive parents, whether mothers or fathers.

From an egalitarian feminist standpoint, real motherhood may be defined as encompassing different demands and degrees of lifegiving, both qualitatively and quantitatively. As we saw in the previous chapter, genes as well as environment figure significantly in the determination of individual traits. In cloning, the individual's genetic endowment is determined by one parent, whether male or female. But the ovum in which that parent's DNA is inserted represents a significant environmental influence on development, and the mitochondrial DNA adds a genetic component to the environment of the nuclear DNA. The individual who provides the egg is another parent, always female and therefore a mother, who undergoes greater risk and discomfort through her lifegiving than does the genetic parent. Another crucial environmental influence is the individual who gestates and gives birth, one who may be described as another parent and another mother, who undergoes greater risk and discomfort through her lifegiving than either of the other parents. In human somatic cell nuclear transfer, a lactating mother is another significant environmental influence, but a father or mother who feeds an infant by bottle may be equally significant.

As a child develops, however, whether cloned or not, the most important environmental determinant of the person he or she becomes is the parent or parents who provide care and nurturance toward adulthood, regardless of whether they are biologically related to the child. In time, the adoptive parent becomes more really a parent than any of the others. A real mother, then, is first and foremost a woman who cares for a child, from any stage of development, until the child no longer needs that care. A real father is a man who does the same when he can, which is after the child is born.

Ordinarily, real parents contribute to their children both biologically and environmentally. When they are not biologically related, their parenthood is real to the extent that they contribute themselves—their love, work, thought, income, communication, and so on—throughout the child's lifetime. By this rationale, if I were asked to compare the different mothers involved in cloning, I would probably resort to the traditional definition by saying the woman who gives birth is the real mother at that point. For some time after birth, a lactating mother could be a real mother as well. But an adoptive mother would in time be more real a mother than any of the others, regardless of the lack of a biological tie to her child.

From an egalitarian feminist standpoint, it is hard to see how genetic ties alone ever provide an adequate basis for defining real mothers *or* real fathers.

Notes

1. Ronald Kotulak, "First Mammal Is Cloned," *Chicago Tribune*, February 23, 1997, pp. 1, 8; Gina Kolata, "Scientist Reports First Cloning Ever of Adult Mammal," *New York Times*, February 23, 1997, pp. 1, 20. I put the name "Dolly" in quotation marks as a means of calling attention to the fact the name chosen by the researchers has offended some people, albeit not the person in whose "honor" the lamb was named. Reportedly, "Dolly" was named after Dolly Parton because the lamb was cloned from mammary tissue and Ms. Parton is well known for her mammary tissue.

2. E.g., a ban on human cloning has been signed by 19 European nations, including France, Italy, Greece, Spain, Portugal, Sweden, Denmark, and Norway. Britain and Germany declined to sign the ban, the former considering it too strict and the latter considering it too mild. President William Clinton urged the U.S. Congress to join the international ban. Joseph Schuman, "19 European Nations Ban Human Cloning," *Chicago Sun-Times*, January 13, 1998, p. 17.

3. E.g., Carey Goldberg, "Scientists Announce Births of Cows Cloned in New Way," *New York Times*, January 21, 1998, p. A14. Except for Dolly, attempts to clone from adult cells have not yet led to live birth of offspring. See also Robert Lee Hotz, "Wis. Scientists Clone 5 Species," *Chicago Sun-Times*, January 19, 1998, p. 3.

4. T. Wakayama, A. C. F. Perry, M. Zuccotti, K. R. Johnson, and R. Yanagimachi, "Full-Term Development of Mice from Enucleated Oocytes Injected with Cumulus Cell Nuclei," *Nature* 394 (1998): 369–74, and Yoko Kato, Tetsuya Tani, Yusuke Sotomaru, K. Kurokawa, J. Keto, H. Doguchi, H. Yasue and Y. Tsunoda, "Eight Calves Cloned from Somatic Cells of a Single Adult," *Science* 282 (1998): 2095–98.

5. J. Madeleine Nash, "Was Dolly a Mistake?" *Time*, March 2, 1998, p. 65.

6. David Ashworth, Matthew Bishop, Keith Campbell, Alan Colman, Alex Kind, A. Schnieke, S. Blott, H. Griffin, C. Haley, J. McWhir, and I. Wilmut, "DNA Microsatellite Analysis of Dolly," *Nature* 394 (1998): 329. DNA Fingerprinting led to the same conclusion from a different set of investigators. Esther N. Signer, Juri E. Dubrova, Alec J. Jeffreys, Colin Wilde, Lynn M. B. Finch, M. Wells, and M. Peaker, "DNA Fingerprinting Dolly," *Nature* 394 (1998): 329–30.

7. Sheryl WuDunn, "South Korean Scientists Say They Cloned a Human Cell," *New York Times*, December 17, 1998, p. A12.

8. According to R. Michael Roberts, Japanese scientists claim to have cloned a prize bull, but this has not been reported in the scientific literature. Gina Kolata, "Japanese Scientists Clone a Cow, Making 8 Copies," *New York Times,* December 9, 1998, p. A8.

9. Jacques Cohen has challenged the description of identical twins derived from embryos as clones, whether they occur naturally or through in vitro manipulation. He calls the latter a "twinning technique" and defines cloning more narrowly: "taking the nucleus of a cell from the body of an adult and transferring it to an unfertilized egg, destroying the genome of the oocyte of the egg, and letting it develop." Rebecca Voelker, "A Clone by Any Other Name Is Still an Ethical Concern," *Journal of the American Medical Association* 271 (1994): 332.

10. Recombinant DNA technology involves the combining of DNA from different species; this is possible because all living species use the same genetic code. The DNA of bacteria, for example, may be combined with human DNA, to develop many copies or clones of the human DNA that investigators wish to examine. Ricki Lewis, *Human Genetics: Concepts and Applications,* 2nd ed. (Dubuque, IA: Wm. C. Brown Publishers, 1997), pp. 316–17.

11. Donald S. Fredrickson, "Asilomar and Recombinant DNA: The End of the Beginning," in Kathi E. Hanna, ed., *Biomedical Politics* (Washington, DC: National Academy Press, 1991), pp. 274–84.

12. Howard W. Jones Jr., Robert G. Edwards, and George E. Seidel Jr., "On Attempts at Cloning in the Human," *Fertility and Sterility* 61, 3 (1994): 423–26.

13. Jones et al., p. 434. This criticism may not apply to somatic cell nuclear transfer, whether used for cattle or humans. Some scientists believe that this technique may be at least as efficient as in vitro fertilization of cows. Kolata, "Japanese Scientists Clone a Cow."

14. J. L. Hall, D. Engel, P. R. Gindoff, G. L. Mottla, and R. J. Stillman, "Experimental Cloning of Human Polyploid Embryos Using an Artificial Zona Pellucida," Paper presented at the Conjoint Annual Meeting of the American Fertility Society and the Canadian Fertility and Andrology Society, General Program Prize Paper, October 13, 1993. Montreal, Quebec. Abstract cited by Jones.

15. Lori B. Andrews puts this point most forcefully when she compares cloning to incest, identifying the risk it entails as "hubris" or "abuse of power." Andrews, "Mom, Dad, Clone: Implications for Reproductive Privacy," *Cambridge Quarterly of Healthcare Ethics* 7 (1998): 183. This article recapitulates the major arguments for and against human somatic cell nuclear transplantation (pp. 176–86).

16. Jones et al., p. 424.

17. Ian Wilmut, A. E., Schnieke, J. McWhir, A. J. Kind, and K. H. S. Campbell, "Viable Offspring Derived from Fetal and Adult Mammalian Cells," *Nature* 385, 27 (1997): 810–13.

18. Elizabeth Pennisi, "Cloned Mice Provide Company for Dolly," *Science* 281 (1998): 495–96; Wakayama et al., Kato et al.

19. Of the three types of adult cells from which mouse cloning was attempted, cumulus (from females), Sertoli (from males), and neural cells (from either sex), only the cumulus cells yielded successful results. Wakayama et al., p. 369.

20. R. C. Lewontin, "The Confusion over Cloning," *New York Review of Books,* October 23, 1997, pp. 18–23.

21. In the plant world, "genetically identical copies of whole organisms are . . . commonly referred to as 'varieties' rather than clones." *Cloning Human Beings, Report and Recommendations of the National Bioethics Advisory Commission* (Rockville, MD: National Bioethics Advisory Commission, 1997), pp. 13–14.

22. Embryo stem cells, which can be produced from blastocysts derived from human clones, may also make it possible to grow healthy tissue or organs, rather than whole organisms, to replace their unhealthy counterparts in the cloned individual. Eliot Marshall, "Use of Stem Cells Still Legally Murky, but Hearing Offers Hope," *Science* 282 (1998): 1962–63. If the human blastocyst from which the replacement develops in vitro has no moral status, this application is less problematic than the deliberate development of whole organisms solely for the purpose of their serving as organ or tissue donors. Development of whole organisms can occur only through women's bodies. But the development of replaceable tissue or organs in the laboratory also depends on women for provision of the oocytes in which the cloned DNA can grow.

23. Sally Ann Stewart, "Toddler May Be Sister's Lifesaver," *USA Today,* June 4, 1991, p. A3.

24. Bob Brown, "20/20," ABC News, November 6, 1997.

25. Transplant Sisters Celebrate a Wedding," *Boston Globe,* June 6, 1992, sec. 11, p. 4.

26. E.g., John A. Robertson, *Children of Choice* (Princeton, NJ: Princeton University Press, 1994).

27. *Cloning Human Beings,* p. 79.

28. *Cloning Human Beings,* p. 79.

29. The dying son from whom a new son is cloned may also be considered the genetic father and mother of his identical twin.

30. Jane E. Brody, "Genetic Ties May Be Factor in Violence in Stepfamilies," *New York Times on the Web,* February 10, 1998, www.nytimes.com.

31. In contrast to the availability of sperm, eggs are in short supply, requiring potential recipients to wait a year or more for donor eggs. To entice egg donors, one infertility clinic has raised its payment to them to $5000 for a month's worth of eggs. This is 20 times what donors were typically paid when the practice began over a decade ago. Clinicians may encourage use of donor eggs from younger women because it improves their success rate in treating older women, attracting more infertility patients. Gina Kolata, "Soaring Price of Donor Eggs Sets Off Debate," *New York Times on the Web,* February 25, 1998, www.nytimes.com.

32. Genesis 16:1–2.

33. *Otakar Kirchner v. John and Jane Doe and Baby Boy "Richard,"* No. 78101 (Supreme Court of Illinois, 1994).

34. The basis for the ruling against the child's adoptive parents was the fact that the biological father had not consented to the adoption. Opposition to the ruling was mainly based on the fact that the child's best interests should have been the grounds for determining his placement. *Edward J. O'Connell Guardian ad Litem for Baby Boy Richard* v. *Otakar Kirchner,* Application for Stay to U.S. Supreme Court, Feb. 13, 1995.

35. Associated Press and Chicago Tribune, "Father of 'Baby Richard' Leaves Wife and Boy, Now 5," *Seattle Times,* January 21, 1997, and Mark Brown and Adrienne Drell, "Baby Richard Battle Back in Court," *Chicago Sun-Times,* July 17, 1997, p. 1.

36. E.g., New York law states that the husband of a woman who is artificially inseminated with donor sperm is the legal father of any child born after the insemination, so long as the procedure was performed by a licensed physician with the husband's consent. New York State Task Force on Life and the Law, *Assisted Reproductive Technologies: Analysis and Recommendations for Public Policy* (New York, NY: New York State Task Force on Life and the Law, 1998), p. 328.

37. The decision was challenged by its critics for failing to take into account the best

interest of the child. From a systemic perspective, it is important to notify genetic fathers who are not sperm donors so as to promote their support of children for whom placement resources are limited. In this case, however, by the time the genetic father learned of his birth and pursued custody, the child had already been legally placed.

38. Some sperm donors have expressed this sentiment as a means of acknowledging their lack of involvement in the parental role. Genetic information relevant to the sperm donor is usually provided by him without compromising his desired anonymity. This information is communicated to the infertile couple or to the woman who is inseminated, to be available to the child who may be born as a result of the insemination.

39. If the motivation of gamete "donors" is to obtain money, the term "donor" is misleading. Although the money that a gamete provider receives in exchange for his or her gametes is (legally and clinically) described as compensation rather than remuneration, whether it is one or the other depends on the amount of the "compensation" vis-à-vis the risk and discomfort for which the provider is "compensated," as well as the economic status and motive of the gamete provider. In most cases of sperm "donation" and some cases of egg "donation," the term "vendor" more accurately describes the gamete provider.

40. Gina Kolata, "In the Game of Cloning, Women Hold All the Cards," *New York Times Week in Review,* February 22, 1998, p. 6.

Conclusion

TOWARD GENDER EQUALITY IN GENETICS

THIS book has a simple rationale: to explore gender equality in genetics. Throughout the text I have interwoven the empirical and theoretical parts because I believe one cannot be adequately understood without the other. The empirical part was my delineation of numerous ways in which research in genetics and its applications affect women differently than they affect men. These involve unchangeable differences, mainly rooted in biology, and changeable differences, mainly associated with psychosocial attitudes and practices that are sometimes but not always related to the biological differences between the sexes. As advances in genetics continue, I believe it necessary to continue to identify the gender differences that occur in their clinical and social applications to individuals.

The theoretical part of the book involved an elaboration of a feminist standpoint that is also egalitarian. Underlying this view is a notion of equality that attributes the same value to all human beings, while acknowledging and respecting their many differences. The differences, I believe, can and should enrich the lives of individuals and society without advantaging some people vis-à-vis others. Consistent with the literature on standpoint theory, my account rejects the presumption of impartiality in ethics and objectivity in science as achievable from the perspective of those who represent the dominant gender, color, class, sexual orientation, and set of abilities. It argues for granting a "privileged status" to the standpoint of those who are not dominant, particularly when they are most affected by the decisions and policies formulated by the dominant group, so that the inevitable limitations of the dominant perspective may be reduced.

Using the term "feminist" throughout my account has been a risk. Although I have personally and professionally identified with the term for decades, I know that its meaning is often misunderstood and simplistically interpreted to represent the view of a small group of advantaged women who are apparently unable to recognize their own advantage. Frequently, a stereotypic view of feminism also involves the notion of hostility toward men. Unfortunately, these simplistic, stereotypic understandings of feminism have led to its being marginalized in public and professional discourse. In philosophical and bioethics circles, this marginalization is evident in a tendency to invite someone like me to present "feminist philosophy" or "feminist bioethics," as if these categories were parallel to specific philosophical frameworks (such as Kantian philosophy or utilitarianism) or bioethical approaches (such as casuistry or principlism).[1] But feminist philosophers may subscribe to any number of philosophical frameworks or any number of bioethical approaches. The only common denominator among us is a commitment to gender justice, which, as a subset of justice, is included in any adequate account of ethics or bioethics. Admittedly, justice and gender justice have different meanings to different people. But whatever their meanings, if the defining element of feminism is gender justice, all philosophers and all bioethicists are or should be feminists.

In light of both biological and psychosocial differences between the sexes, it seems clear that the impact of advances in genetics has been greater for women than for men. The escalation of these advances will surely expand the options and benefits available to some women; for the majority, however, the advances in genetics will probably make little difference in their lives, and for some the advances may in fact prove more burdensome than advantageous, increasing pressures to conform to the preferences of others. What David Peters refers to as "the dark side" of the development and proliferation of genetic testing is likely to affect more women than men because women are less likely than men to be able to pay for health insurance.[2] Peters suggests that if current practice prevails and insurance costs escalate for those who test positive for specific conditions, some people will be forced to forgo coverage because they cannot afford it. Since insurance is the ordinary route by which individuals in the United States pay for their health care, genetic testing would thus indirectly contribute to a lesser degree of health for many of them. The brighter side of advances in genetics could surely be expanded even now through government-mandated health coverage for everyone. It is doubtful, however, that the gender inequities that already exist in society will be exacerbated or reduced by progress in genetics; in the short run, they are more likely to be exacerbated.

Whether or not this rather pessimistic expectation is fulfilled, the identification of gender differences in the impact of genetics is but a first step of any adequate attempt to maximize gender justice in particular and justice in general in American society or in the world at large. The second necessary step is to apply the two distinctions from which a practical plan for maximizing justice may be formulated: the distinction between the differences that are associated with inequity and those that are not, and between those that are changeable and those that are not. The first cut, happily, narrows the ethical task by setting aside the differences that enrich us all individually and in our interactions with one another. What remains constitutes the entire agenda of gender justice: to change the changeable differences associated with gender inequity so that their inequitable impact is reduced, and to develop social measures that reduce the inequitable impact of the differences that cannot be changed.

A climate of "political correctness" seems to have inhibited the first step, which is based on realization that genetics is not gender-neutral in the burdens and benefits of its impact. The material presented here is intended to serve as a catalyst to overcome that inhibition. In no way do the empirical gender differences that I have described constitute a comprehensive list even of currently relevant differences associated with genetics. With the exception of human cloning, my account does not mention gender differences that have not as yet been realized but are bound to occur as advances in genetic information and technology proliferate.[3] But present as well as future gender differences can and need to be identified before their potential for injustice can be addressed. To pretend that they do not or cannot exist because of a wrongheaded notion of equality as sameness is to facilitate genetic discrimination.

I have taken the second step with regard to some of the issues identified in the book. For example, my egalitarian feminist standpoint has led me to develop positions that attribute privileged status to women on issues such as disclosure of misattributed paternity to husbands and carrier testing of pregnant women without partner testing. Regarding the former, I believe that the woman is the primary client and that her interests generally override the husband's right to know. Regarding the latter, I believe that pregnant women have a right to be tested whether or not their partners are tested. In both situations, women's interests, both autonomy-based and welfare-based, trump the interests of others because women are likely to be more significantly affected by the outcome. However, these positions could be altered in particular cases if their impact on different individuals proved to be inequitable. For example, if disclosure of misattributed paternity were to deprive someone of information that is highly relevant to his own reproductive plans, disclosure would be justifiable so long as it did not present a disproportionate risk to his partner. Similarly, although sex selection is morally objectionable in most instances because it is sexist, I can envision instances in which it is justifiable on nonsexist grounds.

On some issues, my account is inconclusive because different positions are defensible in response to different assumptions as well as different variables. For example, different assumptions about the moral status of the fetus or embryo, in vivo or in vitro, yield different positions about the compatibility between advocacy for the disabled and the right to abortion. Variables such as cost, coverage, risk, invasiveness, intention, available alternatives, and definitiveness of the anticipated information are all relevant to determination of whether a particular method of genetic diagnosis is supportable by policies that reflect feminist and egalitarian concerns. Citing the U.S. Department of Defense initiative as a model, I have recommended a specific strategy for addressing these concerns.

If justice, including gender justice, is a social goal for genetics, both first and second steps need to be taken by more people than I. This account, I believe, is less nearsighted than it might be because of my experience of nondominance by gender, but it does not purport to be a complete or even a totally reliable account of the issues identified. As a means of reducing its limitations, I have drawn on the standpoints of other nondominant groups and individuals. My hope is that others, particularly those who hold positions of responsibility for the clinical and social implications of genetics, will do the same.

Notes

1. Philosophers and bioethicists who are women are sometimes assumed to be feminists, and those who are men are assumed not to be feminists, without any attention to whether their writings reflect a feminist or nonfeminist point of view. Moreover, women who are feminists are often assumed to embrace a "feminine" or "care-based ethic," without attending to whether their writings reflect that point of view. For example, I was once invited to join a panel of men to discuss a specific case at a session that had been organized to illustrate different philosophical perspectives. The organizer assumed that I would articulate "an ethic of care," which would not only coincide with "feminist ethics" but would differ from the approaches taken by the other panelists. At that point I had published nothing on a care-based ethic, but many of my writings had been explicitly feminist. My approach to the case was not necessarily different from that of panelists who, while not identifying their views as feminist, considered justice a fundamental principle of bioethics.

2. David A. Peters, "Risk Classification, Genetic Testing, and Health Care: A Conflict between Libertarian and Egalitarian Values," in Ted Peters, ed., *Genetics: Issues of Social Justice* (Cleveland: Pilgrim Press, 1998), p. 206.

3. As mentioned in the previous chapter, somatic cell nuclear human cloning to the four-cell stage has been reported in the popular press but has not been verified by scientific review and publication. There have been no published reports that somatic cell nuclear cloning has produced a live-born human.

NAME INDEX

SUBJECT INDEX